The Archaeology Coursebook

Second Edition

'Expanded and revised, the Coursebook is an excellent resources for archaeology AS and A Level courses. It is clear, easy to read and has an interesting range of case studies. It will be a boon, not just for students but for anyone wanting a handy introduction to archaeology' – *Don Henson, Education and Outreach Co-Ordinator, Council for British Archaeology*

This fully updated and revised new edition of the bestselling *The Archaeology Coursebook* is a guide to students studying archaeology for the first time, providing pre-university students and teachers as well as undergraduates and enthusiasts with the skills and technical concepts necessary to grasp the subject. Specially designed to assist learning, it:

- *introduces* the most commonly examined archaeological methods, concepts, and themes, and provides the necessary skills to understand them
- *explains* how to interpret the material students may meet in examinations and how to succeed with different types of assignments and exam questions
- *supports* study with case studies, key sites, key terms, tasks and skills development
- *illustrates* concepts and commentary with over 300 photos and drawings of excavation sites, methodology and processes, tools and equipment
- *links* from its own website at www.routledge/textbooks/archaeologycoursebook to other key websites in archaeology at the right level
- contains new material on British Prehistory and the Roman Empire; new case studies, methods, examples, boxes, over 100 new photographs and diagrams, as well as updates on examination changes for pre-university students

Jim Grant is a Principal Examiner in A Level Archaeology and Assistant Principal at Cirencester College. He is also a member of the subject advisory panel for archaeology at the Higher Education Academy for teaching and learning and has experience as an archaeologist in the field. **Sam Gorin** is a Principal Examiner in A Level Archaeology and head of general studies at Newark and Sherwood College. He was previously a professional archaeologist. **Neil Fleming** is Chief Examiner in A Level Archaeology and Upper Sixth Housemaster at Christ's Hospital School, Horsham.

The Archaeology Coursebook

Second Edition

An introduction to Study Skills, Topics and Methods

Jim Grant, Sam Gorin and **Neil Fleming**

LONDON AND NEW YORK

First published 2005
by Routledge
2 Park Square, Milton Park, Abingdon, Oxon OX14 4RN

Simultaneously published in the USA and Canada
by Routledge
270 Madison Ave, New York, NY 10016

Routledge is an imprint of the Taylor & Francis Group

Typeset in Garamond by
Florence Production Ltd, Stoodleigh, Devon
Printed and bound in Great Britain by
Bell & Bain Ltd, Glasgow

British Library Cataloguing in Publication Data
A catalogue record for this book is available from the British Library

Library of Congress Cataloging in Publication Data
Grant, Jim, 1958–
The archaeology coursebook : an introduction to study skills, topics, and methods / Jim Grant, Sam Gorin, Neil Fleming – 2nd ed.
p. cm.
Includes bibliographical references (p.) and index.
1. Archaeology – Study and teaching (Higher) 2. Archaeology Methodology. 3. Archaeology – Examinations – Study Guides.
I. Gorin, Sam, 1946– II. Fleming, Neil, 1955– III. Title.
CC83 .G7 2001
930.1′0711 – dc21 2001019758

ISBN 0–416–36076–5 (hbk)
ISBN 0–415–36077–3 (pbk)

Brief Contents

Contents

Figures

Index of Skills

Throughout *The Archaeology Coursebook* we have linked skills to content. However, as you may want to focus on the suggestions for skill development outside this sequence, we have listed them separately. These are generic skills which should apply to most parts of your course.

Acknowledgements

Once again we would like to thank those who contributed to the original book, much of which is retained here. In particular Mick Jones, James Megoran, Toni, Christina, Paloma and Javier in Barcelona, Royston Clark, Sarah Cole, Don Henson, Richard Reece, Nick Trustram-Eve, Vicky Peters, Moira Taylor and Robin Wichard.

Our students at Cirencester College, Christ's Hospital School and Newark and Sherwood College have continued to be guinea pigs for much of the material and in some cases provided illustrations for the book. We've also had lots of useful feedback from students and teachers of archaeology about what you would like to see more or less of. Hopefully you will find this edition even more useful than the first. Neil and Sam would like to reiterate their thanks to Marlene and Russell Fleming who have clearly spent most of their holidays visiting sites and to Sally Gorin who shared in excavations and site visits with Sam and provided help with research.

Revising a book has proved almost as hard as writing one in the first place and thanks are due to Moira Taylor once again and Geraldine Martin at T&F Informa for guidance and patience and to Richard Stoneman for backing the project. One of the things we wanted in this edition was better illustrations and many people have helped us out. In particular Julie Gardner at Wessex Archaeology provided many photos from their archives including the Amesbury Archer. Dave Jones, Amanda Hart and Brona Langton were also particularly helpful. The reconstruction of Tybrind Vig will quickly find its way onto overheads and Powerpoint presentations everywhere!

Finally I'd like to thank my family. William and Irene for giving me the work ethic to get it finished and especially Dawn, Zack and Marnie for allowing me to opt out of family life long enough to write it and being phenomenally patient when every journey seems to take use close to yet another site.

So once more this book is dedicated with love and thanks to our families.

Jim Grant
May 2005

Illustration Acknowledgements

We are very grateful to those below for supplying illustrations and permission to use them. All other illustrations are the Authors.

Ginny Baddiley, Nottinghamshire SMR (1.4)
Mary Baxter (8.24)
Paul Brooker (1.10)
Royston Clarke (3.15, 9.6, 9.7)
Sarah Cole (5.10)
Controller of Her Majesty's Stationery Office (1.21)
Empingham Archive (2.5, 6.13, 8.11)
Martin Green (2.7)
Gwilym Hughes (2.20)
Mick Jones, Lincoln Unit (2.19)
David Knight (2.32 and 2.33)
Harold Mytum (6.15 and 6.16)
Norfolk Archaeology and Environment Division (2.21)
Joshua Pollard, Negotiating Avebury Project (2.2)
Francesca Radcliffe (1.19 and 9.13)
Jim Russell (7.5)
Roger Thomas (12.7)
Jane Timby (2.4)
Nick Trustram-Eve (1.5, 1.8, 12.2, 12.4, 12.10, 12.11, 12.12)
University of Cambridge Air Photos (1.23 and 1.24)
Robin Wichard (2.8, 5.2, 8.37, 9.21)
Brian Williams (3.12)
Kate Walton (3.23, 3.28, 8.2, 8.16, 12.6 (after Lake))
Colin Jarvis (12.9)
Willam Kilbride (ADS) (12.8)
Julie Gardner – Wessex Archaeology (1.13, 2.6, 2.23, 2.27, 3.3, 3.7, 3.10, 3.19, 3.20, 4.1, 4.4, 6.17, 11.15)
Dan Schofield (3.9 and 3.22)
Aidan Scott (10.7 and 11.10)

Brona Langton (1.11, 2.1, 2.25, 5.15)
John Dewar (11.18)
Dave Jones (1.12, 2.11, 2.12, 2.13, 2.14, 2.31, 3.11)
Chris Butler (1.18 and 5.9)
Jonathan Tubb (10.8 and 10.9)
Amanda Hart and Jude Barratt, Corinium Museum (8.40, 9.10, 11.9)
Andy Payne (English Heritage) (1.17)
Sarah Scott (3.6, 3.18, 4.2, 5.14 (after Reynolds and Klausmeyer), 7.6, 9.2, 9.16 (after Drewett), 10.6, 11.8)
Jamie Gibson (7.1)
Clive Ruggles (7.4)
Christina Cliff (9.11)

Introduction

The Archaeology Coursebook is about archaeological literacy. Whether you are a student or someone who wants to know more about archaeology, you probably have not studied it previously. This means that you have a whole new technical language and set of concepts to grasp. This text will enable you to get to grips with them. It does not pretend to cover the whole of a degree programme nor is it a specialist guide to archaeological methods. There is a fantastic array of books and websites already available which fulfil these functions. The aim of this book is to get you started with archaeology and to help you succeed in your academic study. It does this by:

- providing brief introductions to the most commonly examined archaeological methods, concepts and themes. Whole books have been written on the meanings of particular terms and there may not be consensus on their use. We will concentrate on providing you with working definitions and examples rather than debating meaning
- explaining how to interpret the sort of archaeological material you may meet in examinations
- showing you how to succeed with different types of assignments and examination questions
- providing succinct and relevant case studies which you can use in your own work
- providing links to easily accessible sources including internet sites.

As authors our collective experience includes professional and amateur archaeology and teaching in schools in both state and private sectors and in colleges. More importantly, we are all current teachers and examiners of archaeology with long experience of successfully preparing students of all ages for GCSE, A Level, Access and HE programmes. In preparing this new edition we have responded to feedback from students, teachers and general readers of the *Archaeology Coursebook* about what they liked and what was less useful. Amongst the changes are:

- Introductions to religion and ritual in the late prehistory of the British Isles and of the Roman Empire.
- Longer case studies with more cross-referencing between them.
- More illustrations and more use made of them. We have tried to avoid the most frequently used examples.
- Updated methods sections to reflect continuing changes in archaeology.

This book is designed as a handbook. That is, it will be of use to you at every stage of your course, from understanding new terminology to producing your major study. The structure of the book loosely follows the AS and A2 Level Archaeology courses studied by students in England and Wales. However, it is intended to be relevant and useful for all students studying the subject up to first-year undergraduate level. If it equips you to produce pass-level essays and to understand what is being discussed in lectures and seminars it will have done its job. You will, of course, need other sources too. For A level and first year of university you will need case studies and to look at examples of fieldwork reports. From year 2 of university you will need greater depth of material. However, by then you will know everything that is in this book!

We have organised the book into three broad sections:

- *Part I Understanding archaeological resources* is an introduction to how archaeologists work. How they find sites, excavate them and analyse and interpret the material they recover and how we get archaeological knowledge. It also looks at how archaeological knowledge is presented and the role of archaeology today.
- *Part II Studying themes in archaeology* covers the broad topics of religion and ritual, settlement, economics and material culture and society. These will be relevant to you whether your course follows a period-based or thematic approach. We have concentrated on providing examples defining key terms and highlighting the sources and methods used to explore these themes.
- *Part III Examination success and beyond* guides you through how to produce a successful archaeological project and helps you find ways of preparing to pass your exams. It also provides some models for you to follow. The final chapter is a guide to some additional sources of information and further study opportunities.

The study skills you will need to succeed are introduced gradually throughout the book rather than in a separate section. Each chapter includes

Figure 0.1 *Ecofact or Artefact?*

These are two of the first new terms you will learn. This wooden effigy from Ireland is of natural material. However, it was transformed from ecofact to artefact through modification by people during the late Bronze or Iron Age. It may be one of the earliest effigies of a god we have or simply a rather scary doll.

learning goals to develop your skills as well as your understanding. In the early chapters key skills boxes show you how to find information and use it to tackle short tasks. Some of these are closely linked to examination success, others are activities to reinforce your understanding and to stimulate your ability to make connections between content and methods. Later in the book, they guide you through evaluative tasks and ways to approach extended pieces of academic writing. To enable you to rapidly find this advice we have included a skills list as well as a contents list. To be studying at this level you must already have sound general academic skills. However, you will need to adapt these to archaeology and also to develop them further. We have therefore made suggestions on how to improve these rather than just showing you how to do them.

To succeed in your courses you need to develop in three broad areas: general skills, higher level academic skills and archaeological understanding.

HOW TO USE THIS TEXT

There are so many different ways in which lecturers can structure courses that it is unlikely you will follow the exact order of our contents sequence in your own study. We have taken this into account by providing a full index and contents list which includes all the main subheadings. We have also used a system of cross-referencing throughout the book from one topic to related topics. Content, skills and resources are all linked. Look out for the following signposts which all provide links from the text immediately preceding them.

▶ (arrowhead) guides you to related material on another page
• (bullet) indicates a key website or other resource
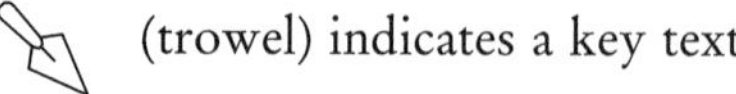 (trowel) indicates a key text

Examples are given for most of the points we make and a range of case studies is provided to deepen your understanding of the ideas and methods discussed. Where they are relevant to your course [they are about the right length and detail for essays up to year 2 at university] you can use them as content to support your written work. We have introduced and defined key terms as they have arisen in the text. The glossary on p. 331 contains a working definition of all the words printed in **bold** in the text. You should look

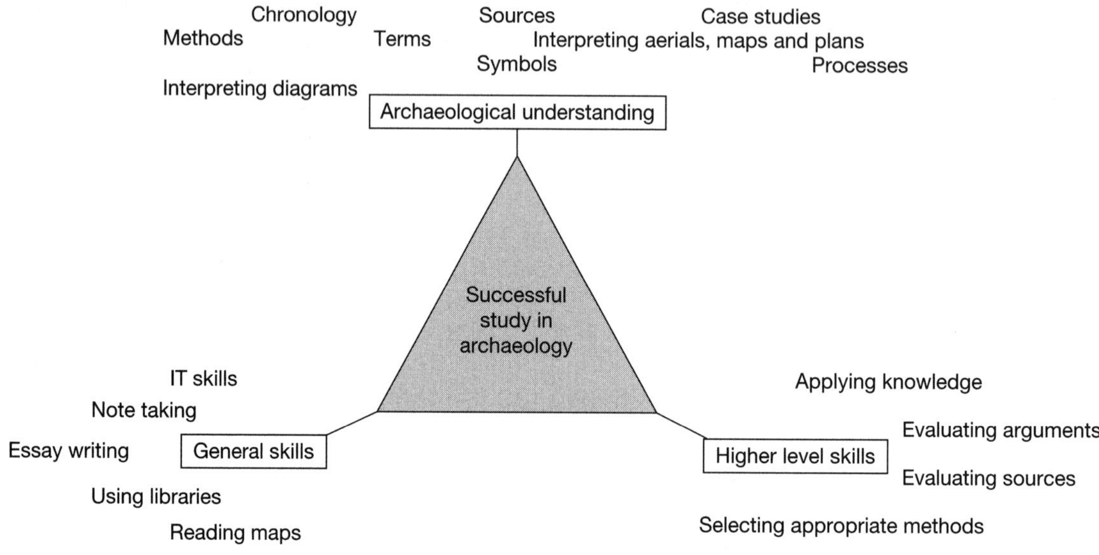

Figure 0.2 *The triangle of success – the keys to succeeding on your course*

KEY SKILL

What you have to learn to be successful

This will probably be the first time you have studied archaeology. As with all subjects, there are a range of things you must know and understand in order to succeed. For example:

You need to:	*In order to:*	*Examples:*	*By:*
Learn definitions	Understand questions and explanations	Mortuary, excarnation	Memorising and testing
Understand concepts	Understand explanations and argue	Characterisation, relative dating	Using them and testing
Understand processes	Assess the limits of evidence	Taphonomy, organic preservation	Using diagrams, explaining
Know case studies	Support your answers	Danebury, Sutton Hoo	Using mind maps, noting
Link methods, themes and examples	Maximise the use of your material	Boxgrove–usewear–hunting-tools	Practice
Apply understanding	Interpret sources	Aerial photos, plans	Practice

there first whenever anything new arises. You may find it helpful to find an example from your own course for each relevant word or phrase in the glossary.

Where you need specific content for your course you should be getting it from your lessons and the detailed books in your library. You should also keep a file of newspaper cuttings on recent archaeological discoveries. We have also assumed that you have access to the internet. A key feature of this book is that it is designed to be used alongside your PC. It provides explanations and gives you a range of websites to look at for examples and illustration. Archaeology is such a visual subject and so well served by many excellent sources on the Net that it is foolish not to use it.

A new feature in this edition is the use of icons to indicate where a case study in one section would also be useful in another. You will find them in the top left of each site box.

 Social archaeology

 Economics and material culture

 Settlement

 Religion

Part One

Understanding Archaeological Resources

Chapter 1

Archaeological Reconnaissance

YOUR GOALS

You need to be able to

- understand the key methods used by archaeologists to locate and define sites
- identify some strengths and limitations of the most important techniques
- suggest appropriate methods for locating and exploring sites in particular circumstances
- establish your own system of note-taking for the course.

Archaeologists use a wide range of reconnaissance techniques to locate archaeological sites and to investigate sites without excavating them. Some archaeologists predict that future advances in non-invasive, and non-destructive, methods will see them emerge as an alternative to excavation. Reconnaissance techniques are also used to map evidence of human activity in the landscape.

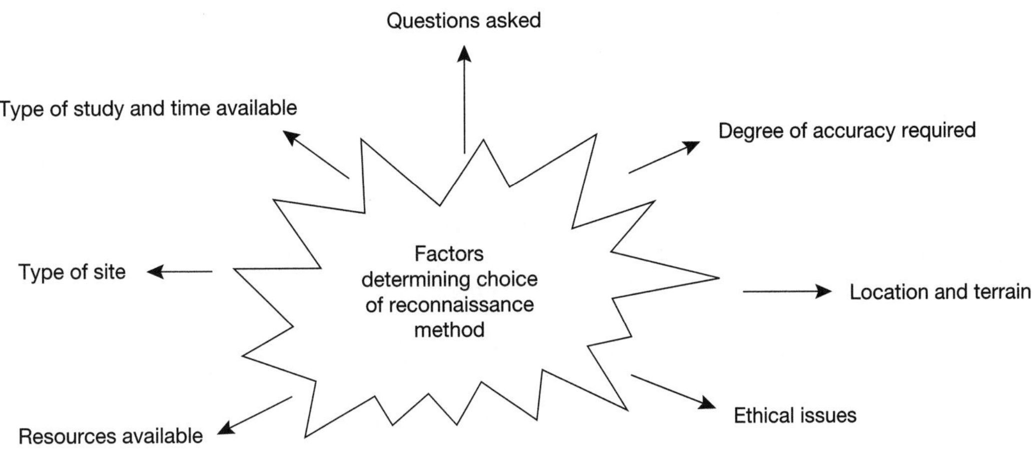

Figure 1.1 *Factors influencing the choice of reconnaissance methods*

KEY SKILL

Successful note-taking

Right from the first day of your archaeology course you should be taking and filing notes on what you have learnt. You have probably already developed your own style of note-taking but it is worth considering alternative forms of note-taking depending on what is required of you and the purpose of the information you are recording. For example, the type of information you need to record as the raw material for a major essay is likely to be very different from what is required to remind you of the meaning of a concept. It is as easy to accumulate too many notes as too few. The acid test is whether they are useful for their purpose. As Figure 1.2 makes clear, different styles of notes are appropriate to different situations.

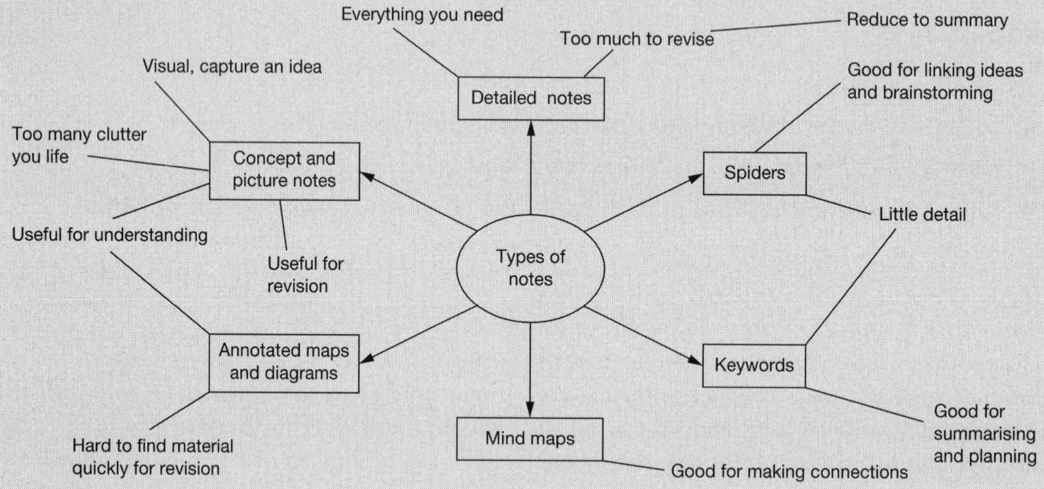

Figure 1.2 *The strengths and weaknesses of different types of notes. Always try to supplement the notes in this book from other texts and websites*

Detailed written notes may be necessary when you are working from library texts on a major project. If you take notes from texts you always have access to, such as *The Archaeology Coursebook*, then you are wasting your time. What you want instead are brief notes which remind you of key points and direct you to places in your texts where the detail is. Try to experiment with a range of notes when preparing for discussion, revising and planning. Many people learn better from visual notes than they do from dense written passages. You may be one of them. We have used these types of notes throughout the text. You can find examples on the following pages:

- Spider diagram p. 4
- Mind map pp. 212, 265
- Flow diagram p. 61
- Target diagram p. 223
- Force field diagram p. 234
- Picture or concept notes pp. 225, 289
- Keyword notes p. 315
- Grids p. 72

The appropriate methods in each case will relate to the time and resources available as well as the particular case being investigated.

Every year hundreds of new sites are located. Some are spotted from the air or even from satellites in space, others through the discovery of artefacts by metal detectorists. Quarrying, dredging and peat cutting all regularly produce unexpected finds while some of the most important have come about completely by chance.

The discoveries of the body of Otzi the Ice Man by skiers and of the Altamira cave art by children are classic examples. So too was the discovery of the Neolithic tomb at Crantit in Orkney, which was found when a digger fell through the roof!

Equally, some sites were never 'lost' to begin with. Stonehenge and the Pyramids were well known before the development of archaeology and many of the buildings of the last 200 years are still in use. Other named sites were documented by historians and located by using written sources. Schliemann's discovery of Troy is the classic example but many historic battlefields also fall into this category. In addition, a considerable number of new discoveries are made during the exploration of known sites.

To locate or explore sites through research or ahead of development there are four broad and complementary categories of methods that are commonly used:

- desktop study
- surface survey
- geophysical or geochemical survey
- aerial survey

In addition there are a range of newer techniques, most of which can be labelled **remote sensing**.

Reconnaissance should not be seen simply as the precursor to the real business of digging. In some cases it can provide all or most of the evidence needed to answer questions. The pioneering Shapwick project which investigated the development of an estate owned by Glastonbury Abbey used a battery of reconnaissance methods alongside limited sampling of deposits through shovel pit testing, geochemical survey and excavation. The results when combined with evidence from maps, historical sources, and environmental data enabled the production of regression maps showing the development of settlement in the area.

DESKTOP STUDY

As its name suggests, this is an office-based investigation using existing records. Some archaeologists, usually concerned with shipwrecks, aircraft or the investigation of historical individuals, continue to use written sources to track down or identify particular sites. More generally, most excavations and all research in Britain today begins with a search of information that has already been recorded. The majority of these investigations are part of the planning process. Their purpose is to determine whether there are likely to be archaeological remains which might be threatened by development (▶ p. 120).

Desktop study involves researching maps and historical or archaeological documents including aerial photographs about the area under investigation. If they are not in private hands, these are most likely to be held in planning departments, county records offices, historic environment record, local **Sites and Monuments Record (SMRs)** or the **National Monuments Record (NMR)** offices.

Historical documents

A diverse assortment of documents may be of value to the archaeologist. These will vary by county, area and period. In much of the country known documents are archived or recorded in the County Records Office. In many areas, useful sources have also been catalogued in a volume of the Victoria County History (VCR). This is often the first resource researchers turn to. Only a fraction of early records have survived and those that

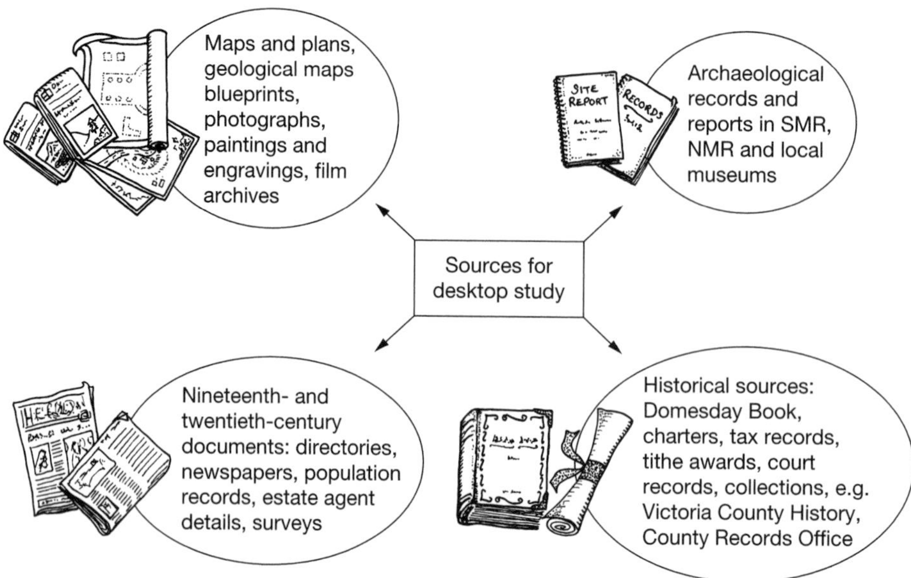

Figure 1.3 *Sources commonly used for desktop study*

have need translation and interpretation. Amongst the potential range available, the following categories are important.

Legal documents. Records of ownership such as Anglo-Saxon charters or court records of disputes often included physical description of boundaries and occasionally land use. Wills and inventories which can be linked to particular buildings may provide lists of contents. These can provide clues to that buildings' use.

Tax records. These are particularly valuable in helping to identify landowning units and their economic uses. The Domesday Book is the best known but later tax surveys and tithe awards are often of more direct use.

Economic records. Order and sales books are invaluable to industrial archaeologists while nineteenth-century directories are useful in exploring functions of buildings. Estate agents' bills are increasingly being preserved to record changes in important buildings.

Pictorial records. Paintings, engravings and photographs can be of value both in identification and in tracing changes. They are particularly valuable when studying standing buildings. Archives of aerial photographs (APs) such as the RAF 'or Luftwaffe' surveys of Britain in the 1940s are key documents in tracing landscape change in the last sixty years. They are often the only record of many sites.

Written accounts. Descriptions of places in books, diaries and travelogues are of use in identifying the function, construction methods and identity of many sites. The work of early antiquarians such as Stukeley is particularly valuable for descriptions of monuments as they were before the modern period.

Archaeological records. There are three main sources here. If there are early excavation or survey results they can often be accessed through libraries or local museums. Local collections of finds and reports will also be held in local museums. Details of previous archaeological work

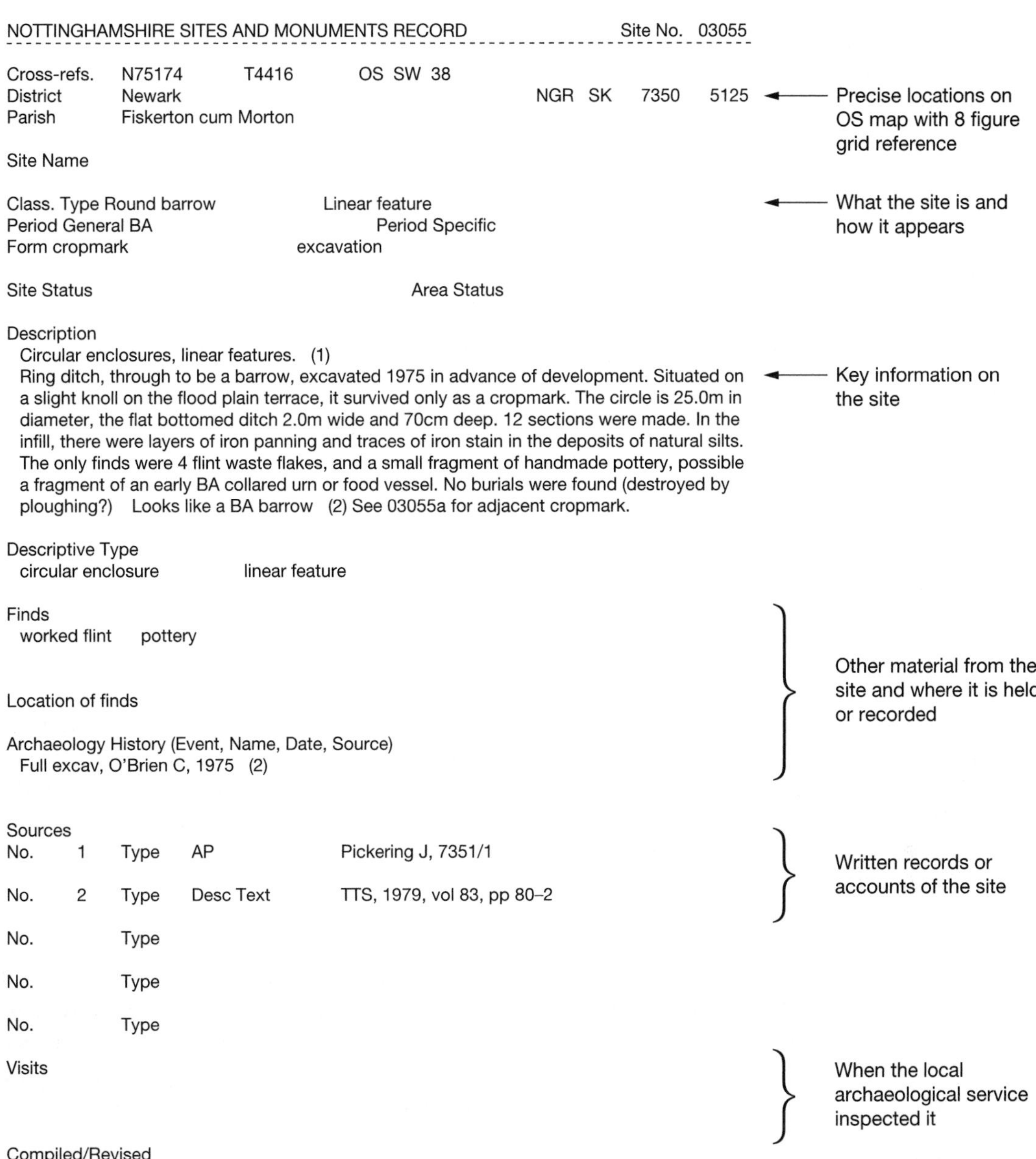

NOTTINGHAMSHIRE SITES AND MONUMENTS RECORD Site No. 03055

Cross-refs. N75174 T4416 OS SW 38
District Newark NGR SK 7350 5125
Parish Fiskerton cum Morton

Site Name

Class. Type Round barrow Linear feature
Period General BA Period Specific
Form cropmark excavation

Site Status Area Status

Description
Circular enclosures, linear features. (1)
Ring ditch, through to be a barrow, excavated 1975 in advance of development. Situated on a slight knoll on the flood plain terrace, it survived only as a cropmark. The circle is 25.0m in diameter, the flat bottomed ditch 2.0m wide and 70cm deep. 12 sections were made. In the infill, there were layers of iron panning and traces of iron stain in the deposits of natural silts. The only finds were 4 flint waste flakes, and a small fragment of handmade pottery, possible a fragment of an early BA collared urn or food vessel. No burials were found (destroyed by ploughing?) Looks like a BA barrow (2) See 03055a for adjacent cropmark.

Descriptive Type
circular enclosure linear feature

Finds
worked flint pottery

Location of finds

Archaeology History (Event, Name, Date, Source)
Full excav, O'Brien C, 1975 (2)

Sources
No. 1 Type AP Pickering J, 7351/1
No. 2 Type Desc Text TTS, 1979, vol 83, pp 80–2
No. Type
No. Type
No. Type

Visits

Compiled/Revised
24/08/1987 VB

Figure 1.4 *How to read an SMR printout*

and stray finds for much of Britain are held in local SMRs. These records are increasingly computerised and a national version is being built up at the various NMR offices. Printouts which include lists of earlier research can be made by inputting grid references.

Oral accounts. While living people may provide clues to the use and location of recent buildings, farmers and others who work on the land or the built environment may have valuable knowledge for archaeologists. Farmers, for example, may be able to identify areas where building rubble has been ploughed up or where dressed stones have been removed. Sometimes estate management records may hold this information for earlier periods.

Maps

Maps are amongst the most basic tools and sources used by archaeologists. They are used to locate and explore sites and to answer questions about previous use of the landscape. They are of particular value in tracking changes through time (settlement shape and location, boundaries, land units, fields and hedges). They can also be used to relate sites to geology and topography. Medieval archaeologists are often able to produce their own maps for periods before mapping began. They do this by working back from the oldest available map and cross-referencing historical sources and fieldnames. This technique is known as **regression**.

A wide variety of maps are used by archaeologists, including the following.

Early maps

Maps from the sixteenth century tend to show the properties of the rich. They are not always to scale but may provide visual information such as illustrations of specific buildings. From the seventeenth century there are also route maps such as Ogilvy's Road Book, which is a series of linear strips. Maps were produced to show the proposed routes of turnpikes, canals and railways in order to gain permission from parliament for building to take place.

Changes in rural landownership from the eighteenth century onwards were recorded on enclosure award maps, while taxes owed to the church by landowners were sometimes written on tithe award maps. Occasionally these can be cross-referenced and both can provide information about fieldnames, routes and boundaries, which are vital for landscape archaeology. Other maps show landscaped gardens, battlefields or provide plans of factories and mines.

These early maps are often held in county record offices. Some may be in private hands or belong to churches.

Ordnance Survey (OS) maps

During the early nineteenth century the OS mapped each county at 1 inch to 1 mile. From the 1880s OS 6 inch to 1 mile maps provided more detail of individual buildings and even hedge species. OS maps established a new standard in accuracy and a comprehensive system of coding and keys for features. A grid system was used which covered the whole country and enabled precise references to be given. By examining a succession of maps for any area, changes in land use and the built environment can be easily seen.

• www.ordsvy.gov.uk

Maps used in archaeological

The OS 1:25000 Pathfinder or Leisure series show the location of some archaeological sites but planning maps that use the OS grid system are needed for investigations. 1:10000 (old 6 inch) maps are sometimes the most detailed available for mountainous, remote and some rural areas but 1:2500 (old 25 inch 1 mile) rural or 1:1250 urban planning maps are normally used. For field walking 1:10000 or 1:2500 is used and for excavation the 1:2500 or 1:1250 provides a base. A 1:2500 map allows you to identify individual metre squares with a

10-figure grid reference. These maps are held in county or district planning offices.

Other maps sometimes used include the Geological Survey series, street maps, factory plans, vegetation and climatic maps, land use and classification, soil surveys and specialist archaeological maps. Increasingly archaeologists are using computerised mapping systems based around Geographical Information Systems (**GIS**).

As an archaeology student you need some basic map skills including the ability to:

- identify and interpret common archaeological features from maps
- 'read' contours and hachures
- use scales and at least 6-figure grid references
- produce basic cross-sectional sketches from maps
- interpret simple archaeological plans and diagrams
- use other evidence such as photographs and written accounts to interpret maps and plans.

SURFACE SURVEYS

This term can be used to encompass **fieldwalking, surveying** and even planned aerial photography. We will use it to describe non-destructive visual surveys at ground level. These can range from slow, painstaking searches on foot to quite rapid examinations of a landscape by Landrover, looking for upstanding earthworks. Since most sites lack visible features, the former is more common. Fieldwalking is largely concerned with finding traces of unrecorded sites. Scatters of building rubble or artefacts or slight undulations in the surface can reveal where there are buried walls or house platforms. Differences in soil or vegetation may also be indicative of past human activity. For studies of the **Mesolithic** and **Neolithic** in Britain, scatters of flint and animal bone are often the only traces of human activity visible in the landscape. To study the activities of these mobile populations, careful identification and plotting of these scatters is essential. A variation on this is the study of hedges and woodlands

KEY TERM

Geographic Information Systems (GIS)

This refers to powerful databases which can store many layers of data against individual map grid references. This can include details of topography, geology and vegetation as well as archaeological data. GIS can integrate data from satellites with field recordings. It can produce topographic maps and site plans in three dimensions and perform complex statistical analysis. It is revolutionising the presentation and interrogation of archaeological data. It can even be used to predict site locations based on known patterns.

- http://www.esri.com/industries/archaeology/index.html

KEY TASK

Sourcing information

Take each of the following examples and list the types of source you might find useful in investigating it.

Next take a real example of one of them and find out what actual sources exist. You may be surprised.

A round barrow or cairn

A Roman villa or Saxon church

A deserted medieval village or abbey

An eighteenth-century farm or canal

A nineteenth-century railway line or factory

A twentieth-century pillbox or airfield

for traces of past economic activities and to help locate settlement areas (▶ p. 201). Surface surveys can cover large areas such as Webster and Sanders' work in the Copan Valley of Mexico or woods such as the Thetford Forest project in East Anglia.

- http://www.wkac.ac.uk/archaeology/index.htm
- www.nottingham.ac.uk/archaeology/research/huancaco/

Surface investigations of known sites include **micro-contour surveys** of the topography. These involve detailed and precise use of surveying tools to build up a picture of variations in height and levels. Data is increasingly being entered on databases to enable computer enhancement of the landscape. These surveys can often reveal hidden features that could not be detected with the naked eye.

In most studies, the areas to be surveyed are measured using surveying equipment or Global Positioning Systems and often set out with rows or squares of pegs, cane or marker poles. This is to enable accurate sampling and recording.

Recording standing buildings

One specialised area of archaeological surveying focuses on the built environment and links archaeology to architectural science. Detailed studies of the material and construction techniques of structures are made both to enhance knowledge of the development of buildings and to provide a record

Figure 1.5 *Rock art survey using GPS and GIS*

The survey of rock carvings or petroglyphs illustrates many aspects of reconnaissance and recording techniques. In addition to a detailed record being made by tracing and photograph, the position of each petroglyph is identified by GPS. Its height above sea level and orientation are also measured and the information entered into a GIS database. This enables 3D presentations to permit study of relationships between petroglyphs and topography or each other.

KEY TERM

Sampling

Whatever is deposited is a fragment of past material culture. Dependent upon the material, a variable portion of these deposits will survive. Archaeologists will recover a sample of these. Not every site can be fieldwalked, let alone excavated. Choices have to be made. If these choices are arbitrary (non-probabilistic) they could lead to bias in the **archaeological record** with certain types of evidence being neglected and others over-represented. For example, if archaeologists chose only to study hill forts from the Iron Age or, as often happens, if development only permitted excavation in one part of a town, it might create an unrepresentative picture of life in the past.

When archaeologists design research strategies they use some form of probabilistic sampling to reduce bias in recovery. This means that the chance of anything being recovered is known. Rigorous sampling is used in most aspects of archaeological reconnaissance and excavation.

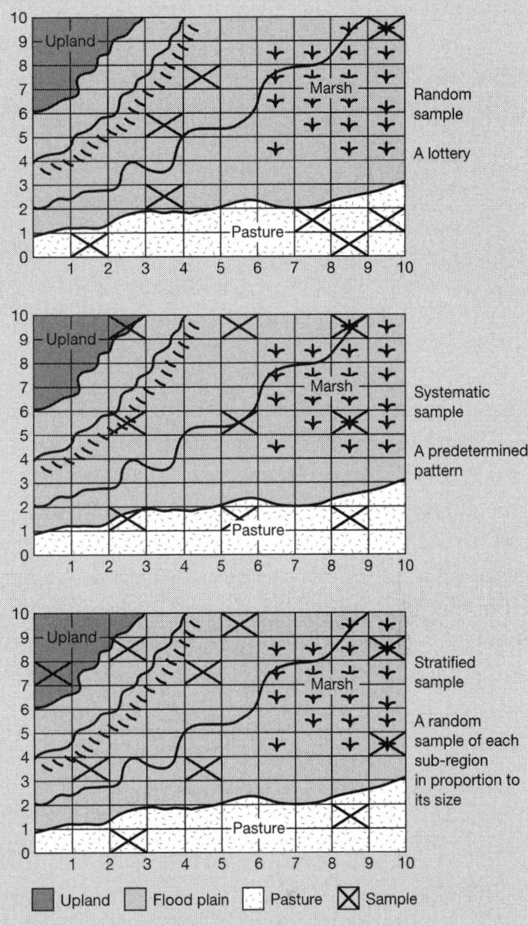

Figure 1.6 *Models of different approaches to sampling*

Firstly the plan of the total area or site to be surveyed is divided up either into a grid pattern of numbered squares or a series of equidistant parallel lines or transects (▶ p. 13). Both are usually aligned north–south to link into the national survey grid although sometimes grids in fields are aligned on a particular boundary. With large areas it is common to select a sample of grids and then use transects within them. The scale varies according to the task. An initial surface survey of a whole landscape might start with 100 metre or kilometre squares and then have transects between 10 and 50 metres apart depending on terrain and resources. For test pitting on a known site the initial grid might be 1 metre square. You need to understand four basic approaches to sampling. Our illustration is for grids but the principles are the same for transects.

A simple *random sample* works like a lottery. The numbered units are selected by computer or number table. This is fair as each unit has an equal chance of being selected, but it can also lead to clustering and thus miss features.

Stratified sampling overcomes clustering bias by first dividing the sample universe into sections. For example, if the site has natural zones such as hills, valley and plain then numbers are selected randomly for each zone in proportion to its area.

KEY TERM *cont.*

Sampling

Systematic sampling overcomes clustering by selecting at evenly spaced intervals, for example every third grid or every 10 metres. This ensures a more even selection although it could miss things that are regularly distributed. It usually requires a higher number of samples.

Stratified systematic sampling combines the last two methods and could be used to take more samples in particular zones than others.

- http://www.utexas/edu/courses/denbow/labs/survey.htm

against future destruction or decay. For example laser scanning is used in some buildings which are covered with lichen to see how they are constructed. Records will range from written description to CAD (computer-aided design) based recording of every brick or stone. Most recording of buildings occurs as part of the planning process (▶ p. 126) or during conservation work. A recent example is the Defence of Britain project, which collected records on surviving defensive monuments of the Second World War.

- www.britarch.ac.uk/projects/dob/index.html

Fieldwalking

Fieldwalking, or **surface collection**, involves systematic collection of artefacts from the ploughsoil which might be indicative of human settlement. This is based on the reasoning that material on the surface reflects buried remains. Sometimes high density scatters of particular materials such as building rubble or broken pottery enable specific sites such as buildings or kilns to be identified. More typically, the method helps identify areas of settlement or activities such as hunting. Ceramics and worked stone are the most commonly gathered but metal, bone and burnt stone are often also collected. The method is destructive in that archaeological material is removed, but as it has been disturbed by ploughing, it is not in its original context anyway.

Decisions about sampling have to be made when planning fieldwalking. Not everything will be collected, particularly when building rubble is involved. For instance, will all ceramics be collected or just diagnostic pieces? Decisions also have to be taken about the width of transects or size of grids.

Timing is important. Ideally ploughed soil should have been broken down by weathering and recent rain will have cleared dust from the surface. Walkers either proceed along a transect in a series of stints or search a grid. These have been carefully set out with marker flags or poles. Grids tend to be used when total coverage of a field is required. The material collected is bagged and tagged with the number of the grid or stint for processing and analysis.

Once washed and identified, finds are counted for each grid or stint. This can then be plotted on a distribution map to show patterns and concentrations. There are many ways of displaying this information. Phase maps or a series of clear plastic overlays for each period or type of find are commonly used. Computer displays using GIS have an edge here since several types of data can be linked to any point and comparisons easily made.

Fieldwalking is a well established method because it has many strengths. It is a relatively cheap way of surveying large areas since volunteer labour can be used to collect and wash finds. It can help establish the function and period of a

Figure 1.7 *A Level students fieldwalking*

The experience and training of fieldwalkers and the conditions on the day are factors affecting what is recovered (▶ p. 109).

KEY TERMS

Transects, traverses and stints.

A transect is a sampling line which could be across a single site or an entire landscape. It is usually aligned north–south and tied into the national grid. In fieldwalking transects are usually divided up into manageable chunks or stints of 10 to 50 metres where one walker will use one collecting bag. 'Traverse' is a term used largely in geophysics and sometimes aerial photography to describe the straight, parallel paths passed over by the surveyor. So a magnetometer survey might use traverses set at 0.5 metres apart.

site without excavation and provide insights into location and exchange.

Fieldwalking can indicate the spread and foci of evidence. It does, however, have important limitations too. It is only really useful on arable land where access has been granted and then only at certain times in the agricultural cycle. In addition, its results cannot be taken at face value. For example, medieval manuring practices transferred much domestic refuse to the ploughsoil, creating a doughnut shape pattern of pottery distribution. Chris Gerrard's work on the Shapwick Project has explored two other major limitations.

Different materials behave differently in the same soil. In Shapwick, rewalking the same fields and monitoring ceramics in them showed that some material migrates further than others. Patterns for pottery from different periods were also

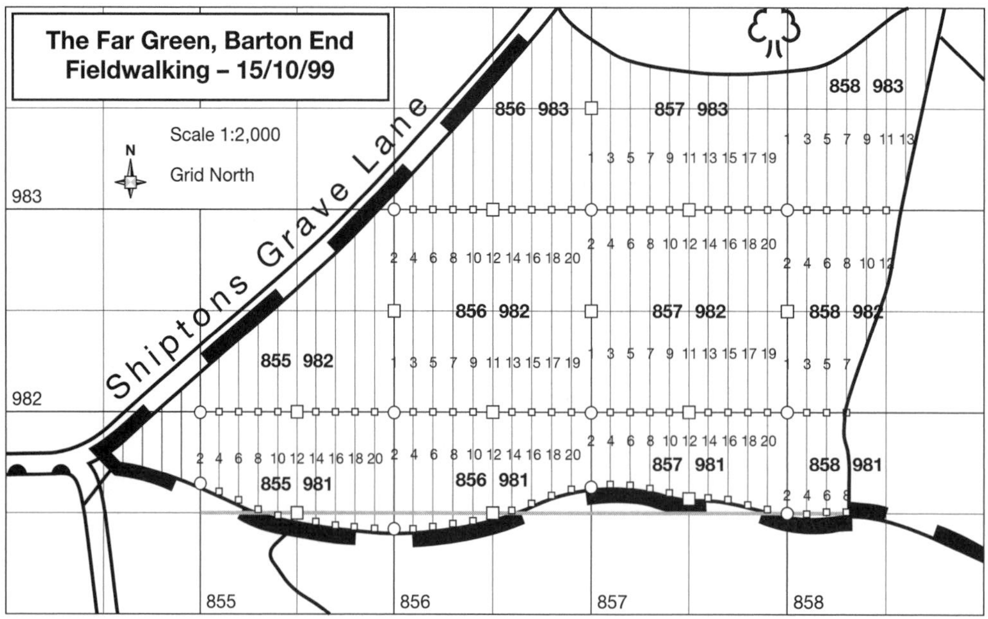

Figure 1.8 *A planned fieldwalk which has been linked to the national grid system. Transects are 10m apart with 50m stints*

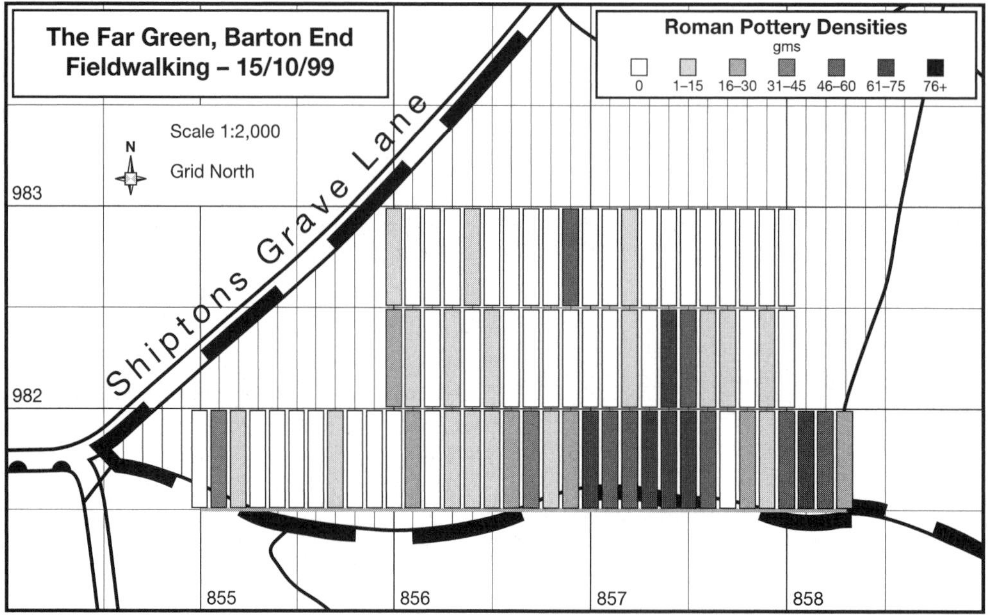

Figure 1.9 *The density of one category of finds plotted in relation to each fieldwalker's stint*

Amounts of selected materials can also be shown with shapes or dots where the size and colour or shading represent the numbers of finds.

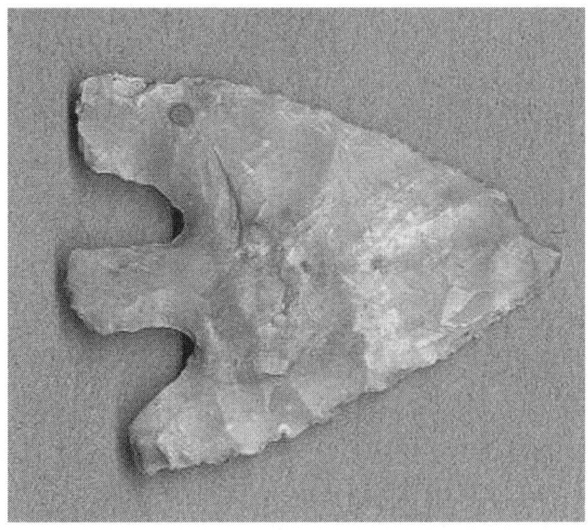

Figure 1.10 *An excellent example of a flint arrowhead recovered during fieldwalking at Thetford*

very different. It was not always a good indication of settlement. A second variable was the differential collection by different fieldwalkers. Analysis of their finds showed that some were good at recognising and collecting one type of material but poor with another. This applied to experienced walkers as well as novices. Their performance varied according to weather and slope. Taken together it means that what is recovered is a sample of what was in the topsoil and the topsoil holds a sample of what lies below. In both cases the sample varies for each type of find. Fieldwalking results therefore need to be cross-checked with other data before conclusions can be drawn.

There are a number of other prospection methods which provide alternatives to fieldwalking although all are more destructive. **Shovel pit testing** can take place in woods, pasture and

Figure 1.11 *A total station surveying coastal settlement in Dubai*

The total station combines the functions of theodolite, EDM and data logger. It is highly accurate in calculating heights, angles and distances and can be used to rapidly set out grids or to record the position of hundreds of points. These can later be downloaded and with the right software, used to produce 3D maps of the survey area.

Figure 1.12 *Shovel pit testing*

This approach to sampling is very common in the USA. Only the top few centimetres are sampled. In each sample a standard volume of soil is sieved through a fine mesh for ecofacts and artefacts.

gardens where fieldwalking is impossible. It may be a more reliable guide to settlement location if the area has not been ploughed in modern times.

Coring and **augering** are also used to sample the subsoil. This can provide a snapshot of the stratigraphy and the sample can be examined for artefactual or environmental evidence. **Probing,** which involves driving a rod into the ground, is more useful for tracing shallow buried features such as walls on known sites.

GEOCHEMICAL PROSPECTION

These relatively new methods and expensive techniques attempt to locate areas of past human activity by detecting differences in the chemical properties of the soil. All living things produce organic phosphate as waste or through decay. Unlike phosphate in fertiliser, this remains in the soil where it was deposited. Samples of soil are taken and levels of phosphate measured in a laboratory. Once plotted, concentrations of organic phosphate may indicate settlements or animal enclosures. Similar principles apply to heavy minerals such as lead and cadmium and to lipids (fats). These may become increasingly important in the future. One possibility is that different chemical combinations could identify 'signatures' (▶ p. 117) for different activities.

GEOPHYSICAL SURVEYS

This term covers techniques that detect features through their physical differences with the surrounding soil. The most common techniques detect magnetic and electrical anomalies and

Figure 1.13 *Taking a core sample during an inter-tidal survey*

A device such as a bucket auger is driven or screwed into the ground. It extracts a sample of the subsoil in much the same way as an apple corer.

require considerable skill to interpret. With the increasing involvement of archaeology in planning development and a shift in emphasis amongst archaeologists in favour of preservation rather than excavation, these techniques are now commonplace. The manufacture of increasingly reliable instruments for archaeology has seen magnetometry become a standard technique.

- http://www.geoscan-research.co.uk
- www.brad.ac.uk/acad/archsci/sbject/archpros.htm

Resistivity survey

There are differences in the ability of different soils to conduct electricity. This can be detected by passing an electric current through the ground and comparing readings. Electricity is conducted through the soil by mineral salts contained in water. The more moisture there is the better the conductivity of the soil. A buried ditch or grave will generally retain water better than the surrounding soil. A buried wall or road will conduct poorly and therefore resist the current more than the surrounding soil. Electrical current flows close to the surface so it can be measured using shallow probes. The method works better with some soils than others. Clay retains moisture well, so differences in resistance between the soil and buried ditches or pits may be impossible to detect. This also applies to many soils if they become waterlogged in wintertime. Plants, rocks and variations in the depths of soils can also create misleading readings.

Resistivity can also be used to create pseudo sections of buried features. This involves taking a series of readings from a line of probes placed across a buried feature such as a ditch. Wider spacing produces data on deeper parts of the feature than narrowly spaced probes. The depth to which this technology penetrates the soil is limited and readings require considerable interpretation, as the sensitivity of the meters is not great. At Hindwell in Wales, a 4-metre wide ditch identified by resistivity turned out after excavation to be a series of massive postholes with construction ramps.

Magnetometer surveying

The earth's magnetic field is generally uniform in any one place. However, local magnetic distortions can be caused by past human activity. Topsoil contains haematite (Fe_2O_3), an iron oxide. In some forms its crystals are magnetic. A ditch which has filled up with topsoil will contain more haematite than the surrounding area. Its' fill will therefore be slightly different magnetically and may be detected by sensitive, modern magnetometers.

A second type of distortion is caused where topsoil has been subject to considerable heat. This

Figure 1.14 *Resistivity surveying on the Long Man of Wilmington*

Meters are usually mounted on a 'zimmer-like' frame and have a data logger on board to record results. While relatively easy to use they are not fast and are best suited to detailed exploration of a site rather than initial prospecting. In this case a student is surveying the outline of the Long Man of Wilmington. Recent evidence based on soil erosion suggests that this version of Europe's tallest figure may date to the sixteenth century rather than prehistory.

RESISTIVITY

The resistivity meter works by detecting anomalies (differences) in the ability of subsurface remains to conduct electricity compared with the surrounding soil.

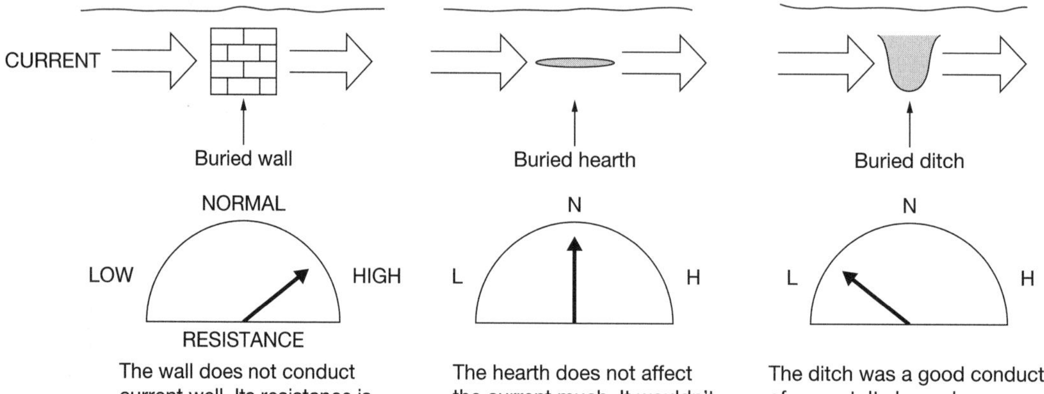

Figure 1.15 *A simplified diagram illustrating the principles of resistivity*

erases the magnetic properties of the iron oxides. For Haematite 675 °C is required. When the soil cools the iron oxides become permanently magnetised according to the polarity of the earth's magnetic field at that time. Since this field changes over time the sites of kilns and hearths appear as magnetic anomalies.

The earliest magnetometers were cumbersome and slow to use. The development of hand-held fluxgate gradiometers has enabled the technique to be used to rapidly scan quite large areas to highlight anomalies. Magnetometers are also used in detailed site investigations where they can detect small features up to 1 metre down and provide images of some buried features. For very detailed work traverses are set 0.5 metres apart with samples every 0.5 metres. 1 metre gaps and sample intervals are more common.

- http://www.archaeotechnics.co.uk/

To be able to detect anomalies, the magnetic background of the soil has to be measured and magnetometers calibrated against it. The measuring of this **magnetic susceptibility** of the topsoil can also be used as a crude but rapid survey technique in its own right. Magnetic hotspots suggest areas of past settlement or industrial activity, which could be surveyed using other methods.

- http://ds.dial.pipex.com/town/terrace/ld36/magsus.htm

Sensitive magnetic instruments are easily disturbed by iron, including nails, pipes and wire fences as well as the zips and piercings of the archaeologist. A further limitation can be background interference from magnetic bedrock or where a long period of occupation has left a magnetic layer over a wide area. Sandy and clay soils often do not provide sufficient contrast.

Figure 1.16 *A hand held magnetometer*

A hand held magnetometer used on the same survey as Figure 1.14. Note how much less cumbersome and easier it is to move it is.

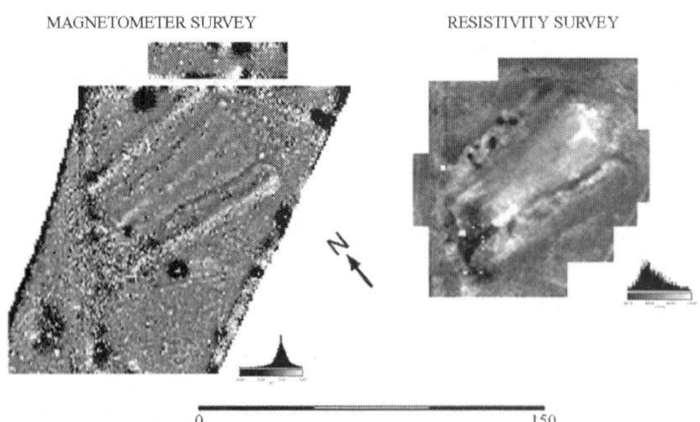

Figure 1.17 *Resistance and Magnetometer plots compared*

The essential complementary nature of these techniques can be seen in these plots from English Heritage's survey of White Barrow.

For larger version see p. 341.

KEY TASK

Test your understanding of geophysics

Which of the two main geophysical methods would normally be effective in detecting these buried features? Answers on p. 330.

1 Hearths
2 Cobbled floors
3 Stone walls
4 Graves
5 Kilns
6 Large pits
7 Stakeholes
8 Building platforms
9 Small pits
10 Ditches

Fluctuations in the earth's magnetic field also have to be taken into account. It requires considerable skill and experience to interpret the results.

Caesium vapour (CV) magnetometers

These are many times more sensitive than conventional magnetometers and are more commonly used in Germany and Austria. Typically several machines are used close together on a large handcart. They work by pumping caesium vapour and taking rapid measurements at around 25cm intervals. This alkali is sensitive to minute variations in magnetism. It is so sensitive that it can define shapes along the edges of buried features formed by magnetite (an Iron Oxide Fe_3O_4) concentrated in the remains of bacteria which have consumed wooden structures such as posts. Recent work at Stanton Drew revealed the 'ghosts' of hundreds of postholes in concentric circles. However, at £40,000 per machine and perhaps four on a cart, this technique is expensive.

Other methods

Metal detectors are useful for metal objects down to about 15 cm. Some archaeologists use them on site to provide information in advance of digging such as the position of burial deposits. Skill is required to avoid time being wasted exploring buried slag or modern metal debris. Similarly they can sweep areas in advance of detailed geophysics to identify concentrations of metal that might distort readings.

Ground penetrating radar (GPR) which was developed for defence and engineering is starting to be used in archaeology. Aerial versions can highlight buried landscapes and rivers. GPR works by transmitting pulses of energy into the ground and recording the time taken and strength of the return signal. This can indicate the density and depth of buried deposits. Data based on different energy wavelengths can be plotted as a series of 'time slices' to build up a 3D picture of buried remains.

Sonar, which was developed to detect submarines is a form of acoustic sensing. Side scan sonar measures sound waves as they 'bounce back' and can map the sea bed and reveal the depth and form of sunken structures. *Bosing* is a crude form of acoustic sensing used on land. It involves hitting the ground with a mallet and listening for variations in resonant sounds. These may indicate buried ditches or walls.

Finally there is *dowsing*. This is a traditional method by which skilled dowsers use wooden rods to detect water or archaeology underground.

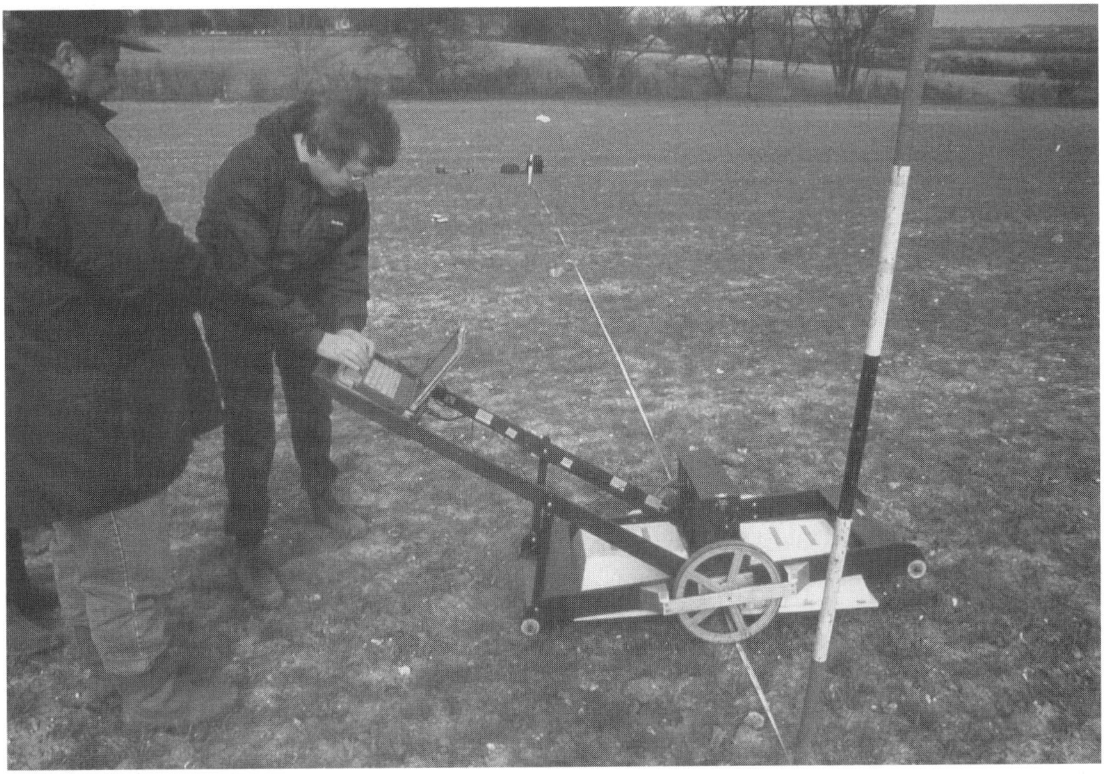

Figure 1.18 *Handcart mounted GPR*

Ground versions of GPR are useful for detecting buried floors, voids and walls. It has been particularly effective in revealing the internal structures of buildings and exploring burials. It is the only effective geophysics technique in city centres where it can even penetrate tarmac. Due to its cost and the availability of quicker methods it has not been used widely outside urban areas in the UK although this is starting to change. It also works poorly on clay soils.

KEY SKILL

Comparing methods

Construct your own table for geophysics and geochemical methods to summarise and compare strengths and weaknesses as shown below. Research and add an additional example to each.

Method	*Strengths*	*Limitations*	*Example*
Resistivity			
Magnetometry			

All of these geophysical techniques are limited in the type of work they can do and they should therefore be seen as complementary. None of them are particularly useful on waterlogged sites. Their value is often in pinpointing or exploring features rather than finding new sites.

AERIAL PHOTOGRAPHY

The first aerial photographs (APs) were taken from balloons. Today, most photographs are taken from light aircraft although even kites or balloons are used on occasions. APs are used for mapping, finding new sites rapidly over large areas and illustrating and exploring known sites. Substantial archives of aerial photographs are available publicly and commercially so new pictures may not always be needed.

- http://aarg.univie.ac.at/
- www.evidenceincamera.co.uk/
- http://www.nmia.com/~jaybird/AANewsletter/

Verticals and obliques

Aerial photographs used for mapping are taken with the camera pointing straight down at the ground (*verticals*) with the aircraft flying along grid lines. Often these are taken from high altitude. This is the case with the RAF archives dating from the 1940s which are now housed at the NMR. These also provide an excellent desktop source for initial study of landscape developments. Overlapping vertical photographs can be viewed through a stereoscope to see the landscape in 3D. Their main value is in planning and illustrating sites. Where some dimensions in the photograph are known, reasonably accurate plans can be drawn of sites, including their contours. This is known as photogrammetric mapping.

Oblique photographs are the most widely used in archaeology to locate sites and illustrate features. These are taken from low-flying aircraft with the picture taken at an angle to the ground. Aerial reconaissance usually precedes field survey. While is is fast and gives good coverage, it can be expensive and can miss features if their **signatures** are not visible from the air. Equally, there may be features which are invisible at ground level and this provides the only means of recording them. There are three main ways in which archaeological sites show up from the air.

Shadow sites

In low light, either at the start or end of the day, shadows are at their longest and even quite minor variations in ground level cast shadows, for instance ploughed out barrows or the remains of early field systems.

APs taken from a low-flying aircraft and recorded with a camera pointed into the sun have a distorted perspective which emphasises shadows. The technique is best used for illustrating existing sites and locating details within them, for example features inside a hill fort. However, shadows are also created where crops are at different heights (▶ p. 23) and occasionally new sites can be detected. Winter is the best season for photography as the sun is low and vegetation which might mask sites has often died down. Snowfall and flooding can accentuate the appearance of hollows and earthworks and create some of the most dramatic images of **shadow sites**.

Cropmarks

The ripening and growth rate of crops is related to the amount of moisture their root systems can access. Plants with better access to moisture will often grow taller and turn a different tone or colour than those plants around them. If there are buried archaeological features under a field this can result in patterns showing in the crop. A buried ditch with its infill of humus and topsoil will often hold moisture, creating a dark green line in the crop above. This 'positive' **cropmark** is visible from the air. The opposite occurs in plants

Figure 1.19 *An excellent view of the deserted medieval village (DMV) of Bingham's Melcombe, which shows up because of shadows cast by low sunlight. Traces of houses, enclosures and trackways are all visible*

Note how features at right angles to the sun show up best.

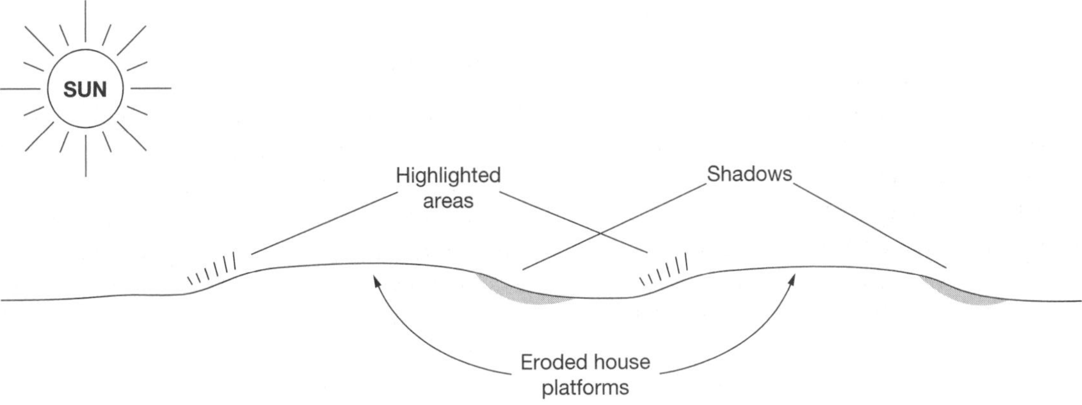

Figure 1.20 *Why earthworks are visible as 'shadow sites'*

over a buried wall. They are likely to be stunted and produce a yellowish, 'negative' cropmark. 'Parch marks' show on grass for the same reason.

Cropmarks sometimes only show for a few days a year. Repeatedly flying over areas over time can pick up new and different features. Some only show up in drought conditions when crops with access to moisture have the greatest advantage and colour contrast is exaggerated. The technique works best on quickly draining soils such as river gravels but is less good on clay or areas of deeper topsoil, where the soil retains moisture well. Cropmarks show up best in cereal crops such as wheat and particularly barley. They do not show up in many crops, for example peas and beans, and the effect of differential moisture can be overcome or masked by irrigation or fertiliser. Care has to be taken with interpretation, as geological features such as periglacial cracks and modern field drainage and underground pipelines also create cropmarks. Trial excavation is often the only way to firmly identify many sites. Cropmarks are the most prolific source of new sites, particularly for the late Neolithic to early medieval periods, and are also used to investigate existing sites such as the extent of the harbour at Fishbourne Palace.

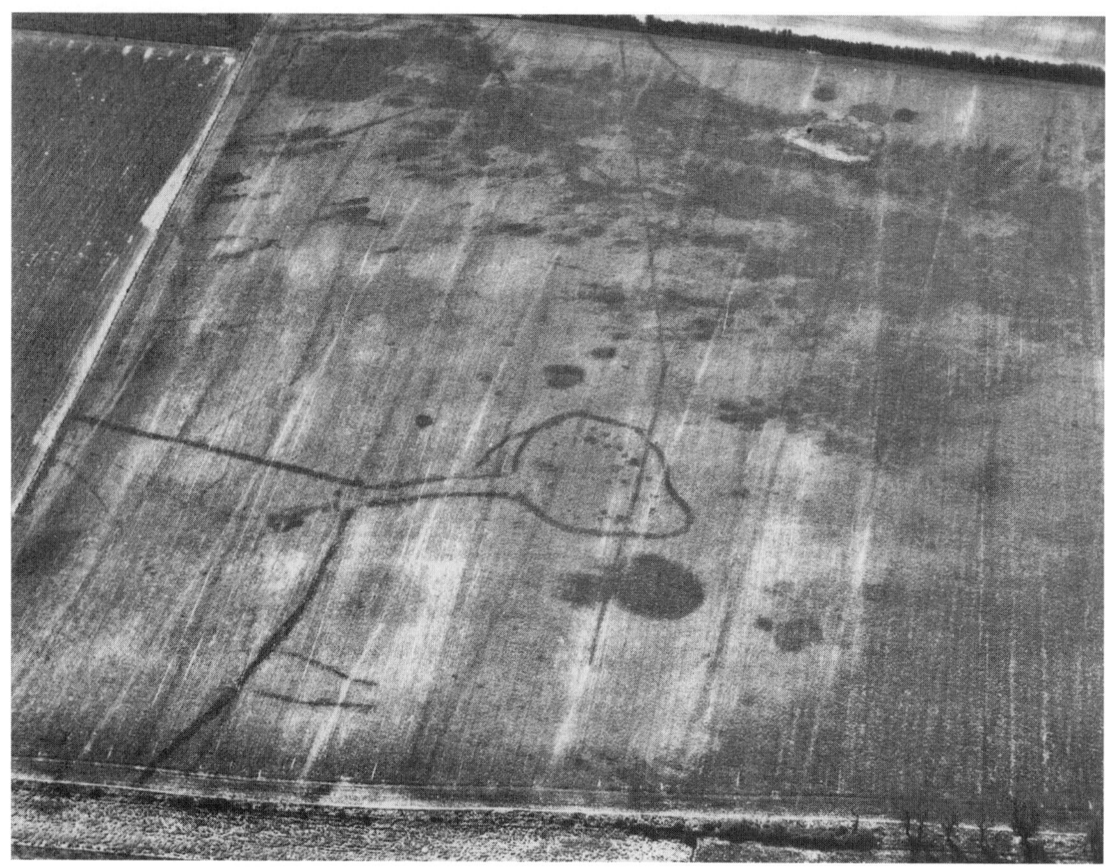

Figure 1.21 *An Iron Age 'banjo' enclosure on Cranborne Chase showing as a dark cropmark*

The crops growing over the ditches of the feature are darker because their roots have better access to moisture than the surrounding crops. Crown Copyright 1955 & 1959/MOD.

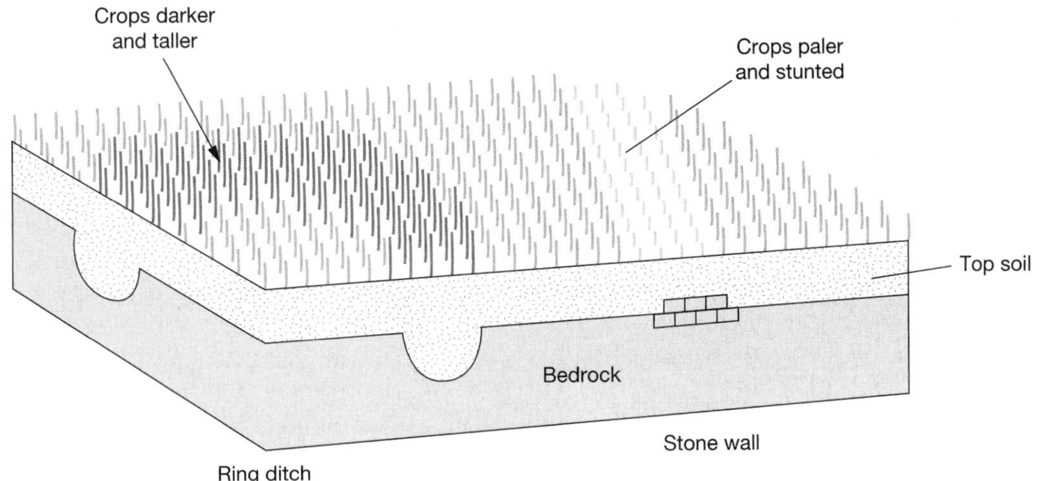

Figure 1.22 *Three-dimensional cross section of cropmarks*

Soil marks

On soils where there is a marked contrast between the colour of the topsoil and subsoil, evidence of ploughed-out monuments can occur as **soil marks**. On chalk, the dark brown of ditch infill will contrast with the chalk rubble of a bank and the lighter brown of the plough soil. At Flag Fen a Roman road appeared as an orangish stripe against the black peat soil. Soil marks are sharpest in winter when vegetation is low.

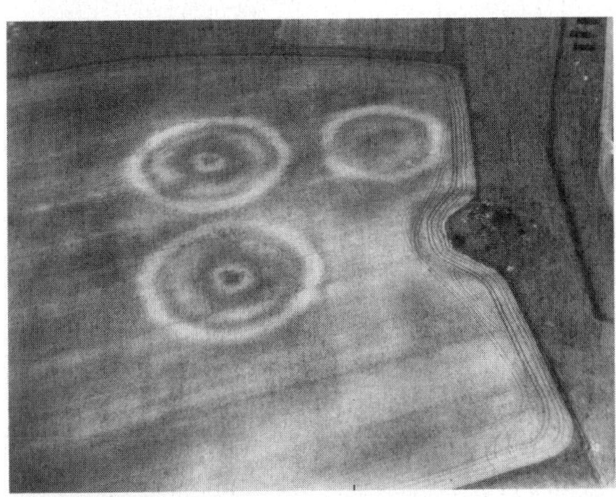

Figure 1.23 *Winterbourne Stoke round barrow cemetery showing as soil marks*

The difference in tone between the top soil and the material used for the barrow provides a clear contrast. The monuments would not be easily detected on the ground.

Remote sensing

This can be a rather confusing term. Usually it is used to distinguish between the imaging techniques used from planes and satellites and those of ground based prospection. Sometimes it is used to describe all techniques that don't remove material. When you come across it, be sure to check which sense it is being used in. We are using it in the first sense. The results of all these techniques need to be checked at ground level.

- http://www.arcl.ed.ac.uk/arch/remotesense/

A variety of airborne and satellite techniques, including thermal imaging and infrared photography, are able to record temperature, dew and frost dispersal variations invisible to light-sensitive film. They all work on the principle that anomalies such as disturbed earth or buried walls will absorb and retain heat or moisture at different rates to the surrounding ground. Commercial equipment is really only suitable for large features although military developments to increase sensitivity will no doubt filter through to archaeology. Currently such equipment is too expensive for most archaeological surveys.

Radar has been used to find sites both on land and at sea. Its ability to penetrate both clouds and dense jungle has made it particularly useful in Mesoamerica.

KEY SKILL

Short questions test

This exercise is in the format of part of AS Level Archaeology paper 1.

Examine the aerial photograph below.

1a Describe the markings you can see in the field. *2 mks*
1b Why do these marks show up? *5 mks*
1c What non-invasive investigation could archaeologists undertake to help identify these features? *7 mks*

A suggested mark scheme is on ▶ p. 330.

Figure 1.24 *Aerial photo of Wyke Down*

Chapter 2

Excavation

YOUR GOALS

You need to understand

- why and when excavation is undertaken
- what can be achieved by excavation
- the advantages and disadvantages of common excavation strategies
- the principles of stratigraphy
- how artefacts and faunal and floral material are recovered during excavations
- the techniques of recording used in excavation.

To many people, archaeology simply means excavation. Often their interest in archaeology stems from witnessing an excavation or viewing one on television. Excavation is often the public face of archaeology. It is only when people 'dig' deeper into the subject that they are able to recognise the role that excavation plays in the wider nature of the discipline. It has its own methodology, which constantly changes to reflect current thinking and improving technologies. There can never be one set of rules for excavation although there is general agreement on key elements of the process. This chapter will try to reflect that current consensus.

WHY EXCAVATE?

Any removal of the accumulated evidence of the past is a finite act. Once disturbed, trowelled, shovelled and bucketed away that material cannot be replaced as it was before the excavator removed it. Hence it has been frequently said that 'all excavation is destruction'. Today no one condones excavation as it took place in the nineteenth century: for the pleasure of the excavators and to establish collections of artefacts. In all but those extreme circumstances, where chance discovery of remains demands a prompt response, there should be controlled planning. This should establish the rationale for excavation and formulate a series of questions, which it is hoped, the excavation might answer.

Often the record of a site can be remarkably full if a wide range of reconnaissance methods has been applied and there are sufficient clues about hidden features or structures. In many cases, once the record of such survey activities is carefully housed in an appropriate archive, for example the local SMR, archaeologists leave the physical remains untouched. If, however, a decision is made to excavate, it should be viewed as a very serious step. While most scientific experiments can be repeated over and over again in the laboratory, archaeological excavation, although scientific in its approach, does not, by its very nature, allow a second chance. Some excavation procedures, somewhat confusingly referred to as sampling strategies, have been developed to try and ensure that not all the evidence is removed in the primary investigation of a feature or deposit. Nevertheless, in essence, excavation means destruction. However, that 'destruction' is minimised if the archaeologist pays appropriate care and attention to the way the excavation is conducted and particularly to the quality of the records kept. This is sometimes referred to as 'preservation by record'

There are other considerations. A balance must be struck between the desire to protect archaeological remains for future generations and the need to develop the discipline and advance our knowledge through excavation. It is also important that archaeology is kept sufficiently in the public eye to receive the support it needs in the wider political forum. All these issues are explored further in Chapter 6.

Today, excavators are expected to:

- provide justifications for digging a site
- use survey techniques to plan excavation strategies

Figure 2.1 *No it isn't a row of onions*

The reuse of ceramic containers for drainage purposes in the town walls at Cremona in Italy presents an archaeological dilemma. Should all the vessels be recorded in situ and excavated by hand or treated as fill and a sample of complete and diagnostic pieces kept and the rest discarded?

KEY SITE

Avebury

Recent research at Avebury demonstrates the way new questions and techniques can reveal new information about one of Britains best known monuments.

The West Kennet Avenue, a double line of stones running to Avebury from the Sanctuary, is well known but in the eighteenth century the antiquarian Stukeley recorded a second avenue leading past Beckhampton. Today only two of the hundreds of stones he drew survive. Investigation to test his account began with investigation of a cropmark of what appeared to be an oval enclosure lying adjacent to the suspected line of the avenue at 'Longstones'. Three universities assisted by English Heritage took part. Trial trenches revealed that the enclosure seemed to be a hybrid of several types. Its 1m deep ditch with an internal bank was segmented like causewayed enclosures but was associated with grooved ware and feasting debris like late Neolithic timber enclosures. Furthermore, it had been deliberately back-filled after a short period. Around 2500BC the Beckhampton Avenue was built over it. Following geophysics surveys, excavation exposed shallow stone sockets and stones buried in the medieval period. A complex 'cove' which had been remodelled several times was also discovered. Possibly this was a stone version of the sanctuary. It seems Stukeley had been right.

In Figure 2.2 the AP plot of the oval enclosure is shown as a dotted line. Trenches 11–15 section the ditch of the enclosure. To the east an area excavation investigates the stone settings.

Elsewhere, a new survey of the gap in the West Kennet Avenue by Pollard found that far from stones having been removed, they may never have existed there. In the 'gap' natural sarsens were lying in a dry valley. Perhaps they were a staging point on a processional route to Avebury. Pottery and flint was found there and also in larger amounts in a midden discovered under the avenue just south of Avebury. It might seem strange to walk through rubbish but this might have significance as a place of ancestors and fertility.

Investigation also occurred at the cove (Figure 2.3) where engineering work was undertaken to straighten a huge megalith which appeared in danger of toppling. Amazingly, there were another 3 metres of it underground and it was probably quite stable. It weighed between 50 and 100 tons and must have been a significant landmark before it was brought to this site and erected. Its date of 3000BC suggested it could have pre-dated the henge. Curiously, its packing included lumps of clay brought from over 10 miles away.

- http://www.stonehenge-avebury.net/
- http://www.eng-h.gov.uk/reports/beckhampton/
- *Current Archaeology* 167

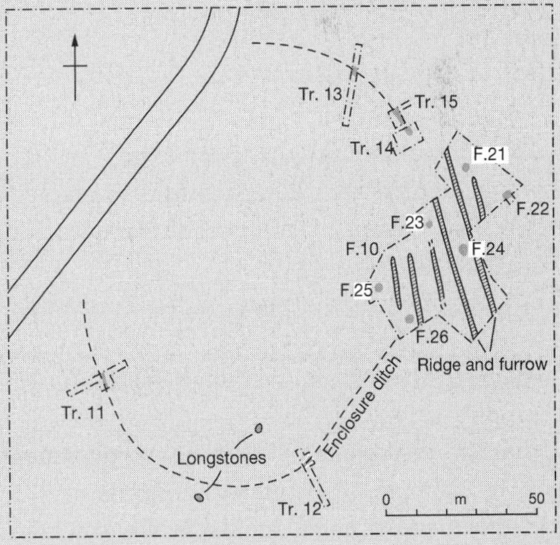

Figure 2.2 *Plan of the Longstones excavations*

KEY SITE *cont.*

Avebury

Figure 2.3 *The cove at Avebury*

- adjust to subsequent changes on site
- put a complete recording system is in place
- select and maintain appropriate samples for analysis
- have facilities for all aspects of post-excavation work
- interpret a site from a limited excavation or sample
- 'publish' the results of the work so that they are available to other interested parties
- maintain professional standards while working under time and economic constraints.

If this is done then excavation can move beyond the possible results of survey and get to the real core of archaeology – the hard evidence left by previous people of their existence.

TYPES OF EXCAVATION

Excavations today usually fall into one of two broad categories depending on the main reason for them: research or rescue.

Research excavations

These are usually excavations on sites where there is no immediate threat of destruction. The site is selected by archaeologists for its suitability to answer the questions they wish to answer. It can be excavated according to archaeological needs rather than prompted by the threat of development. Research excavation is only undertaken when the perceived benefits to archaeological understanding outweigh the loss of the original site, or part of it, to future generations.

There is little public or commercial funding of research excavation so archaeologists have to finance themselves by alternative means. For instance, universities that run 'training excavations' for their undergraduates may also accept paying 'volunteers'. (▶ p. 123) Applied research agencies, for example the British Academy, provide some support for this type of long-term research.

Rescue excavations

'Rescue excavation' was a term coined in the 1960s when much of our archaeological heritage was destroyed by development and road building. It involved trying to excavate and record as much as possible in the time before the builders began work. Occasionally sites were not discovered until bulldozing began. Rapid recording and rushed excavation in these circumstances was often the best that could be done. This was often called '*salvage archaeology*'. Some excavations in inter-tidal areas (▶ p. 54) still fall into this category. The term is used in the USA interchangeably with 'rescue archaeology'.

Today most digs are rescue excavation. These take place within the framework of the planning process. (▶ See Chapter 6.) Exploratory excavations are often used alongside remote sensing to establish the nature and extent of archaeological deposits. These '*impact assessments*' inform discussions between archaeologists, planners and contractors. To avoid the heavy costs and delays in construction caused by full excavation, a series of '*mitigation strategies*' (▶ p. 129) are often adopted. These involve building whilst trying to minimize damage to archaeology. This is known as '*preservation in situ*' (▶ p. 129). However, where excavation does go ahead, archaeologists will often set their priorities against research questions as well as time and cost considerations. Unless they miscalculate or uncover unexpected remains they have time to carry out their work according to proper archaeological principles. Once the bulldozers move in, archaeologists keep a '*watching brief*' (▶ p. 129). This means that they can stop building work to record archaeology which turns up unexpectedly.

Amongst the key differences between the two approaches is the ability of research archaeologists to select sites and also to fully excavate all sites. Rescue archaeology has sometimes resulted in many tiny 'keyhole' excavations into parts of sites rather than always revealing large parts of them. However, sometimes the differences can be overstated. The Channel Tunnel rail link from London to Dover resulted in the largest archaeological project to date in the UK. Engineers and archaeologists from eight different groups worked together to ensure that archaeological issues were fully considered. All forms of survey work were carried out; over 2,000 trial trenches and test pits were dug. Fieldwork informed the setting of priorities about where to excavate. Some 55 hectares of the route were identified as requiring detailed archaeological investigation. Planning of the work gave archaeologists time to 'painstakingly' record the archaeological deposits on the sites selected for detailed work. Other areas were subject to watching briefs. In this particular scheme the archaeologists were empowered to stop construction work if 'features of significance' were identified. Over forty sites were excavated with dates ranging from the Palaeolithic to the Second World War. The impact of the new evidence will alter many current perceptions of Kent's archaeology.

• See *Current Archaeology 168.*

KEY SITE

Empingham, Rutland

The excavation of this site provides an insight into excavation before modern planning rules. The valley of the river Gwash was of little interest to people outside Rutland until planners in the 1970s decided to build a dam across it. The area flooded would create Rutland Water – one of England's largest lakes. The chance find of an Anglo-Saxon brooch and the discovery through fieldwalking of two Romano-British sites in the area enabled archaeologists to plan rescue excavations on an Anglo-Saxon cemetery, a Romano-British farmstead and a villa. Despite the looming engineering development, excavations over three seasons were designed and conducted with adequate time for the removal and recording of features and finds. When the developers began work a watching brief was negotiated (▶ p. 129) but then the nature of the archaeological work changed considerably.

Mechanical scrapers systematically stripped the landscape of its topsoil on both sides of the river for 2 kilometres back from the dam. Watching archaeologists made a whole series of unexpected discoveries. These included:

- two burials in stone coffins
- a third major Romano-British site
- an Iron Age roundhouse
- two Anglo-Saxon grubenhauser
- a sunken Iron Age trackway
- a large Anglo-Saxon inhumation cemetery with 130 burials.

An excavation team and resources had to be gathered at short notice to deal with the situation. The Romano-British site and burials were excavated rapidly as they lay right in the path of

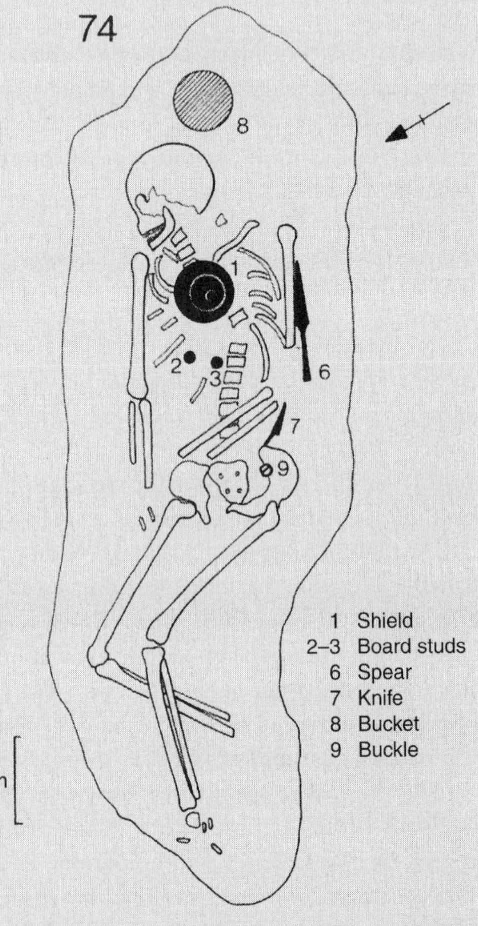

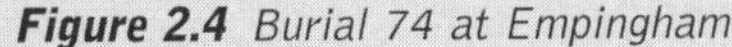

Figure 2.4 *Burial 74 at Empingham*

A plan of a skeleton in the grave to show positions of bones and grave goods. The skeleton of a male aged about 25–30 years old was accompanied by a shield boss; two boards studs, a spearhead, an iron knife, a copper alloy-bound wooden bucket and an iron buckle. Preserved wood remains in the spear socket were identified as willow and poplar and in the bucket as yew. See drawing of finds in Figure 3.13 (▶ p. 71).

KEY SITE *cont.*

Empingham, Rutland

the diggers and no further delays were possible. This is an example of 'salvage archaeology'. The developers agreed to 'work around' the archaeologists which enabled a higher level of excavation and recording.

Cooper 2000

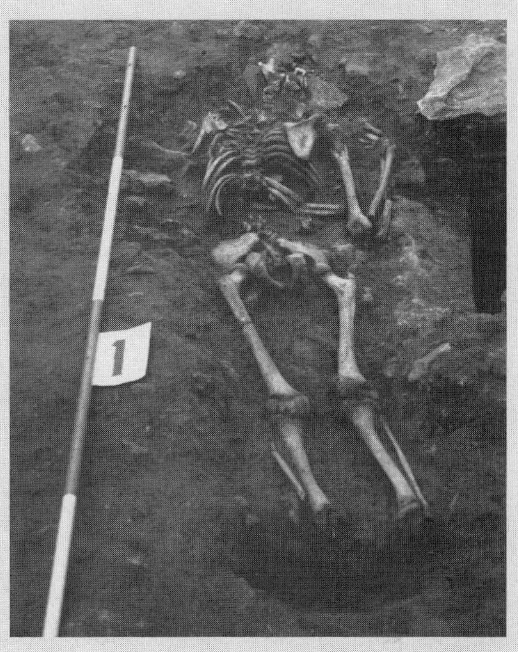

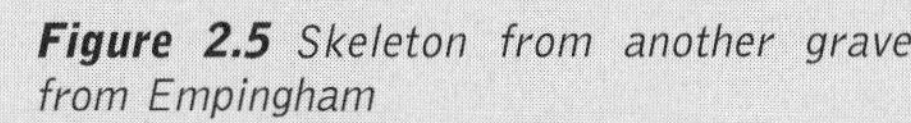

Figure 2.5 *Skeleton from another grave from Empingham*

Note the different information provided by plan on p.32 and this photograph.

EXCAVATION STRATEGIES AND THE PROCESS OF EXCAVATION

The decision to dig will originate either in a research project or because remains are due to be destroyed. In either case the excavation director will make plans based on what is known from desktop surveys and reconnaissance. These plans will aim to answer a series of questions at different levels. An example of a question linked to wider debates might be 'Did towns decay early in the 4th century AD?' A more specific question might be 'Why was this site abandoned?' Below that might be a whole series of questions such as establishing the date of deposits and understanding site formation processes (▶ p. 105). These

Figure 2.6 *Rescue excavation of a Roman barn*

The M6 Toll motorway created a huge transect across the West Midlands. Many sites were located and recorded along the route including the post settings of this Roman barn.

KEY TERMS

Features and cuts

Features are traces in the soil of past human activity. A distinction can be made between

* Constructed features which were deliberately built such as a wall, fish trap or pond
* Cumulative features which develop from repeated actions. Middens, hollow-ways and the shallow gullies known as drip rings which encircled round houses are good examples.

While some features are obvious, many are not. Only the faintest traces of a stakehole may survive as slight variations in the colour or texture of soil only detectable by an experienced excavator. Many small features such as ditches or postholes may in fact be elements in one larger feature which is only revealed when excavation recording is complete. The term 'cut' is increasingly used to describe dug features such as pits, ditches and postholes.

The site below is seen topstripped before Green's (2000) research dig. The major features or cuts are revealed as discolorations in the chalk but excavation was required to identify them. They proved to be a ring of pits with a central pit 10m wide and 1.5m deep. Hidden in this pit was a burial of a woman and three children and a 7m deep shaft down to a seam of flint.

Figure 2.7 *Features at Neolithic ritual site at Monkton Up Wimborne*

questions along with constraints of time and money will lead to decisions about where and how to dig.

Defining the site in question is the first issue (▶ p. 194). In excavation terms some 'sites' are in fact a series of smaller 'sites' in themselves. For example, cropmarks may indicate a series of **features** (enclosures, pits, tracks) which can be separated out for investigation while a Roman town has a street plan and a variety of public and private buildings each capable of individual excavation. Sites are set within a landscape context and a successful excavation needs to take note of that factor too. So the director needs to decide whether it is the entirety of the site that is the focus of their attention or whether concentration on certain parts offers the best chance to answer their questions.

If there are many similar features it is likely that a number will be sampled rather than excavating every one. This can mean that some deposits are not recorded to the same extent as others. For example Georgian housing might be relatively neglected because the main interest is in an underlying Roman forum.

- http://museums.ncl.ac.uk/raunds/
- http://www.jungsteinsite.de/2000_gibson/hindwell.htm

There is no set manual for archaeological field practices either in relation to where to put the holes in the ground or in how to proceed once the excavation trench is underway. This is not because archaeologists have a laissez-faire attitude to standards and procedures but because of variety in the nature of sites, evidence and questions asked. Most texts on excavation express their ideas about appropriate 'good practice' and as new methods evolve so they too appear in print. The archaeological world constantly shares its experiences and a general consensus of current good practice is evident when one looks at images of modern excavations. Practitioners learn from one another and try to keep their methods in line with current thinking and therefore ensure that their results, when published, stand up to scrutiny and are accepted by their peers. For example, many archaeological units use the Museum of London excavation manual.

The nature of the archaeological record in the ground is often complex. Human nature and life circumstances ensure that most sites have a developmental history, which the archaeologist needs to unravel. The people who left the evidence went about their daily business without a thought for how their activities might leave traces for future investigators. They were not simply creating 'features' much of the time, nor did they often build a structure and leave it unaltered. However, their constructional or daily activities will have created a sequence of deposits, layers or **contexts** (the words are often used interchangeably) which build up to create the archaeological record. Contained within these deposits, which are linked to features and structures, are the **artefacts** of pottery, metalwork, etc. and **ecofacts**, which provide sources for understanding the chronological, cultural and environmental nature of the site.

One further issue which excavators have to be aware of is the health and safety of their diggers. Precautions range from hardhats and reflective clothing on developer sites to ensuring that deep trenches are properly shored up or have stepped sides. Safety issues are most evident on underwater sites where air supply, currents, cold and sharks are amongst the potential hazards not faced on land.

How to dig?

The excavation methodology debate centres on the fact that all sites have two key elements. A vertical sequence of layers containing structures and finds, and the horizontal layout of an occupation area or individual structure. It is difficult for a method to explore both equally well but to record both elements is vital. Unless the archaeologist can establish the correct succession of levels

KEY CONCEPTS

Stratigraphy, contexts and phases

In any text about archaeological sites you will come across terms such as level, layer, deposit, stratum. They describe the make-up of the excavated ground in terms of layers. These were created either by people or nature. Archaeologists attempt to carefully record these strata – the **stratification**. By studying their relationship they can build up a sequence of events on the site. The study of the strata is known as stratigraphy.

If no intrusive features are present (for example a pit dug from an upper/recent layer down through lower/older layers) it would be safe to assume that layers at the bottom of any sequence are older than those at the top. Each successive layer was deposited after the one directly below it. This is sometimes referred to as 'the law of **superposition**'. But life and archaeological sites are not usually that simple. Archaeologists need to establish which layers overlie others and which cut into earlier layers or are cut by later ones.

Figure 2.8 *A picture that demonstrates how the law of superposition can tell a story*

The female skeleton is lying above the mosaic at Kingscote and covered by building debris. The interpretation is that she was one of a number of 'squatters' who occupied the derelict villa building but was killed, apparently trying to escape, when it collapsed.

It is within the layers that the artefactual, environmental and dating evidence is located. Layers are a time capsule. Materials in any layer are likely to be broadly contemporary and can be dated by association with dateable evidence from that layer. The layer holds the clues to the immediate context of finds and structures. Plotting the position of each layer within the site helps determine chronological patterns. Other archaeologists will use published data about the stratification to assure themselves of the authenticity of the conclusions reached about phasing on a site.

Increasingly **context** is used for both layers and features. Each individual element in the stratigraphy is a context. A context might result from a single event such as a fire or roof collapse or a build up of soil against a wall over several years. The task of the digger is to identify each context and to trace the boundaries or 'interfaces' between contexts. This may only be detectable by minute changes in the colour, texture or composition of the soil. Typically contexts will be identified in the side of a trench by nails and labels. (▶ p. 40). A description is also noted on a **context sheet** (▶ p. 47). Once recorded, the stratigraphic relationship between contexts can be determined and a vertical, chronological sequence based on successive 'events' established. Stratigraphy is usually

KEY CONCEPTS *cont.*

Stratigraphy, contexts and phases

recorded in section drawings (▶ p. 49). However, since 1973 the Harris Matrix has revolutionized the presentation of the sequences in schematic diagrams. This interpretative system can be applied to standing buildings and rock art as well as to excavated remains.

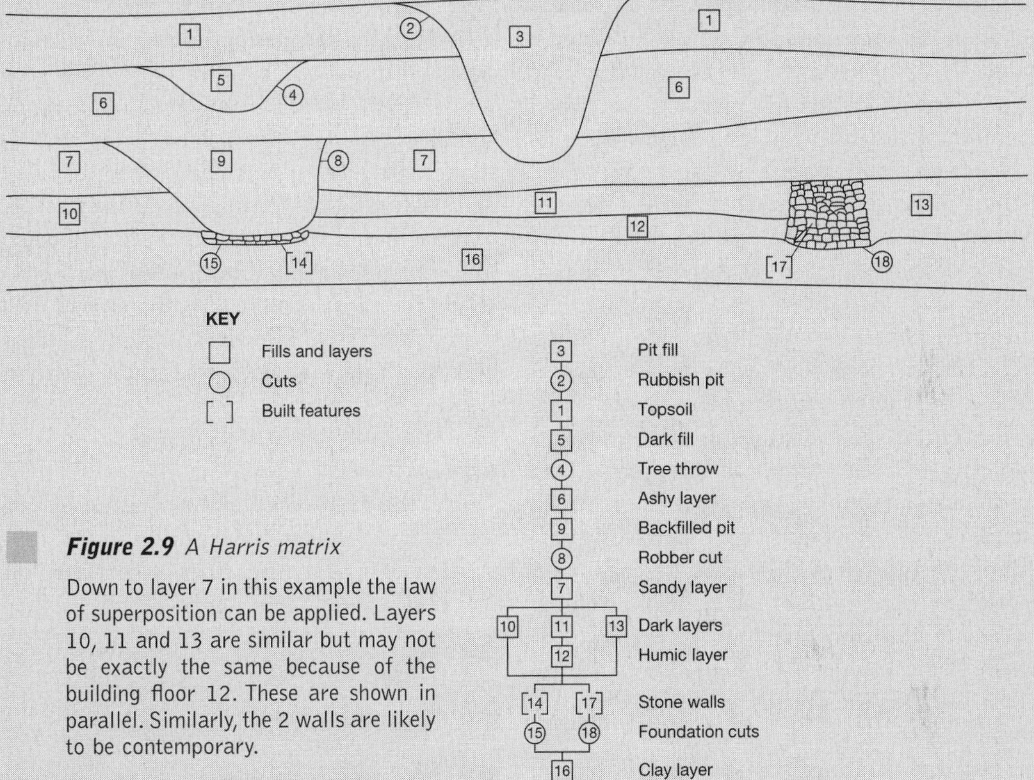

Figure 2.9 *A Harris matrix*

Down to layer 7 in this example the law of superposition can be applied. Layers 10, 11 and 13 are similar but may not be exactly the same because of the building floor 12. These are shown in parallel. Similarly, the 2 walls are likely to be contemporary.

Context is also used in a general sense when talking about finds and their relationship to layers. This is based on the principle that objects found together in the same layer are roughly from the same period and can be dated by association with dateable evidence from that deposit (▶ p. 90). Associated finds may also have a relationship. They may help to explain each other because they were used in the same activity or process. If the context of an artefact is not known, it is usually of little use to archaeologists.

Once sequences and associations of finds are established, different phases of the site can be determined. This relies on recognizing significant changes in the assemblages of artefacts or ecofacts or type of structures. For example, the first phase with pottery on a site might be preceded with a final aceramic phase.

http://www.harrismatrix.com

an excavation will have limited, if any, value. Similarly the inability to produce the plan (layout) of a building or a cemetery leaves the researcher well short of the required results. Archaeologists have therefore developed a series of methods appropriate to different types of site.

Trenches and test pits

The term 'trench' has been applied to any linear excavation and sometimes to any hole cut into the ground by archaeologists, whatever its surface shape. A stricter definition is a rectangular shaped excavation of variable width and length. Test pits or 'sondages' are essentially square trenches, usually 1 metre square. Trenches and test pits are used either to evaluate the stratigraphy of a site before a decision is made on whether or not to excavate or as part of an excavation sampling strategy. By digging down either to bedrock or the top of the archaeological deposits the vertical profile of part of the site can be examined. This provides information about depth of deposits and complexity of contexts. It can also provide an opportunity for sampling environmental remains. Sometimes mechanical diggers are used to dig part or all of the trench in which case the trench is 1.5 metres wide – the width of the digger bucket.

Those of you who have watched the TV programme 'Time Team' will be familiar with the use of trial trenches to investigate possible features identified by reconnaissance methods. This is also done on many sites after 'top-stripping' of topsoil (▶ p. 43). In very large sites trenches are used to investigate linear archaeological features such as defensive **earthworks** by being placed at 90° to the alignment of the feature. The trenches cut by Alcock through the defences of South Cadbury hill fort in Somerset provide a classic example. By strategically placing a series of 2-metre wide trenches around the hill he was able to study and report on the developmental sequence of the site's fortifications. This had the added bonus of disturbing a small proportion of the site in return for a large volume of evidence. Most of the site was left undamaged for future archaeologists. Other linear features such as roads and boundaries can be cross-sectioned in this way. Offa's Dyke, an early medieval feature running from north to south Wales, has been the focus of a long-term study by Manchester University and over 100 trenches have been put across it to check and confirm details of its construction.

Sometimes test pitting is the main method used. The site is gridded with 1 metre squares and sampling used to select a number of locations to dig. This produced a series of vertical profiles across the site which gives some idea of the horizontal plan. On very shallow sites with little stratigraphy, shovel pit testing (◀ p. 16) is sometimes used for this. Cutting lots of test pits or trial trenches into a site is quick, cheap and provides valuable information about stratigraphy. For this reason they are the most common type of excavation in the UK. However, they are relatively poor as a means to understand how a site fitted together.

Area excavation

This is the most common form of excavation of whole sites as can be seen in most reports or archaeological magazines. 'Area' or 'open-

Figure 2.10 *A 'cut' feature quartered in order to give four internal section profiles*

This will enable excavators to determine the depth, shape and fill of the pit as well as any internal stratigraphy.

stripping' occurs where the extent of the features to be uncovered determines the size of the excavation. This does not mean that whole sites are always laid bare. This can be an outcome but more frequently other factors limit the total recovery of evidence or perhaps development only threatens part of the site and the rest is left 'in situ'. On some research digs such as those run by universities digging may take place over several seasons. Different parts of the site are dug and recorded each year. Danebury hill fort is a well known example of this strategy (▶ p. 112). Finally there may be research considerations. Only a sample of the site may be needed to answer the director's questions. Financial constraints may limit the amount of digging.

Although destructive, area excavation has become the key approved method for several reasons.

- Complete structures can be studied.
- Complex relationships between features can be clarified.
- It provides excellent recording possibilities.
- A total understanding of horizontal relationships is possible.

When area excavation became fashionable there was criticism from those traditionalists who had used trenches. The sides of trenches have the advantage of revealing the vertical sequence of deposits (stratigraphy) and there was concern that

Figure 2.11 *Area excavation at Goldfields Farm*

The training dig (▶ p. 133) on this Romano-British site has adopted an area approach. Once topstripped the individual features such as the ditch in the foreground are sectioned or excavated. Barrow runways ensure spoil is quickly and safely removed and protect the surface.

this essential record might be lost. The depth of deposits can vary and the issue is of great significance where the stratification is deeper and more complicated. This problem can be addressed by leaving baulks (undug strips of ground) at strategic points or, increasingly, by carefully recording the horizontal picture of a site layer by layer and feeding the data into a computer. This data can be interrogated to produce sections along any chosen line. The problem is that without baulks no check is left in place if the director wishes to refer back, so the recording systems must be of the highest quality.

Box-grid or quadrant systems

These sit in an intermediate position between trenches and area excavation. They offer archaeologists the better aspects of each by giving access to both the horizontal view and the vertical cut simultaneously.

The box-grid system owes its origins to the work of Sir Mortimer Wheeler in the first half of the twentieth century. He would set out a grid of square 'boxes' to be excavated with baulks left in between them. This resulted in a dig resembling a patchwork quilt. An advantage was the chance to record four sections for every 'box'. Removal of spoil was also easier as baulks provided barrow runs. However, the whole layout of a site was not revealed until the baulks were finally removed. Important relationships between features or structures would not be understood while digging, which might depend on such an understanding, was progressing. The system was complex, costly of time and manpower and of little use on sites with very deep stratigraphy. It is little used in the UK today except for large pit features although it is still popular in other countries, particularly India.

The 'quadrant system' is a similar approach that is still sometimes employed. It is particularly relevant in the case of sites that are approximately circular in nature, such as round barrows, (▶ p. 49) although a smaller scale version of this

Figure 2.12 *Recording a section across an excavated ditch*

This approach to features is typical of area excavations. The planning frame against the vertical section helps the recorder to produce an accurate profile on gridded paper. The context labels on the face of the section ensure that slight changes in the fill which might be very difficult to see or photograph are recorded.

KEY SITE

Boxgrove

The chance discovery in 1993 of a human shin bone in a quarry by Mark Roberts led him to initiate the most famous recent example of box-grid excavation. The ongoing excavations have revealed much about the lifestyle and environment of Homo Heidelbergensis, one of the earliest of our ancestors to reach Britain. The bone enabled scientists to suggest that these hominids were large and heavily built like a modern sprinter. Cut marks on two human teeth found nearby showed that they used their teeth to hold meat while they cut it. The geology revealed that the site had been a beach backed by chalk cliffs. A spring at the foot of the cliffs fed a small fresh water pool that attracted animals. In and around the pool were scatters of animal bones and flint tools including 450 well made hand axes and hammer stones (for removing marrow from bone). Many of the bones had cut marks from the tools and even fragments of flint in a knife cut.

Figure 2.13 *Box sections*

Box sections enabled precise cross referencing of the freshwater sediments laid down by the stream. Chalk ensured excellent preservation and enabled scatters of flint and bones to be studied where they had fallen. Some of the silts were so fine grained that individual episodes could be recorded and in one case it was possible to tell from waste flakes how the flint knapper was sitting.

KEY SITE *cont.*

Boxgrove

SEM examination of a rhinoceros bone revealed human butchery marks under the tooth marks of a scavenging carnivore. In other words, the human had got there first. Hunting evidence came in the form of a horse scapula with a very neat circular perforation on the outside and a splintered 'exit wound'. This suggested a high velocity projectile, perhaps a fire-hardened wooden spear such as the ones discovered at Lehringen. Experimental archaeology (▶ p. 117) involving a javelin thrower and a deer carcass produced very similar damage to excavated bones. This suggests that these hominids were hunters rather than scavengers. They used speed and throwing weapons to kill and strip the meat from the horses, deer and possibly rhinoceros visiting the pool. The hominids repeatedly exploited their understanding of animal behaviour at the waterhole while evading other predators. Their presence is evident from wolf teeth marks on the shin bone.

The base of each section was marked with the site grid to ensure precise planning. Each find was given a coloured flag depending on the material and both compass direction and angle of dip recorded in order to determine whether water movement had moved them (▶ p. 105). Figure 2.14 illustrates spit level sections.

Faunal dating (▶ p. 94) showed that the site was in use during a warm interglacial period 500,000 years ago. Lions, elephants and tuna bones suggest a warmer climate than today. As well as bones of large grazing animals, wet sieving enabled the recovery of bird and fish bone and the remains of extinct water voles. These tiny rodents evolve rapidly. Over time their teeth lost their roots. The level of development of vole teeth enabled Boxgrove to be compared to examples from sites dated using absolute methods (▶ p. 95). The 'vole clock' showed that Boxgrove was older than 478,000 BC.

The find of an 'antler hammer' potentially provides a new perspective on human mental capacity and behaviour for this period. It suggests a degree of planning, forethought and 'curation' that was believed to be beyond the capacity of hominids at this stage in evolution. The hammer also provided corroborative faunal dating evidence. The antler came from a giant elk which became extinct around 500,000 years ago.

Figure 2.14 *Living floor*

Figure 2.15 *A quadrant excavation of a mound demonstrated at the Quest Project.*

You can enhance your understanding of excavation procedures by attempting a quadrant excavation of a gateau placed on a patterned plate. You should reveal enough of the plate to recognise patterns and see clearly the layers of sponge and cream in the excavated sections!

KEY TASK

Testing the law of superposition

When you have been working at your desk for a while or after, say, half an hour of a lesson look at the way your books, papers, pencil case, sweet wrappers (or those of your fellow students) have combined in an overlapping manner. If you pick your way backwards through the evidence it should be possible to establish in reverse order the sequence of events that led to the accumulated material being in position. This will not tell you when the build up of items took place but should establish the order. The floor of your room provides an alternative site to examine.

method can be used on hearths, pits or even post-holes. The feature is cut into four quarters by lines intersecting at the middle. Opposing quadrants are excavated first. It is possible after only removing half the remains to see patterns of features in plan (which if they show common elements suggest that they continue under the undug areas) and to totally record the vertical profile of the site in two directions.

THE PROCESS OF EXCAVATION

Archaeologists have developed a variety of methods for removing archaeological deposits from the ground in which they have lain to suit the varying circumstances of archaeological sites. The topsoil is removed by mechanically topstripping with a digger or by using picks, mattocks and shovels. This is either bulldozed or wheelbarrowed away to start a spoil heap. This has to be far enough away to avoid it spilling over and contaminating deeper layers or burying the diggers. Although mechanical diggers can be used for trial trenches, most excavation is by hand. According to the time available and the nature of the deposits, tools could range from shovels to dentistry instruments for recovering tiny fragments of material. The most familiar toolkit includes a mattock, a short pointed trowel, a dustbrush, a coalshovel and a bucket. In the USA long handled shovels are used which are better for a digger's back than spades, while in some countries hand hoes are an alternative to trowels. Eventually, and very neatly, what was an archaeological resource is converted into a hole in the ground. The extracted evidence must be subjected to a rigorous recording process or the excavation will have destroyed the site and its potential. Recording requirements will vary for sites with less obvious collectable material or with particular distributions of evidence.

Layers of deposits in the ground are recognised, labelled and removed in sequence. On many sites such as Roman or medieval where pottery sherds and animal bones are common, their collection is linked to the contexts in which the material is found. They are collected in labelled 'finds trays' so that all the finds from each layer can be put together. They will subsequently be washed, dried and coded to their particular layer for recording.

On the same sites less common objects like metal, worked bone or stone will usually be classified as special or key 'finds'. A distinct and more comprehensive recording system will ensure that the precise location of each find is recorded in three dimensions by triangulation and depth measurements. They are collected in finds trays or plastic bags and given unique reference numbers. On a working floor associated with a prehistoric flint-knapper careful plotting of each flake is necessary to recreate the sequence of the earlier activity. Sometimes their position in a layer is marked by a small flag so that distribution patterns can be recorded. These finds will be kept separately and the nature and fragility of each object will determine their post-excavation scientific treatment.

Recovery of environmental material

Not all the material to be retrieved can be recovered by trowelling. The ground contains much smaller and less obvious evidence, in particular faunal (animal) and floral (plant) evidence such as snail shells, small fish or bird bones, insect remains, seeds and pollen grains. Not all of these are visible to the naked eye. Tiny fragments of metal or worked material such as flint or glass present the same problem. This material can be recovered on-site by using sieving or flotation or by taking strategically selected soil samples for later analysis.

Dry sieving small amounts of soil is carried out in the same way as shovel pit testing (◀ p. 15). On larger sites buckets of soil samples are tipped into a large sieve usually suspended from a frame and riddled over a barrow to ensure that finds not detected in the digging process are retrieved. A series of sieves with increasingly finer mesh improve collection chances and also collect different sized material in each sieve. The introduction of water to create 'wet-sieving', whether by spray or dipping into a tank, helps to remove the soil particles. Wet material is often easier to identify and locate by colour contrast.

Soil sampling

Some recovery of environmental remains occurs off-site. Bags of soil samples are taken from selected locations such as pits, ditches or other similar diagnostic features or layers. On peat sites, long sampling tins are hammered vertically into the sides of freshly dug sections, removed and quickly sealed in plastic to avoid contamination. They are then placed in cold storage before detailed analysis in the laboratory. The pollens and plant remains in them will be used to provide vegetation sequences and help date the site. Soil may also be sampled for chemical analysis, particularly for phosphates (◀ p. 16).

Flotation

This involves putting soil samples into water. Lighter materials such as plant remains float to the surface while the soil drops to the bottom of the container. Improvements to this basic methodology include adding oil to hold tiny particles on the surface and bubbling air from below the water to create a froth, which holds and separates lighter organic material. Water is drained from the top through a sequence of increasingly finely meshed sieves.

Metal detection

On some excavations, and directly under the control of the director, it is appropriate to use metal detectors. They can be employed as part of the initial survey as a piece of geophysical equipment but they can also be used to check the spoil dump for finds. This would be applicable if the site had been stripped by machine rather than by hand or if soil removal had been by pick and shovel without subsequent sieving. Any such finds would be classed as unstratified. Metal detectors can also be used to alert diggers to potentially fragile metal objects in areas they are trowelling.

Figure 2.16 *Flotation bins*

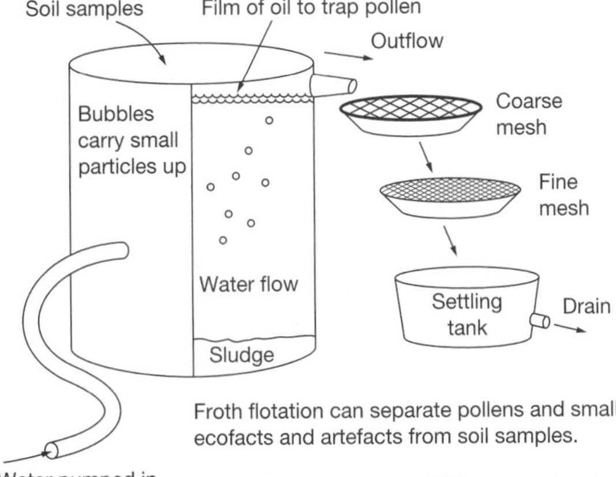

Figure 2.17 *How a flotation bin works*

Figure 2.18 *A metal detector on site*

In whatever way the finds are identified and collected it is vital that the methods used allow their full potential to be exploited in post-excavation analysis and dating procedures. Individual directors of excavations have to make valid decisions about the processes they adopt in order to balance the needs of the dig to make sufficient progress with the demands of post-excavation studies.

WHAT RECORDS DO ARCHAEOLOGISTS CREATE?

Different directors will approach the task of recording, as they will the excavation itself, from slightly different standpoints. But certain common themes will feature: context sheets, plans, sections, photographs, artefact collection systems and, increasingly, the use of on-site computer technology. They also make use of a range of surveying equipment to plot the exact positions of finds and features. Each excavation has a complex reference system. A grid allows each point surveyed and key find to be linked to the national grid. Finds are numbered and linked to contexts. Each context has its own distinct number. Alidades, plane tables and theodolites are still in use alongside Electronic Distance Measures (EDMs) but increasingly **total stations** (◀ p. 15) are superseding them.

Context sheets

These provide detailed records of layers and other elements of the stratigraphy of the site. They also allow associations between finds to be explored post-excavation. They will be used in post-excavation analysis to reconstruct the phases of use of the site and its features.

Plans

Detailed plans are used to show the location and spread of features, artefacts and structures. Large-scale plans are used to illustrate individual features. For example, an excavation of an Anglo-Saxon cemetery requires an overall plan to show the relationships between graves and associated features. A detailed plan drawing will be required of each individual grave to show the position of skeletal remains and the location of grave goods. The position of some of the artefacts may be better explained by a close-up drawing featuring, perhaps, the chest area of the burial.

- http://www.gla.ac.uk/archaeology/staff/

All these drawings relate to the fixed recording grid on the site. Their position is plotted using surveying equipment and their dimensions carefully scaled onto paper. This usually involves placing a planning frame over the feature to assist the production of accurately measured drawings (▶ p. 50). Considerable effort after the excavation often goes into producing cleaned up versions of these plans for publication. Often finds and features will be plotted on a series of overlays related to soil and topography. Increasingly, plans are plotted onto computers because of the flexibility in presenting data they allow. GIS is revolutionising this process. Its 3D database enables the production of any section or plan and the testing of complex models.

Section drawings

The sides of excavation trenches, strategically placed baulks or cuts through the fill of features such as ditches, pits or postholes offer vertical slices through the constituent layers of an archaeological site.

Although methods of recording the horizontal spread and depth of each deposit have improved over recent decades it still remains true that an accurate scaled depiction of the vertical relationship of layers is commonly used to demonstrate the development of a site or feature. For example, the relationship of a 'post pipe' – the evidence for the location of the post itself – within a posthole and to any packing material is best related in drawn form. As with plans, a key advantage of section drawings is that they can highlight subtle differences in the colour, texture or composition of layers. These are difficult to pick up with photographs. Before drawing it is essential that the face of the section is cleaned up and in some instances sprayed with water to improve contrast. Soil structure and Munsell colour charts are sometimes used to enable specific and standardised descriptions.

Where a section results from a continuous period of excavation it may be some time before it is ready for recording. Archaeologists note the presence of layers as the dig proceeds by pinning labels to the side of the excavation with context numbers to ensure that when the section is drawn

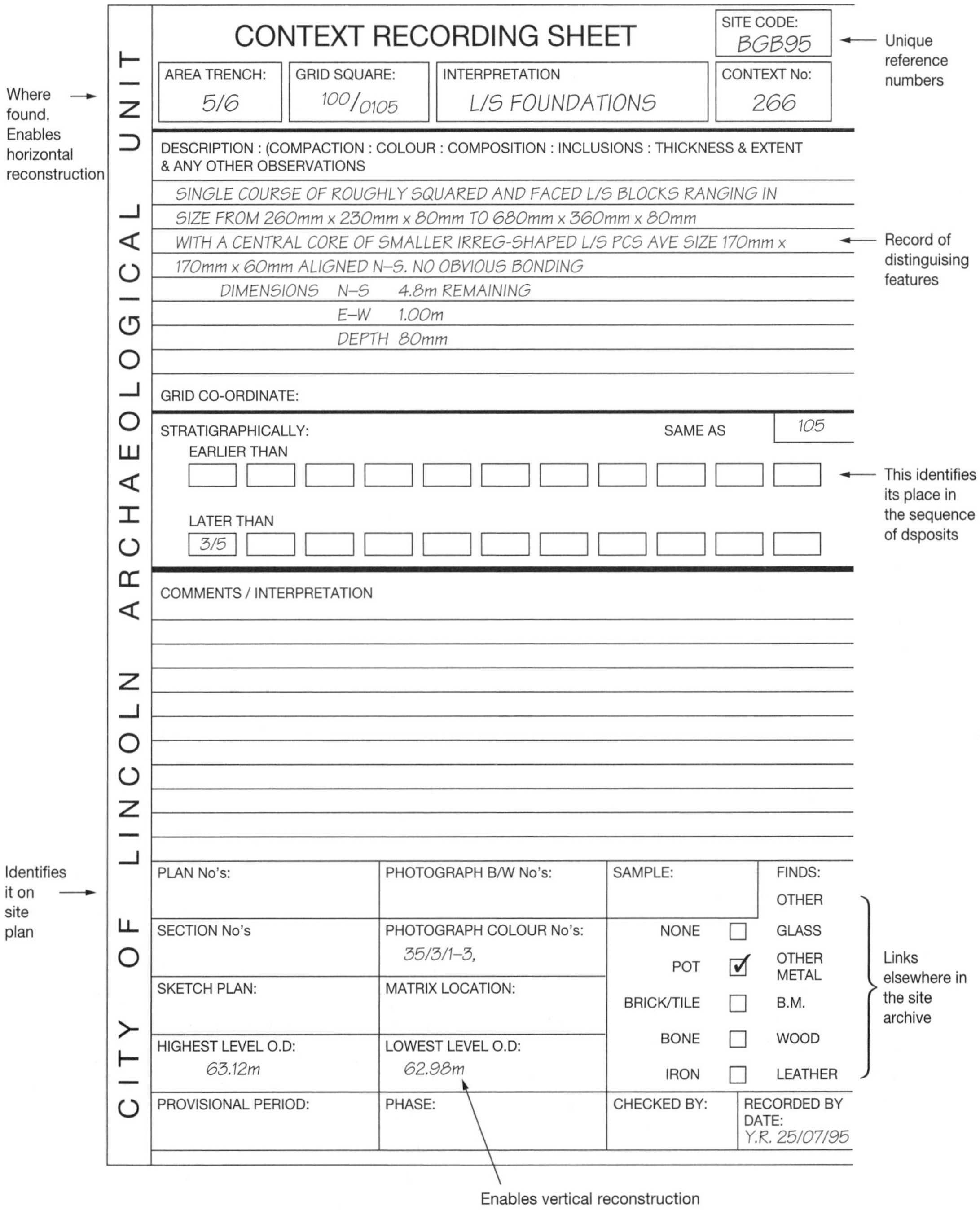

CITY OF LINCOLN ARCHAEOLOGICAL UNIT

CONTEXT RECORDING SHEET

SITE CODE:	BGB95

← Unique reference numbers

AREA TRENCH:	GRID SQUARE:	INTERPRETATION	CONTEXT No:
5/6	100/0105	L/S FOUNDATIONS	266

Where found. Enables horizontal reconstruction →

DESCRIPTION : (COMPACTION : COLOUR : COMPOSITION : INCLUSIONS : THICKNESS & EXTENT & ANY OTHER OBSERVATIONS

SINGLE COURSE OF ROUGHLY SQUARED AND FACED L/S BLOCKS RANGING IN
SIZE FROM 260mm x 230mm x 80mm TO 680mm x 360mm x 80mm
WITH A CENTRAL CORE OF SMALLER IRREG-SHAPED L/S PCS AVE SIZE 170mm x
170mm x 60mm ALIGNED N–S. NO OBVIOUS BONDING

DIMENSIONS N–S 4.8m REMAINING
E–W 1.00m
DEPTH 80mm

← Record of distinguishing features

GRID CO-ORDINATE:

STRATIGRAPHICALLY: SAME AS 105

EARLIER THAN

LATER THAN 3/5

← This identifies its place in the sequence of dsposits

COMMENTS / INTERPRETATION

PLAN No's:	PHOTOGRAPH B/W No's:	SAMPLE:	FINDS:
			OTHER
SECTION No's	PHOTOGRAPH COLOUR No's: 35/3/1–3,	NONE ☐	GLASS
		POT ☑	OTHER METAL
SKETCH PLAN:	MATRIX LOCATION:	BRICK/TILE ☐	B.M.
		BONE ☐	WOOD
HIGHEST LEVEL O.D: 63.12m	LOWEST LEVEL O.D: 62.98m	IRON ☐	LEATHER
PROVISIONAL PERIOD:	PHASE:	CHECKED BY:	RECORDED BY DATE: Y.R. 25/07/95

Identifies it on site plan →

Links elsewhere in the site archive

Enables vertical reconstruction

Figure 2.19 *How to interpret a context sheet*

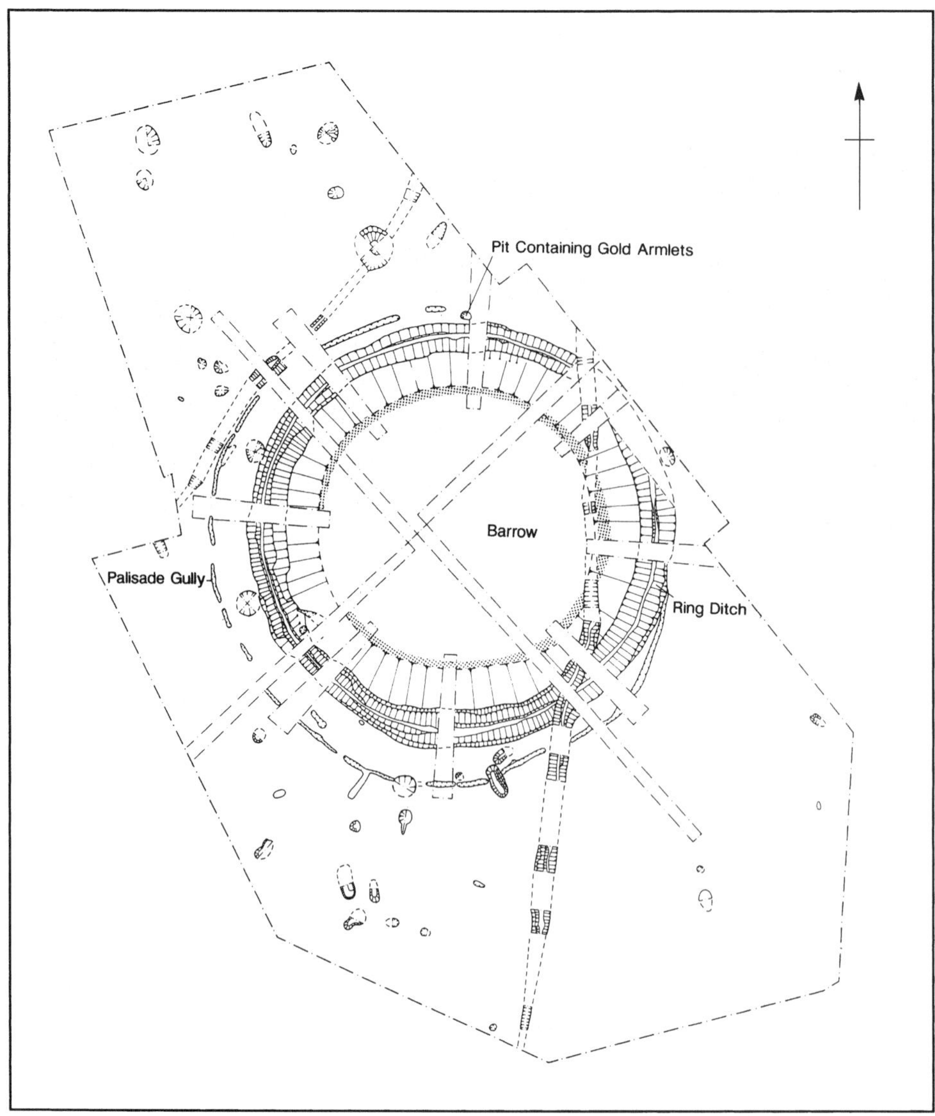

Figure 2.20 *Plan of an excavated barrow at Lockington using the quadrant method of mound removal*

Circular features such as the surrounding ring ditch and palisade gully are revealed in each quadrant. Eight narrow baulks are left for extra sections. A pit containing gold armlets was located on the edge of the barrow. Although clearly important, no relationship could be established by the processes of excavation to link this pit and its contents to the barrow and the cremation burial below it.

Figure 2.21 *A quartered barrow seen in profile. The picture also shows the familiar wheelbarrow runs used to remove spoil from the excavation itself*

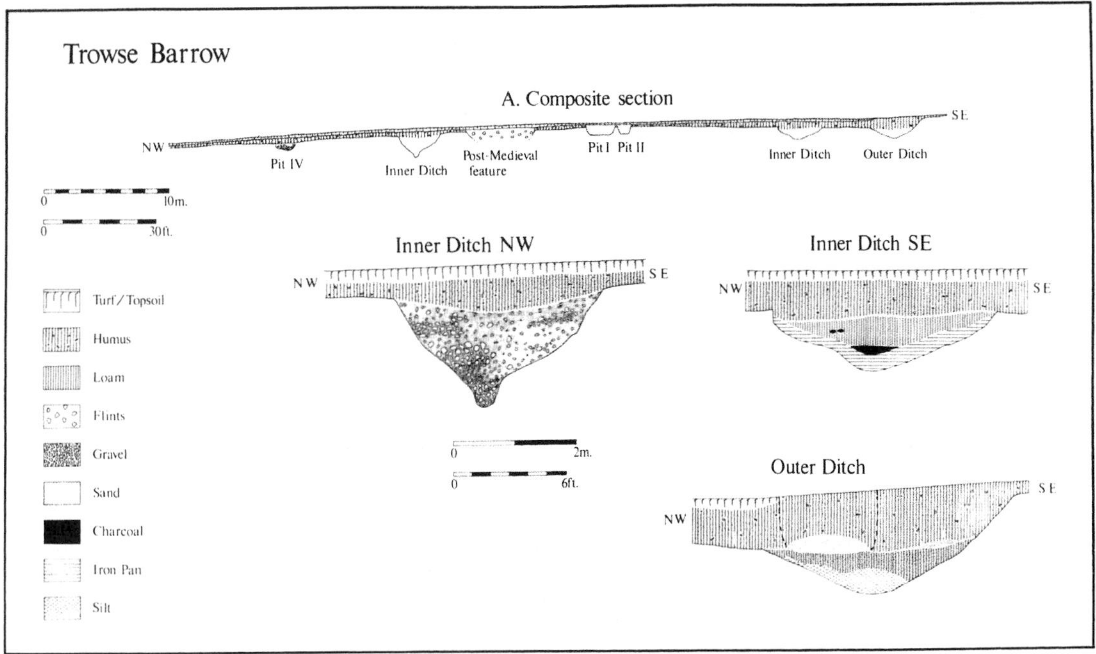

Figure 2.22 *A section drawing of Trowse Round Barrow*

This barrow has two incomplete ditches surrounding it. The main composite cross-section shows the inner ditch twice, the outer ditch once and several other features. The inner and outer ditch sections are enlarged to give greater detail. A key is provided to demonstrate the soil types present. Reproduced with the permission of the copyright holder, Norfolk Archaeology & Environment Division.

Figure 2.23 *Using gridlines to plan a skeleton*

In this example the soil covering the skeleton has been carefully excavated prior to recording. The gridlines make it easier for the recorder to keep to scale. Measurements are frequently taken during drawing to ensure the finished record is as accurate as possible. Following recording the skeleton will be excavated.

it is still possible to recognise the finer points of the stratification. Such labels are frequently seen on site photographs.

Once completed, drawings are usually accompanied by an interpretation offered in textual or schematic form such as the Harris Matrix. It must be stressed that drawings are always interpretations and the quality of on-site drawings does vary according to the skill of the recorder and the conditions they are working under. Back-up photographs can provide an additional record.

Photographs

The camera is a key aid to recording although archaeologists believe that it is less comprehensive in the detail it can show than the drawn record. Although rulers or ranging rods are usually seen in photographs to give an idea of scale, distances are distorted and film cannot be used to provide precise measurements. The camera clearly offers the chance of accurate views of features and sections whereas the draughtsperson can accentuate elements that the camera might obscure, for example similar coloured soils which have different textures. The camera also provides back up in case the drawings are poor. The two methods complement each other and both are normally used. Most archaeologists continue to use conventional black and white film for recording. Slides have been used to film the dig in progress and for lectures afterwards. However, the superior quality of slide film it is increasingly being replaced by digital photography and video, particularly as a support to the site diary. Digital recording also enables the excavation to be viewed online.

The essence of site photography lies in ensuring that the parts to be captured on film are clean, edges of individual structures or bones are well established and careful spraying is used to accentuate coloration changes and contrasts. The use of photographic towers or other means to get a camera above the excavation is common. Vertical photographs with scales can be used as an aid in the creation of plans.

- http://www.brad.ac.uk/acad/archsci/field_proj/scat/
- http://www.woodnet.org.uk/woodlandweb/enjoy/excavat.htm

Figure 2.24 *Recording using photography*

This section at Barcombe Roman villa is being carefully photographed to complement the drawn record. To counteract the effects of perspective a horizontal and vertical scale have been placed on the section. Also in view are a north pointer and a board with the feature or context number to enable identification and location afterwards.

SPECIAL CASES

Most of the points in this chapter apply to all sites but there are some issues that apply to particular types of sites.

Archaeology of standing buildings

In 'traditional' archaeology, interpretation of excavated evidence relies on the basic principle that the deeper the deposit, the earlier it is – the basis of relative dating by stratigraphy. Although standing buildings require a different approach to their study, the basic principles remain the same. One of the objectives of recording is to enable the developmental sequence of the building to be traced. Where a feature has been inserted into an existing one (for example a window or door inserted into a standing wall) it follows that the inserted feature is later than that into which it was inserted. Similarly, later walls may be of different construction to the original or may be butt-jointed (simply butted up against earlier walls rather than properly bonded). All of these clues help archaeologists to build up a sequence of development in the same way as on an excavation. Recording standing buildings may involve reconnaissance techniques (◀ p. 10), dismantling, excavation or a combination of these approaches. The amount of information which may be recovered from a building will depend on many factors. Cosmetic renovation of a structure may give only a few clues (for example glimpses beneath floor boards or behind small areas of plaster) whereas a building undergoing substantial alterations or even demolition will be far more exposed to study. The aim should be to

Figure 2.25 *Recording inside a building under excavation*

Much the same techniques are being applied as to any other excavation.

identify the earliest structural remains on the site and then, having plotted them, begin to add in later stages of development. Additions or changes to a building are never random: they will always serve a clear purpose which archaeologists try to detect, for example the extending of a room or rebuilding of a façade.

The recording of standing buildings should be every bit as rigorous as the recording of an excavation. Alongside drawings and written descriptions a full photographic record should be maintained, indicating scale and the exact point on a master plan from which the view was taken, along with any other relevant information. Sampling should include examples of different mortars and plasters. Substantial timbers may be sampled for **dendrochronology**. (▶ p. 95) Details of the fabric and construction of the building, alterations and dating evidence are gathered through drawing and photography. Elevations of buildings are often drawn stone by stone using grids as the completed drawing can often reveal patterns not obvious to the naked eye. Very precise photographic recording to within 10mm can be achieved using photogrammetry. In this technique, also used for aerial photography, two precision cameras are used together to create a 'stereo' recording. When combined with readings from an EDM, specialists can use CAD to produce a 3D record of the building, including very fine decorative or architectural detail. It is considerably faster than traditional recording and is both cost effective and accurate. It is particularly used where historic buildings are being restored.

Wetland archaeology

Waterlogged sites are where the natural water table has maintained a wet or damp environment since the deposition of the evidence. They have been a major factor in adding to our knowledge of past cultures. **Anaerobic** conditions, which prevent or impede normal bacterial and chemical decay processes, can result in widespread survival of organic material such as wood, leather and textiles which would normally perish. Strategies for excavation, conservation and post-excavation analysis on wetland sites need to take into account the time and cost of dealing with additional evidence as well as the particular problems associated with waterlogged sites. In particular there are often large quantities of environmental material, especially plant remains. While the complete removal of all material for close examination is not usually a viable proposition much emphasis is put on the selection of large numbers of samples of site deposits for laboratory analysis. This has been

Figure 2.26 *Reconstruction of Oakbank Iron Age Crannog*

Crannogs are artificial islands with a wooden platform supported by piles driven into lakebeds or boulders dumped on the lakebed. They were used for some 5000 years until the seventeenth century in Scotland and Ireland as farmsteads, halls and defensive refuges. At Oakbank underwater archaeologists were able to recover organic remains including food, artefacts and structural timbers. Exceptional finds included a butter dish containing butter and a canoe paddle. Like many wet sites, Oakbank has shed light on the extent to which large timbers were felled, shaped and moved in the past.

the case with excavations of London's waterfront. Huge amounts of large timbers could not all be preserved. Those selected for recovery enabled the development of carpentry and construction techniques over a long period to be studied. This revealed the way older timber buildings were recycled by builders. Once out of water, organic material will be stored in tanks of water prior to conservation.

The consequence is that while the information from 'wet' sites is considered a real bonus in archaeological study, the costs of obtaining it considerably outstrip those of excavating 'dry' sites.

Unlike 'dry' sites where you can walk carefully across the site, pressure on wetland deposits can cause considerable damage. Excavators at Flag Fen erected a series of platforms on scaffolding to allow diggers to lie above the features they were excavating. Such restriction to movement makes digging, cleaning, planning and photography all the more difficult.

- http://www.crannog.co.uk/

Figure 2.27 *Inter-tidal archaeology presents another specific range of challenges*

Organic material exposed between tides such as shipwrecks or structures has often been well preserved but will rapidly decay. It needs to be excavated and recorded quickly but twice a day it is submerged, covering the site with sand or mud. This makes work difficult or dangerous. A salvage approach is usually adopted with material where possible being removed from immediate danger for study in a laboratory. Unfortunately this action can also destroy the context of the site.

- http://www.arch.soton.ac.uk/Projects/projects.asp?ProjectID=4

Underwater archaeology

Although underwater sites follow the same basic rules as dry sites – the need for survey, careful excavation and recording – being below water presents additional challenges. The excavators usually require watertight diving suits, air tanks and weights. In extreme depths remotely controlled vehicles may be used. In addition to underwater hazards, cold temperatures may make it difficult to remain stationary for long periods while poor visibility may require excavation using touch rather than sight!

To inform excavation strategy a form of sampling is often employed to gain a feel for the site. One example of this is the Tudor warship the *Mary Rose* whose position and condition was examined and investigated for several years before a full enough understanding enabled full excavation. Where little or no wooden remains are present and finds are in a dispersed state, plans are drawn and trial trenches excavated to determine the extent of the deposits.

- http://www.abc.se/~m10354/uwa/
- http://www.maryrose.org/

Removal of spoil can employ a combination of hand movement and water dispersal but special tools are usually required. A water lance can shred sediment while a range of water vacuum cleaners can help excavate spoil and keep a site clear of sediment for recording. Objects may have suffered corrosion and created concretions that need to be broken apart. Decisions have to be made as to whether to use hammer and chisel below water or to bring the whole mass to the surface. Ordinary finds are placed in open containers, fragile finds in sealed ones and larger objects lifted by the use of inflated air bags. As with waterlogged sites, organic material is susceptible to damage if it is allowed, even briefly, to dry out during excavation. Once such material is removed from the water it must be quickly put into appropriate storage.

Plastic 2 × 2 or 4 × 4 metre recording grids are set out and the usual land-based methods of planning, context sheets and photography employed where possible. Synthetic paper enables ordinary pens to be used underwater. Photography is likely to be limited to close-up shots or carefully rigged photogrammetry rather than general views. One

Key

1 Pipe sucking sediment and spoil away
2 Laminated recording sheets
3 Suspended polythene tube grids
4 Finds box
5 Ranging pole
6 Water lance and tube
7 Section (close-up below)
8 Organic materials

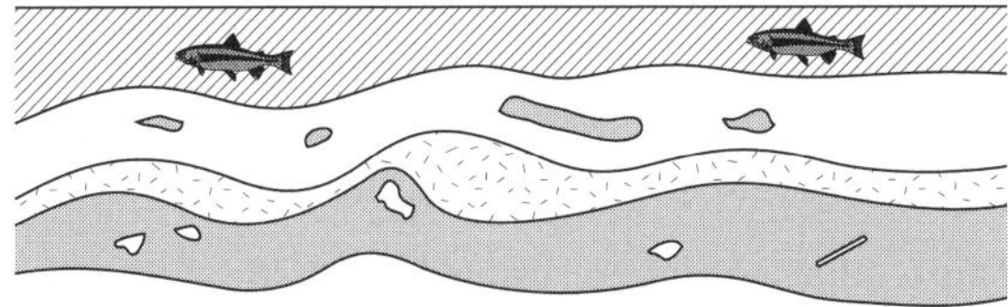

Figure 2.28 *Diagram illustrating some of the equipment used in underwater archaeology (after Thomasen in Andersen 1985)*

advantage of underwater excavation is that the archaeologist can cross the site without treading on a trowelled surface!

Urban archaeology

While it is clear that there is a great variety in the nature of archaeological sites in rural areas, archaeologists working on urban sites face very different challenges.

In urban areas open ground is at a premium and so it is usually the clearance of a site for development that provides archaeological opportunities. The area involved is often tightly constrained by other buildings and therefore only parts of buried sites are available for study. These do not necessarily correspond to areas which archaeologists would choose if they were making the site selection on academic grounds, a good example of rescue archaeology being dictated by

Figure 2.29 *An area excavation of the medieval burial grounds at Spitalfields market in London*

Note the cover over the site, both for protection of the remains and out of respect for the burials. The relatively confined space is typical of most urban excavations.

developer activity. Such excavations are like keyholes into the past because a full view cannot be obtained. The depth of stratification is usually much greater than on rural sites because of frequent reuse of the same site over time. It is particularly difficult to forecast the range of features, that will be encountered and the time it will take to excavate them all properly. Deep excavation also presents additional safety hazards.

Survey methods applicable to rural sites such as aerial photography and many of the geophysical procedures are ineffectual or inappropriate in preparatory work. Indeed, at a large excavation in London at Number 1, Poultry in the 1990s the evaluation consisted of a desktop survey and four shafts between 3 m and 5 m deep to reach the top of the natural geology. These gave indications of the sequences and structures which might be encountered. The excavation also produced 'wet' archaeology including about 1,500 datable (by dendrochronology) Roman timbers. This extensive urban excavation (the on-site budget exceeded £2m) continued for twelve months below the construction of the new building. Normally archaeologists have to

Figure 2.30 *Using a total station to rapidly plot the position of finds*

At Spitalfields, so many skeletons were discovered that digital means of recording their position were used including barcodes.

complete their work before the building contractors arrive on site.

- *Current Archaeology* 143 and 158

KEY TASK

Comparative study of survey and excavation methods

Take either an excavation report or an article from *Current Archaeology, British Archaeology* or *Rescue News*. Make notes under the following headings:

- Name of site
- Reason for excavation
- Was this a research, rescue or salvage excavation?
- Source of funding
- Prior knowledge of site and survey methods employed prior to excavation
- Style and strategy of excavation
- Key finds
- Post-excavation scientific activity
- Dating methods employed

If a group of students follow this information gathering process, valuable comparative data will emerge to inform discussion on a series of key issues relating to current practice in archaeology.

AFTER EXCAVATION

Once the digging is completed attention switches to the laboratories and the processing of finds and site records. This is dealt with in Chapters 3 and 4. The eventual outcome of the excavation used to be a full excavation report with text on the features and structures, catalogues and drawings of finds and specialists' reports. Today the emphasis is on producing a quality 'archive' which can then be adapted as appropriate into reports, more popular publications or to provide research opportunities. Increasingly records are stored digitally which offers tremendous potential for disseminating data to different audiences in different ways.

Figure 2.31 *Removing a skeleton*

The excavator has dressed to minimise DNA contamination of the remains. Each bone is carefully recovered, sometimes using dental tools. In this instance the body had actually been placed in the grave in pieces.

KEY SKILL

Tackling structured, source-based questions

These questions are found at AS Level and sometimes at university. You will usually have several sources to work with at the same time. These will be drawn from archaeological plans, sections, illustrations, tables, maps, photographs and reports. Four common areas are outlined below. Two essential pieces of equipment which you can take into the exam are a ruler and a magnifying glass. Be sure to use them.

Interpreting plans

Begin with an accurate description of the relevant sites, features and artefacts in order to build up a picture of overall function or changes. Always refer to context numbers where they are given. You should consider:

- size and orientation
- spatial distribution of features
- phases of use: discuss any stratigraphic evidence for different periods of activity
- assess individual features to identify site function
- boundaries: are they defensive or just a demarcation line – a physical or a spiritual barrier?

Interpreting aerial photographs

Read all the questions concerned with these first. They will probably ask about method as well as interpretation and you need to match the right response to a question. For interpretation start by describing what you can see. Is it a cropmark, soil mark or shadows? What size and shape is it? Is it a boundary, structure or some other type of feature. How is it aligned?

Only when you have done this, suggest specific site or period. This way you will get some marks even where you get it wrong. Questions about methods usually require an account of why features are visible and can be recorded and why they do not show up in all areas (◀ pp. 22–5).

Appraising methods

You need to understand the basic techniques for each type of material you are likely to be tested on, for example stone, pottery, metal, and what it can tell us. Ensure you know the main principles and some of their strengths and limitations. In the case of dating and reconnaissance methods it is sensible to test yourself on their application to different types of material and sites. In all cases, one good example is useful.

Interpreting organic remains

Questions will focus on what could be learned from the remains. You need to be familiar with common ways of presenting such data and what terms such as MNI mean. Always consider the sample size. Are there sufficient examples to say much at all? Also comment on their survival: why have they survived and how might they have been transformed by taphonomy (▶ p. 107)?

KEY TASK

Test your understanding of methods

Examine the diagrams from an excavated site at Gamston. Figure 2.32 contrasts what was seen in aerial photographs and after excavation.

1a Why would this site have shown up from the air? *2 mks*

1b Why do the excavation plans show different evidence from the cropmark diagram? *6 mks*

Now examine Figure 2.33

1c What evidence would have allowed the archaeologists to construct these diagrams? *8 mks*

Suggested mark scheme on ▶ p. 330.

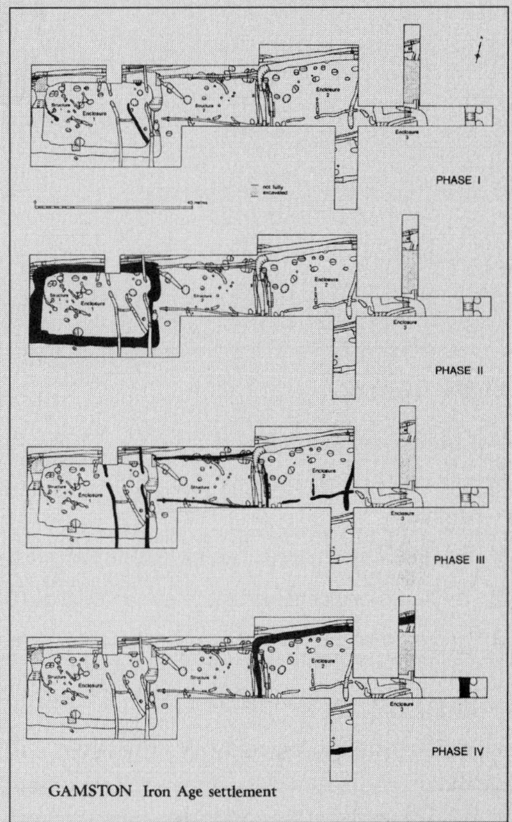

Figure 2.33 *Gamston drawing 2*

Figure 2.32 *Gamston drawing 1. Gamston was an Iron Age settlement and field system in the Trent Valley*

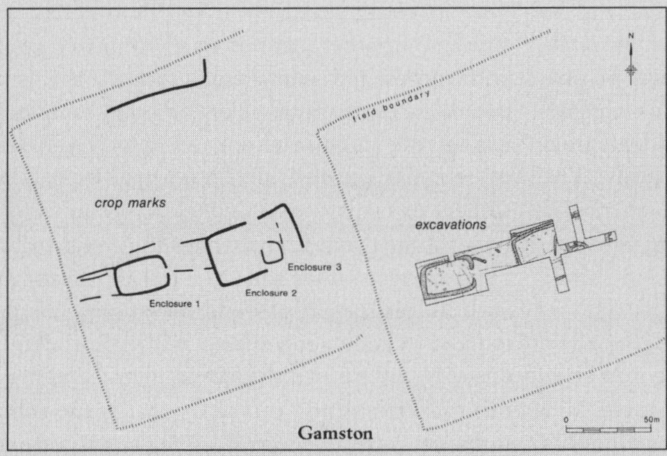

Chapter 3

Post-excavation Analysis

YOUR GOALS

You need to understand

- the range of specialisms involved in post excavation work and what they can contribute to site archives
- the types of analysis carried out on the most commonly analysed materials
- the basic principles of the main analytical techniques
- how to integrate a grasp of analytical techniques with specific examples

Analytical techniques are often the parts of archaeology courses which most students find difficult. The bulleted points above are sufficient for AS/A Level and some first year undergraduate courses which do not require detailed scientific knowledge. Most degree-level courses will at some point require a greater depth of understanding of scientific techniques and many will involve practical work. The first half of this chapter explains general approaches and some widely used methods applied to a range of materials. The second half considers issues related to particular types of material and illustrates what analysis can achieve. Further examples can be found in Part II of this book.

Post excavation or 'post-ex' encompasses all of the processes and interpretation that go on after the dig has ended and the material stored in a temporary archive. The focus now moves indoors to the specialist's rooms at the excavation team's base. Wessex Archaeology's headquarters in a converted RAF command centre near Salisbury is one such location. At one end of the building corridors are lined with archive boxes, labelled with site and context codes while in the main work area pots are being reassembled and flints sorted and labelled. Another suite of small rooms equipped with sieves and microscopes houses the 'snail people'. They patiently sieve through samples to extract the molluscan remains which will help to reconstruct past environments (▶ p. 196). Other specialists deal with beetles or animal bones. One room is given over to careful technical drawings of finds and of crucial site documents such as plans, sections and elevations, complemented where appropriate with photographs. Close by are housed the site archives from previous excavations and projects – that is the collections of context sheets and registers normally stored in a series of ring-binders until needed for

Figure 3.1 *Post-excavation processes normally take longer, cost more and involve more people than excavation. It is the hidden face of archaeology. This desk is set up for the identification and recording of samples*

publication. Finally there is the suite of computers in the publishing room which produces the finished site reports. Other teams may have more or less than this. In all cases there will always be some processes they have to outsource. Palynologists (pollen), pathologists and geologists are just some of the specialists who are contracted to analyse material. Radiocarbon dating is also undertaken in more specialist facilities.

- www.wessexarch.co.uk/

On arrival materials are treated differently according to their properties. Robust artefacts such as flint tools or pottery are cleaned in water unless analysis of residues or wear is to be undertaken. Fragile bones, metals artefacts and wood are handled with delicacy and may require conservation work before analysis can begin. For example, bone may require treatment with polyvinyl acetate (PVA) to stop it crumbling while organic samples may require mild fungicides to halt decay. The conditions they are kept in will also vary depending on their original context.

ARCHAEOMETRY

Scientific advances have a major impact on archaeology with those in dating DNA and reconnaissance being the best known. However, just as inventions such as sonar and GPS were developed

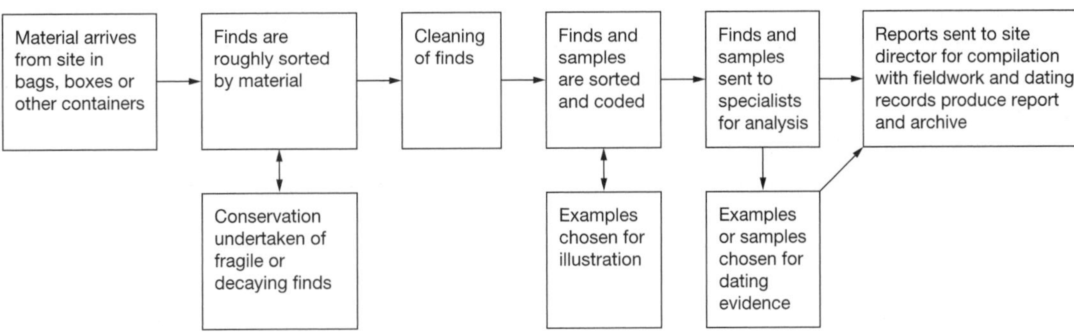

Figure 3.2 *Simplified diagram of the post-excavation process*

Figure 3.3 *A painstakingly reconstructed beaker from Boscombe Down*

The convention is for plain clay to be infilled in the gaps to recreate the solid shape while making clear which parts are original. Compare with the Cretan house (▶ p. 217). Beakers are associated with the cross-over between Neolithic and early Bronze Age. In Europe this is often called the Copper Age or Chalcolithic.

for military rather than archaeological purposes, archaeologists have adopted an impressive range of techniques from other disciplines. The growth of **archaeometry**, the scientific analysis of archaeological materials, has led to the creation of a whole range of new archaeological specialisms as well as archaeological science degree courses.

Scientific analysis offers many insights into ancient objects and ecofacts including:

1 Identification of finds or specimens
2 Determining numbers of finds or specimens from particular categories
3 Identifying how materials were produced and used
4 Identifying sources of artefacts and raw materials
5 Providing data on the local environment

New scientific techniques can analyse and present data rapidly. However, they are usually expensive and are used sparingly. Only selected materials are sent to laboratories and only with clear questions in mind which help address overall research questions.

Is archaeology a science?

The adoption of scientific techniques and the overlap between archaeology and biology in the study of human origins led some archaeologists to claim that archaeology was now a science. This would have advantages for university departments since science enjoys higher status and better funding than the humanities. However, the use of scientific techniques in itself doesn't make a subject a science. To be accepted as a science archaeology would have to demonstrate that it is following the principles of empirical methods with a view to establishing 'laws', or 'middle range theory' as it is often called. Although many research archaeologists have adopted the scientific model of generating a hypothesis and then testing, it is difficult for archaeologists to form law-like generalisations from their findings. While the relationships explored by scientists in laboratory experiments can be repeatedly tested under controlled conditions, archaeologists investigate unique events from the past and deal with material which, once removed from its context, can never be re-excavated.

VISUAL EXAMINATION

The first analytical stage for most materials involves categorization. Artefacts will be sorted according to physical characteristics or attributes into categories by material and typology. Specialists use their knowledge to categorise finds but they will also have a set of diagnostic sherds or illustrations to aid identification. These are sometimes called parallels. Experts will also use the feel of artefacts to assist them. Characteristics such as grittiness or greasiness are best determined by touch. Some materials, particularly metals will require further tests. Microscope examination of marks on some materials can also provide clues to their use. Each category can then be counted in order to say something about relative amounts in the archive and to identify on-site distribution of materials. Environmental samples, once removed from soil, are identified by species and then analysed in similar ways, using microscopes for plant and invertebrate remains. Once identified and categorized material is quantified and recorded through drawing or photography. A descriptive report is then produced by the specialist undertaking the work.

Figure 3.4 *Sorting pottery according to attributes*

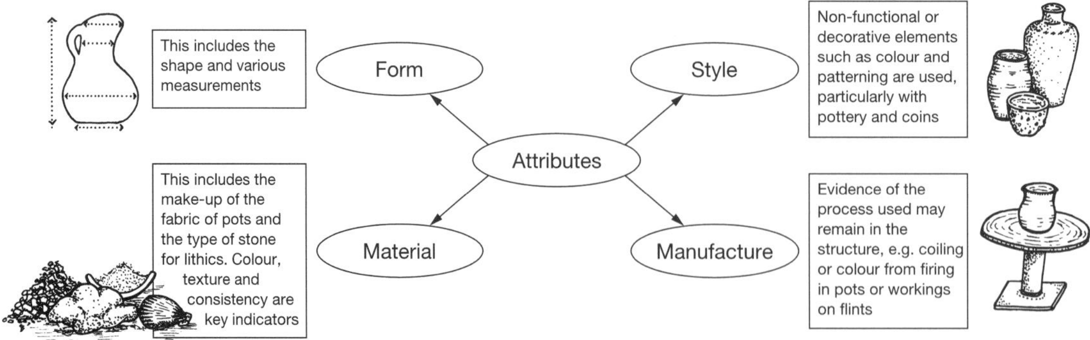

Figure 3.5 *Examples of attributes which could be used to sort material*

Figure 3.6 *Early Minoan 'Myrtos style' jug*

Some pottery is easily identified by material and decoration and do not require further typological analysis. In this case the fabric and the red lines on light background would be enough. Note how artefact styles are normally named after the site where they were first recognised.

SCIENTIFIC ANALYSIS OF ARTEFACTS

Laboratory investigation of artefacts can determine their composition, structure and manufacturing history. The type of analysis selected in any particular case will depend on factors including cost, the importance of the individual artefact and the questions the archaeologists are asking. For example, **petrology** is relatively cheap, but it is also destructive. **X-ray fluorescence** provides a dearer alternative, which doesn't cause damage, but it can only analyse the surface of objects. An excellent range of links for scientific methods is at

- http://www.brad.ac.uk/acad/archsci/

Characterisation studies

Scientific analysis of artefacts and building material can reveal their chemical make-up. This is valuable because while stone or metal of the same type is largely composed of the same elements, their exact chemical composition varies. Each stone or metal ore was extracted from a specific location under particular geological conditions. These unique circumstances mean that they contain slightly different combinations and quantities of 'impurities'. Copper, for example, may contain minute amounts of arsenic, silver and lead. These **'trace elements'** occur as a few parts per million and may have negligible effects on the material, but they provide it with a distinctive 'chemical fingerprint'. Where the geological sources of metal, clay or stone have been mapped, archaeologists may be able to identify the location from which the materials were quarried.

Petrology

This is a geological technique for locating the source of minerals. A **thin section** of a stone or ceramic (▶ p. 67) artefact is cut, ground and polished till it is about 0.02 mm thick. It is then examined by microscope. The crystals of each mineral have a distinctive colour and structure. The particular combinations of key minerals enable the original source to be established with reference to geological maps. Thin sections of pottery can also be studied to provide information about manufacturing techniques.

Petrology has contributed greatly to our understanding of exchange. For instance the sources for the early medieval period trade in lava quernstones throughout north-west Europe have been traced back to quarries in the Eiffel Mountains of Germany. The technique can be used for building materials including stone and, in some cases, brick. It has been used extensively in Egypt to identify the quarries used to build the temples at Karnak and the pyramid complex at Giza. Distribution patterns based on extensive studies such as these have helped us understand the complexity of ancient trade routes, transport systems and economic organisation.

Petrology does not work in all cases. Thin sections of **obsidian** and flint look remarkably similar regardless of where they originated. Similarly, ceramics, which lack distinctive mineral tempers, require other techniques in order to source them.

Spectrometry

Spectrometry covers a range of methods that derive from physics and involve using radiation (for example X-rays) to force a small sample of material to produce light (another form of radiation) which can be measured through spectrographic analysis. In the way that sunlight can be split into a rainbow, the light emitted by different elements shows different characteristic patterns when split by a prism into a spectrum. This is projected onto a viewing screen or photographic plate, so that information can be recorded. In a compound of elements, the balance of those elements is shown by the intensity of the lines in the spectrum. This is compared with control spectrums of known composition produced under the same conditions. Trace elements of a few parts per million can be recorded in this way. Spectrometry is a very accurate method for quantitative analysis and only requires small samples (less than 10 milligrams) to be taken. This makes it suitable for valuable archaeological material. It is widely employed for metal analysis but is also used for glass, faience, pottery, obsidian and occasionally flint.

X-ray fluorescence

This technique is one of the cheapest and quickest methods of analysing the surface composition of materials, particularly metals and pottery glazes. It is also non-destructive. A beam of X-rays forces the material to re-emit X-rays. The intensity of energy given off can be measured to indicate the chemicals present and their relative abundance. Since the method does not penetrate deeply it is of little use where materials have a coating of another mineral. A more advanced method uses protons to penetrate more deeply but it is also more expensive.

Neutron activation analysis (NAA)

This is the most accurate and reliable **characterisation** technique. Tiny samples are ground down and then bombarded with neutrons in a reactor. Elements in the sample become unstable isotopes and give off distinctive patterns of radiation, which can be measured. The technique is so

Figure 3.7 *Copper knives from the Amesbury Archer burial*

These knives would have had wooden handles. They were made out of pure copper which was repeatedly heated and hammered into shape. NAA would be the most accurate test of composition but would damage them. For such thin objects XRF might produce the required results. One knife was Spanish, another French, which provided clues to the origin of the bowman.

Figure 3.8 *Copper 'oxhide ingots' from Minoan Crete*

Copper was exchanged across the eastern Mediterranean in the early Bronze Age. These distinctive ingots are found at palace sites and also shipwrecks (▶ p. 252). Shape, moulding marks and inscriptions have been studied to identify patterns but lead isotope studies were able to locate the mines to Cyprus.

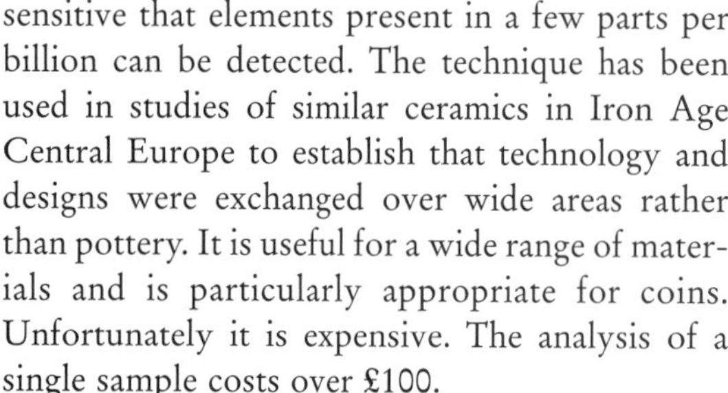

sensitive that elements present in a few parts per billion can be detected. The technique has been used in studies of similar ceramics in Iron Age Central Europe to establish that technology and designs were exchanged over wide areas rather than pottery. It is useful for a wide range of materials and is particularly appropriate for coins. Unfortunately it is expensive. The analysis of a single sample costs over £100.

Isotopic analysis

Atoms of the same element which have the same number of neutrons and electrons but different numbers of protons, are called isotopes. Copper, lead, oxygen and carbon all have several different isotopes for example carbon 12, 13 and 14. By determining what isotopes are present, and in what proportions, materials can be linked to known sources with the same ratios. This technique was used to analyse metal artefacts from early Bronze Age Crete. These had distinctive Cretan styles but there are no metal ores found on Crete. Ratios for lead isotopes in bronze and silver artefacts enabled the material to be traced to sources on the mainland. This showed that raw materials rather than finished objects were being traded. Trade in copper and marble around the Mediterranean has also been traced using isotopic analysis. In the case of marble, petrology had been unable to do so.

ANALYSIS OF PARTICULAR INORGANIC MATERIALS

Ceramic analysis

Pottery is very important to archaeology from the Neolithic onwards because it survives well in almost any environment. It provides dating evidence and can be used to make inferences about exchange, economy and society. To categorise sherds, colour is described by reference to the Munsell Soil Colour Charts. There are similar charts for hardness and the grain size of inclusions in the temper. Such analysis may require the use of polarising microscopes. Manufacturing by hand, coil or wheel methods can usually be determined visually, as can form. The key indicators here are sherds from the rim, neck and base of vessels. Where possible pots are reassembled by specialists for recording.

Clay is almost entirely formed from eroded sedimentary rocks, but a tiny percentage of the material is made up of trace elements. Petrology and other characterisation techniques can be applied to pottery and bricks although 'fingerprinting' clay sources is much more difficult and well developed than is the case with rocks. In many cases, experts on regional pottery will be able to suggest the origin of artefacts from the temper and inclusions in the pottery, which they identify from visual or microscopic examination.

Refiring experiments and ethnography (▶ p. 114) can provide insights into manufacturing techniques. The fabric colour and hardness provide clues to firing temperatures. Clay often contains iron, which forms a red oxide if it is heated in an oxygen rich environment or a black/grey oxide if it is oxygen poor. The colour of the molecules of clay indicates which was the case. If the clay is vitrified (where minerals have melted and fused together) it indicates that firing occurred in a kiln at temperatures in excess of 1100°C. Slips and glazes provide additional clues to origins and period.

In quantifying pottery finds there is debate amongst archaeologists over whether the number or weight of sherds is more useful. On most sites it is rare to recover entire pots either intact or in pieces. A large urn may break into several large but heavy pieces while a small pot may shatter into many small light fragments. Depending on which measure is chosen the results can be widely different. Increasingly archaeologists measure both, but weight used in conjunction with average sherd weight can be used to reduce variability caused by different sizes of vessels. Various attempts have also been made to work out 'estimated vessel equivalents' (EVE) or 'minimum number of vessels' (MNV). Techniques vary from counting elements which only occur once such as the base to dividing the total angles of rim sherds by 360 degrees. The Ashmolean Museum website has an excellent guide to the value of pottery to archaeologists.

- http://www.ashmol.ox.ac.uk/PotWeb/

Organic residue analysis

This exciting new technique uses chemical solvents and reagents to dissolve and extract traces of organic materials left in the fabric of pottery sherds. The resulting solution can be tested for sugars, lipids (fats) and proteins. The results can be matched to 'fingerprints' known from commodities such as honey, olive oil and plant resins. A team from Bradford University has used this technique to study the bulk import of liquids into Bronze Age Egypt through analysis of amphorae sherds. Other researchers are examining the development of dairying. Unfortunately the process is too expensive to be widely used. Some sites produce thousands of sherds and the analysis of a single sample would cost around £10.

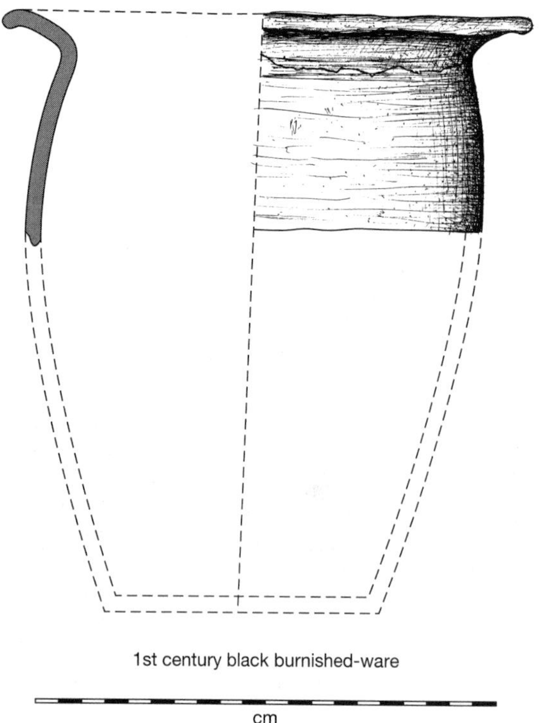

Figure 3.9 *The standard way to record and illustrate ceramics is to draw the whole vessel in outline but with one quarter cut away. This enables one half to provide a cross-section to show internal and external shape and dimensions. The other half shows external appearance. Sometimes the area of decoration is limited to the area of the actual sherd recovered.*

KEY TERM

Use wear analysis

For some artefacts, including stone tools, tiny scratches and traces are left from past activity. For example, half an hour cutting cereals will leave a polish on a flint blade. Expert analysis backed by examples from experimental archaeology (▶ p. 117) can sometimes identify the signatures of different activities. However, this may only reveal the *last* activity the tool was used for. The detection and description of wear marks can be greatly assisted by the use of a scanning electron microscope (SEM). This sweeps a band of electrons over the surface of the tool being studied and gives much improved depth of focus and higher magnification. This enhanced image can then be displayed on a screen. Recent work has involved the study of starch grains on stone blades in Polynesia and the analysis of blood residues on some of the equipment carried by Otzi the Ice Man.

Lithic analysis

Lithics or stone tools are virtually indestructible. They have been used for all but the earliest stages of human development and for many sites and periods are the only definite sign of human activity. Examination of their surface can determine whether they were manufactured by fracturing, pecking or polishing the original stone. Reference to experimental or ethnographic examples (▶ Chapter 5) can help identify signs of techniques such as indirect percussion and pressure flaking. Artefacts can be sorted by type of stone, colour and **typology**. Specialists will use reference material for relative dating and suggestion of function. Manufacturing debris (debitage) is of particular value. It provides evidence of raw materials, the production process and the tools used. Sometimes debitage can be refitted to show the sequence of manufacturing and even whether the knapper was sitting or standing, left- or right-handed. Petrology has been the most widely used means of characterisation for lithics although the other techniques are increasingly used.

Metallurgical analysis

Some metal artefacts require special treatment to remove corrosion. They may also need X-raying to see the shape of the artefact beneath a crust of oxidised material or to identify cracks or seams

Figure 3.10 *Lithics*

The examples in this photograph are particularly fine examples of the flint knapper's art. These flint arrow heads with tangs for secure fastening into the shaft were state of the art hunting and possibly fighting tools in the early Bronze Age. These come from the Amesbury Archer burial. The drawn record would aim to show size, depth, shape and how they were formed including direction of flaking.

where several pieces of metal were joined to form complex artefacts. Metallurgists use microscopes to explore manufacturing techniques. **Metallography** includes examination of the size and shape of the grains of minerals in the material for traces of heating, working and alloying. Where they are available, SEMs are preferred. Their magnification at 1000x may be similar to the best optical microscopes but the depth of field they provide enables fine detail to be identified. This is particularly important when exploring the manufacturing techniques used in jewellery or weapons making. The manufacture of iron sword blades often involved hammering folded layers of metal. This process can be detected by examining a cross-section of the blade. Analysis of the carbon content may reveal enrichment due to roasting in charcoal in order to produce resilient weapons.

The first recorded use of metal is in the form of jewellery and ritual items. These were made from 'soft' metals (gold and copper) which would be worked by hammering. Early metal artefacts were relatively simple and tended to imitate stone ones. It was not till smiths learnt how to use bellows to reach the high temperatures needed to smelt ores in crucibles that the potential of metals could be

Figure 3.11 *Bloom*

Finds of material from various stages in the production of metals are crucial to understanding manufacturing technology. In this experiment the cooling metal or bloom is being lifted out of the furnace leaving slag behind.

realized. This also enabled the production of alloys which were blends of two or more minerals. The most significant was bronze made from copper and tin. One and two piece moulds enabled new shapes including socketed weapons to be produced. A key development was the 'lost wax process' where a model of the desired tool was made in wax and then fired inside a casing of clay. The wax melted when the clay was fired leaving a void in the shape of the tool into which molten metal could be poured. Evidence for this technology comes from stone and clay moulds, crucibles, slag and waste metal as well as the finished products. Artefacts themselves provide evidence of casting errors, mould seams, cold working after casting and decorative techniques.

Metal objects were frequently ornamented by means of a range of engraving tools or punches whose shapes may be identified when magnified. The Gundestrup Cauldron, a magnificent, silver Iron Age feasting pot found in a bog in Denmark was examined in this way. Analysis of punchmarks with a SEM suggested that several toolkits had been used. Taylor was able to compare manufacturing techniques and imagery to identify Transylvania as the likely location for the workshop and to suggest the ethnic origins of the craftsmen.

- Taylor 1997

Besides the characterisation techniques already discussed a number of other methods are used with metals. Measuring the specific gravity of artefacts and comparing with known examples can identify alloys of gold. A more precise technique is **atomic absorption spectrometry** (AAS).

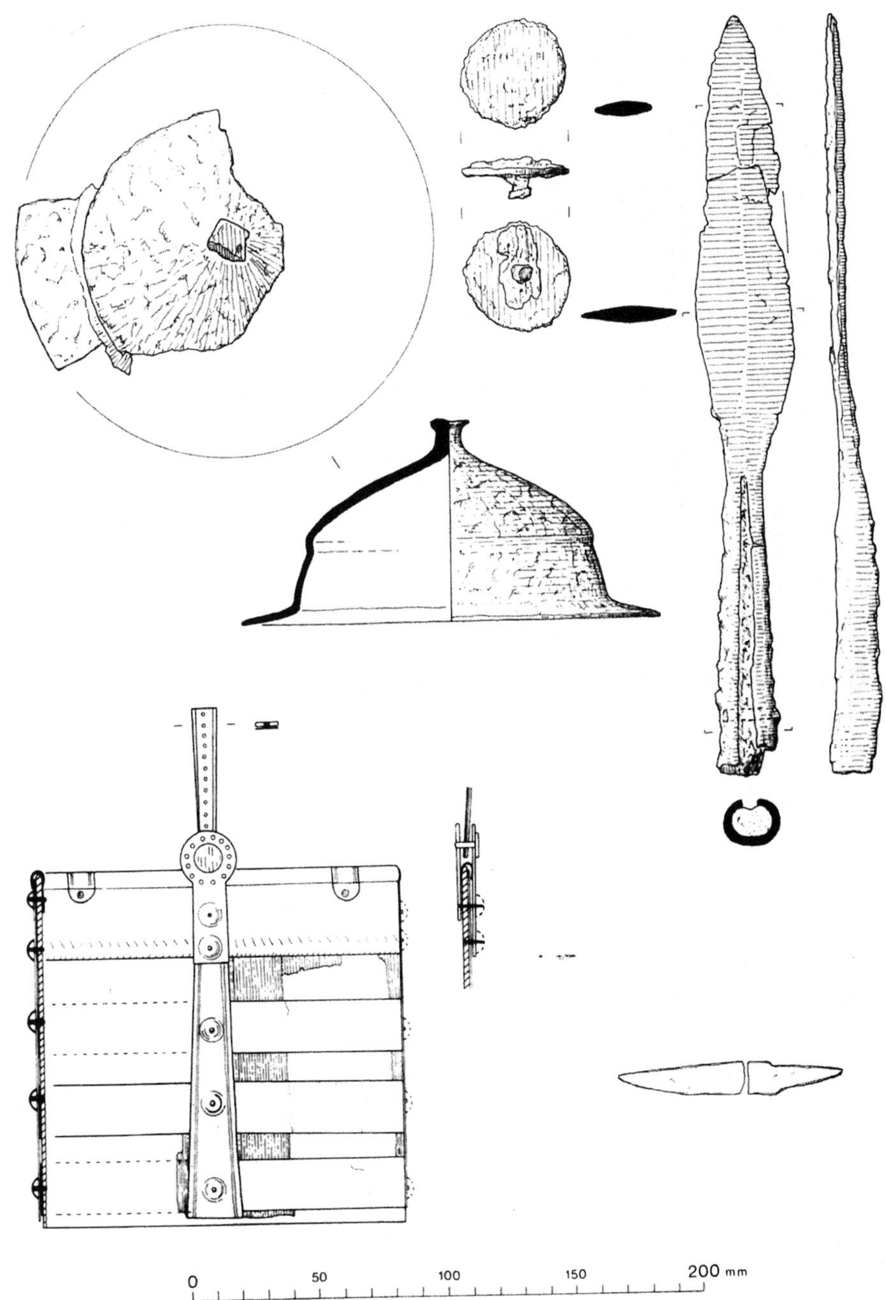

Figure 3.12 *Anglo-Saxon grave goods from Empingham*

This illustrates many of the conventions for drawing inorganic artefacts. The shield boss is shown partly reconstructed as with pottery. The button and spear are shown in several views so that shape is communicated. Compare this with the photographs and grave plans (◀ p. 32). Aside from the bucket this might look like a warrior grave. However, there is some evidence that such grave goods were a mark of ethnic identity in the early medieval period rather than a direct link with what a person did (▶ p. 282).

KEY SKILL

Noting methods of analysis

The vast range of scientific methods used by archaeologists to analyse materials looks very daunting at first site. The key to starting to grasp them is to learn some of the principle in simple terms before you tackle specialist texts. We have adopted this approach in the selection presented in this text. After reading this section, you should make some notes to clarify points in your own mind. One way is to draw your own impression of the processes involved in each method.

Which analytical methods are appropriate for which material?

	Ceramics	*Stone*	*Flint*	*Copper*	*Iron*	*Glass*
Thin section						
Petrology						
Spectrometry						
Isotopic analysis						
Use wear analysis						
AAS						

Test yourself by copying this table and ticking approprate methods for each material. You can add to the list as you become familiar with a greater range of techniques.

A minute sample is dissolved in acid and then vaporised. When light of known wavelengths is passed through the gas, the amount that is absorbed indicates the minerals present. This technique has been used to trace the seventh-century debasement of coins in the Merovingian Empire. AAS is also widely used for bronze and copper. A limitation of this technique is that where metal artefacts were made from several sources the 'fingerprint' is obscured. In the ancient world, valuable commodities such as bronze were often recycled with new artefacts made from scrap from a variety of sources.

The study of coins is a very specialised area. The analytical techniques already described provide information on the metals used. The degree of debasement in gold and silver Roman coins can be used as an approximate form of dating although the images and inscriptions on the surface are usually more valuable. Coins have been used to explore topics as diverse as trade, territories and particular events.

ANALYSIS OF ORGANIC REMAINS

Soil

The chemistry of soil can provide clues to the type of vegetation and by extension, fauna and agriculture it could support. The early farmers in central Europe, for example, seemed to favour particular soil types for their farming settlements. Soil change can also record the impact of humans on the land. Sediments in valleys in Cyprus were used to explain the abandonment of Bronze Age sites. Deforestation or overgrazing had led to erosion of topsoil on the hillsides which had then been deposited in the valleys. Soil is also analysed for what it holds. Pollen, invertebrates and even microbes can be recovered to provide clues about environment and economy.

Soils differ in their ability to preserve materials. Pollen survives well in acidic contexts whereas alkaline environments are better for snail shells.

Faunal remains

Archaeozoology or zooarchaeology is the study of the remains of animals from archaeological contexts. Humans interact with animals in several ways including their use for human food or other resources and indirectly as the occupants of ecological niches alongside humans. Faunal (which includes fish and birds as well as mammals) remains are vital to archaeologists in two ways: to reconstruct past environments (▶ p. 197) and to identify the contribution which animals made to the human economy (▶ p. 224).

Figure 3.13 *Animal bones after washing*

The mineral element in bones can survives well in alkaline soils such as sand or gravel. Acid soils usually dissolve all but burnt bone although in certain conditions, bone collagen can sometimes be recovered. Waterlogged, arid and frozen sites provide the best preservation. This means that some sites may have vast amounts of bone whilst others have very little. This bias applies to different types of bone. Larger bones and teeth enamel survive far longer than small bones. Similarly tiny fish and bird bones don't survive as well as cattle bones. Even where they survive, they are rarely recovered unless sieving or flotation is used.

The first task for bone specialists is to identify the type of bone and then the species of animal from which they came. Mammals have similar numbers and types of bones so reference collections supplement the expert's knowledge. This also applies to fish and birds. To understand the significance of particular species in an **assemblage** the number of animals represented has to be determined. However, it is rare for complete skeletons to be recovered so several different ways of counting the bones of each species are used.

- NISP. The number of identified specimens (bones) present. However, only parts of some animals may have been taken to a site.
- Weight. This is biased to animals with heavier bones.
- MMI. Minimum number of individuals. Working out the smallest number of animals which could produce the assemblage. This is done by counting bones which only occur once such as skulls or pelvis.

The raw data only shows the relative abundance of a particular species not how important it was to people and their economy. There is more meat on a cow than on a sheep, so while the MNI for sheep may be greater than for cows, they may contribute much less to the overall diet. Several additional measures have been developed to assess dietary contribution such as meat weight versus bone weight. A further complication arises when we consider the body elements that are present. Some animals may not have been slaughtered on-site and bones that are low in meat, such as the spine and feet, may have been discarded off-site. Careful examination of butchery marks can reveal the process by which animal bone reached the site of deposition.

Establishing the age and sex of the animals represented in a bone assemblage can help reconstruct the system of hunting or agriculture practised (▶ p. 226). For example, the sex ratio and age structure in herds of cattle kept for dairy products are different from those kept for meat. The sex of bones can be identified from anatomical features such as antlers (deer), large canines (pig) and penis bone (dog) in males and pelvic shape and structure in females. The dimensions of bones can also be used as males are larger in many species. The ratio between two or more measurements from one bone is used rather than a single measure (for example length) as size may be dependent on the age of the animal. Identification of changes in the skeleton is useful for establishing age especially patterns of teeth eruption, growth and wear and bone fusion. The ends of long bones are called epiphyses. In a young animal these are joined to the bone by cartilage. As the animal ages this calcifies until by a process

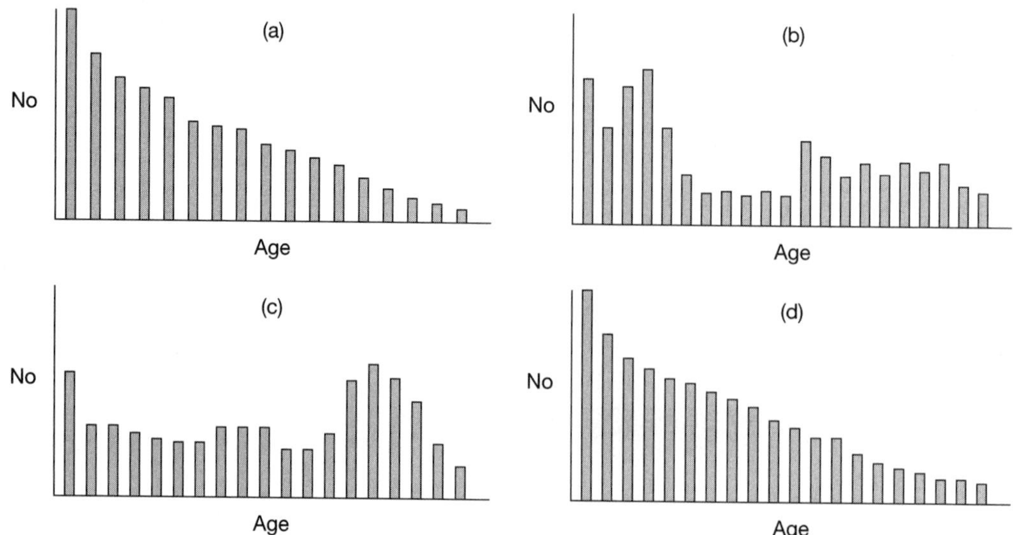

Profiles which plot the age of animals from surviving bones against the number found in each age group.

(a) The age profile of a modern herd of similar animals. This provides the 'norm' for comparison.

(b) A profile caused by selective butchery or hunting. A disproportionate number of animals are killed as they reach maturity (probably male) and when they are beyond breeding age. Animals in their prime, particularly females, would be spared.

(c) A dairying herd. There is a rise in the proportion killed as they cease to supply milk.

(d) A catastrophic profile. The whole herd has died. Possibly caused by stampeding over a cliff.

Figure 3.14 *Simplified diagrams to illustrate catastrophic and attritional profiles in animal bone assemblages*

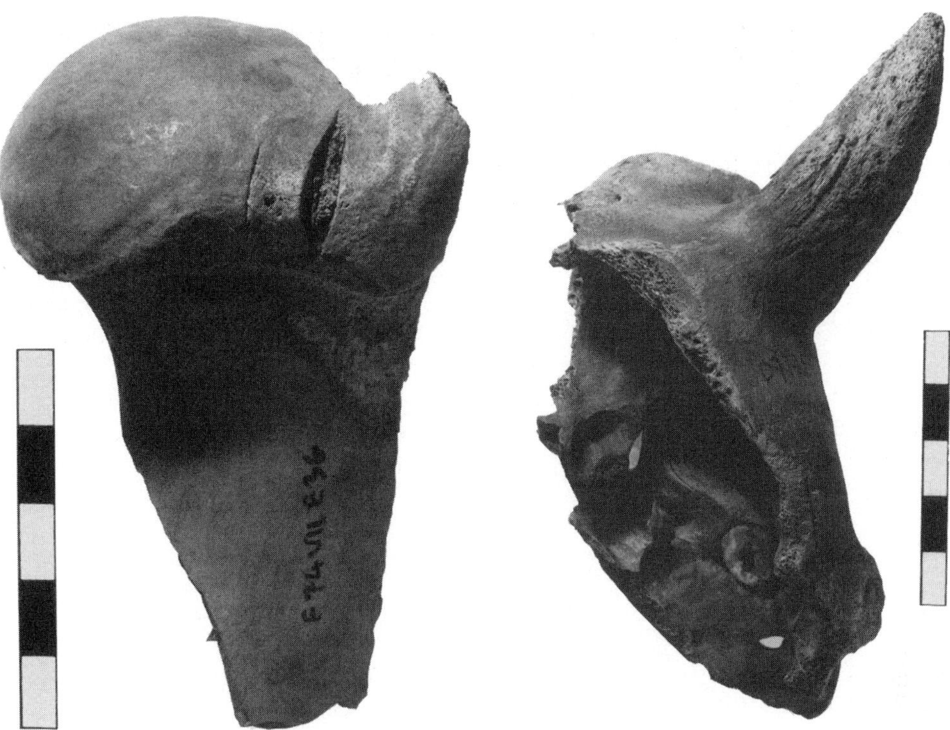

Figure 3.15 *Neolithic animal bone with evidence of human butchery. The cattle bone on the left has cut marks while the sheep skull on the right has been split open with a sharp tool*

known as epiphysial fusion the ends and bones are joined. This allows adults and juveniles to be differentiated. Tooth eruption and antler shedding may also establish the season of death of the animals. However, such analysis is not always reliable, as bones may not have been deposited at the time the animals were killed. Note that Star Carr was thought to be a winter site from antler evidence, but recent discoveries of stork and crane bones suggest it was used in summer.

Biostratigraphy, the principle of using fossil animals to date layers, has been used by archaeologists to help date sites. For example, reindeer bones might indicate a period during the last Ice Age. Smaller mammals such as voles, which evolve quickly, are often the most useful for this **faunal dating**. It is also possible to analyse bone collagen for dating and for environmental information from the minerals and amino acids it contains. Animals provide clues to the environment although we cannot always be certain that they occupied similar habitats to today's animals. Bones can also provide insights into human behaviour. The spread of species may be related to trade or human migration. DNA studies will soon shed light on the origins of modern animal species. Analysis of damage to bones provides data on hunting, butchery and craft technology.

Human remains

Human remains can be divided into two major categories: hard and soft tissue. The evidence that these two types provide and the conditions in which they are preserved vary considerably.

Figure 3.16 *A latrine at Housesteads fort. Analysis of soil at similar sites has provided valuable evidence about the diets of legionaries*

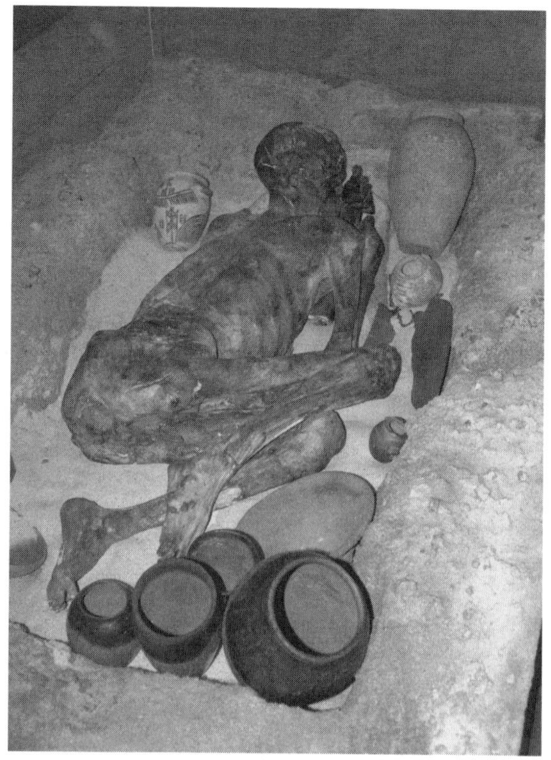

Figure 3.17 *'Ginger'*

Nicknamed from his colour, this naturally mummified Egyptian from around 3400BC is testimony to the preserving power of arid conditions. The hot sand dessicated the body by absorbing its water content. As a dried out piece of leather there was no moisture for the flesh eating bacteria which cause decay. Ginger is surrounded by pre-Dynastic grave goods.

Soft tissue

Like other organic remains, soft tissue is only usually recovered on sites with unusually good preservation. They are not likely to be a representative sample of the wider population but are useful none the less.

Desiccated bodies such as Egyptian mummies often preserve facial features well, if a little distorted from the drying process, together with internal organs, nails and hair. Accurate sexing of the body can usually be done from the external sexual organs, or from facial hair. There are always exceptions. 'Mummy 1770', which had probably spent some time in the Nile as a result of an unfortunate encounter with a crocodile, could not be sexed at the time of mummification by the priests. He/she was therefore prepared for either eventuality in the afterlife by being given both a false penis made of a roll of bandage, and gold nipples. In addition to providing details of clothing and **mortuary practices**, tissue samples can be rehydrated to give useful evidence about disease, for example the sand pneumoconiosis suffered by one of 'The Brothers' in Manchester Museum. Dry sites sometimes also provide coprolites. Analysis of these can recover hair, bone, seed and parasites to reveal information about diet and health. Analysis of deposits from the latrines at Bearsden Roman Fort revealed little trace of cholesterol but lots of wheat bran, suggesting that the legionaries ate little meat. The Dungfile website provides all the links you might want.

- http://www.ualberta.ca/~abeaudoi/stuff/dung/human.htm

Frozen corpses like Otzi the Ice Man and the Pazyryk 'Ice Maiden' provide similar evidence to dry bodies except that stomach contents are often preserved as well. The general level of distortion and decay is often so low that these bodies can almost seem asleep, not dead. The Peruvian Inca children are especially extraordinary in this respect. In one case the trauma that caused death – a blow to the head – could still be identified in a CAT scan. In another example the red-stained vomit from the symbolic 'achiote' dye that the child had been forced to ingest still marked his face and the front of his clothing. Without Otzi's preserved skin we would not have known about his tattoos, which may be the earliest evidence of medicinal acupuncture.

Bodies from anaerobic conditions such as the famous 'bog bodies' of northern Europe, including Lindow and Tollund Man, have been used to study diet, internal parasites and trauma. The acid nature of bogs can lead to the almost complete demineralisation of bone while tanning the skin to perfection.

- http://www.archaeology.org/online/features/bog/index.html
- http://www.pbs.org/wgbh/nova/peru/
- http://www.nationalgeographic.com/mummy/index.html
- http://www.gla.ac.uk/Acad/IBLS/DEEB/jd/otzi.htm
- http://www.bps.org/wgbh/nova/icemummies/iceman.html

In some soil conditions, in East Anglia for example, where the soil is damp and acid, neither hard nor soft tissue survives well. The only surviving trace of a body may be a stain in the bottom of the grave that provides a silhouette of the original corpse. The 'sand man' in Mound 1 at Sutton Hoo may have been such a burial.

- http://www.suttonhoo.org/

Hard tissue

Bone is much more frequently recovered by archaeologists than soft tissue. Similar analysis to that used on faunal remains is carried out to determine the composition of assemblages of human remains. Many techniques for ageing and sexing humans are also similar. However, due to widespread variation amongst males and females no physical method is totally reliable and it is almost impossible to sex children. DNA testing is accurate, but is very expensive. Using wear on bones to estimate age for older individuals is also notoriously unreliable. Theya Molleson made a comparative study on the collection from Spitalfields Crypt where the actual ages were known from the coffin plates. In the case of Louisa Courtauld, the archaeological estimate of her age using bone was wrong by over twenty years. However, a newer technique of thin-sectioning teeth, which relies on measuring the amount of translucence in the root, provided a much closer estimate.

Health. Where a large sample of human bones is recovered one can *start* to gain some tentative insights into age structure and health of the population. Some diseases leave marks on bones. These include polio, tuberculosis and genetic disorders such as cleft palate, along with syphilis and various types of cancer. Early medical treatments such as trepanation (cutting or drilling a hole in the skull) can sometimes be identified.

Damage to the skeleton through accidents, activities undertaken during life, murder and warfare injuries and even childbirth can all be evidenced by physical traces left on bone. Female skeletons at Tell Abu Hureyra (▶ p. 231) were shown to have traces of arthritis from using grindstones, while the murder of prisoners at the Battle of Towton (▶ p. 287) has recently been investigated through meticulous examination of skeletons from a pit near the battle site.

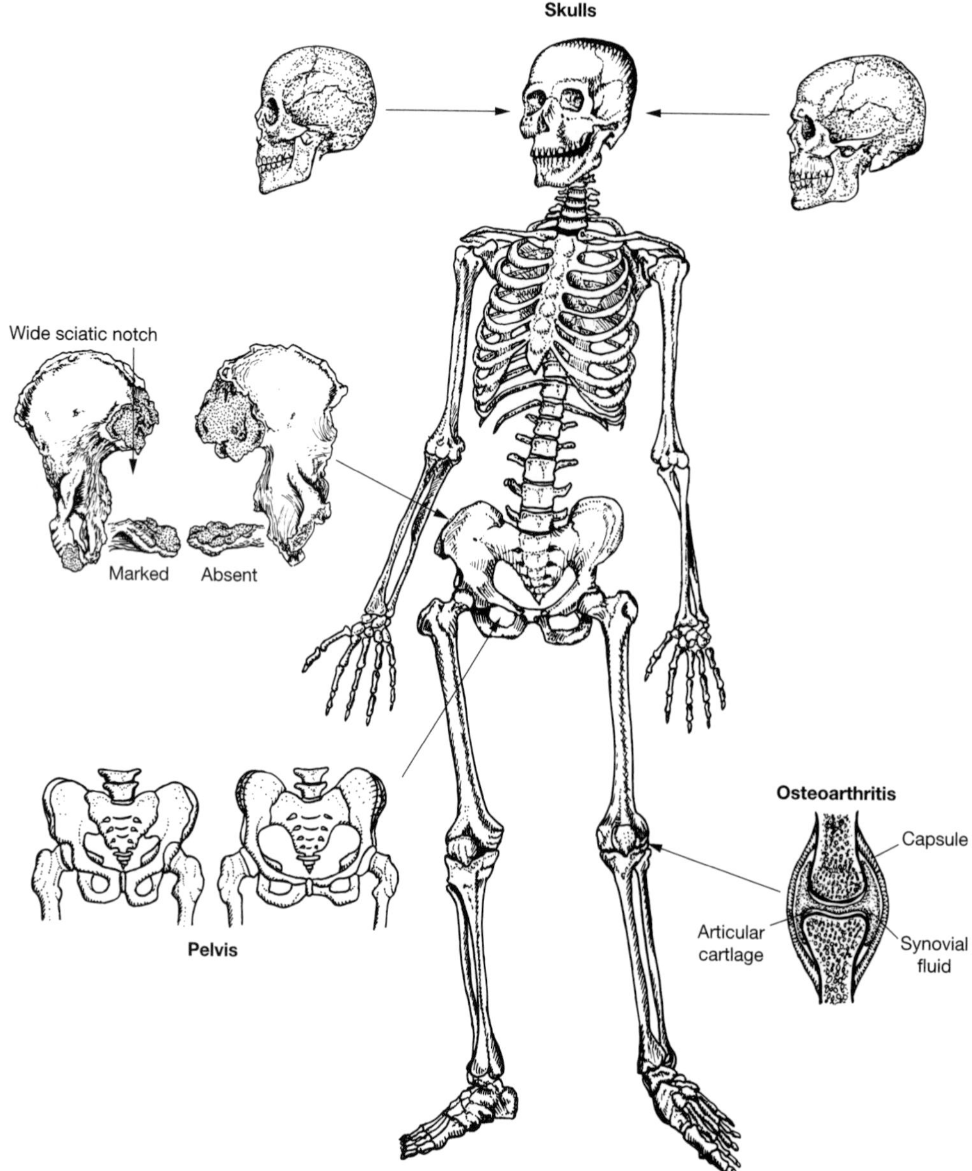

Figure 3.18 *Drawings of human skeleton*

The key parts of the skeleton used by archaeologists to sex and age the body are labelled. The close-up of the pelvis indicates the difference between the narrow arch of males and the wider arch in females to allow for the passage of the baby's head during birth. In the blade of the pelvis, below the socket for the hipbone (femur), is the sciatic notch. The rough 'rule of thumb' of the forensic anthropologist Rebecca Storey is, 'You stick your thumb in and if it wiggles it's female and if it doesn't it's male!' The skulls illustrate potential variation between male and female skulls although there is more of a continuum here. Generally male brow ridges are heavier with larger mandibles (jaws) and skulls. The best guide to age is tooth eruption stages and epiphysial fusion. Bones fuse at different rates during an individual's life until full maturity in a person's twenties. There are also changes in bone structure as we age although microscopic analysis would be required to assess it.

KEY SITE

The 'Amesbury Archer'

During housing development in the Stonehenge area, Wessex Archaeology made one of the most significant discoveries of recent years. A burial which was dated to 2300BC contained the richest assemblage of grave goods found from the period including the earliest gold found in Britain. Most beaker burials have one or two vessels and one archery kit. This man was buried in a wood lined cist with over 100 artefacts (▶ p. 92) including five beakers, two archery sets and an array of rare metal objects. These included copper knives and two gold hair tresses (▶ p. 277). Shortly after this discovery a second grave was found. This man did not have so many goods but he too had a pair of gold tresses, discovered during micro-excavation of his jaw! These were spectacular finds but analysis of their skeletal remains was to reveal much more.

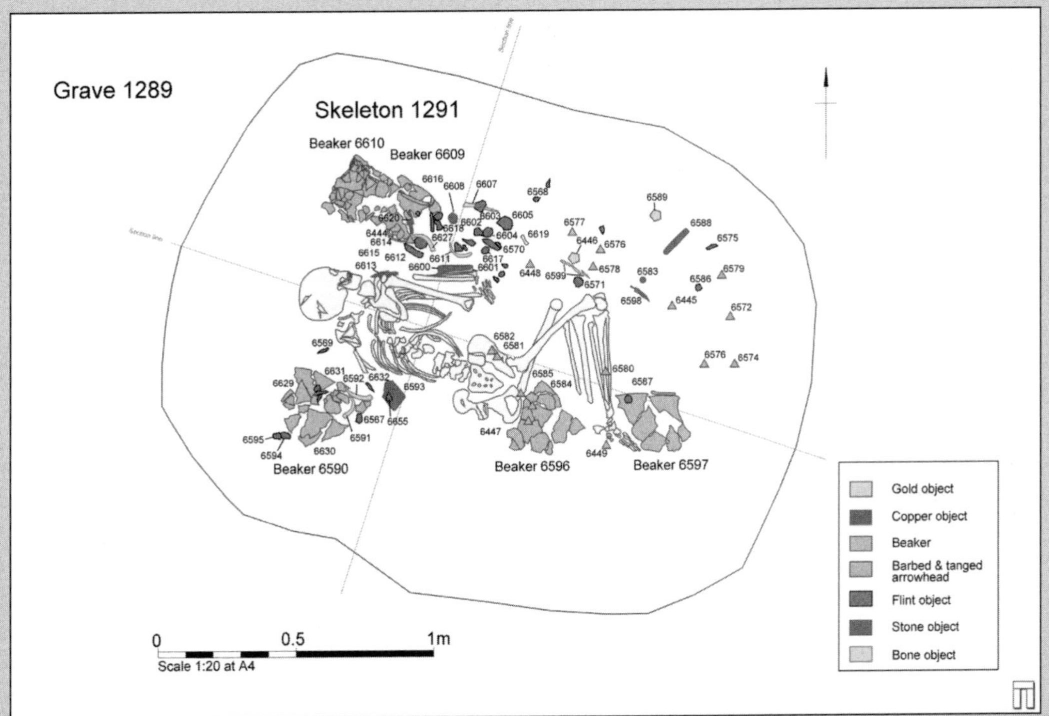

Figure 3.19 *The grave of the Amesbury Archer*

- Oesteoarchaeological examination suggested the archer was 35–40. He was a robust individual about 5′8″ in height with a badly damaged left knee. His leg would have been withered and oozed with pus. It would have been awkward and may have smelled bad. The second man was in his 20s when he died.

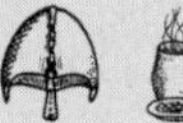

KEY SITE *cont.*

The 'Amesbury Archer'

- The men shared a number of distinctive anatomical traits including similar shaped heads and a rare deformity of their heels. They were related, possibly father and son.
- Carbon isotope analysis suggested that they had eaten diets based around cereals.
- When growing, teeth enamel locks in oxygen from local drinking water. Isotopic analysis showed that the archer's teeth had developed in Europe, possibly in the alps. In contrast, the younger man had grown up in southern England.

Analysis of the gold suggested it came from at least 100 miles away-.possibly from Europe as were two knives. His shale bracelet was from the Dorset coast and other artefacts had also come from some distance. So who was this man with such exotic possessions? The press quickly dubbed him 'the king of Stonehenge' and suggested that he built it. Since Stonehenge is far older that is impossible although he may have been involved in one of its later phases.

The beaker assemblages are one clue. Beakers from the grave have been compared to others from both Europe and Scotland. The origins of the beaker assemblage lie in the central European corded ware tradition (Sherratt, 1997) of individual burials with battle axes, beakers and flint dagger. In the bell-beaker development which reached Britain, archery equipment replaced the battleaxe. This male warrior drinking assemblage might reflect life roles or it might simply be the 'right way' to be buried. Either way, the archer was one of the earliest of such burials so he may have been involved in importing such ideas. He also had equipment for metal working – some of it similar to the Upton Lovell burial (▶ p. 260). Perhaps his status (and wealth) was derived from his craft which initially must have seemed close to sorcery.

Diet. The main approach to diet relies upon studies of isotopic traces in bone. Particular diets such as one dependent on marine foods or one heavy in maize consumption will leave a signature in the bone collagen. A Homo Erectus from Lake Turkana was found to have an extra scab of bone around its femur. The most likely cause was an excess of vitamin A caused by eating too much raw meat, especially liver; a reminder that the transition of our species from plant eaters to meat eaters was not without its problems. Tooth wear is also used to demonstrate gritty diets while earth from the abdominal area of buried skeletons can be analysed for pollen and seeds which may have been in the stomach.

- http://www.brad.ac.uk/acad/archsci/depart/resgrp/palaeodiet/

Genetic links. Shared genetic differences in populations often have a visible effect on bone, which allows people with this trait to be grouped together. Much work has been done on this in the USA in order to establish tribal affiliations for government programmes to repatriate bones from museums to their tribal homelands and also to trace the origins of diseases currently affecting native populations. Through the application of PCR (polymerase chain reaction) genetic scientists have amplified small amounts of genetic material found in archaeological contexts. This has enabled human evolution to be traced. Through the study of mitochondrial DNA, the identity of the female founder of our species, the 'African Eve', has been established. DNA was able to establish that the woman from Monkton

Up Wimborne (◀ p. 34) was the mother of one of the girls but unrelated to the other two children who were brother and sister. Isotope analysis revealed that she had come from the Mendips and had eaten mainly dairy products.

Organic artefacts

Organic artefacts are far rarer in archaeology than those made of stone and clay. Inevitably this has distorted our view of the past because so much material culture is invisible to us. Sites where organic finds survive in large amounts are unusual and in some cases may not be 'typical' sites. However, they do provide tantalising glimpses of the skills, culture and economics of the periods in the past from which they came.

Plants

For the archaeologist samples of plant remains divide into the microscopic and the macroscopic. Both types usually require specialised methods of conservation and analysis. Plants can tell the archaeologist about past climate, economic practices, the nature of past environment and environmental change. We can explore the exploitation of plants for food, medicinal and narcotic purposes while the study of wood leads us into construction, carpentry and woodland management.

Plant macrofossils

Plant macrofossils are specimens that are visible to the naked eye. They include seeds, leaves and

Figure 3.20 *Alder cones*

These magnified plant remains were part of a huge sample of environmental remains which enabled archaeologists to reconstruct the landscape around Britain's oldest known bridge (1500BC) in Hampshire. This is possible since soil type is fairly constant and we know the habitat of each plant and insect.

twigs. They are usually preserved in the following unusual conditions:

- Waterlogged, where wet anaerobic conditions inhibit the growth of the bacteria that cause decomposition. For example, bran in Lindow Man's stomach or moss used as 'toilet paper' in Viking York.
- Carbonised, where charring has converted material to inorganic carbon which is less susceptible to the forces of decay, for example grain in the pits at Danebury. Some plants are more likely than others to have become carbonized during processing which can distort samples (▶ p. 106).
- Mineralised, where the organic content of the specimen is replaced by minerals such as iron and manganese from groundwater in the soil.
- Frozen, usually in conditions of permafrost when the ground is always frozen and organic remains within it can be perfectly preserved. For example coriander seeds in the 'Ice Maiden's' grave or the stomach contents of Siberian mammoths.
- As impressions in mudbrick, pottery or daub, for example corn cobs at Ceren and olives at Pompeii.

Wood

Dealing with wood from archaeological contexts presents huge problems, but may also offer sources of evidence unavailable elsewhere. Wood survives on wet or dessicated sites and in carbonized form. The cellular structure of trees varies so it is possible to identify different species using a microscope. Leaving aside its use for dating through dendrochronology, wood is valuable as physical evidence for structure and artefacts. Living trees are discussed in chapter 9. Archaeologists cannot study carpentry practices from the past, which involved complex joinery, without part of a ship or building to show how the joint was made. The discovery of wooden structures is also important in revealing the huge range of uses to which wood was put in the past.

Shipwrecks (▶ p. 252) such as the Wasa or Mary Rose are time capsules: a moment frozen in time. Inside these two warships were a bewildering array of wooden artefacts from mundane spoons and bowls to sophisticated navigational aids.

- http://dover.gov.uk/museum/boat/home.htm

All of this material derived from wet contexts. The wood, though flimsy and insubstantial, retains much of its form and details such as axe marks. Wood from dry contexts also sometimes survives but is frequently warped and distorted. Once wood is removed from a wet environment, decay sets in rapidly unless proactive measures are taken. Observations at Oakbank (◀ p. 53) showed that excavated wood when freshly broken retained the colour of fresh timber, but once exposed to the air the wood turned black in about twenty seconds. In the short term wood is kept wet with biocides added to the water to prevent fungal growth. Longer term conservation may involve freeze-drying but this is only a viable option for artefacts and small timbers. Larger specimens require different techniques. Replacing the water in the cells of the wood with a soluble wax such as PEG (polyethylene glycol) treats shipwreck timbers, which have the consistency of wet cardboard and consist of 80–90 per cent water. This treatment can be very time-consuming. The *Mary Rose*, which has been treated with PEG, is still not ready for display more than ten years after she was raised.

Indirect evidence for the use of wood can also be detected. At Sutton Hoo the imprint of an Anglo-Saxon ship's timbers remained in the sand while at Garton Slack there was a stain from the vanished spokes of a chariot's wheels. Charcoal is a common find on many archaeological sites. In addition to providing samples for radiocarbon dating (▶ p. 96) it can reveal much about local environments. Microscopic analysis can reveal not only species but even whether firewood came from coppiced trees.

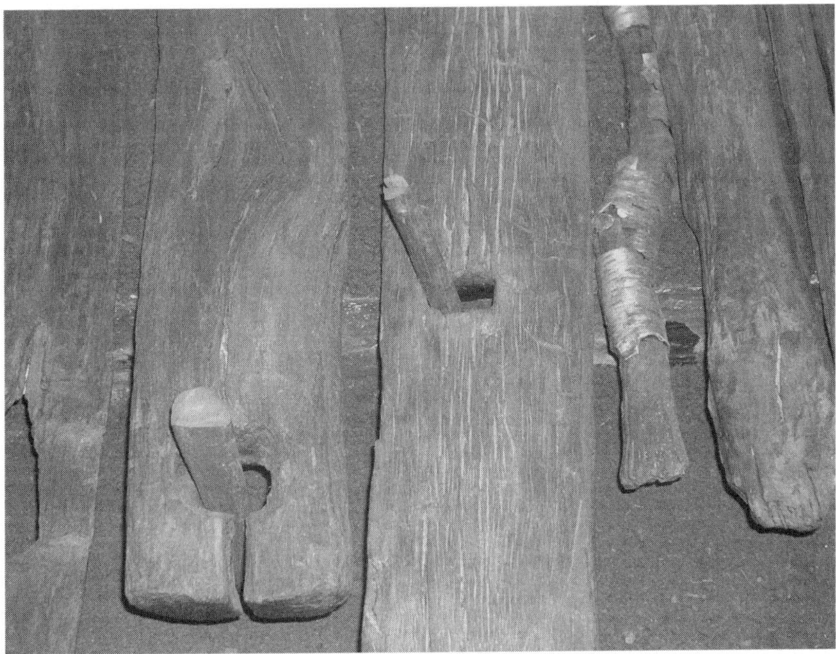

Figure 3.21 *Wood from the Corlea Trackway*

Wooden structures not only tell us about carpentry and construction techniques but also about woodland management. In most cases research reveals that specific tree species were selected for specific tasks. At Corlea in 148 BC a 2 km long track way was built across a bog. The timber for the road came from 370 oak trees. This was laid on alder and elm runners above a platform of brushwood. The planks were split skilfully with wooden wedges and were anchored down with pegs through mortices. Causeways are common in the area and are mentioned in Celtic stories such as the Wooing of Etain. However, the scale of Corlea is exceptional and would have required a high degree of social organization to construct. Possibly at tribal level (▶ p. 265). There are no ruts from carts or wear on the surface and unlike the Sweet Track (▶ p. 255) the Corlea sank within a decade. Its purpose can only be guessed at but may relate to ostentatious display.

Other plant macrofossils

The quantity of plant material in natural sediments is usually low but on archaeological sites can be abnormally high, especially where activities such as deposition of food waste and human faeces (**coprolites**) or food processing and storage has have taken place. Archaeologists must also take care in presenting data if the sheer quantity of small seeds produced by some species is not to artificially dominate an assemblage at the expense of other species which produce fewer and larger seeds. A comparison between the size of poppy seeds and almonds makes this point.

On most sites archaeologists will want to know about the local environment and the use of plant foods including crops (▶ Chapter 10). However, biases can occur in samples for a number of reasons. Differential survival may distort the range of plants known from a particular period because some plants do not preserve well or because they grow in locations lacking suitable conditions for preservation. People may also have

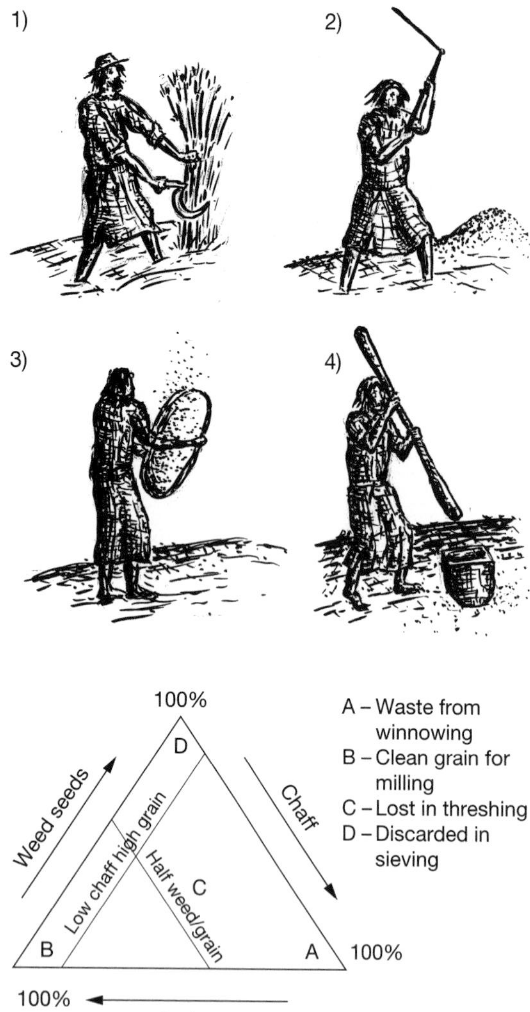

***Figure 3.22** Stages in grain processing and the resulting assemblages*

Through ethnographic study (▶ p. 117) of contemporary societies that rely on simple technology, archaeologists can understand the main stages of grain processing. Each stage produces a signature assemblage of plant macrofossils from the waste or what is left. After reaping (1) ears, bits of stalk and various weeds are taken to the farm. Threshing (2) breaks up the ear and separates the grain from the chaff. Winnowing (3) removes straw and husks – often to be fed to animals. Pounding (4) starts to break up the grains. Singeing to remove waste and sieving to remove smaller weed seeds may occur before storage and finally grinding.

introduced plants into the site either deliberately through plant collecting or cultivation or by accident as in the case of Otzi the Ice Man, in the form of cereal grains adhering to his grass cape. This means that the archaeologist must study very carefully the formation processes (▶ Chapter 5) that led to the creation of the deposit that contains the plant remains under consideration.

Plant microfossils

Plant microfossils are remains that can usually be studied only using microscopes. Three types that are important to archaeologists are pollens, diatoms and phytoliths.

Pollen

The study of pollen is known as **palynology**. The species of individual grains of pollen are readily identifiable by palynologists through their characteristic shapes. They survive well, especially in wet, acid conditions, because they possess a tough outer case. Pollen can be retrieved from most soil samples but is most useful when taken by coring or from a column of samples from a ditch or pit to show vegetation changes. Species frequency in samples can be counted and the numerical data plotted to show relative quantities. Some species produce more pollen then others, so depending on wind, animal and human action a particular assemblage of pollen may represent a very local or a more regional sample.

The relative quantities of pollens provide a record of environmental change. In well-researched areas it has been possible to define pollen zones which characterise particular periods according to the relative amounts of each species. These pollen assemblages can be used to assign relative dates to samples from other sites according to where they match the established environmental sequence. This is known as **pollen dating** (▶ p. 93). The samples can also be dated using radiocarbon dating.

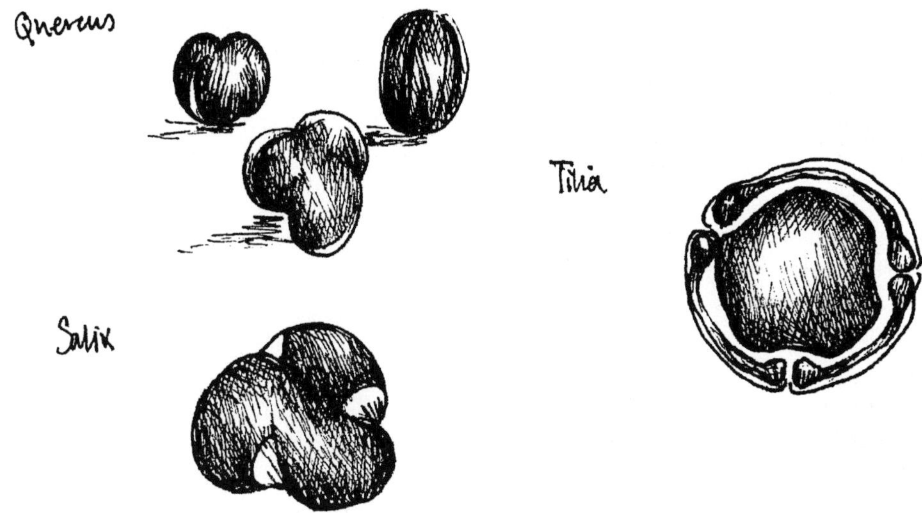

Figure 3.23 *Drawings of examples of magnified pollen grains of oak, lime and willow illustrating the different shapes for each species*

Diatoms

Diatoms are microscopic single-celled plants usually found in open water or in wet conditions such as bogs and waterlogged soils. They are very sensitive to changes in their local water. Their hard outer shell survives well in alkaline or anaerobic conditions. Changes caused by human action such as deforestation or pollution can be inferred from changes in the species of diatom. They have been invaluable in studies around London in determining where the braided channels of the Thames were in prehistory and whether they were tidal.

Phytoliths

Phytoliths are silica from the cells of plants. They survive well enough in alkaline soils to be identified to particular groups of plants. It has been suggested that sickle gloss on flint blades from the early Neolithic in the Near East is indirect evidence of abrasive cereal phytoliths, while in Mesoamerica maize phytoliths have been used to demonstrate the spread of agriculture.

Invertebrates

The shells of many tiny living creatures are surprisingly resilient. They provide evidence of the local environment and in some cases human diet and activity, as with the layers of seashells in coastal middens. Two important categories are beetles and snails.

Beetles

Beetles (or Coleoptera) are one of the most diverse types of invertebrate and they can be found in virtually every environment. In evolutionary terms, beetles have changed very little for tens of thousands of years, so comparison of samples with modern reference collections is relatively straightforward. The large number of types of beetle can make species lists rather unhelpful as there may be up to fifty species present in a collection of 100 specimens with only one or two in each category. A more profitable approach has been to group species together by their food or habitat preferences into classes such as 'phytophages' (plant eater) or 'obligate

KEY STUDY

The decline of the Maya

Rue (1989) collected samples by coring a peat bog to produce a long thin column of sediment which encapsulated the environmental history of the Copan valley. Once processed the data revealed a surprise. The general view was that Maya society declined rapidly after AD 800 so Rue expected this would be reflected in the pollen evidence with maize being less prominent and tree pollen becoming dominant as the forest cover regenerated. In fact maize continued to be planted until at least AD 1100 and only after that did hardwoods like the mahogany, suggestive of fully established rainforest, became apparent on a large scale. Either the standard textbooks about the Maya were wrong or Rue's data were. His results were supported by Freter, who was working on obsidian hydration dating of blades found on Maya sites of this period. Her dates also suggested a long drawn out decline over several hundred years rather than a cataclysmic demise for the Maya. This provided a new 'model' to explain the end of Maya civilisation. It also highlights the view of modern archaeology as a discipline made up of many subdisciplines which often provide complementary evidence and new ways of looking at established ideas.

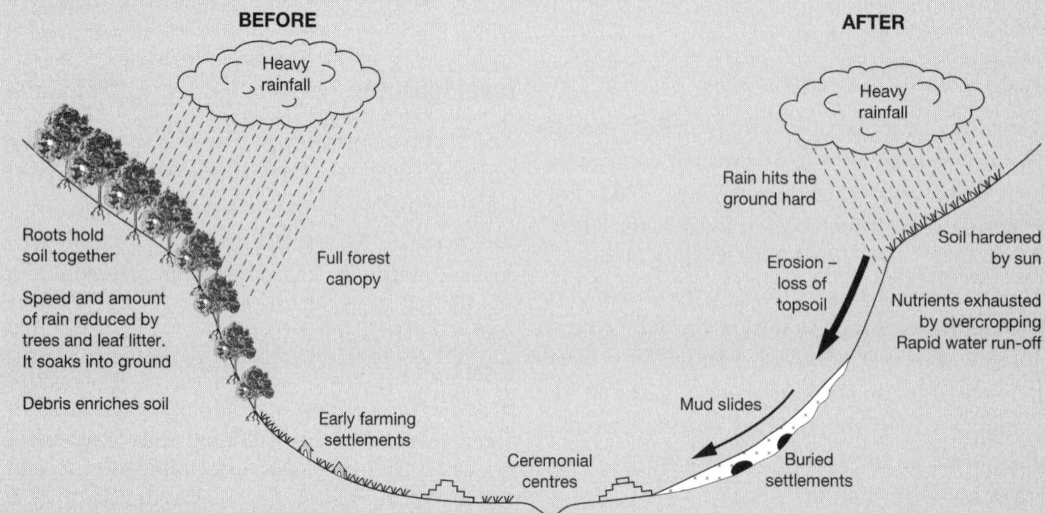

Figure 3.24 *Ecological disaster at Copan*

The extension of farming onto thin hillside soils and removal of tree cover led to environmental damage. Rain washed nutrients from the hill soils. The sediments covering valley settlements were caused by topsoil sliding down from the hills.

Figure 3.25 *Drawing of a beetle*

The crunchiness of beetles is due to their hard shell. This 'exoskeleton' is very resistant to decay and sufficiently variable to allow identification down to species level. In this example the thorax and wing casings would survive.

aquatics' (living in water). Archaeologists can then discover their local habitat and what taphonomic processes (▶ p. 107) led to their decomposition in a particular deposit. The kind of archaeological information provided by the beetles can be summarised as follows:

- Reconstruction of ground surface conditions. Buckland (1976) used beetles to analyse the floors of houses at Reykholb in order to infer the use of different rooms.
- Reconstruction of vegetation and climate. The discovery of Oodes gracilis in southern Britain during the Palaeolithic has been used to infer the existence of much cooler conditions during glacial periods since this species now has a largely Arctic distribution.
- Information about stored products and the utilisation of plants resources. In Roman granaries at York grain beetles have been discovered which prove the exploitation of cereals even though there is no physical evidence of the plants themselves.

Molluscs

Land snail shells are preserved in calcareous, chalky soils because their shells are made of calcium carbonate (chalk). Most snails are so small (around 2 mm) that you can't normally see them. Those larger snails you may have seen, or even eaten, are much bigger and represent only three or four varieties of the hundreds of species of snail. Snails are especially useful to archaeologists as different species have particular vegetation habitats.

Microscopic shells are carefully sieved out of the soil (rather like seeds), identified and counted by the specialist. All snails need shade as they must not dry out, but some species are more tolerant to areas with less shade. This

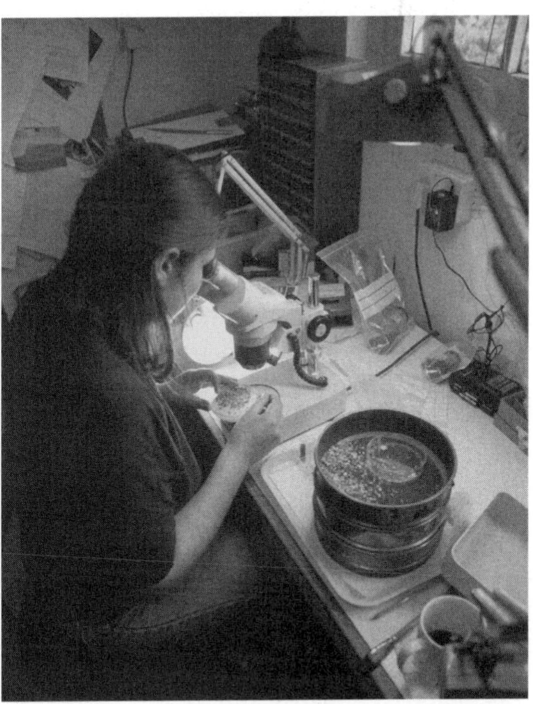

Figure 3.26 *Laboratory examination of snails. A microscope is used to identify the different species to provide insights into local habitats*

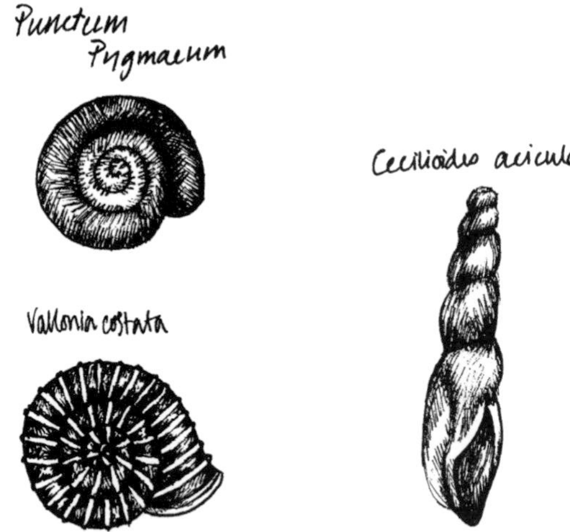

Figure 3.27 *Drawing of magnified snails to illustrate the varied shapes which enable each species to be identified*

enables classification into three broad groups. Open country species can survive in grassland areas with little shade, unlike the woodland group. A catholic group is frequently found in both habitats, but some have quite specific preferences. Snails do not move far so although you cannot tell what any past habitat was like from just one or two shells, you can from a whole assemblage.

AFTER ANALYSIS

Finally all the reports are united with the dating evidence and the fieldwork record as a complete site archive. At this point the archaeological record becomes a collection of written, graphical and electronic data. It still needs to be interpreted. (▶ p. 103) In the tradition of scientific reporting, published archaeological reports tend to be descriptive and analytical with a fairly minimal amount of assessment and interpretation. The archive is there for others to draw their conclusions from. For members of the public and many students, reports are often frustrating. What they want are the works of synthesis and interpretation that are largely produced by academic rather than field archaeologists. The examples and discussions in Part II of this book are largely drawn from these interpretative accounts.

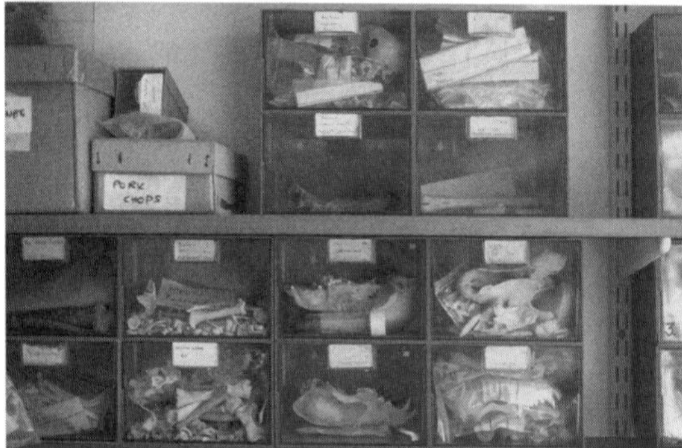

Figure 3.28 *After excavation, finds are stored in archive boxes. This enables future researchers to access them*

KEY SKILL

Reinforcing class learning of methods

Learning methods can sometimes be dull, and comparing and contrasting them can be difficult. One approach is to use games. Two examples follow:

Balloon debate. Several students are each given the name of a different development in archaeology. They have to prepare in advance to answer questions on it, including providing examples. On the day of the debate the chosen students have to argue 'X has been the most important contribution to archaeology in the last 100 years.' The rest of the class have to each ask a question and will then vote for the winner. Over the course, similar debates could be used to ensure that all students have a go. The game builds up skills in argument too.

Rizla! Papers are dealt out with methods written on them. Without looking at it, one student sticks their paper to their forehead. They then have ten questions to guess what they are. The other students can only answer yes or no.

Chapter 4

Understanding Dating in Archaeology

YOUR GOALS

You need to understand

- the underlying principles of dating
- the essence of how the more common techniques work
- reasons why particular techniques are appropriate for specific situations
- how to 'read' some of the more common types of charts and diagrams used to present dating data.

Archaeologists have used many different techniques to work out the age of artefacts and sites for which they have no historical dates and the order in which they were used. These dating techniques can be broadly subdivided into two groups:

- **Relative dating** techniques which identify the order in which sites or artefacts were used in a sequence from earliest to latest.
- **Absolute** (or chronometric) **dating** techniques that try to establish an exact or approximate calendar date for a site or artefact.

The techniques selected depend on the specific task and evidence as well as practical considerations such as cost. Many of the scientific techniques are expensive and require high levels of technical skill to use and to interpret. The span of human history studied by archaeologists is so vast and environments so varied that techniques suitable for one place and period may be unsuitable for another.

Historical dating

For sites less than 5,000 years old there may be written or artistic evidence which can provide precise dates as long as the original language can be decoded. For example, coins, seals, inscriptions and clay tablets were used by the civilisations of the Mediterranean and Middle East. Sometimes historical records such as dates, calendars or lists of rulers are available. These have allowed sites such as Egyptian tombs or Mayan temples to be precisely dated. When artefacts from these civilisations appear in non-literate areas they can be used to provide approximate dates in those areas.

Figure 4.1 *Roman coin from the reign of Nero*

Coins have often been used to establish TPQ dates. In this case, the layer with the coin could not have been earlier than 54–68AD (the reign of Nero). To help remember the difference between TPQ and TAQ think 'you have to post a letter before it can arrive'.

For more recent periods the exact dates for the introduction of many artefacts from clay pipes to beer bottles are known and can be used to date sites. Where artefacts are used for dating it is critical that their precise position within the stratigraphy is accurately recorded. Such 'indirect dating' of sites provides two types of date:

- *Terminus post quem* (**TPQ**): the earliest possible date for an archaeological deposit
- *Terminus ante quem* (**TAQ**):the latest possible date for the deposit

RELATIVE DATING

Typology

In its simplest form, this involves putting a number of finds into chronological order. On a site with a clear and undisturbed stratigraphy, items from lower levels are older than those in higher levels. In the nineteenth century, observations about the types of artefact from different

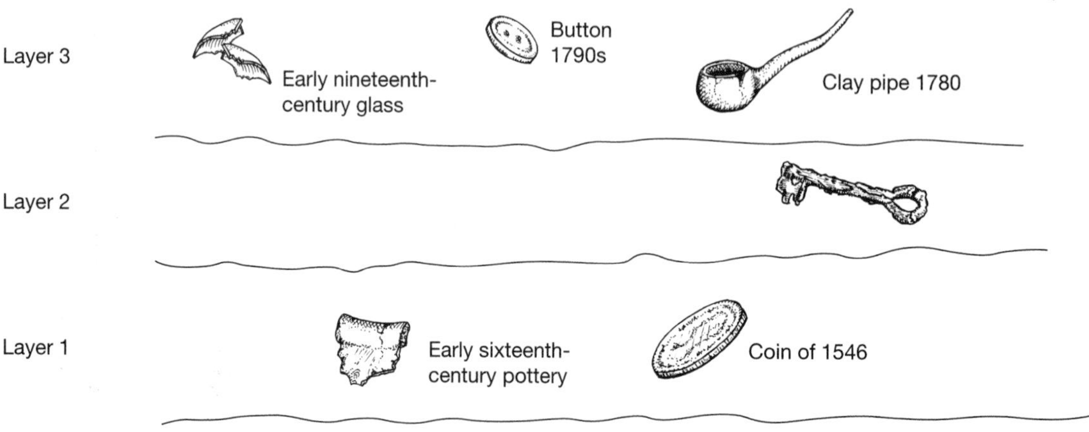

Figure 4.2 *The use of finds to provide earliest and latest dates for a layer. The key can be dated by association (◀ p. 36) to the layer*

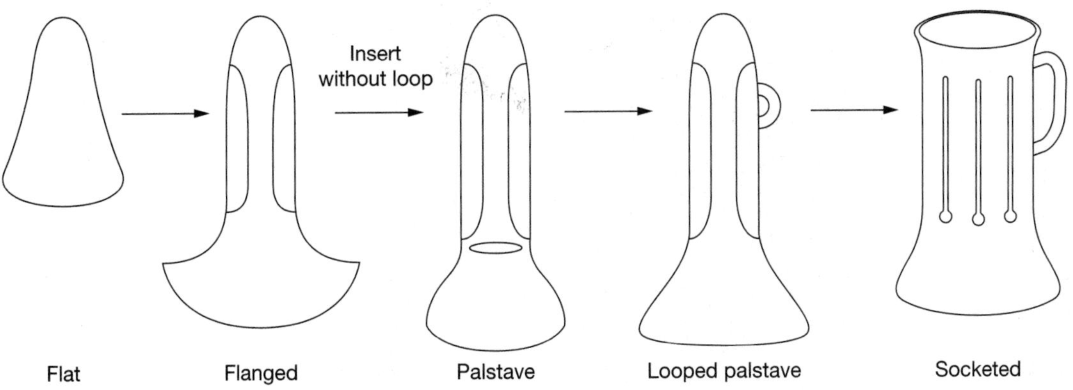

Figure 4.3 *An example of a typological sequence: the development of copper and bronze axes*

layers led to the creation of a time frame for prehistory known as the '3 age system', based on the introduction of tools made from stone then bronze then iron. Today many flaws are apparent in this scheme but the terms are still used to distinguish different 'periods' in the past. A more sophisticated technique was popularised by Flinders Petrie in the 1900s. He noted that the design and decoration of pottery from the Egyptian tombs he excavated changed gradually over time. He was able to place the different types into a chronological sequence. Once a good typological sequence for an area is established it can be referred to when new finds and sites are discovered and used to 'cross-date' them.

In addition to design, the fabric or material used to make the artefact is also analysed. If you take a piece of pottery into your local museum, typology will be used to assign your sherd to a particular period.

Successive groups (or assemblages) of contemporary artefacts, which are commonly found together, have been used to form culture sequences over wide periods. Before the advent of absolute dating techniques this technique enabled a timetable of the spread of 'cultures' across Europe in later prehistory to be constructed, based on changing combinations of grave goods.

Seriation

Most artefact styles appear rarely at first in the archaeological record, then become more common and eventually dwindle in numbers again. This pattern has enabled a sophisticated statistical technique known as seriation (ordering) to be used. Information from a variety of dated sites across a long period is brought together. The frequency with which each form of artefact appears can be plotted as bars on a timeline. Ideally this will produce a shape known as a 'battleship curve' because it looks like an aerial view of a battleship. The changing popularity of each form will appear as a sequence of battleship curves. Other sites can be dated relative to the first site by comparing their seriation.

Problems with these techniques

- Although they can put sites and artefacts into order, they can only be used to provide calendar dates where elements of the sequences are tied to historical data.
- The advent of radiocarbon dating showed that archaeologists had underestimated timespans in prehistory. They had mistakenly constructed sequences to fit their assumptions that all developments happened around the Mediterranean and then spread north and west to 'less civilised' areas.

Figure 4.4 *Beaker Assemblage*

This view show the burial goods of the Amesbury Archer after processing but before reassembly. It incorporates the classic assemblage artefacts of beaker, arrowheads, dagger and wrist brace.

- One type of artefact doesn't always succeed another. For many years it was thought that pointed hand axes were earlier than oval ones after they were found in lower levels on some sites. However, at Boxgrove both were found together suggesting that other influences on

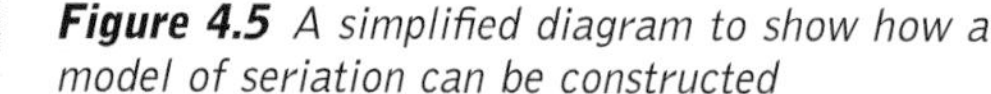

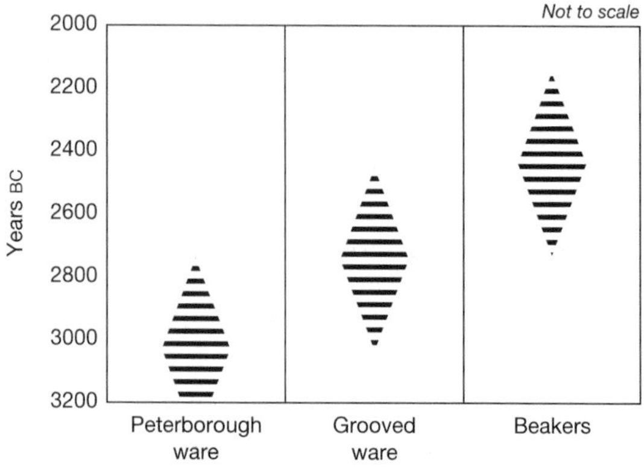

Figure 4.5 *A simplified diagram to show how a model of seriation can be constructed*

The relative proportions of pottery types at a new site would be compared with the seriation chart to give it an approximate date. On our diagram, a site with lots of Grooved ware but only one beaker might be relatively dated to soon after 2800BC.

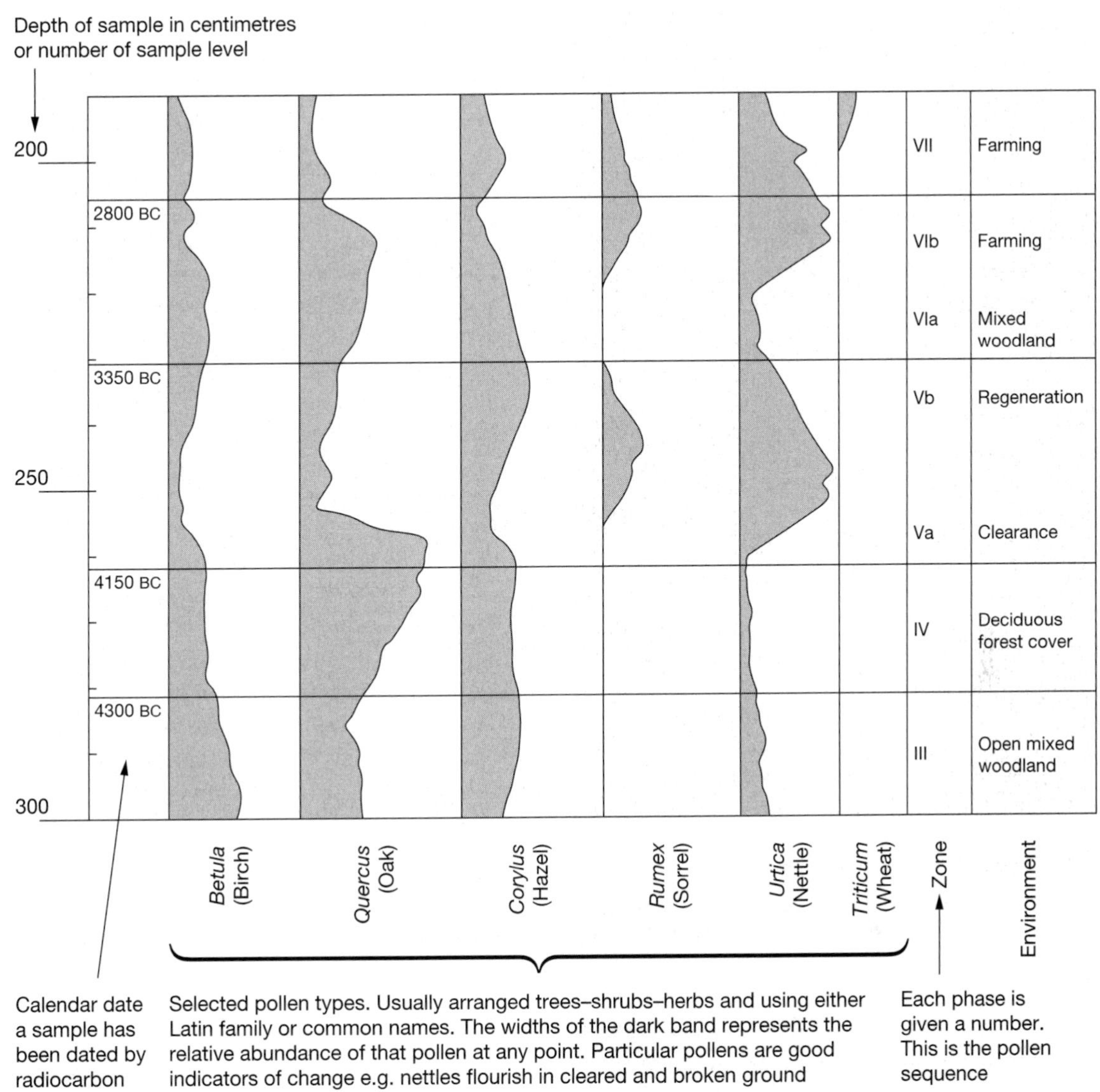

Figure 4.6 *How to read a pollen dating diagram*

choice were important. Seriation assumes that new artefacts are phased in gradually as others are phased out. This does not always happen.

- **Curation**, the preservation of valued artefacts, can lead to items being deposited a long time after their manufacture. Basing dates on a few isolated artefacts could lead to errors.

Geoarchaeological dating

For early periods of prehistory archaeologists have borrowed techniques from the earth sciences to reconstruct the environments of early people and also to establish relative chronologies based on environmental changes. As the climate alters, so too do the types and relative numbers of different plants and animals. Where organic preservation is

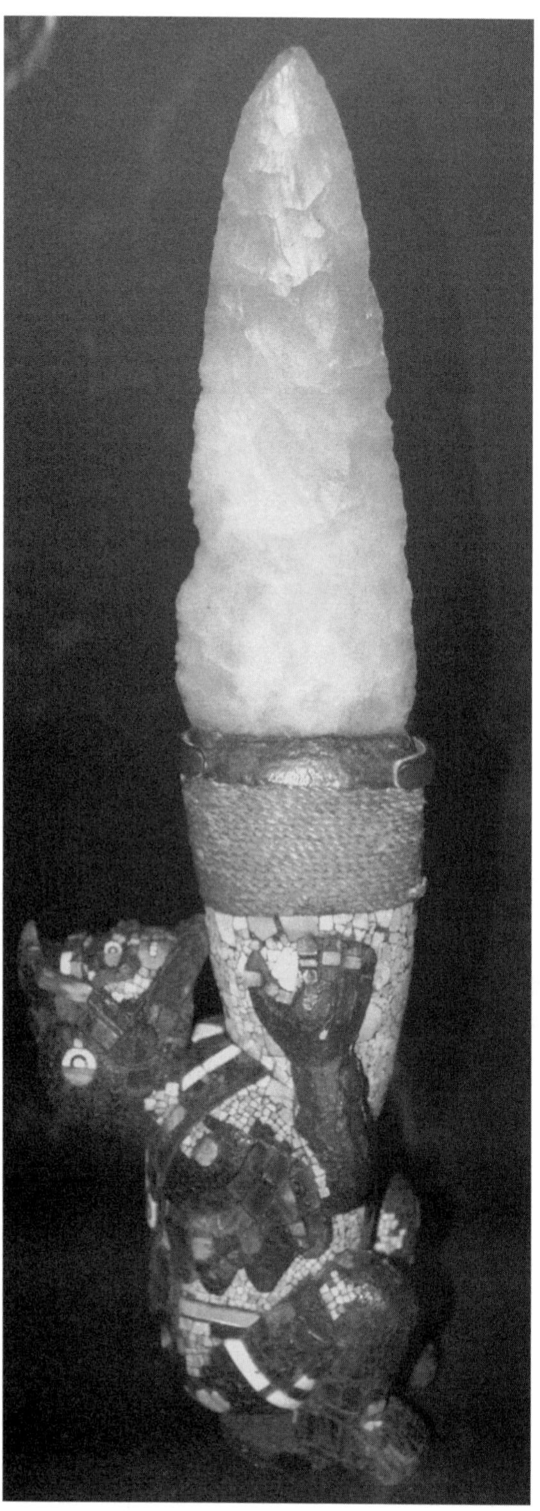

Figure 4.7 *Obsidian blade*

This example is too precious to subject to hydration dating. It illustrates one of the other properties of obsidian – its razor-sharp cutting edge. This Aztec ritual blade was used to remove hearts from sacrificial victims.

good, changes can be traced by analysing pollen (◀ p. 84) contained in sediments and animal bones. (◀ p. 73) To provide a pollen sequence a core through a deposit such as peat is taken and for each layer the proportions of different types of pollen are identified. Sites within these deposits can then be cross-dated to particular phases of climate history in local sequences. Analysis has to take account of many factors including the different amounts of pollen produced by each plant and the different distances the pollen travels. Similarly, sites can be relatively dated from the type of animal bones present (◀ p. 42). This is particularly useful where the sequence of the appearance or extinction of species (for example mammoths) is known. Absolute techniques are needed to date these sequences. For the relative dating of major climatic sequences, deep sea cores and varves (lake deposits) are used.

Obsidian hydration

Obsidian is a volcanic glass that can be worked to provide razor-sharp cutting edges. In the Middle East and Mesoamerica it performed a similar function to flint in northern Europe. As soon as a piece of obsidian is broken it begins to absorb water from the atmosphere at a known rate (in much the same way as a stick of rock which goes soft on the outside). By measuring how far water has penetrated (hydration) into the obsidian on one site a relative date can be estimated compared to other sites. In some cases, results can be calibrated to provide absolute dates but that requires considerable additional data since the speed of hydration varies with local temperatures and the chemical make-up of the obsidian. This is one of the cheaper laboratory dating techniques.

- http://obsidian.pahma.berkeley.edu/anth131.htm

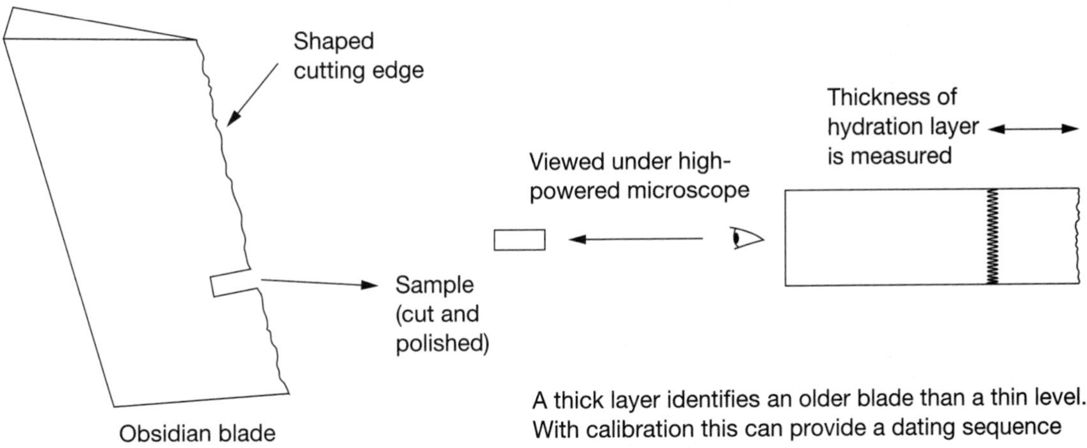

Figure 4.8 *How obsidian hydration works*

Chemical dating of bones

Buried bones absorb fluorine and uranium from water in the ground whilst their nitrogen content declines as collagen in the bones decays. These processes occur at uniform rates so it is possible to establish the relative age of different bones by measuring the proportions of these chemicals.

ABSOLUTE OR CHRONOMETRIC DATING

Since the middle of the twentieth century new methods have been used to provide calendar dates. With the exception of dendrochronology, they all have margins of error and are expensive to use.

Dendrochronology (tree ring dating)

This is the most accurate chronometric dating method. Every year trees produce a visible ring of new wood under their bark. Early in the annual growing season trees produce thin-walled 'early-wood' cells. Towards the end of the year thick-walled 'latewood' cells are produced. This cycle produces a visible 'ring' in the wood each year. The rings are wider in good weather conditions than in poor ones and can provide a record of local climatic variation. Trees in the same area will have similar ring patterns which means wood from different periods can be matched in overlapping sequences. These are tied to historical dates by modern trees. Californian Bristlecone Pines, which live for 4,000 years, were used to construct sequences over 7,000 years in the USA while oaks preserved in bogs have been used in Europe to create master sequences going back 10,000 years. The precision of the method is such that the felling date of the central stump of Seahenge (▶ p. 111) which had its bark attached has been pinpointed to between April and June 2050 BC.

Sometimes carpenters discard the softer sapwood just under the bark. This is important as in England there may be 15–55 or so 'sapwood' rings on an oak. In such cases researchers can only estimate an 'earliest possible felling date'. However, the method has limitations. Not all areas have sufficiently varied seasons or enough surviving timber to be able to construct sequences. To effectively date wood around fifty years of tree rings are needed. Since this represents quite a thick piece of wood, the technique is better for dating building timbers than artefacts. Its direct use is from the Neolithic onwards when buildings were used and it has been widely used on medieval ships and buildings. Dendrochronology actually

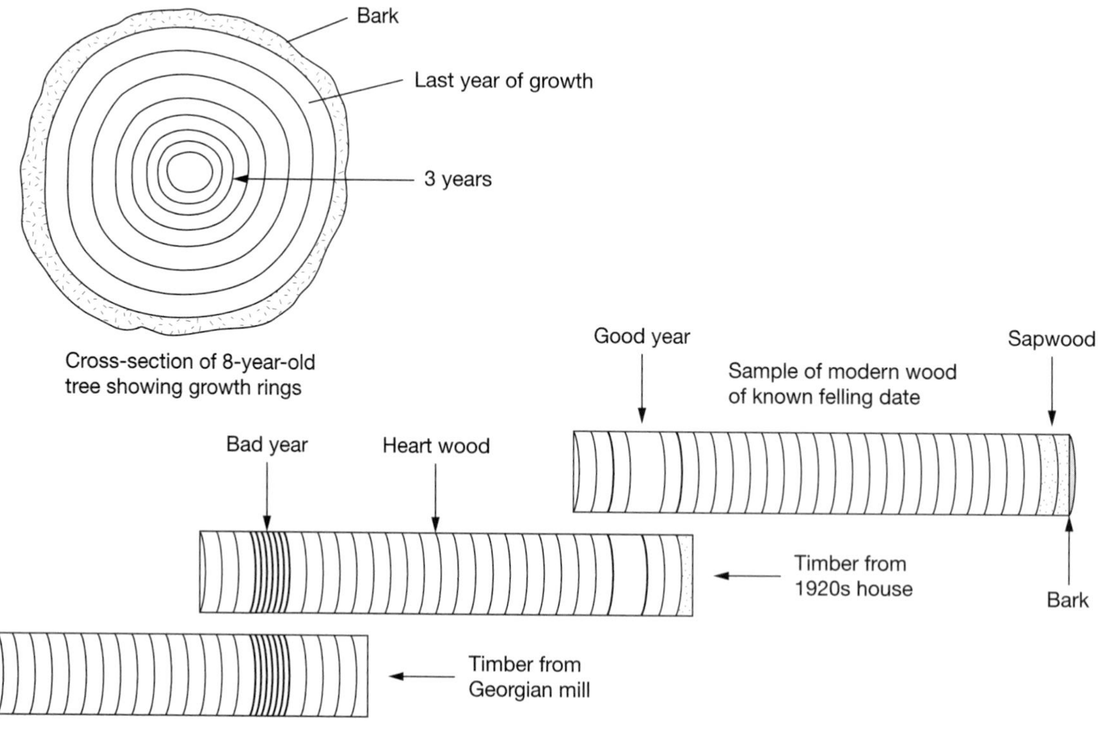

Figure 4.9 *The key principles of dendrochronology*

Principle of tree ring dating: overlaps are matched to take the sequence back from a known date to date old timbers. Samples are taken at 90 degrees to the grain and numbers of rings and their thickness measured by eye or computer.

dates when the tree died or was felled. Where wood has been reused, as often happened with structural timbers in the past, this method can overestimate the age of a structure. However, dendrochronology is also the key method for calibrating radiocarbon dates and therefore is indirectly used in dating a wide range of organic materials for up to 11,500 years.

- http://www.shef.ac.uk/uni/academic/A-C/ap/dendro/dendro.html
- http://www.ltrr.arizona.edu/

Radiocarbon dating

All living things absorb several types of carbon isotope from the atmosphere in similar ratios. About 1 per cent of this carbon is an unstable isotope known as carbon 14 (C-14) which decays at a known rate. By comparing the weight of remaining C-14 with amounts of other carbon isotopes in organic samples it is possible to work out how much C-14 has decayed. This indicates how long it has been since decay began (and the creature or plant was alive). It was thought that the dates produced by radiocarbon dating were precise until it was recognised that amounts of carbon in the atmosphere have varied over time. Dates for the last 8000 years were underestimated. For 5000 BC this was by around 800 years! To get round this problem, radiocarbon dates are calibrated.

Radiocarbon dates are never exact. Even after calibration there is a margin of error that is calculated statistically. This usually means that there is a 68 per cent chance or 'level of confidence' (LOC) that the real date is within the range indicated and a 95 per cent LOC that it is within twice the range. C-14 is mainly used to date organic materials including bone, shell and plant remains. It does not work on cremated bone although it will work for charred bone. It is more precise with wood samples from twigs and nuts than from trees that may have lived for hundreds of years. Radiocarbon's practical use is for periods from 200 to about 10,000 years with less reliability to around 40,000 years. Until recently at least 10 grams of charcoal or 200 grams of bone were needed for results. The development of accelerator mass spectrometry (AMS) has enabled samples as tiny as one grain of cereal to be dated. This expensive technique uses energy to accelerate the carbon molecules in such a way that they can be separated by weight and then counted.

- http://www.radiocarbon.org/
- http://www.c14dating.com/

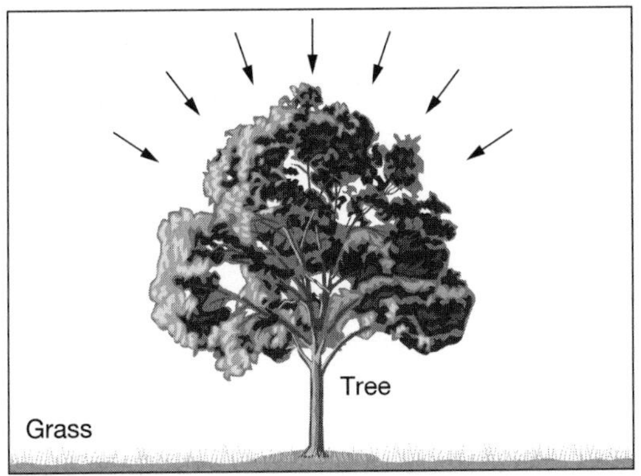

C-14 is formed by cosmic radiation in the atmosphere and absorbed by plants through photosynthesis.

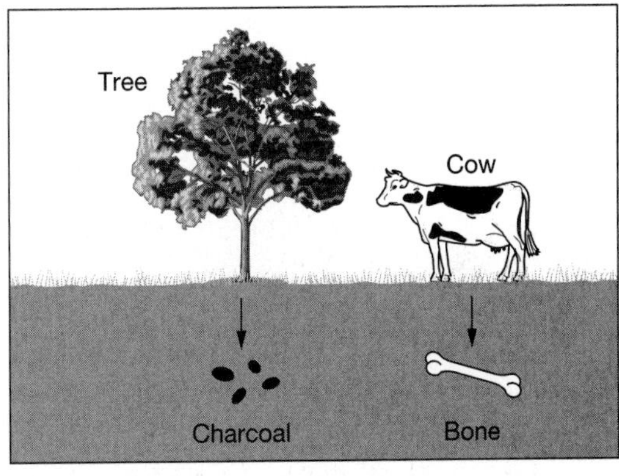

C-14 is absorbed by animals from plants. It enters the archaeological record in burnt wood (charcoal) or bones.

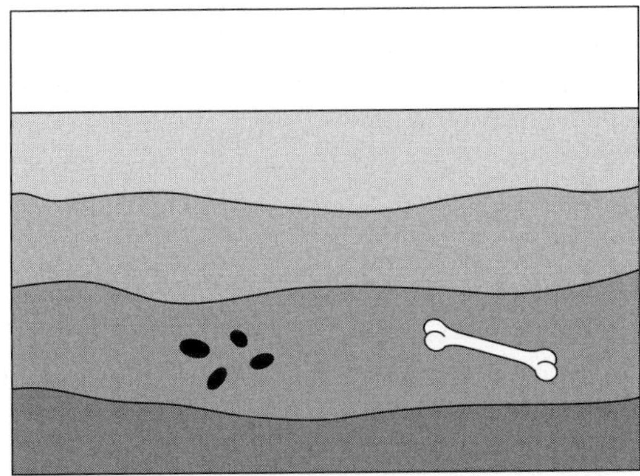

Archaeologists recover charcoal and bone samples to date a layer. Great care is taken to avoid contamination.

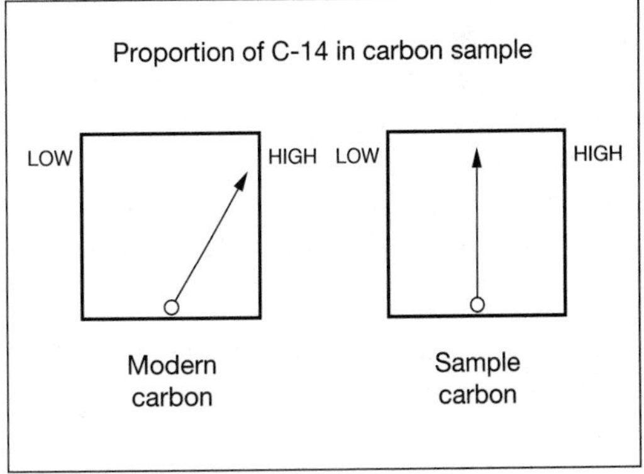

Laboratory analysis gives time since animal or plant died and C-14 decay began.

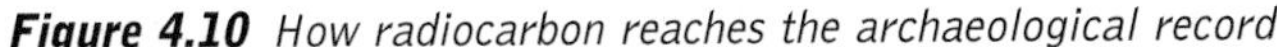

Figure 4.10 *How radiocarbon reaches the archaeological record*

C-14 dates are expressed in the following ways:

- Lower case letters are often, but not always, used to show that dates are uncalibrated, whereas capitals should mean they have been calibrated. Increasingly 'Cal' is added to a calibrated date to avoid any confusion.
- Calendar dates are expressed as ad or bc (uncalibrated) and BC, AD, Cal BC, Cal AD (calibrated)
- Radiocarbon dates are expressed as BP or Cal BP (calibrated). **BP** means 'before present' (1950) and is often preferred for early prehistoric periods for which BC and AD are relatively meaningless.

KEY TERM

Calibration

Calibration involves turning measures of time into calendar dates by comparing results from one method with dates from a more precise method. Dendrochronology is the most widely used method for calibration. Essentially, wood of a known age is tested for its C-14 date and the two dates compared. Once a large range of comparisons has been made a chart can be produced which enables scientists to read off a calendar year against a sample date.

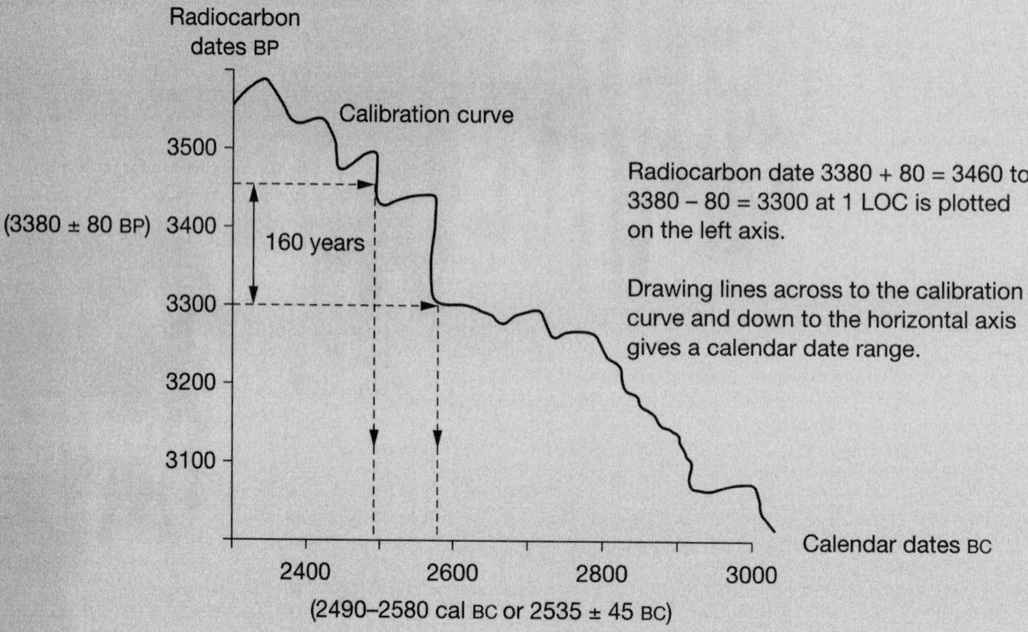

Figure 4.11 *How calibration works*

This diagram is intended simply to illustrate principles. In the example plotted you can see that where the calibration curve is steeper, raw dates are converted to a relatively short range of calibrated dates while where the curve is shallow the range would be much longer.

Thermoluminescence (TL)

Radioactive decay in the quartz crystals found in clay leads to a build up of electric charge at a known rate. The electrical charge is released as light when the crystals are heated. When pottery is heated in a laboratory the energy in the flash of light is measured and used to calculate the time since it was fired. Each reheating resets the clock. The technique can be used for materials such as glass and burnt flint or stone for periods from the present to around 400,000 years ago. It is significantly less accurate than C-14 dating and can give false readings due to radiation from the soil or if the initial firing was at low temperature. However, it is useful for older periods and instances where there are no organic remains such as dating Upper

Figure 4.12 *Understanding a radiocarbon date*

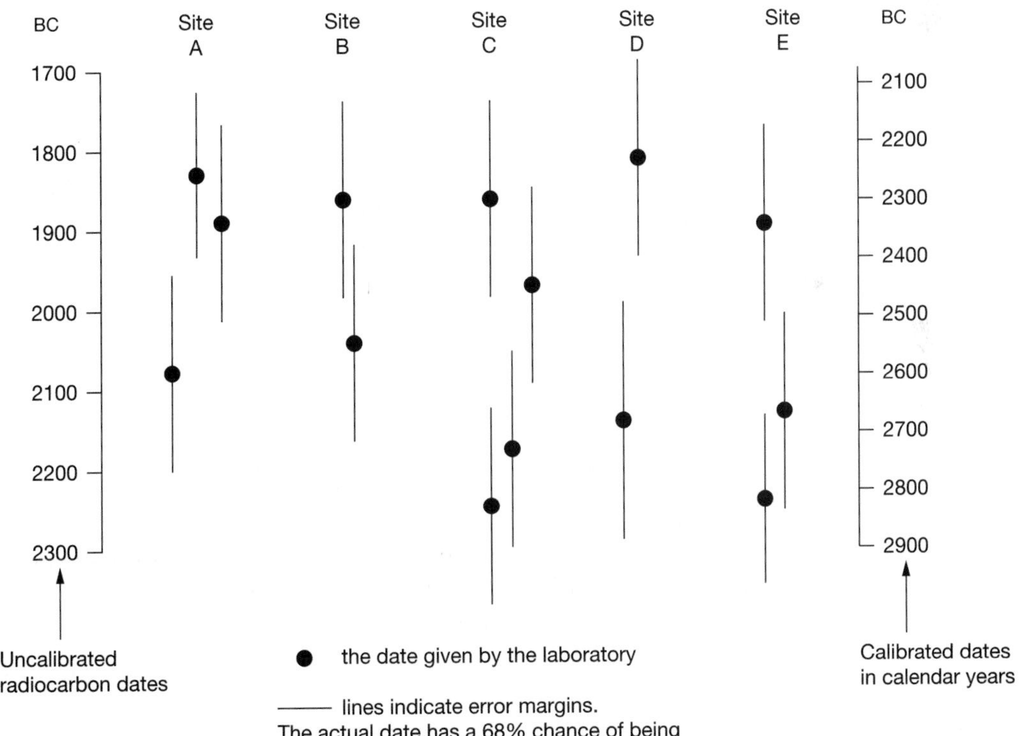

Figure 4.13 *Reading a radiocarbon table*

Palaeolithic figurines from Dolni Vestonice. A similar principle underlies **Optically Stimulated Luminescence (OSL)**. Electrons from decaying radioactive elements are trapped in crystals of quartz or feldspar which form part of many sediments. When stimulated with light, the electrons free themselves, giving of luminescence (light energy) in the process. The amount released can be used to date the last 'clock setting event'. Dates from 50 to a million years can be calculated with more accuracy than TL.

- http://www.info.ox.ac.uk/departments/rlaha/

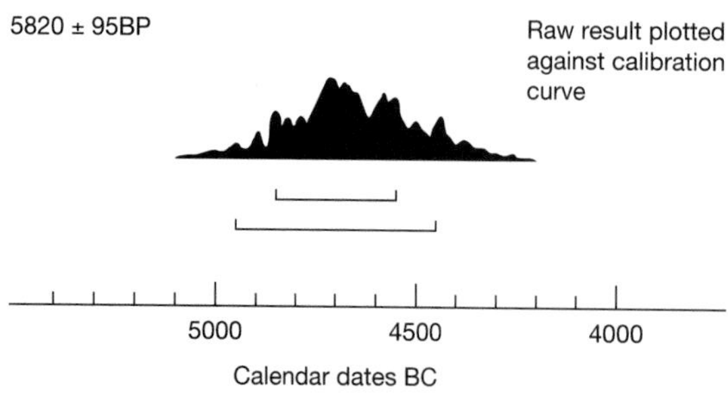

Figure 4.14 *A 'cloud' diagram*

An alternative mode of plotting RC dates shows the date range graphically. Lines underneath indicate 1 and 2 LOC.

Potassium–argon dating

As potassium in rock crystals decays it produces argon gas at a known rate. Measuring the amounts and ratios in a laboratory provides a date at which the crystal was formed. It has been used in volcanic regions to date layers of rock which sandwich human remains. For instance, at Koobi Fora

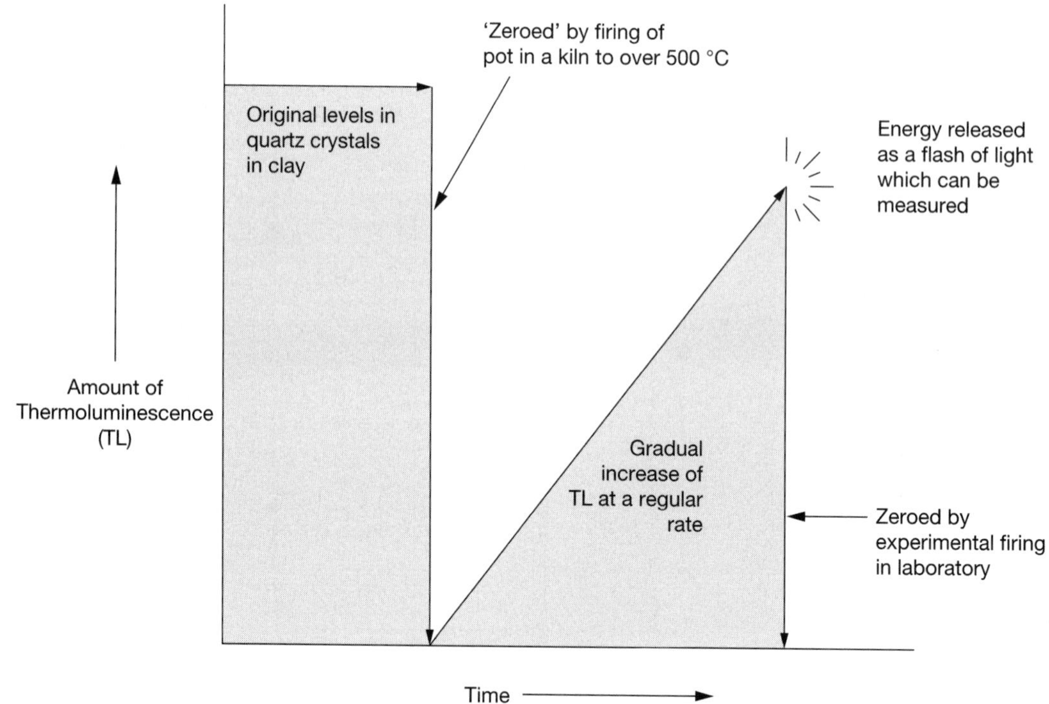

Figure 4.15 *How thermoluminescence works*

	How it works	*What it can be used for*	*What periods it is used for*	*Comments/limitations*	*Examples*
Amino acid racemization	The chemical structures of the amino acids found in all living things change slowly over time at a known rate	Bones, teeth and shell	1000 to 1 million years	Must not be cooked Needs calibrating Varies with climate	Ostrich eggs on Paleolithic sites in Africa
Archeomagnetism	The earth's magnetic field changes over time. When iron oxide is heated to around 600 °C and cools, it records the magnetic field at that time. Variations in the earth's field have been calculated which enables the date of initial heating to be established	Ceramics, lava, hearths and kilns that contain iron oxide	Up to 5,000 years	Local variations in magnetism Sites must be undisturbed when measured. Needs to be calibrated, e.g. by varves Can provide inaccurate dates where the same polarity occurred more than once	Clay ovens in south-west USA
Electron spin resonance (ESR)	Electrical charges build up at a known rate in some crystal structures. The time since the process began can be calculated by measuring the charge	Teeth enamel, shells calcite deposits in caves	50,000 to 1 million years	Works best in dry environments Wide error margins	Palaeolithic sites in Israel and Africa
Fission track dating	Uranium decays regularly through fission (splitting) which releases energy and damages crystalline structures, leaving a 'track'. Tracks or holes are counted to estimate the time the process of decay has taken	Glass, burned obsidian, heated stones containing uranium Sites sandwiched between volcanic layers	Mainly 100,000 to several million years although some recent glass has been dated	Difficulty in differentiating tracks from crystal defects Over 10% error margins	Homo Habilis bones at Olduvai Gorge from around 2 million years ago
Uranium series	Uranium isotopes U235 and U238 are soluble in water and decay to produce deposits of thorium and protactinium at known rates. By measuring the ratios of the elements the date at which the deposits was laid down can be established	Analysing calcium carbonate deposits where water containing uranium has seeped into caves and been deposited (e.g. as stalactites) Teeth enamel, shells	Early human sites in Europe 50,000 to 500,000 years	Prone to ambiguous results Needs a high uranium content	Dentine on Neanderthal/ early human teeth in Israel
Varves	Melt-water from glaciers lays down different sediment at different times of year. This creates annual layers like tree rings. Changing climate will lead to changing deposits which can then be cross-referenced over large areas	Analysing cores taken from ancient lake beds. Where they contain pollen they can be tied to geoarchaeological sequences	Up to 20,000 years	Key dating role is by calibrating other techniques such as radiocarbon and archaeomagnetism	A sequence of 17,000 years has been established in Scandinavia and 20,000 in the USA

Figure 4.16 *Comparison of other major scientific dating methods*

in East Africa early hominid remains were dated to 1.89 million years BP ±0.01 million years. The technique can be used for periods from around 200,000 to several million years ago but it is limited to sites with the right geology.

Other absolute dating techniques

Figure 4.16 covers less commonly used methods, some of which are still at an experimental stage. You do not need to know them in detail although you should be aware of the situations where they might be used. Like radiocarbon dating, most of them rely on data showing known rates of chemical change or decay that can be measured in laboratories. Several of them measure the age of layers rather than the archaeological deposits themselves and are thus limited to particular types of geology. Most methods are used in combination to cross-check dates.

KEY TASK

Test your grasp of dating methods

1 Which methods might you use to date the following? Check your answers on p. 330.

- A wooden spear tip from 200,000 years ago
- Shells from a Mesolithic midden
- Seeds from a Roman well
- Burnt flint from a paleolithic hearth
- Walls made from baked mud bricks from an ancient house
- Human bones from a Saxon cemetery
- An Aztec kiln site from Mexico
- Bison bones found in cave deposits
- A terracotta figurine from a Roman temple
- Timbers from a Bronze Age boat

2 Construct a bar chart to show which methods are useful for which period in the past.

- List each method on the vertical axis at regularly spaced intervals.
- List the following dates (in years BP) on the horizontal axis at regularly spaced intervals: 0, 100, 500, 1,000, 5,000, 10,000, 50,000, 100,000, 500,000, 1,000,000, 5,000,000.
- Shade the period for which each method is useful in the relevant row.

Chapter 5

Archaeological Interpretation

YOUR GOALS

You need to understand

- why the way in which the archaeological record is formed is so important
- the basis of some ideas which archaeologists use to interpret archaeological remains
- the strengths and weaknesses of some of these ideas.

As humans, we use ideas and models to interpret the world around us. It is impossible to describe something or another person without likening them to something or somebody else. The same is true for archaeology. The goal of archaeology is to explain (not really reconstruct) past behaviour, but archaeologists do not dig up behaviour. They excavate material remains from the past and assume that behaviour and the ideas that motivated behaviour will be reflected in these remains. They then use theories from the present to make sense of the archaeological record. For example, you need theory to interpret a dark circular mark as a posthole or a particular burial as that of a chieftain. This way of thinking, which links material remains to their interpretation as evidence, is known as middle-range theory.

KEY TERM

The archaeological record

This is the raw data for archaeology. The physical remains of past activities include features, artefacts and ecofacts (including human remains). The archaeological record comprises these remains in the contexts in which they come down to us. It is not static and constantly changes.

Debates between archaeologists often stem from differences in their assumptions about how the archaeological record was created and how one should interpret it. On degree-level programmes you will encounter a variety of theories of archaeological knowledge. Before then you don't need to know about specific theories. However a basic grasp of aspects of middle-range theory can help you assess the strengths and weaknesses of different interpretations.

Figure 5.1 *Excavation of this dark circle of earth can define shape, dimension and content. Establishing what it once was will always require interpretation. This example was a lime kiln*

In order to interpret data, and determine its significance, archaeologists have to know which materials go together and can be used to provide evidence of past behaviour. For example, a clustering of broken pottery, burnt stones and processed animal bones could represent a cooking area or it could be the result of people spreading their domestic rubbish on a field as fertiliser. This is where archaeology becomes detective work. To determine which explanation is most likely to be correct we need to understand the processes by which data reached us. Not all the materials used in human activity enter the archaeological record. Once there, some materials survive, others do not. Finally, some archaeologists are better at recovering some materials than others.

Figure 5.2 *Sites contain, and are made up of, features. This stone-built feature from Kingscote Roman Villa was identified as a kiln or corn dryer through reference to other sites, ethnographic example and experiment*

KEY CONCEPT

Relativist theories of knowledge

There are a wealth of texts on this subject and on the debates between rival schools of thought. In recent years, as in most academic disciplines, relativist ideas have become very influential. They share a belief that there are no absolute facts since all knowledge is subjective. For example, the values and assumptions we hold determine the way we think. The way we think structures what we see in such a way that it makes sense to us. So when we think we are discovering patterns in archaeological data, what we are really doing is organising data so that it reflects the structures already in our minds. For example, a female skeleton in a prehistoric burial with a flint arrowhead by her neck might be automatically interpreted as a victim if you have already assumed that only men fired arrows. Archaeologists with other assumptions might *see* her as a hunter or warrior.

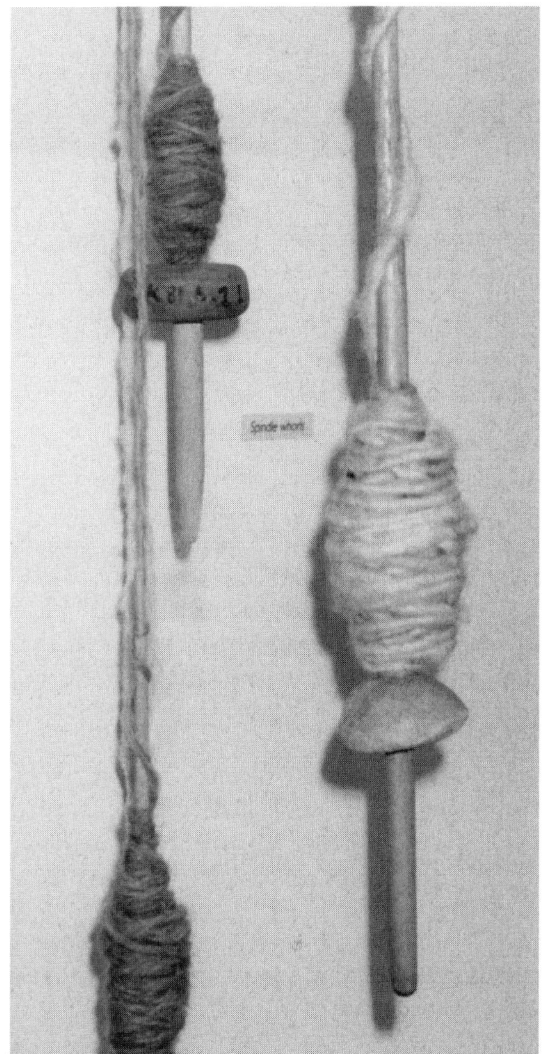

Figure 5.3 *Spindles*

These composite artefacts for twisting wool into thread is made of both organic and inorganic materials. Only the clay or stone 'whorl' is likely to survive. Interpretation is needed to reconstruct it.

TRANSFORMATION PROCESSES

These processes include all the stages by which human behaviour from the past is translated into the data recorded in archaeological reports and all the human and natural forces that shaped that data.

Formation processes

Archaeological data can be used to explain past human behaviour because people helped create that data. This applies to artefacts, ecofacts and much environment data. The formation of archaeological materials is a complex process involving four broad stages. These need to be understood since evidence can enter the archaeological record at any point.

Depositional processes are the ways in which remains actually find their way into the ground. If humans are responsible, we need to try and understand their logic. Why was an artefact discarded rather than being reused, recycled, repaired or

KEY TASK

Understanding formation processes

Produce your own table (like Figure 5.4) or illustration to show your understanding of **formation processes**. Use one of the following examples:

1 Remains of a hunted animal
2 A Roman amphora

KEY TERM

Curation

Deliberately keeping and preserving something. It accounts for why old artefacts sometimes turn up amid much more recent material. Artefacts might be curated for sentimental reasons, rarity, beauty or because they were particularly useful. What has been curated in your home? Curation can distort the record, for example in early medieval Europe fine classical pottery often continued in use while metal vessels were recycled.

curated? These questions also apply to structures and ecofacts.

Some historical sources were created specifically to deceive. While there have been odd instances of faking such as 'Piltdown Man', it is highly unlikely that archaeological material has been buried to fool later generations. However, there are still codes to be broken. Archaeologists carefully map buried finds to see if there are patterns. Where these exist they may indicate 'structured' rather than random deposition. Natural forces may also have caused particular deposits. These might include erosion, flooding or volcanic activity. By understanding formation and transformation processes, archaeologists learn to differentiate between what was due to humans and what was due to nature.

Post-depositional factors

Once buried, further modifications take place. The archaeological record is not a safe place for

Stage of formation process	*Example*	*We need to know*	*May enter the archaeological record as*
Acquisition	Collecting flint, feathers and resin, cutting wood	Where and how the materials were gathered? Why were they chosen?	Flint mine
Manufacture	Shaping the flint, feathers and wood to make an arrow Heating the resin the make glue	What techniques and tools were used?	Waste flakes Antler tools
Use/purpose	Used to hunt animals	How it was used, which creatures it was used on?	Lost or broken points
Discard	Buried with its owner or in the remains of an animal	Was it thrown away, lost or deliberately abandoned?	Arrowhead in burial or bone debris

Figure 5.4 *Example of the way in which a flint-tipped arrow might enter the archaeological record*

KEY TERM

Structured deposition

Most human societies, including our own, dispose of materials in ways determined by their beliefs and knowledge. By trying to uncover the patterns in which material was deliberately deposited in the past, archaeologists hope to reveal elements of past beliefs. Structured deposition has been particularly influential in recent studies of ritual practices in European prehistory, for example at Flag Fen. Here, the sacrificed bones of dogs were found on the seaward side of an artificial causeway.

Figure 5.5 *Shears from Flag Fen*

This perfect pair of clippers from Flag Fen shows us that Bronze Age shepherds already had technology which would be in use until the nineteenth century. They were not lost or casually discarded. These valuable items complete with their wooden case were deposited from a wooden causeway as ritual offerings. Hundreds of other valuable finds from jewellery through swords to millstones belonged to these structured deposits.

artefacts or ecofacts. The causes of these changes are usually grouped as:

- natural forces or 'N transforms,' including bacteria, acid, water, erosion, ice, worms, sunlight, roots, freezing and thawing, drying out (desiccation), silting, gnawing and oxidisation
- human or cultural 'C Transforms,' including grave robbing, looting, shelling, mining, reuse, ploughing, collecting, trampling, building and draining.

These factors can result in changes including movement, destruction, partial decay, colour loss, texture and shape changes, and alteration of chemical composition. The extent of change varies between different materials. Inorganic materials are preserved best. Stone, pottery and bronze, for example, are particularly durable. Consequently, there is a systematic bias in the archaeological record towards tools made from these materials. By contrast, organic materials such as wool, wood and bodies are far less likely to survive. Where they do it may reflect particular environmental conditions as much as what happened in the past. **Taphonomy** (the law of burial) is the name commonly given to the study of the effects of such processes on animal and plant remains. The size of buried objects; their depth of burial, climate and the nature of the soil further complicate these basic distinctions. Bones, for example, will decay more slowly than normal in dry soil

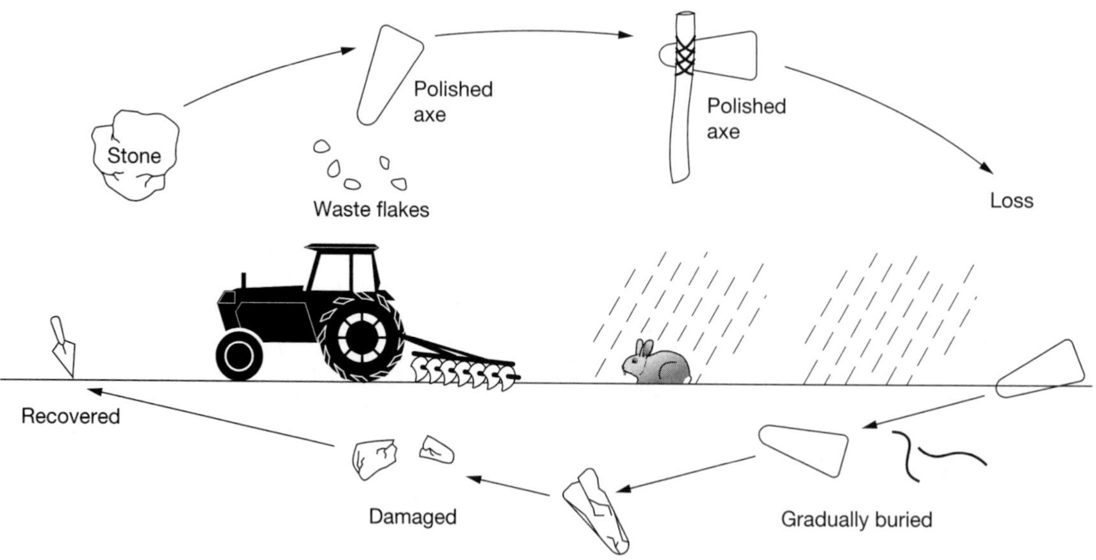

Figure 5.6 *Examples of transformation processes affecting a polished stone axe*

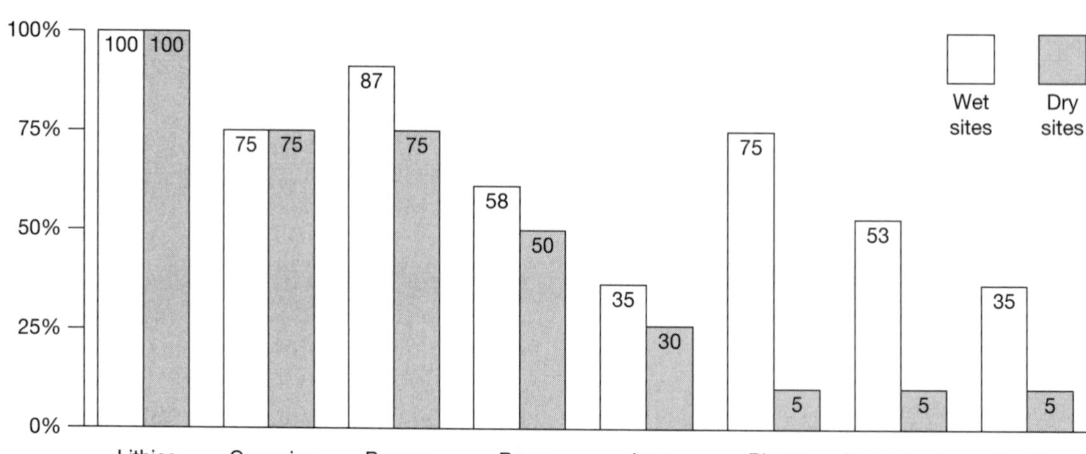

Figure 5.7 *Examples of differential survival of materials on wet and dry sites*

such as sand and in soils with little oxygen such as clay.

We can get some idea of the wealth of material that is usually lost by studying finds from sites with exceptionally good organic preservation. In these cases remains are protected from the bacteria which normally consume organic material by climatic conditions or low oxygen levels (anaerobic conditions). While these sites remind us that absence of evidence is not evidence of absence, we cannot assume that they are typical sites from their period.

Figure 5.8 *Wooden bucket*

Wet sites often produce extensive ranges of wooden artefacts including everyday items which are less likely to survive otherwise. This bucket is from Medieval Dublin.

- Arid sites, often in desert regions, can lead to remains drying out (desiccation) before they have a chance to decay. In the case of bodies, this process creates natural mummies. Classic examples include Mesa Verde in the south-west USA where wooden and leather items were preserved.
- Waterlogged sites including lakes and peat bogs have been particularly important in European archaeology. Examples include Flag Fen, Tybrind Vig (▶ p. 229) and the wreck of the *Mary Rose*.
- Frozen sites have produced some incredible finds in recent years. Perhaps the most well known are the bodies of Otzi the Ice Man from the Alps and the Pazyryk 'Ice Maiden' from Siberia. Their skin has been so well preserved that tattoos and acupuncture marks can be studied.
- Rapidly buried sites can also reveal much that is normally lost. Examples include Pompeii (▶ p. 281) volcanic ash, Copan (▶ p. 159) earthquake and Ozette in the USA where mudslides also preserved organic material.

KEY TASK

Group activity on transformation processes

Brainstorm ideas about what might be left for future generations of archaeologists if a disaster struck your class today. Consider what the effect of post-depositional forces would be. Present your findings in a visual format.

Recovery factors

As if these processes were not enough, there is one final hurdle for archaeological remains to cross before they can be used to explain the past. Archaeologists themselves structure the archaeological record in the way they recover data. This results in some materials or sites being better represented than others. Sometimes this may simply be due to chance factors such as discovery or whether archaeologists can get access to particular sites. Decisions about how much of a site to excavate, which samples to take and what period to prioritise (◀ p. 28) all 'structure' what is recorded. Similarly, while pottery and metals finds are usually recorded, animal bone is sometimes not. The techniques available for recovery are also important. Not all excavations will use flotation techniques to recover pollen and small bone fragments or have the laboratory support to analyse them. Finally there is the quality of the diggers

Figure 5.9 *Dry sieving at Barcombe Roman Villa*

Depending on the mesh size, sieving can dramatically increase the recovery of earth coloured pottery, coins, lithics and organic remains. However, even a large riddle like this is relatively slow to process soil and they are not used as widely in Britain as in the USA.

and those recording the finds. Inevitably there are some variations. Once away from the site, the care taken in analysis and storage may continue to transform the record.

The net result of all these processes is that archaeologists do not simply piece together recorded data to produce a picture of the past. Archaeological evidence cannot speak for itself and needs interpretation. Whatever was deposited was a fraction of the material used by people in the past. Only some elements of this will survive and only a sample of them will be recovered. By understanding transformation processes, archaeologists gain insights into what shaped the various samples. This enables them to identify which of the patterns in their data are really the result of human behaviour and to begin interpreting them. For example, human skeletons are often found with the head turned to one side. At face value this might seem significant. However, forensic science has revealed that the slumping of corpses' heads is due to natural processes of decay rather than burial rites.

Partly because these factors and the limitations of our analytical techniques, archaeological reports often contain minimal amounts of interpretation. Their writers follow a scientific tradition of reporting their findings and analysis of data but leaving interpretation to others.

Analysing spatial patterns

Having identified archaeological material and taken account of various transformation processes, archaeologists try to identify what human behaviour lies behind any patterns that they can detect. Initially this involves plotting vertical and horizontal relationships between finds, structures

KEY STUDY

Seahenge

The Bronze Age timber ritual site dated by dendrochronology to 2050 BC illustrates both differential survival and recovery. Until erosion by the sea the timbers and land surface had been preserved, perhaps with associated deposits. By the time it was discovered in 1999 much damage had been done and English Heritage felt it was not worth rescuing. Under pressure from archaeologists they relented and began a fairly basic salvaging of the main timbers amid mud, tides and some angry pagans who saw excavation as sacrilege. Each of the 55 timbers was at least 30cms across which meant that the circle was almost closed and focused on a massive upturned oak stump. Little else was recovered and it provides a good contrast with recovery at Boxgrove (◀ p. 41). In 2007 the conserved timbers will be partially reconstructed in a new museum.

Figure 5.10 *Seahenge*

- http://www.channel4.com/history/timeteam/archive/2000seahenge.html

KEY TERM

Assemblage

Sub-assemblage: a repeated pattern of artefacts associated with one activity. Think of it as a toolkit.

Assemblage: the range of toolkits used by a particular community.

and sites. Patterning is taken to be evidence for behaviour. For example, a scatter of flint tools amidst the bones of an animal might indicate a butchery or kill site involving humans in scavenging or hunting. The toolkit used is termed a sub-assemblage.

MAKING SENSE OF THE DATA

The next stage of archaeological interpretation tends to vary according to the ideas about knowledge held by the archaeologist. In most cases they will use **analogies** or models to formulate theories about what the data can provide evidence of.

Our society does not include all the rich variety of human activity and culture that has existed. To rely on it as the sole source of analogies would be limiting and lead to Eurocentric and anachronistic interpretations. Increasingly, archaeologists have drawn on three major sources of analogies.

KEY SITES

Danebury and Butser

The Hillfort of Danebury had a huge storage capacity. This took two forms. Amongst 18,000 post-holes were hundreds of four and six post structures and 5000 pits. Both forms are common on Iron Age sites but rarely in such amounts. Carbonised grain was recovered from the pits while seeds and snails were recovered from soil samples by flotation and wet sieving. Analysis and interpretation of these finds revealed much about the farming economy.

Microscopic examination of plant assemblages identified the main crops as einkorn and emmer wheat, but also found over 40 types of weed. This suggested that wheat was brought to Danebury unprocessed since weeds had come too. It also showed that wheat came from a wide area since many weeds are particular to certain soil types and locations. Assemblages also contained much chaff which is a by-product of processing (◀ p. 84).

Ethnographic analogy (▶ p. 116) suggested that the four posters might have been raised granaries. To test this idea several full scale models were built at Butser Ancient Farm. This innovative open air laboratory had already been one of the first places to experiment with 'constructs' based on excavation floor-plans. Apart from the post holes another clue was provided by traces of wattle and daub panels which might have been the walls of these structures. The Butser model made sense as it kept grain out of reach of rats and allowed air to circulate to prevent damp. The walls, beams and roof itself are the product of experimentation based on knowledge of Iron Age carpentry and engineering. Building roundhouses has enabled the exploration of ideas about roof slope, light, efficiency of fires and whether a smoke hole is needed. It has also answered questions about how long a roundhouse might last and the amount of woodland needed to build and maintain it. The site also experiments with Iron Age crop growing and animal husbandry.

Figure 5.11 *Four poster granaries*

  **KEY SITES** *cont.*

Danebury and Butser

Many of the pits cut into the solid chalk were bell-shaped. They were a metre wide and up to 2 metres deep with a capacity of over 2 tonnes each. Initially it was thought that the pits had been sealed and covered with a basketwork lid so that their contents would last over the winter. How they did this without rotting was unclear. To investigate, the archaeobotanist Hillson conducted a micro-excavation in his lab of a sample of carbonized grain from a pit. As he removed and counted the seeds layer by layer he discovered that there were more germinated seeds at the bottom, next to the chalk.

Reynolds (1979) tested Hillson's findings had found by digging a 1.5m pit and filling it with grain. Instruments were inserted to measure humidity, temperature and gas exchange. The pit was sealed with an airtight layer of clay. The results were impressive. The grain around the edges, especially when it was in contact with the chalk, began to germinate and produced shoots. This gradually used up the available oxygen and produced carbon dioxide creating an anaerobic environment and germination ceased. While the seal remained intact the grain lay dormant and survived the winter in good condition. When the pit was opened most of the grain could be used except for that around the edges, which was full of mould and fungi. If the pit was to be used again this waste had to be disposed of. Reynolds suggested that it was burnt in the pit, which accounted for the carbonised grain at the bottom. It is likely that the grain was taken out in one go, perhaps for sowing or trading, rather than used as a larder for food.

The zones where grain would germinate and spoil are shown in Figure 5.13. Ladders and baskets or buckets would be needed to empty a pit of this depth. Excavation on contemporary sites suggested that pits were usually backfilled to preserve their narrow entrances from collapse and not present a hazard. It was easier to re-dig them than start a new pit. Curiously this seems to have been rare at

Figure 5.12
View of Butser Ancient Farm

KEY SITES *cont.*

Danebury and Butser

Danebury where many pits contained strange ritual deposits (▶ p. 185).

Compared with the huge number of pits at Danebury a magnetometer survey of the nearby hill fort of Woolbury contained very few. Cunliffe, the excavator, used this finding to support his idea that Danebury was a high status site with a redistributive (▶ p. 247) function.

- Cunliffe 1995
- http://www.butser.org.uk/

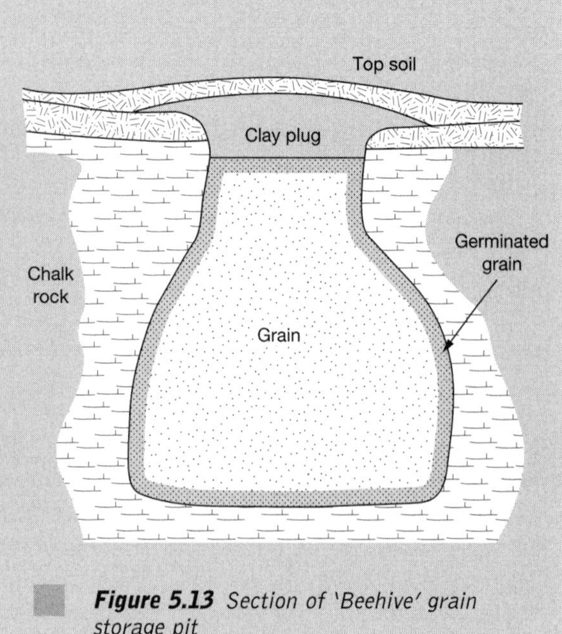

Figure 5.13 *Section of 'Beehive' grain storage pit*

KEY TERM

Analogy

This involves using something with which we are familiar to interpret a new thing or phenomena. It is based on the idea that if two things are similar in one way then they may be similar in others. When we describe an artefact as a hand-axe or an enclosure as a hill fort, we are using analogies. Analogies range from interpretations of how something was made or worn to what the social systems or patterns of religious belief in the past might have been. Analogies cannot prove anything about the past but they can tell us much about what was possible. They can widen our horizons, generate new lines of enquiry and provide theories to be tested against further evidence to see how robust they are.

Historical accounts or documents of past societies

- Classical accounts of the world such as the descriptions of Ancient Egypt by Herodotus
- Literary and artistic sources such as the poetry of early medieval Europe
- Travelogues written by the first western people to visit areas largely unaffected by European culture. For example, reports by Catholic missionaries on the peoples of Mesoamerica in the sixteenth century. These accounts are often called ethno-histories
- Where there is continuity in population, environment and some cultural forms, the direct historical approach (**DHA**) uses studies of, or oral accounts from, current peoples.

Ethnography or anthropology

Ethnography is the study of people in the world today while **anthropology** compares human

KEY STUDY

San Jose Mogote

Flannery and Marcus used several key interpretive methods in their exploration of beliefs from the Zapotec civilisation that flourished in the Oaxaca Valley of southern Mexico between 200 BC and AD 700. There was evidence of great continuity in local populations from Zapotec times until the Spanish conquest in the sixteenth century. The archaeologists were able to use what they termed a direct historical approach (DHA). Spanish priests had documented local 'pagan' customs that were used to form a hypothesis for testing by excavation. The archaeologists predicted that anything with breath (pee) would be sacred and that ancestors would be worshipped. The burning of copal incense and sacrifices of blood, jade, living things and exotic goods would be made to petition elemental forces such as earthquake and lightning. They expected to find evidence of priests who lived in two-roomed houses with sacrifices made in the inner room and who used drugs to reach ecstatic states.

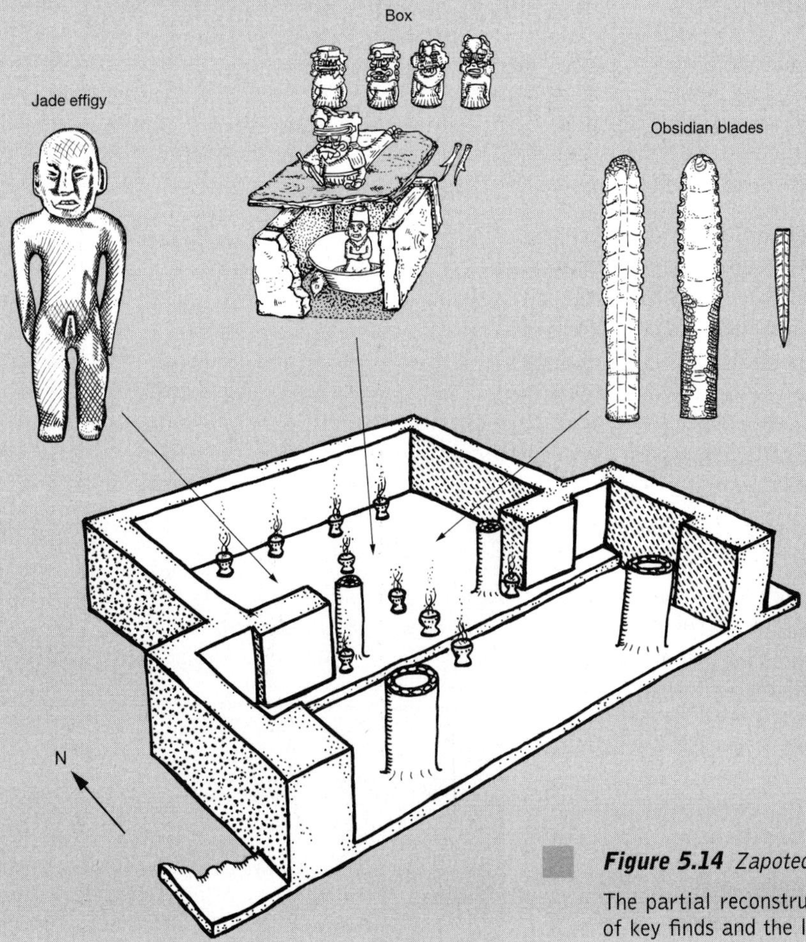

Figure 5.14 *Zapotec temple*

The partial reconstruction shows the position of key finds and the layout of the structure.

KEY STUDY *cont.*

San Jose Mogote

Excavations at San Jose Mogote revealed symbolism in the architecture and repeated patterns of structured deposition. There were a series of two-roomed buildings with the same east–west axis superimposed upon them. The inner rooms had been kept scrupulously clean although there were traces of repeated burning in them. Tiny pieces of debris in the corners were frequently from obsidian blades or stingray stings, used for bloodletting until historic times. Buried in the floor were tiny statues, jade beads and the bones of quail; a bird believed to be pure. The Spanish hadn't recorded this aspect of religion. Underfloor offerings also included effigies of the lightning clouds, hail and wind. Research amongst local people revealed that they called the statuettes 'little people of the clouds'. Ancestors were also known as cloud people. Through a mixture of historical records, analyses of excavated architecture and artefacts, and ethnography, Flannery and Marcus were able to reach conclusions about Zapotec reverence for ancestors and natural forces and the types of ritual practice involved in worship.

- http://www.angelfire.com/ca/humanorigins/religion.html#zapotec
- Marcus and Flannery 1994

cultures to identify general principles. Amongst the most well known ethnographic studies are those of the Hadza and Kalahari bushmen which were used in the 1960s to provide social and economic models for pre-agricultural humans as 'man the hunter'.

Specific analogies have been used to explore particular archaeological phenomena. For example the mortuary practice of the Merina of Madagascar has been used to provide insights into Neolithic beliefs (▶ p. 177).

General models drawing on broad comparisons across many cultures such as Service's band-tribe-chiefdom model of social evolution (▶ p. 266) have been used to categorise and interpret past societies.

Figure 5.15 *Romanian four poster*

Similar ideas to those at Butser have been used in other countries although their own cultural heritage produces very different looks as in these examples from historic buildings in Romania.

KEY TERM

Signature

To help identify features and their functions, archaeologists use mental templates for common activities in the period they are studying. There will be certain recurring patterns at sites, which have already been studied, which are associated with particular activities. For example, fires or hearths usually colour the earth reddish-orange while smelting or metalworking leaves slag and other waste products.

Archaeologists will 'read' these signatures when they come across similar finds or features on new sites.

However, most ethnographic studies come from the twentieth century when most of the world was already influenced in some way by European civilisations. There is often also a huge gulf in time and place between ancient peoples and the modern groups who are the source of analogies. While taking us beyond western models, ethnography can also limit our imagination. It is highly likely that ideas, social organisations and ways of doing things existed in the past that are not present in any current societies. The greater share of variation in human societies has already been lost. Archaeologists also have to resist the temptation to select the single examples that make most sense to them.

Actualistic studies

These studies involve the use of materials similar to those from the past in order to tie observed behaviour to physical remains.

Ethnoarchaeology

This involves studying how contemporary communities use material culture from an archaeological perspective. By correlating modern activities with physical remains we may start to understand what behaviour is reflected in which data. Studying people who manufacture stone tools and the debris they leave can help us identify the signatures left by different processes. Examining the distribution of remains within modern hunting camps may help identify the functions of particular areas (▶ p. 208). **Ethnoarchaeology** may also help reveal 'invisible' influences such as gender or ethnicity.

Experimental Archaeology

This involves forming a hypothesis about a process, artefact or ecofact and testing it using similar materials to those found on archaeological sites.

- Using replica artefacts to discover their functions. For example, testing flint axes to see how effectively they can chop down trees and then comparing the wear patterns with Neolithic examples.
- Reconstructions use data as the basis for models that can be tested. The best known in Britain is probably the constructs of Iron Age roundhouses at Butser Ancient Farm. Where the remains of such an experimental village are examined there might be an overlap with ethnoarchaeology. However, the people in the experiment would clearly be very different from those in archaeological examples. While some recreations are primarily for presenting ideas (▶ p. 150) others are used to test assumptions. The Kon Tiki raft which sailed across the Atlantic to test the possibility that the Ancient Egyptians could have reached Mexico falls into this category. Recreated boats have frequently broadened our understanding of seafaring in the past. The most recent example is the half size replica of the Sutton Hoo ship.
- Recreating taphonomic and other transformation processes to understand patterns on real sites. Experiments in Africa have explored the

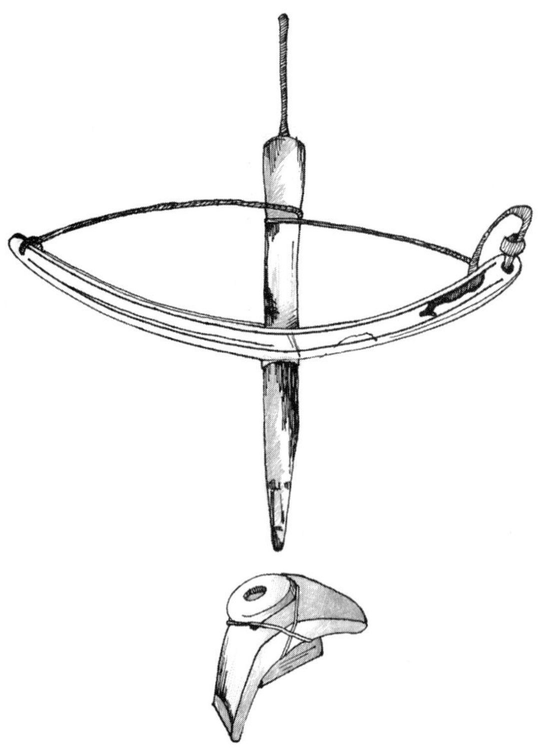

Figure 5.16 Bowdrill

Reconstructions of tools such as bow drills enable researchers to test their effectiveness on a range of materials and to identify signatures for their use. Replica tools are also widely used at archaeological attractions to enable the public to connect with the past by appreciating the skills of past people.

Figure 5.17 Replication as education

effect of scavengers on the distribution of bones from a carcass or the effects of streams on artefact movement. With all experiments replication is a key element in determining their validity. Where several researchers get similar results from similar experiments those results are more widely accepted. The production of lithics falls into this category.

• Schick and Toth 1993

WHY DO ARCHAEOLOGISTS OFFER DIFFERENT INTERPRETATIONS OF THE PAST?

Since archaeologists disagree about how or whether past behaviour can be reconstructed and because the archaeological record is so flawed, it is hardly surprising that their accounts differ. Data is constantly being reinterpreted as archaeologists ask new questions, use new techniques or find new sources of analogs. They also borrow models and methods from other disciplines. In the 1970s geography provided settlement archaeology with site catchment analysis and central place theory. In the 1990s phenomenology and critical theory inspired new interpretations of beliefs and rituals. The continued debate amongst archaeologists is a sign of the subject's vitality.

KEY SKILL

Applying your understanding to your course

Having an appreciation of how the archaeological record is formed should help you to understand archaeological reports and arguments. A grasp of why archaeologists' arguments might differ is necessary to score well on essays which ask you to evaluate a point of view. This is important at A2 and crucial at undergraduate level.

To practise, try to explore a debate between two writers who disagree about a topic you are studying. You may like to work with another student on this to halve the reading.

Start by writing down clearly what it is that they disagree about. Then, for each text list the key points that make up their argument and the key evidence they cite in support of each point. Try to identify where they are making an interpretation.

You will probably find that they will either:

- be using different data which will produce conflicting results
- differ about what the archaeological record actually shows or
- use different analogies to interpret data.

Your task is to explain the difference and then reach a conclusion about which of the explanations you consider more valid. For example, you could argue that some data is better than others for the particular question in hand or you could consult other sources to see which side they tend to support.

Present your findings briefly in bullet point form on a divided side of A4 paper. Add a visual symbol to each half to help you remember them.

Examples of debates:

- Binford vs. Freeman over whether there were elephant hunters at Torralba (Binford 1989)
- Cunliffe (1995) vs. Hill (1996) on whether Celtic chieftains ruled during the Iron Age in Britain

Chapter 6

Managing the Past

YOUR GOALS

You need to understand

- the key threats to our archaeological heritage
- the nature and effectiveness of current protection for archaeological remains
- the roles of the key agencies involved in archaeology and managing heritage
- the key debates about the preservation and ownership of archaeological remains.

THREATS TO ARCHAEOLOGICAL REMAINS

Natural processes (◀ Chapter 5) account for the decay of most archaeological remains once in the soil but the overwhelming threat to surviving monuments, from field systems to buildings, comes from human activity. The rapid growth of towns and road networks since 1945 combined with declining pasture land and more intensive forms of agriculture are largely responsible. Even seemingly minor changes can have significant impacts. For example in the aftermath of 'mad cow disease' many farmers in the upper Severn valley ploughed up old pasture to grow maize which is much more destructive.

Between the 1960s and 1980s most excavation was of sites about to be destroyed through development. Despite the efforts of some government agencies, many volunteer groups and the charity Rescue, only a small proportion were recorded. This was the key factor behind the introduction of the government policy and planning guide PPG 16 (▶ p. 126).

Development continues and debates about the destruction of archaeological remains are rarely out of the media for long. Recently quarrying at Thornborough and the Nine Ladies Henge and the new plan for Stonehenge have all made the news.

- http://www.savestonehenge.org.uk/

Some high profile sites are simply threatened by increasing public interest in our past. Hadrian's Wall and Avebury are two high profile sites that have suffered badly from erosion caused by walkers. As World Heritage Sites (▶ p. 125) detailed management plans have been drawn up to try and resolve the conflict between access and preservation. Avebury's plan can be found at:

- http://www.english-heritage.org.uk/knowledge/archaeology/new-archcommis/archcommis9697/1.html

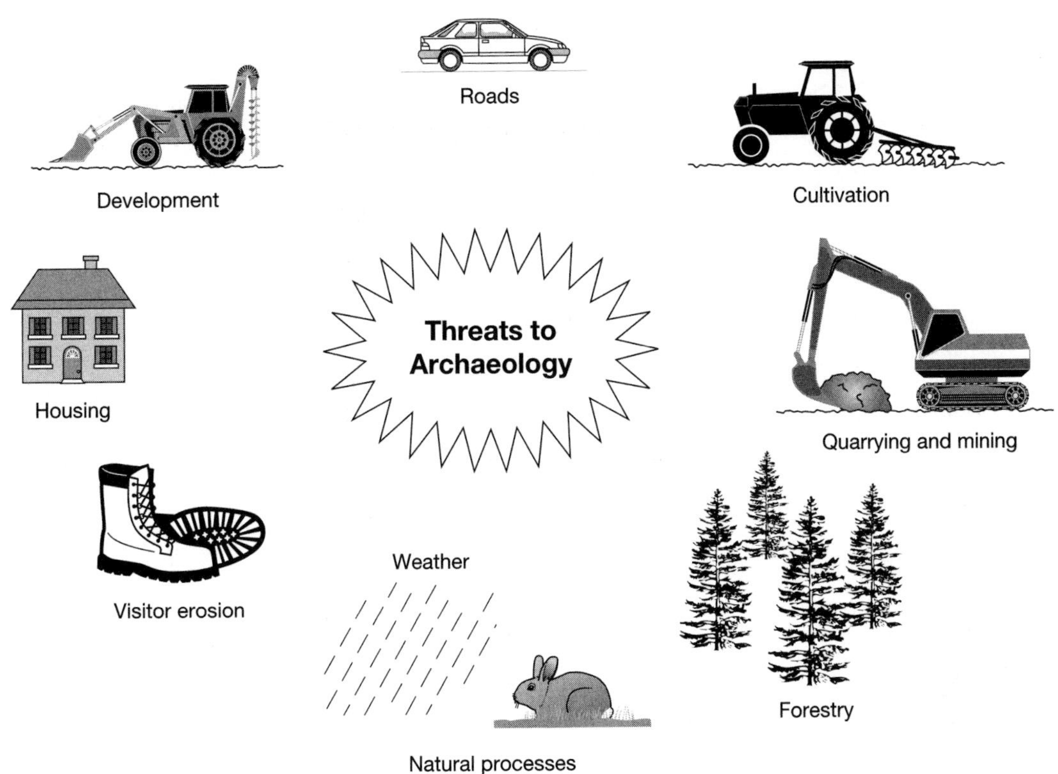

Figure 6.1 *Examples of the threats to archaeological remains*

Naturally public attention focuses on threats to famous monuments and exciting discoveries. However, a massive amount of our visible archaeological heritage continues to disappear with little protest. A glance at aerial photographs from the 1940s will reveal how many hedges, water meadows and medieval field systems have vanished. To landscape archaeologists they provide key evidence about landownership, settlement and use of the environment. Medieval field systems also provided a protective blanket over earlier sites that would otherwise have been eroded.

Global threats to archaeology

The pace of development across the world means thousands of archaeological sites are lost each year. Few countries have the resources to record what is lost. For many, archaeology comes an understandable second to feeding and housing their people. An additional global problem is the looting of archaeological sites to feed the demand of western collectors for artefacts and artwork. Britain has its problems with 'nighthawks' (▶ p. 133) but looting in much of the world is on an industrial scale. At Angkor Wat and other Buddhist temples in Cambodia, power saws have been used to remove statues and reliefs which are then trucked over the border for export. In the west, the blame is often placed with corrupt local officials and the army for colluding or even controlling the trade. The Cambodian government blames the famous auction houses in London for disposing of stolen antiquities. On a much lower scale sites throughout the world are routinely

KEY STUDY

The Monuments at Risk Survey of England (MARS), 1995

Bournemouth University and The Royal Commission on the Historic Monuments of England (RCHME) combined to survey the condition of a 5 per cent random sample of England's 937,484 recorded archaeological sites. The study, which was funded and published by English Heritage, provided a census of the nature, distribution and state of England's archaeological resources.

The study discovered that the South-east had lost the highest proportions of monuments with best survival in the West Midlands. Standing buildings and field systems are most at risk while those protected by legislation are at least risk. In total, 95 per cent of monuments had suffered some damage. Since 1945 an average of one site a day has been destroyed. Over 2 per cent of recorded sites have been lost since the survey. MARS drew on existing records plus its own surveys but inevitably will have missed many buried sites. The numbers of all sites destroyed and at risk will be higher. The table below summarises the key causes of destruction.

Cause of destruction	*Wholesale*	*Piecemeal*
New building and urban growth	27	9
Building repairs, alterations, demolition	20	19
Mineral extraction	12	3
Cultivation	10	30
Road building	9	4
Natural processes, visitors, vandalism	5	24
Unknown	17	11

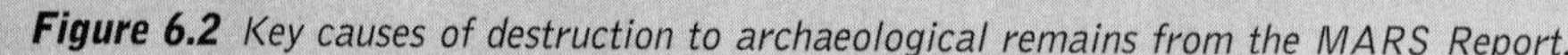

Figure 6.2 *Key causes of destruction to archaeological remains from the MARS Report.*

- http://www.csweb.bournemouth.ac.uk//consci/text_mars/marsint.htm

looted for coins, pottery and other portable artefacts by local people. They supplement low incomes by selling to tourists and dealers. Other tourists join commercial metal detecting tours to help themselves to artefacts. Sometimes monuments are deliberately destroyed for political reasons, as has happened recently in Bosnia and Afghanistan.

- http://www.nationalgeographic.com/features/97/copan/
- http://www.amnh.org/naturalhistory/features/0201_feature.html

Figure 6.3 Example of a damaged site. Spoonley Wood Roman Villa was partially excavated and restored by Victorian antiquarians. Trees and visitors continue to damage the mosaics

THE PROTECTION OF ARCHAEOLOGICAL REMAINS

Archaeology in Britain has not been well served by the law despite the existence of some protection since 1882. Some of the following laws only apply to England although similar measures exist in other parts of the UK.

Ancient Monuments and Archaeological Areas Act 1979 (AMAA)

Legislation before 1979 provided little protection. Even owners of scheduled monuments simply had to give notice if they wanted to change their condition. AMAA replaced earlier laws and provided greater protection. Its key features are:

- the *consent* of the Secretary of State is required before any changes to scheduled monuments

Figure 6.4 Altar Q at the Mayan city of Copan showing the baton of power being passed between a whole dynasty of sixteen kings. Each is represented symbolically by a sacrificed jaguar underneath the altar. On this panel the baton is passing from from the founder Yax K'uk Mo to the last king Yax Pasajh. Despite World Heritage Site status, Copan like many similar monuments, is regularly threatened by looting. Gangs of well-organised (and sometimes armed) looters have removed stone reliefs and statues, sometimes with power-saws. Much of this material is bought by wealthy 'art collectors' in the west

(listed by English Heritage as being of national importance) can be made

- English Heritage has the task of recording, assessing and monitoring monuments. It can recommend endangered sites and the land around them for scheduling to the Secretary of State for Culture, Media and Sport

• http://www.english-heritage.org.uk/

- Part 2 of the Act allowed Areas of Archaeological Importance to be designated where development could be delayed for proper assessment and excavation (government funded)
- the National Heritage Act (1983) amended AMAA to allow industrial areas and gardens to become scheduled monuments.

Pros

- It gave legal protection to some visible monuments after years of destruction.
- The English Heritage monument protection programme is listing other key monuments. Currently about 15,000 are listed (only 2 per cent of known archaeological sites).
- Part 2 established the use of mapping as a tool to protect sites. Developers were 'warned off' sites where their plans might be slowed down or halted.
- Some landowners have signed management agreements to protect sites in return for funding.

Cons

- Sites which are not scheduled as being 'of national importance' (roughly 98 per cent of known sites) are not protected.
- Newly discovered sites are not protected, so these can be lost in development. The process of scheduling is slow (for example only 56 of 40,000 known shipwrecks are scheduled).
- It doesn't cover landscapes.
- It often only protects the visible (earthwork) element of monuments. The mounds of many long barrows survive as islands in ploughed fields while the ditches, pits and post holes are still ploughed.

• http://www.csweb.bournemouth.ac.uk/consci/text_kn/knhome.htm

- Landowners and developers can appeal against scheduling. They can also plead ignorance as an excuse for damaging sites.
- Part 2 of the Act was never brought properly into force. Few areas of towns were scheduled.
- The cost of work fell on local or national government. It was never a priority.
- Monuments can still be ploughed as long as the depth of ploughing isn't increased.

Other protective legislation for sites

These laws were not usually drawn up with archaeology in mind. However they provide some protection for unscheduled sites including archaeological landscapes.

- *The National Parks Act 1949 limited* development within the parks and designated other 'Areas of Outstanding Natural Beauty'. MARS found that survival in these areas was better than elsewhere.
- *The Wildlife and Countryside Act 1981* required local authorities to assess rural areas and draw up plans to manage them. Archaeology *can* be taken into account.
- *The Town and Country Planning Act 1971 allowed* local authorities to take Archaeology into account in planning applications and *required* them to produce structure plans for future development. Further legislation in 1990 created conservation areas.
- *Capital Transfer Tax 1984*. Landowners are exempted from this if they contract to maintain and preserve the land and ensure reasonable access.
- Additionally, legislation about industries including coal mining and electricity includes clauses on archaeology. There are also a growing number of non-statutory categories

KEY TASK

Assessing local monuments

Either of these tasks would make a good personal study project or group task.

- Visit a sample of local monuments to record their condition and threats to them. Compare your findings to the MARS study.
- Investigate the impact of PPG 16 in your area. This could involve interviews with some of those involved and examination of the role of local organisations such as units, SMR, etc.

You may be able to obtain a list from your local SMR.

of designation such as Parks and Gardens and the Battlefield Register. None of these provide secure protection and none ensures funding for archaeological work.

International protection

The United Nations Educational, Scientific and Cultural Organization (UNESCO) has drawn up a World Heritage list of 634 sites of outstanding international value.

Governments of most UN member states have signed up to protect these sites. In itself this provides some protection since it would be embarrassing for a government to authorise development on a listed site. The scheme also enables funds to be channelled to conservation and restoration projects on endangered sites in poorer countries. However, it does not guarantee preservation and only covers a fraction of sites worldwide.

The Valetta Convention (1992)

This European Union Convention came into force in March 2001. It is based on the principle that the archaeological heritage throughout Europe is threatened by development and needs to be protected. It requires governments to protect monuments and regulate archaeology to ensure the proper conservation of excavated sites and the recording and safe-keeping of finds. It also covers the use of metal detectors, the trade in artefacts and the need to raise public awareness of and access to archaeological heritage. Although much of it is similar to existing UK measures (particularly the emphasis on preservation 'in situ'), Article 3, which called for all work to be authorised and carried out by suitably qualified people, caused considerable debate. This was because of fears that it could be used to limit the involvement of amateurs in archaeology.

- http://www.unesco.org/whc/nwhc/pages/sites/main.htm

Countries vary widely in how they manage archaeological resources. This chapter has focused on England but Australia provides an interesting alternative example:

- http://life.csu.edu.au~dspennem/VIRTPAST/VIRTPAST.HTM/

PROTECTION OF ARTEFACTS

Legal protection of artefacts focuses on those few examples of high monetary value. The old laws on treasure trove in England and Wales were replaced by the Treasure Act in 1996. It defines objects and coins as treasure which are over 300 years old and either over ten per cent precious metal or at least ten in number. In 2003 'treasure' was extended to cover all prehistoric metal finds. Items substantially composed of precious metal and less than 300 years old are treasure if it can be shown that they were deposited with the intention of recovering them.

Apart from general legislation on theft and trespass, the law neglects other materials (for example pottery) which may be of greater archaeological value. In the case of treasure, it also means that assemblages can be broken up.

To improve the recording of artefacts which fell outside the scope of the Treasure Act the Portable Antiquities Scheme was introduced in 1997. The Government and Heritage Lottery Fund financed pilot schemes to encourage the recording of all archaeological objects found by members of the public in any site. 'Finds Liaison Officers' provide advice on finds and run 'finds roadshows'. They provide a link between the public, metal detector users and archaeologists and museums. The scheme has been very successful. 47,000 chance finds were reported by the public in 2003–4 including an increasing amount of 'treasure'. Accurate recording enabled details to be added to an online data base. It is expected that the scheme will be extended to all parts of England and Wales.

- www.finds.org.uk/

PROTECTION THROUGH THE PLANNING PROCESS: PPG 16

Planning and Policy Guide note number 16 (1990) is not a law. It is one of many Government guidelines issued to help local planning officials in England when they consider applications to develop land. Another note, PPG 15 (1994), deals with changes to buildings of historic interest. Although PPG 16 is not law, planners need to have good reasons for not following its advice. It advises planners to consider archaeology at an early stage of the development process and to favour the preservation of archaeological remains where possible. PPG 16 advises that the developer should be responsible for funding any archaeological work deemed necessary. It also provides guidance on appeals that can be made to the Secretary of State for the Environment.

PPG 16 broadly divides archaeologists into two groups.

Curators

Local authority (LA) archaeologists advise planners on the sensitivity of each site, following a desktop survey (◀ p. 6) drawing on information held by their Sites and Monuments Record (SMR). They draw up the brief for any archaeological work needed and check that it is done to required standards. Most of the finds from development work are usually deposited with the LA museum service.

Contractors

Developers put out a contract for exploratory work or excavation to competitive tender. They may also hire archaeological consultants to contest the local authority positions. Independent archaeological trusts or commercial 'units' do most of this work. LA units or amateur groups carry out some work in a few areas but this is becoming increasingly rare.

- http://www.britarch.ac.uk/info/contract.html

The effects of PPG 16

PPG 16 has had an enormous impact on archaeology in England and there is considerable debate amongst archaeologists about its positive and negative effects. To gain a taste of the debate, look in the archives of the archaeology email discussion group Britarch.

- britarch@jiscmail.ac.uk

Positive

- The past is now recognised as a finite resource, which requires management and conservation.
- Rescue archaeology is funded by what amounts to a tax on development.
- Archaeological remains are considered by planners. Those which are destroyed are often 'preserved by record'.

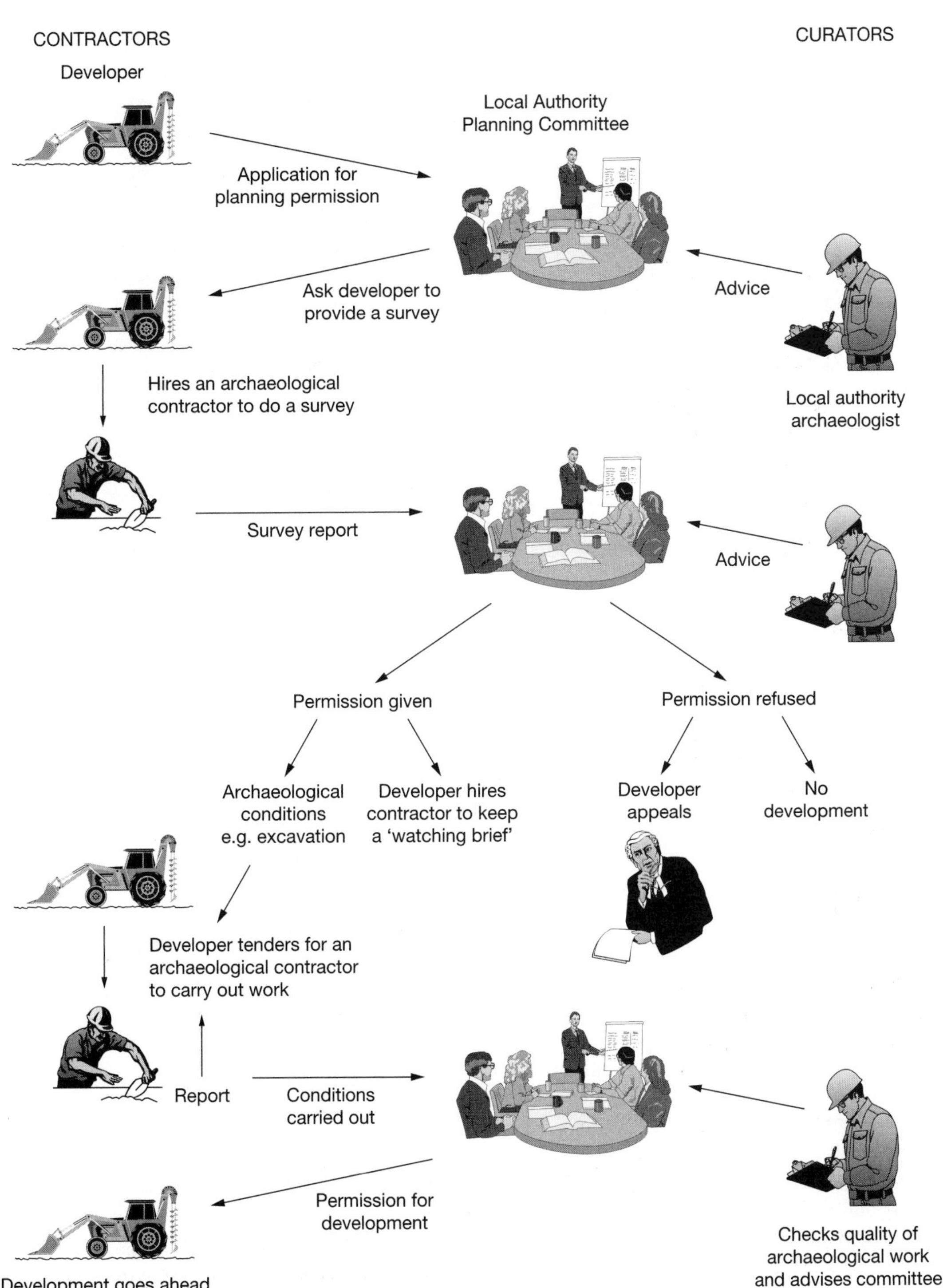

Figure 6.5 *Simplified diagram to show how archaeology is involved in the planning process*

Figure 6.6 *PPG16 in action*

Deposits from the area around the Forum in Cirencester lie around a metre under the surface. Rather than excavate a large area of Roman Britain's second city planners preferred a mitigation strategy. Test pits and a minor excavation down to the top of the Roman road in the foreground established the depth of deposits. In the picture these are being covered in a concrete raft before houses are built on top. Depending on your viewpoint, this is a wasted opportunity or precious remains preserved in situ for a future generation.

- It provides increased employment for professional archaeologists
- SMRs have developed because of the need for detailed records.

Negative

- Sites for excavation are dictated by development rather than research needs.
- It has decreased opportunities for amateur enthusiasts to become involved.
- Inexperienced archaeological units tended to bid too low for contracts during the early 1990s. As a result many struggle to pay staff well.
- The costs of post-excavation work, including the use of specialists and storage of remains, can be under-estimated. This work may have suffered. Some museums are now 'full'.
- Completed excavation reports belong to the developers. They do not have to publish them.
- Some local authorities have used PPG 16 as a way of reducing spending on archaeology. LA archaeologists often spend most of their time on planning matters.

The language of PPG 16

PPG 16 has generated a new range of terminology, which needs to be understood in order to follow archaeologists' discussions:

- *Archaeological assessment or appraisal*: A desktop survey and a look at the site.
- *Field evaluation*: a survey of the site, which usually includes trial trenching to establish the depth, nature and condition of remains.

- *Watching brief*: literally that. An archaeologist will watch as the bulldozers go in to see if any archaeological remains are unearthed and to report on them.
- *Preservation in situ*: Excavation is destructive so PPG 16 advises that archaeological remains should be left where they are (in situ) if possible. This can mean resting buildings on piles driven through deposits. This method is controversial. In Norway, piling, which damages and interferes with the drainage and stratigraphy of sites, is viewed as destruction rather than preservation.

Figure 6.7 *Developer-led archaeology. A major excavation in Cheltenham by Cotswold Archaeology. This was the result of a contract tendered by the developers as part of planning permission for a new superstore. The small team of professional archaeologists dressed in safety gear, worked to tight deadlines through the winter. This is the face of most modern archaeology*

- *Mitigation Strategy*: applies to any measures taken to reduce or prevent the destruction of remains during development.
- *Preservation by record*: the site is destroyed but a proper archaeological record is made through a detailed site report.

Other forms of protection

The protection of archaeological remains is a key aim of many of the organisations listed on p. 134. Official agencies such as English Heritage or Historic Scotland have statutory responsibilities and advise ministers on policy and decisions affecting archaeology.

- http://www.english-heritage.org.uk/
- http://www.historic-scotland.gov.uk/

Campaigns, including lobbying, use of the media and advice for developers and farmers, are also part of the roles of independent organisations, charities and learned bodies such as the Council for British Archaeology (CBA), Rescue and the Prehistoric Society. There is also the Institute of Field Archaeologists which promotes (but cannot enforce) high standards amongst those engaging in excavations. It acts as a professional body for part of the sector.

- http://www.britarch.ac.uk
- http//www.rescue-archaeology.freeserve.co.uk/
- http:www.britarch.ac.uk/prehist
- http://www.archaeologists.net

WHO ARE THE ARCHAEOLOGISTS?

Within archaeology in the UK there is increasing debate about who should engage in practical archaeology. Archaeology's roots lie with the work of enthusiastic amateurs but it has become increasingly professionalised.

Excavation began with the antiquarians from the seventeenth century onwards. Archaeology provided a hobby for landed enthusiasts right up to the 1950s. Some early diggers were little more

KEY SITE

Stonehenge

Britain's most famous archaeological site presents a whole series of problems in balancing access against protection. A landmark for centuries, its visibility on Salisbury Plain ensured it attracted a road junction. It now exists in a traffic island, cut off from its landscape and surrounded by tourist facilities which make few concessions to the nature of the site. Recently the government has accepted that Stonehenge is a national disgrace and in breach of World Heritage conventions and have pushed through plans to redevelop the site. One of the roads will be grassed over and another will run through a tunnel. Visitor facilities will be moved over a mile away, out of sight of the monument. There is much support for reuniting Stonehenge with the ritual landscape of which it is an integral part. Visitors will be able to follow the avenue to the stones, which is probably the route taken in the Bronze Age. However, consensus ends there. There is much opposition amongst archaeologists to the tunnel because it will cut through archaeological deposits and the entrances are near other monuments. Others are unhappy about the 'land trains' which will be used to bring 150 visitors

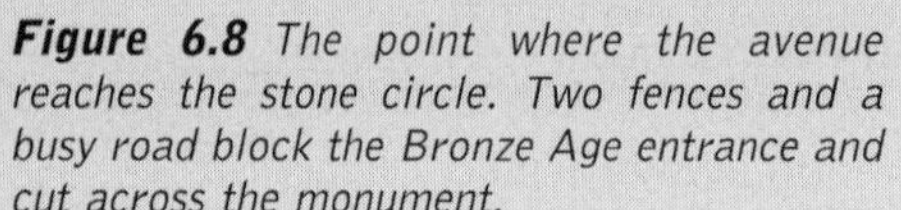

Figure 6.8 *The point where the avenue reaches the stone circle. Two fences and a busy road block the Bronze Age entrance and cut across the monument.*

Figure 6.9 *World class visitor facilities are promised*

Figure 6.10 *The view of Stonehenge from the cursus round barrows*

KEY STUDY *cont.*

Stonehenge

per trip to the site. These pictures illustrate other problems. Look at English Heritage's vision for the site and make up your own mind. You may like to compare with Newgrange (▶ p. 147) and consider the case for 'reconstruction'.

- http://www.english-heritage.org.uk/stonehenge/

Figure 6.11 *This is how you currently enter this world heritage site*

Figure 6.12 *Not the most imaginative interpretation of the three huge Mesolithic post-holes close to Stonehenge. These may have made the location important long before Stonehenge was built*

than grave robbers. However in the twentieth century other amateurs, such as Sir Mortimer Wheeler, pioneered modern excavation techniques.

Learned and excavation societies

By 1900 most parts of the country had societies devoted to gathering archaeological information and communicating it to their members and to the wider public. Most undertook excavations and began journals, many of which continue to this day. Some established museums where their collections could be displayed. This too was largely an upper-class activity, undertaken by those who could afford the time to take part in research excavations. The societies did, however, include more of the public by the 1950s.

The rescue era

The massive urban expansion and road building programmes of the 1960s and 1970s saw a rapid rise in rescue archaeology. Teams of volunteers or low paid diggers sought to record what they could before bulldozers or ploughs destroyed remains. This coincided with a rapid expansion of higher education including the development of new archaeological departments. These developments provided many new opportunities for the public to get involved in archaeology and to follow that interest academically. However, archaeology was poorly resourced. Much of the funding came from charitable efforts and it was difficult to find full time paid work in archaeology. Nevertheless a pool of skilled excavators did develop from diggers who moved from site to site.

The term 'rescue excavations' was coined in the 1960s when so much development was occurring that the earlier pattern of amateur and university summer excavations could not cope with the volume of archaeological sites being threatened and destroyed. Rescue, a charitable trust, dramatised the threat to Britain's archaeology by using as its logo an image of Stonehenge being scooped up in a bulldozer's bucket. This overstates destruction but what was recognised was that the scale and pace of development meant that much valuable evidence was in danger of being lost if it could not be excavated and recorded. Excavation teams were needed all year round.

- http//www.rescue-archaeology.freeserve.co.uk/

Some teams were centrally based within government agencies while others were formed locally to combat specific threats. Often these were amateur groups. The M5 Rescue Committee is a good example of a group founded with a clear

Figure 6.13 *How it used to be: amateur involvement in archaeology. The Empingham excavation (**◀ p. 32**) involved a small number of professionals working alongside volunteers. Since the 1970s, amateurs have been gradually squeezed out of much excavation work by professionalisation and the terms of developer contracts*

but essentially time-constrained focus. From these late 1960s/early 1970s teams most of today's archaeological **units** have developed.

Originally, rescue teams identified potential threats to archaeological sites from planned developments such as road building, gravel extraction or pipelines, and submitted bids for public funding to excavate before development began. Today planning authorities, guided by PPG 16, require developers to prepare impact assessments and may also demand a formal site evaluation. Depending on the findings there may be excavation in advance of development and/or a watching brief (◀ p. 129) during construction. On the principle of 'the polluter pays' the cost is increasingly passed on to developers.

Archaeology today

In the 1980s and 1990s archaeology underwent huge changes. Funding came initially through government job creation schemes at a time of high unemployment. After PPG 16 developers had to pay for work. They expected to hire qualified workers and commercial standards of health and safety to be applied. Commercial units of professional archaeologists developed in response. Unit archaeologists had to compete for business to survive. This left little time for the traditional professional role of supervising and training volunteers. Opportunities for amateur involvement in digging began to decline as a result. At the same time archaeology became more specialised. The application of scientific techniques for prospecting, recording and analysing was in most cases beyond the resources of rescue committees and enthusiastic amateurs.

Most excavations now fall into the following three categories:

- Assessments and rescue excavations in advance of developments. These are largely carried out by professional archaeologists in the contracting units.
- Seasonal research excavations run by universities. These are largely open to their own students although some take paying volunteers as training excavations.
- Occasional research excavation by specialists from government heritage agencies.

Amateur archaeology is still thriving in pockets throughout the UK although it is not as widespread as it once was. The Council for Independent Archaeology offers support for amateurs and has pioneered the development of affordable geophysics equipment for amateurs. The journal *Current Archaeology* often covers amateur projects and provides a critique of 'official archaeology'.

- http://www.archaeology.co.uk/cia/default.htm
- http://www.archaeology.co.uk/gateway/thinktank/who/welcome.htm

Metal detecting

The gradual exclusion of amateurs from field archaeology has coincided with an increase in metal detecting. Some professionals remain hostile to all detectorists because of damage that has been done to sites or looting by organised gangs of 'nighthawks'.

However, most detectorists are not intentionally destructive or members of criminal gangs but simply people interested in the physical past. Increasingly there have been moves by county archaeologists to work with detectorists and some archaeologists do use metal detectors on excavations. Issues can be followed up at:

- http://www.britarch.ac.uk/detecting/index.html
- http://www.ukdetectornet.co.uk/

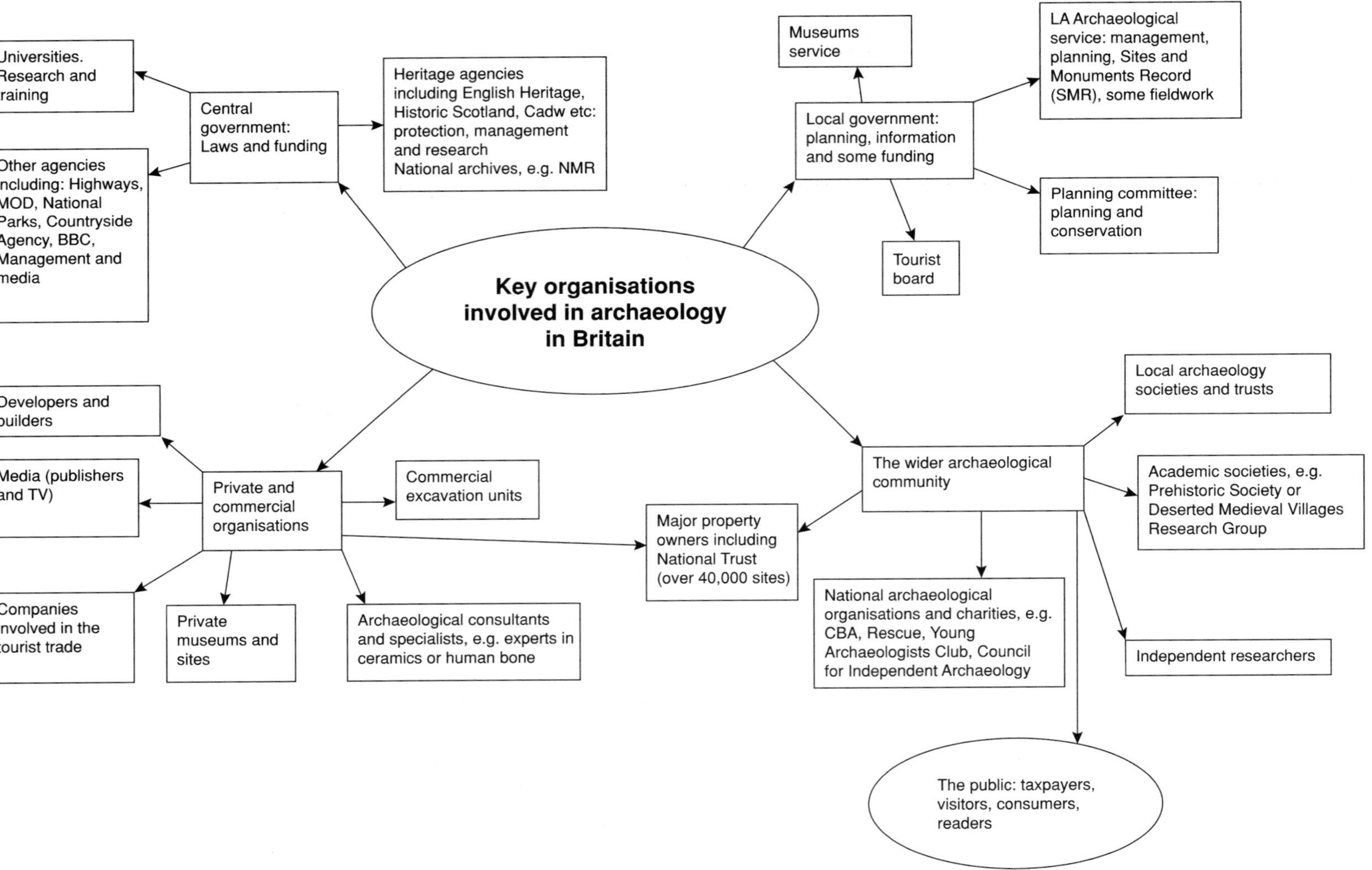

Figure 6.14 *Key organisations involved in British Archaeology*

The popular view of archaeologists is that they spend their time digging. While many do, there are at least an equal number who do not. For those of you who are considering archaeology-related careers, this chart may provide helpful in identifying opportunities.

KEY SITE

Castell Henllys

This small Iron Age hill fort in South West Wales provides an example of a long-term research excavation. It was bought in 1980 by the co-founder of the London Dungeon, who worked to develop it as a tourist attraction with reconstructed Iron Age houses. Subsequently it has been taken over by the Pembrokeshire Coast National Park, which has established a visitors' centre on the site.

It was necessary to excavate the site and recover the evidence on which to base the reconstructions. Students and paying volunteers have helped in the excavations each summer. Over twenty seasons, archaeologists have studied the defensive circuit, the complex phases of the gateway, and almost the whole of the interior of the fort. Reconstructions of four major roundhouses and smaller constructions have been completed.

This research has provided a much fuller understanding of the archaeology of this period and provided a link via its marketing style between archaeologists and the general public.

- *Current Archaeology* 161
- http://www.castelhenllys.com/

Figure 6.15 *An area excavation to reveal the 'chevaux de frise' an Iron Age 'tank trap' protecting the entrance to Castell Henllys, West Wales. Compare with the interpretation*

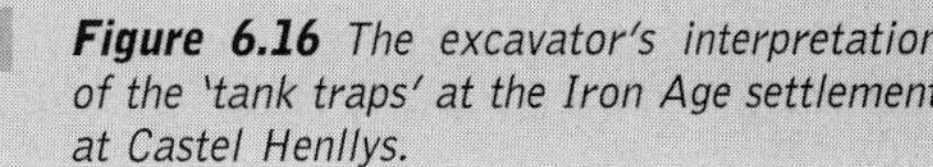

Figure 6.16 *The excavator's interpretation of the 'tank traps' at the Iron Age settlement at Castel Henllys.*

KEY SKILL

Starting to construct arguments

Putting together arguments is a key element in higher level essay writing. One way to approach this is to organise your notes into pro and con lists. Try this for the following question. It would work equally well as a small group task.

Outline the case for and against amateur involvement in excavation

Aim to write three sides of A4. You might like to consider the following points as starters.

- Most archaeologists start out as amateurs.
- Professionals are 'better' than amateurs.
- Can standards be ensured without professionalism?

Tip

Writing pro and con assignments usually leads to one of the following structures.

A	B
Introduction and outline of issue	Introduction and outline of issue
Points and examples for	Point by point for and against
Points and examples against	Weighing up to reach a judgement
Weighing up to reach a judgement	Conclusion
Conclusion	

A is easier to write than *B*, but *B* ensures that you compare for and against on each point. *A* can become descriptive while with *B* you have to be analytical. Whichever you select, try to provide a range of points and support each with a specific example. If you only consider a few points it is difficult to reach the higher levels of mark schemes, however much detail you have included. It is also vital that you say at the end how far you agree with the arguments for and against. Don't worry about what you conclude as long as it is supported by the judgements you make in the body of the assignment.

Alternative assignments:

- Consider the arguments for and against metal detecting.
- Consider the strengths of research archaeology against developer-led archaeology.

Figure 6.17 *Archaeology on a massive scale*

Excavations on the site of the Heathrow extension. Only the largest units are capable of bidding for projects such as this and often only in collaboration with others. Amongst the discoveries on this site was this linear feature, not an earlier runway but the Heathrow Cursus, a Neolithic ritual monument. (See p. 341 for larger version.)

Chapter 7

Presenting the Past

YOUR GOALS

You need to

- understand some of the political and ethical debates about ownership and presentation of the past
- have a knowledge of a range of methods of communicating archaeological understanding
- know some case studies in depth to use as examples
- be able to critically assess the merits of different modes of communication.

WHICH PAST?

Before considering how archaeological remains and knowledge might be best communicated we should reflect on what the social and cultural implications of explanations about the past might be. Archaeological knowledge and the images of the past created by archaeologists are not value free. As with history and literature, the selection of what is significant and how it should be interpreted partly derives from the political and social values and structures in present-day society. Archaeology and history have both been used either consciously or unconsciously to justify particular values and social structures.

The political use of archaeology

Extreme cases are fairly easy to identify. A succession of rulers have sought to justify their regimes and their territorial ambitions by claiming precedent from the past. Mussolini, the Fascist dictator of Italy (1922–45), claimed to be following in the footsteps of the Romans with his plans for an Italian empire in Africa and to turn the Mediterranean into an Italian lake (Mare Nostrum). Saddam Hussein in Iraq drew parallels between his regime and the Assyrian Empire, which dominated the region in the first millennium BC. Israel, Bosnia and the Indian city of Ayodhya are three of many places where archaeology has recently been involved in violent political conflicts. In each case the ability to control what is known about the past is used as a tool to legitimise political, social or economic power.

It is not just dictatorships or extremist political parties which have used archaeology for political ends. Mainstream politicians in many countries have argued over the ownership of cultural

KEY STUDY

Nazi archaeology

Archaeology was enlisted for propaganda purposes by the Nazi government of Germany during the 1930s and 1940s. At this time it was commonplace for archaeologists to associate pottery styles with distinctive ethnic groups and to identify racial differences from skeletal remains. The Nazis used this confusion of race with ethnicity to draw up racial maps of Europe and identify 'superior' races. Their excavations 'revealed' artefacts of Germanic origin in occupied Poland including bowls marked with swastikas. Overlooking the fact that the swastika is an ancient Indian symbol, archaeologists gave these forgeries a scientific stamp of approval. They helped justify Nazi conquests as retaking land which had always been German.

remains. The most famous of these is the dispute over the Elgin Marbles (▶ p. 140). In many parts of the world, native peoples are using archaeology to reclaim rights lost in previous centuries. In some cases this involves claims for the return of cultural artefacts taken from them by foreign museums or art collectors. Increasingly there are also disputes over the disturbance of burials by archaeologists and for the return of human remains to their place of origin for burial. Usually at the heart of these conflicts are two fundamental issues:

- Should (usually western) archaeologists have the right to excavate cultural remains of another culture or are their actions simply a continuation of colonialist exploitation?
- Do excavated remains from the past provide evidence which can be used to sustain claims on the rightful ownership of land?

Archaeology and land rights

In South Africa during the colonial period, a myth was created by Dutch settlers that they had occupied an empty land. Archaeological finds proved that to be false. In Australia, aboriginal groups have been able to use archaeological evidence to prove that their ancestors inhabited particular regions and to demonstrate their right to the land or to compensation for its use by others.

Archaeology and identity

In Britain, there are also political struggles about rights and identity which involve archaeology and assumption drawn from it. In Wales, the selection of sites for preservation and particularly for promotion has generated debate about which version of the past should predominate: the past of English conquest and castle building or the tradition of Welsh independence and resistance? More generally, the way archaeologists have interpreted the past can lead to certain values and arrangements being seen as unchanging and therefore 'normal'.

Until the late twentieth century, many archaeologists associated particular artefacts with homogenous ethnic groups and attributed social changes to the arrivals of new peoples, for example 'the beaker people'. This fitted with the assumptions of many classically educated people that social and technological developments had originated in the Mediterranean and then were spread by colonists into the barbarian lands further north. It also fitted the way in which Europeans viewed their empires in the rest of the world and to some extent justified their role in spreading 'civilisation' to inferior 'races'. Recent advances in archaeology and genetics have undermined the idea that pure ethnic groups existed in the past, while radiocarbon dating has shown that indigenous Neolithic and Bronze Age peoples had achieved a great deal well before the arrival of Mediterranean influences. The building of Stonehenge and the brochs of Scotland and the

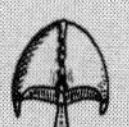

KEY STUDIES

Archaeology and Native Americans

According to historical records, the Pequot Indian tribe of Connecticut died out following a war with European settlers in the seventeenth century. However, archaeologists working with descendants of the Pequots were able to establish cultural continuity between the original tribe and survivors of the war whose descendents continued to live on reservations in the area until recent times. The Pequots were able to use archaeological data to gain recognition as a sovereign nation from the US government in 1987. A treaty was signed and some of their land was returned to them.

By the 1990s the civil rights movements for Native Americans had won a series of legal and political victories. One of these was the 1990 Native American Graves Protection and Repatriation Act (NAGPRA) which provides for the return to tribes of the skeletons and religious artefacts of their ancestors. This has created problems for archaeologists. To some Native Americans, archaeology is grave robbing by an occupying power. A major conflict has arisen since the discovery of human remains at Kennewick on the Columbia River. Scientists who examined the remains dated them to 8410 ± BP and claimed that the anatomy was different from that of Native Americans. 'Kennewick Man' quickly became a political issue. Native Americans wanted the remains to be reburied, not studied. Some feared that if he did prove to be from a people who occupied the area before the current tribes, his existence might be used to challenge the right of Native Americans to that land. Attempts to perform rituals near the bones led to claims that their DNA was deliberately being contaminated. The US Army then dumped rubble over the find-site but were unable to prevent the dispute spreading. For further details on this fascinating case try the following websites:

- http://www.kennewick-man.com/
- http://www.umatilla.nsn.us/ (for the Native American perspective)
- http://www.archaeology.org/ (for the Archaeological Institute of America's view)

Northern Isles (▶ p. 215) are two cases where the achievements of indigenous populations are now recognised.

In a similar way, early archaeologists often identified burials of male and female on the basis of their assumptions about gender roles. For example, a skeleton buried with an axe *must* have been male because men fight and chop down trees. A burial with a mirror or domestic artefacts *must* be female. (▶ p. 278) This kind of analysis has, in turn, tended to reinforce stereotypes about natural roles for men and women. Once again, recent discoveries such as the Pazyryk 'Ice Maiden' and DNA analysis have tended to challenge the traditional view (▶ p. 278). Some museums have begun to re-label displays where the earlier sexing of skeletal remains is in doubt.

New Age and pagan beliefs and the issue of access to ancient monuments

Most books on Stonehenge feature a picture of the Druids, a nineteenth-century order who developed their own ceremonies at the monument based on their interpretation of Iron Age beliefs. Since the 1960s many other groups have also sought to use ancient monuments for rituals and festivals. Pagans have claimed the sites as sacred according to their beliefs and want the right to

Figure 7.0 *The Elgin Marbles*

Perhaps the most famous dispute between nations over archaeology is that of the Elgin Marbles. Bought by Lord Elgin from Ottoman Turks who ruled Greece at that time, the sculptures were brought to London and are in the British Museum. The Greek government wants them back to put in a new Parthenon Museum. Should they stay or should they go?

worship there. For others their demands to hold festivals at the sites symbolise a struggle against an oppressive state. Either way, these demands have led to conflict with those responsible for managing the monuments and archaeologists concerned about damage to remains. In the case of the West Kennet Long Barrow this includes sarsen stone being damaged by candles. In the case of Stonehenge disputes over access have led to public order offences and occasionally violence. More recently the authorities have realised that those wanting to celebrate at the sites do not usually want to see them damaged. This has lead to more inclusive management plans and more emphasis on education about potential threats to the monuments. Many New Age websites provide excellent visual records of sites.

- http://www.themodernantiquarian.com/home/

The common thread that runs through all of these disputes is control of the past. Those who control access to sites and artefacts are best placed to interpret the past for the wider public. It is their values which will be reflected in accounts of the past and their values which in turn are supported by those accounts.

KEY SKILL

Taking notes from contradictory sources

For longer questions, including essays, you will be expected to consider more than one side to any given issue. In order to do this effectively and quickly, you need to become used to understanding arguments. If you find this difficult you could try using this structured approach. Attempt it using the Kennewick websites as your raw material.

For each point of view complete a table such as the one below. State as simply as you can the general argument or claim.

List the key points they make	*What evidence do they give to support this point?*	*Do you find the evidence acceptable?*	*Does this point support their overall argument*

How strong do you think this argument is?

Having done this you may now be able to distinguish between the arguments. Are some of the points in them contradictory? Are some points unsupported or supported by evidence that you feel is unsound? Is the difference one of belief or opinion which you can only decide on a moral basis? You may find that the two parties agree on certain aspects or that you think they are both sound in different ways. This is the kind of information you will need to write down when you move on to discursive essays (▶ p. 293).

Figure 7.1 *A pagan summer solstice at Avebury. This circular gathering at dawn includes both druids and followers of Wicca*

KEY STUDY

The Corinium Museum Cirencester

There has been a revolution in museum design over the last few decades. The Corinium has had a complete makeover courtesy of the National Lottery and exhibits many state of the art features. Families and primary school children are the target audience and little previous knowledge is assumed. Heavy use is made of recreations to explain burials, buildings and technology including hands-on replica clothing and artefacts. Interactive displays allow exhibits and the museum's catalogue to be interrogated at several levels. A particularly innovative feature uses video, sound and lighting in conjunction with tombstones to 'bring the people to life'.

Developments in IT and communications technology have offered archaeologists the opportunities to transform the way they communicate. As a result, the range of methods and modes of communicating archaeological information is rapidly expanding and there is considerable diversity in the way they are used.

Rather than cover all periods, the Corinium has chosen to major in Roman Corinium with a minor in Anglo-Saxon Lechlade (▶ p. 282). This specialisation is a growing feature of British museums.

In Figure 7.2 the Jupiter Column has been re-erected to give a sense of scale. In the foreground is one of the mosaics for which the town was famous and in the background a range of different types of display.

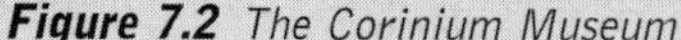

Figure 7.2 *The Corinium Museum*

Figure 7.3 *Interactive displays*

KEY STUDIES

New modes of communication

A Time Team excavation on television

Some professionals despair at the idea of a three-day excavation against the clock but they are not the intended audience for this programme. Its main function is to provide entertainment to a general audience whilst educating them in some aspects of archaeological methods and interpretations. The format of a time-limited challenge to a group of personalities is well established through house and garden makeover shows. Technical language and ideas are communicated simply through computer-generated images while the routine or time-consuming aspects of excavation and post-excavation work are edited out in favour of action involving celebrity diggers. Its entertainment value is attested to by its high ratings. In addition, its website and publications provide opportunities for people to develop their understanding and explore links to educational sites. However, the programme may raise unrealistic expectations about archaeology and the possibility of public involvement that may ultimately frustrate its audience.

- http:///www.channel4.com/nextstep/timeteam/

Figure 7.5 *Tony Robinson of the Time Team*

His programmes have been outstandingly successful in raising public awareness of and interest in archaeology.

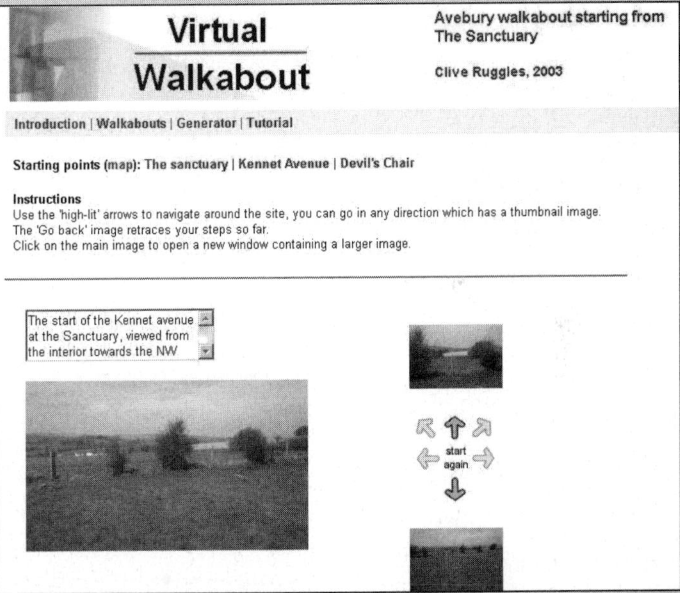

Figure 7.4 *A virtual site visit*

The growth of broadband and digital photography have enabled a range of new site presentations to be developed. One of the most exciting is the virtual tour which lets people explore sites remotely and study relationships between features. Increasingly such sites are interactive with 'visitors' able to decide the depth and level they want to investigate to. In this example created by Clive Ruggles you navigate around Avebury and see (on photos) the views you would actually see. The package from ADS (▶ p. 305) enables you to create your own walkabout – this is likely to become a popular coursework option.

COMMUNICATING ARCHAEOLOGICAL KNOWLEDGE

Before 1990, most archaeological knowledge was communicated via lectures, museum galleries and the printed word. While these are familiar mediums, it is expensive to produce reports and books and there is often a considerable timelag before new ideas and discoveries are widely disseminated.

Increasing diversity reflects the differing audiences for archaeology and the way their requirements vary. Consider how your requirements of a site or museum might differ from those of a researcher or of a class of 5 year olds. As a result, what is a perfectly adequate mode of communication for one person may be inaccessible or too shallow for another. The contrast between a specialist pottery report and an episode of Time Team illustrates this point well.

This is because archaeological reports follow a scientific format. A series of experts present evidence as accurately and precisely as they can. There is often only limited interpretation and rarely speculation. Often only a few hundred are printed and increasingly they are owned by developers. This makes them inaccessible to a general readership. However, they are essential reading to others in the same field who rely on them to provide data for them to compare findings and detect patterns.

Cutting edge technology such as virtual reality displays and GIS systems (◀ p. 9) are still expensive but digital photography and basic websites are now accessible to most people. This has enabled a much wider range of people to produce and disseminate archaeological information. In the future 'electronic' site reports may enable people to interrogate data at very different levels.

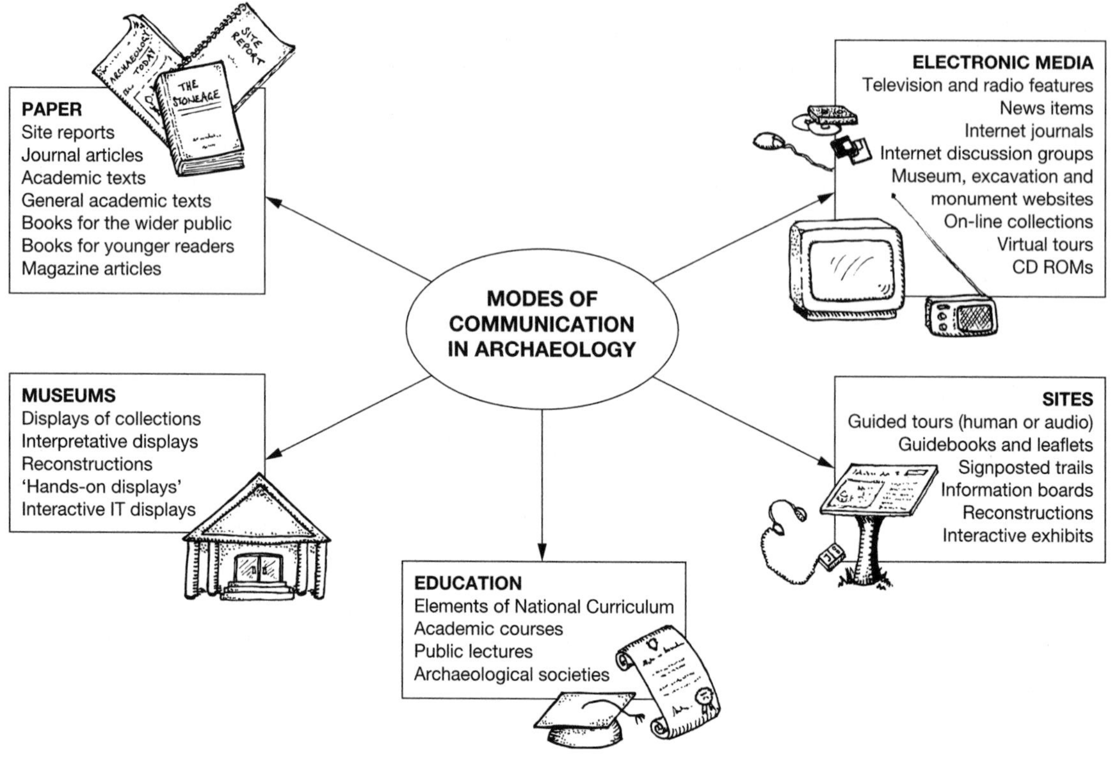

Figure 7.6 *The communication of archaeological information*

KEY SKILL

Assessing modes of communication using the 4 As

Assessing particular modes of communication and display is usually done in relation to specific case studies, for example 'How might archaeologists best communicate the results of a particular excavation?' or 'How could a specific site be better presented to the public?'

In order to address these issues you should consider the following criteria:

- *Audience*: who is it for and what might they hope to get from it?
- *Accessibility*: does its design and location enable it to reach its intended audience(s)?
- *Adequacy*: is it useful for that audience?
- *Alternatives*: would another mode of communication be more effective?

Start by considering the list of possible modes from Figure 7.6. Then select several examples such as a local museum display, a TV programme or a site report. Copy out the grid below on a large sheet of paper and complete it, using yourself as a student on your particular course as the intended audience. Pay particular attention to your reason for using the sources and why it was useful or not.

Examples	*Audience*	*Accessibility*	*Adequacy*	*Alternatives*
	Research for my essays on . . .	Could you get it and understand it?	How did it meet your needs or was it of limited use to you?	Might an alternative mode have worked better?
Local museum				
A local site				
Site report on X				
An academic text				
A website				
A guidebook				

Now repeat the exercise for the same examples but considering a different audience. For example a tourist visiting the area or a primary school group. You should start to gain an awareness of the difficulties of meeting diverse needs within one mode of communication. You could rate the different sites you have visited on your course.

Good examples of several categories are:

- Individual enthusiasts: Stone Pages:
  - http://www.stonepages.com/
- Groups of enthusiasts: the Megalithic Society:
  - http://www.stonehenge-avebury.net/
- University projects: Gardoms Edge
  - http://www.shef.ac.uk/~geap/
- International research projects: Catal Huyuk:
  - http://catal.arch.cam.ac.uk/catal/catal.html
- Museums: National Museums of Scotland at
  - http://www.nms.ac.uk/

The time between recording and presenting to an audience is much reduced. Many excavations now offer daily diaries or webcams on their websites. The numbers visiting most site websites far exceed the numbers of site reports sold. Moreover, the audience is now global rather than largely national.

Hyperlinks embedded in text offer the chance to satisfy more than one audience at the same time. A basic account can be supplemented by detailed discussion in linked documents. Similarly, this can be built into maps and site plans (point and click options) as at Kilmartin.

- http://www.kilmartin.org/

Not only do digital images readily offer high quality colour photographs where their use was previously rationed. They can go beyond the limitations of two-dimensional illustration on A3 paper. Maps and plans can be presented at a larger scale and three-dimensional modelling is possible as at Wroxeter.

- http://www.bufau.bham.ac.uk/newsite/Projects/BT/default.htm

The online journal *Internet Archaeology* is exploring the wider potential of the internet for academic archaeological publishing.

- http://intarch.ac.uk/

Finally you can discuss ideas and seek help from fellow archaeologists through discussion groups such as the CBA's lists for archaeologists and teachers.

- http://www.jiscmail.ac.uk/lists/britarch.html

Problems with using the internet for research

There are, of course, some drawbacks to the new technology. The sheer volume of material available means that you have to be selective but it is often difficult to immediately see what might be relevant. A particular problem for students is that referencing conventions are not applied to the same degree as in printed material. It is often hard to tell what is opinion, fantasy or based on evidence. Often there is no way of checking. If you cite internet sources in essays at undergraduate level, be sure to appraise them thoroughly. A further problem is plagiarism. It is easy to cut and paste someone else's work into your own. Resist this temptation. If you are caught, the penalties can be severe.

Applying communication issues on your course

By now you will appreciate how hard it is to successfully communicate in ways that reach all possible audiences. Some sources will have clearly targeted particular audiences. Others, such as sites or museums, will probably have changed their methods to reach wider audiences. This may have involved diversifying the types of presentation or a wholesale change in the way collections or a site are displayed. If you wished to follow up this topic as a major project on a particular site you should be able to find one of their staff who can explain their thinking on this.

KEY SITE

Newgrange

This massive passage grave was constructed around 3200BC. It measures some 90m in diameter and features a light box above the entrance and a sinuous 19m passage leading to the central chambers. These contained burials and cremations and some of the most important rock art in Europe (▶ p. 174). Newgrange illustrates some of the problems faced by Stonehenge. During excavation in the 1960s the decision was taken to reconstruct the monument to enable visitors to appreciate its original features. The front of the monument was faced with quartz which petrology showed had come from the Wicklow Mountains, a long boat journey to the south, while much of the granite came from the Mountains of Mourne to the north. The 19 metre passage was also realigned to allow the sun to shine through the famous lightbox and penetrate the inner chamber on the winter solstice.

Antiquarian accounts, experiments and engineering principles were used to determine the final shape of the mound. The result has been much criticised. The façade would probably fall down without the concrete holding it in place while the peppering of the quartz with granite pebbles is said to make it look like a cheesecake.

A major interpretation centre was built a short distance away with buses used to transport tourists to the tomb and control numbers. Its massive popularity means visits often have to be booked ahead and a lottery system used to select those to witness the solstice. While many have criticised the 'reconstruction' of Newgrange it serves as a tourist 'honeypot' which reduces pressure on the other major tombs and other monuments in the Boyne Valley. These include the equally large passage tombs at Dowth and Knowth which are currently being excavated.

- http://knowth.powernet.co.uk/neolithic-religion-status.htm

Figure 7.7 *Newgrange entrance showing the reconstructed facade*

KEY STUDY

The 'reconstructed' Anglo-Saxon village of West Stow

West Stow in Suffolk uses a variety of different means to present an excavated and recorded site to the public.

Excavation of this site revealed traces of a number of features including rectangular sunken featured buildings (SFBs), still commonly called grubenhauser. The materials used had not survived in the sandy local soil but postholes, pits and beam slots were preserved, as were a range of inorganic artefacts and animal bones. The site report catalogues and interprets the finds for the archaeological profession. It also discusses the problem of interpreting the above ground structure of the buildings.

Figure 7.8 *An excavated grubenhaus at Lechlade (▶ p. 282)*

Rectangular pits with domestic rubbish are common on early Anglo-Saxon sites. These grubenhauser had previously been interpreted as pit dwellings. In part this reflected the view amongst classically influenced archaeologists that their inhabitants really were barbaric. With increasing knowledge of Anglo-Saxon carpentry and construction techniques, experimental archaeology has developed alternative models. At West Stow several versions were constructed over the excavated features. It is now thought likely that grubenhauser had suspended floors with the rubbish entering the pit after the building's abandonment.

There is also a debate about the internal decoration and use of buildings. The site, which includes a display centre through which visitors enter a recreation of the settlement, addresses these issues and the problem of multiple audiences in a number of ways.

- Several different versions of the buildings were built on the sites of the originals so that visitors could enter each and judge them against the plans in guidebooks and the visitors centre.
- Artefacts are displayed in the visitors centre with pictures and reconstructions alongside to show how they were used.
- Activity areas allow visitors to see how artefacts might have been made.
- Demonstrations by experts in fields such as green woodworking are available to those interested.
- Video presentations show how Anglo-Saxons lived.
- Publications are available at a variety of levels ranging from infant school to professional.

KEY STUDY *cont.*

Figure 7.9 *Experimental Anglo-Saxon houses at West Stow*

A second approach is for you to consider how to present a site which may currently be inaccessible, or has little existing display material. This might typically include sites under excavation or a site that has no upstanding features. In these cases you need to not only draw on your knowledge of different types of communication and their suitability for particular audiences but understand some of the other issues facing museum and site management staff. These include:

- *funding*: the latest high-tech displays might be nice but how realistic is a budget to provide, maintain and secure them? What could be done on a lower budget?
- *impact*: modern interactive displays take up more room than traditional displays of exhibits. In a finite space, what would you remove from display? Visitor centres and display boards may be useful, but will they ruin the visual impact of a site?
- *accuracy*: reconstructions are popular with the public but may be misleading. It may be possible to reconstruct the wooden handle of an iron tool with a reasonable degree of accuracy but rebuilding a Neolithic structure from a mass of postholes will be more problematic. Is it better to show how something was used, even if it may be inaccurate, or provide the evidence and ask people (who are

not specialists) to try to make up their own minds? Two approaches can be found at:

- http://www.archaeolink.co.uk/home.htm
- http://www.history.maelmin.ukf.net/

The world heritage site at Lascaux provides a good example of what can be done with a large budget. The very presence of visitors in the caves was damaging the delicate Palaeolithic wall-paintings there. The response has been to close the cave but to construct a copy nearby for visitors whilst producing an interactive website to enable virtual exploration of the real thing.

- http://www.culture.fr/culture/arcnat/lascaux/fr/p

Figure 7.11 *The Romans were small people*

In order to be commercially successful many ventures have to try and combine education and entertainment. At Archaeolink small children dig in a sandpit for artefacts while adults have a choice of excavated remains, reconstructions, workshops, books and New Age presentations. Those in between can dress up as Romans and throw javelins.

KEY TASK

Outlining a presentation of a site or landscape

Consider a site or a landscape that contains archaeological remains with which you are familiar.

a) Briefly describe the site and outline the types of evidence available. (200 words)
b) Produce a visual presentation to show how it could best be presented to visitors to the area. (800 words)

Your account should include a justification of your selection of key methods of communication and use sketches, diagrams and plans where appropriate to illustrate it. Advertisements or a Powerpoint presentation are alternatives. Remember to consider the 4 As.

This activity offers the chance to meet some national key skill communication objectives at level 3.

Part Two
Studying Themes in Archaeology

The content of archaeology courses can be arranged in many ways. All include methods to some extent. Beyond this they are selective in their areas of archaeological knowledge. Some focus on particular parts of the world, following continuity and change over time, e.g. 'British prehistory'. Others may focus on change but take a whole world perspective, with topics such as 'human origins' or 'the spread of farming'. Some concentrate on particular cultures in more limited periods such as 'the classical world' while others, including A Level, are organised around themes. Whichever course you take you will need to use case studies. In fact the same case studies might be relevant to all these courses (p. xxix). For example, the Iron Age settlement at Hengistbury Head could be used to study:

- the emergence of elites and trade in Iron Age Britain
- the development of towns and commercial trade
- the influence of the Roman Empire
- settlement function, exchange and manufacturing themes.

We have chosen to organise this section thematically partly because it mirrors the A Level syllabus and partly because an understanding of the themes is more transferable. A study of Maya temples may not be immediately useful to a student studying Neolithic Britain and vice versa, but an introduction to concepts of religion and ritual will be useful to both. We have included content, but its function is to illustrate. It may well be in just the right size chunks to put into essays but it is there to provide examples of archaeological ideas and debates.

Chapter 8

Religion and Ritual

YOUR GOALS

You need to understand

- the key concepts drawn from sociology and anthropology that archaeologists use to help define and explain past beliefs and rituals
- the techniques and sources used to interpret evidence of religious belief and practices
- case studies from your chosen period or area of study, which illustrate religion and ritual
- how to use evidence to support longer pieces of writing.

For periods where there are written sources such as Ancient Greece or medieval Europe, archaeologists have tended to use texts as the means to interpret and understand past belief systems. For cultures where there are no written sources, many archaeologists have held the view that uncovering the nature of past religious belief from material remains is beyond their ability. In the 1950s Hawkes argued that there was a hierarchy of inferences which archaeologists could make from their sources. Using material remains they could say a great deal about technology and economics, much less about society and very little about belief. How can you understand thoughts from bones, sherds and postholes? His argument has become known as Hawkes' ladder of inference.

Since the 1960s there has been an explosion of interest amongst the general public in prehistoric religions. The reluctance of many archaeologists to discuss religion left a gap that was filled by a range of other explanations, which fed on public interest in ancient monuments. Often these involved projecting current concerns onto evidence from the past. The most famous was Von Däniken's depiction of God as an astronaut. This view attributed great monuments from the past to aliens. For example, the Nazca lines in Peru became alien landing strips. More recently a New Age version of prehistory has linked together sites from various periods as evidence of a universal cult of an earth goddess. Partly in response, archaeologists have borrowed a battery of analytical techniques and concepts from other disciplines including ethnography, sociology and critical theory to explore religion and ritual. It is now a core element of study for many periods. A particularly influential idea has been the fact that for many cultures religion cannot neatly be

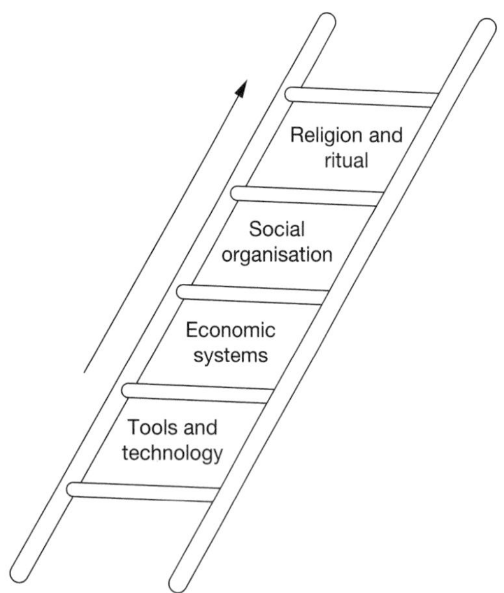

Figure 8.0 *Hawkes' Ladder of Inference (after Hawkes 1954). The higher one goes up the ladder the harder it is to make inferences on the basis of archaeological evidence*

Figure 8.1 *Minoan snake goddess or Potmia Theron (Mistress of the Beasts)*

This idol found in a hidden cist at Knossos with other cult objects may represent a female deity. Some have claimed she is evidence of a mother goddess religion. (c. 1600BC).

separated from social organisation or even economics. It influences the way people behave and therefore leaves traces in their material culture.

The analytical power of computers is increasingly enlisted in searching for patterns, particularly in the disposal of artefacts and the siting of monuments. Use of these techniques has in turn led to criticism of written sources for what they omit and because they are often ambivalent. Archaeology may have much to offer the study of religion in the classical period after all.

In this chapter we have tried to explain some of the more unfamiliar concepts which archaeologists have adopted. We have also provided examples of the methods and insights used by archaeologists to tease out clues about belief and ritual from material remains. To illustrate the contribution of archaeology in the past we have included overviews of religion and ritual in later British and Irish prehistory and also the Roman Empire.

WHAT IS RELIGION?

You are most likely to be familiar with modern world religions. These are atypical. Christianity, Judaism and Islam, for example, are all **monotheistic** (one god) religions which provide codes of conduct for life, have permanent religious institutions and offer life after death to believers. There have been religions that have differed on each of these points. At the other end of the scale from the **states** (▶ p. 268), which have promoted world religions, are hunter-gatherer societies. They tend to see themselves as part of, rather than in control of, nature and their religion may be simply one part of their daily life rather than something done on special occasions. There is far more variety in those small-scale societies which survive today than in world religions. They may provide better insights into the wealth of lost belief systems. After all humans have spent most of history hunting and foraging for food rather than growing it.

Giddens (1989) provides a useful, broad definition of religion as: 'a set of symbols, invoking feelings of reverence or awe . . . linked to rituals or ceremonials practised by a community of believers'. These symbols may be of gods and goddesses, ancestral or nature spirits, or impersonal powers. Rituals can consist of prayers, songs, dances, feasting, drug taking, offerings and sacrifices. People often use them to try to influence supernatural powers and beings to their advantage and to deal with problems that cannot be solved through the application of technology. However, there are some religions without objects of worship. In Confucianism and Taoism, for example, the individual attempts to attain a higher level through correctly following specified principles.

WHAT IS THE FUNCTION OF RELIGION?

Archaeologists are more interested in how religion affected the people practising it rather than whether a particular religion accomplished what its believers hoped. All religions cater to basic human social and psychological needs. Some of these, such as the need to explain what happens when people die, may be universal if we are correct in our interpretation of the archaeological evidence for burial and associated activities from the last 40,000 years. Common functions include:

- Explaining the unknown in order to provide meaning and reduce anxiety. A belief in a divine force can provide hope and comfort in difficult times. The death of a family member may be easier to cope with if they are believed to exist beyond death. Ritual at a time of crisis may give people the confidence to cope with problems, for example, praying before a battle.

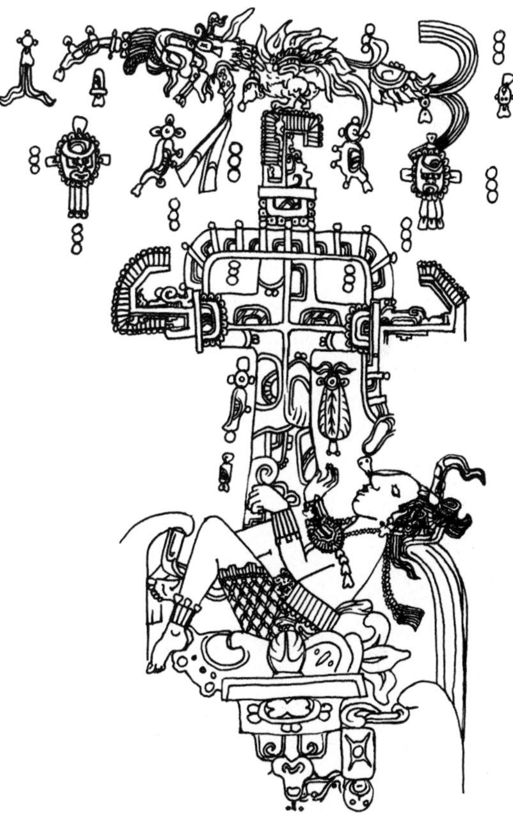

Figure 8.2 *Drawing of the Wakah Kan or 'Raised up sky' from Palenque*

This 'world tree' linked the underworld, the realm of the living and the sky. The king would dress in the image of the Wakah Kan to emphasise the special relationship between the ruler and the spirit world. He provided a conduit for supernatural powers. (The Stela on p. 159 symbolises this too). King Pacal is shown falling into the jaws of the earth monster. Underneath is an altar with a bowl of blood sacrifices burning and thus opening up a portal into another world. The smoking axe in Pacal's forehead is a mark of his divinity and he wears a jade net skirt which reveals that at his moment of death he had become the 'Maize God'. Above him the cross branch of the tree represents the double-headed 'vision serpent' of life and death. This sceptre of power is depicted on altars being handed on from one ruler to the next rather like a relay baton. Von Däniken considered the Wakah Kan was evidence of space travel with the top as the front of the alien craft.

KEY SITE

The Temple of Karnak at Luxor

In Egypt, Amun's great temple of Karnak, through the physical symbolism of the building, offers key insights into the creation myth, the role of the priesthood and the nature of rituals. Every pharaoh felt bound to leave his mark on this temple by lavish construction works of his own such that over time it extended over an area that would encompass more than a dozen medieval cathedrals.

The layout of Karnak was designed as a microcosm of the world at the time of its creation by the god Amun. Its high walls and huge gates or 'pylons' excluded ordinary people. Only priests could enter the temple and they, like all other things dedicated to Amun, had to be pure and clean. They shaved off all their body hair, bathed daily in the Sacred Lake in the heart of the temple and dressed in spotless robes. Rituals depicted in hieroglyphics include the journey of Amun's sacred boat from Karnak to Luxor with attendants singing and dancing. The desire for the maintenance of order is also featured symbolically in the temple reliefs. Battle scenes show foreigners as disorderly mobs until they have been conquered and brought within the civilising influence of Egypt. Then they are shown in neat lines. In the nearby Luxor Temple this contrast is very clear: the Egyptian infantry and chariots at the Battle of Kadesh are immaculately organised in geometric squads while the opposing Hittites are in total disarray.

Figure 8.3 *Bust of Ramesses II at Luxor. Many rulers have used statuary and images of themselves in ritual places to emphasise their special links with the gods and to reinforce their claim to power*

The myth at the heart of the temple is that of the original creation of the world from the waters of chaos. The 'Hypostyle Hall' represented the 'Swamp of Creation' with its forest of columns whose capitals were carved in the shape of plants such as papyrus. Amun came into being in this chaos. He lifted himself out of the water and masturbated himself to produce the two constituent elements of all life: wet and dry. From this act comes the first land in the form of the 'primeval mound' (the temple) and then the sky and later the first inhabitants of that Egyptian 'Eden': Isis and Osiris. In the hidden depths of the temple was the cult statue of Amun. The exact nature of the statue is much disputed due to the damage inflicted on the portraits of Amun in antiquity and the desire of previous generations of scholars to play down the sexual nature of Egyptian iconography. For the Egyptians this statue was a house for the god, a place where he could take up residence to interact with mortals. Through his divine presence it became 'alive' in a very real sense. The priests would

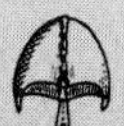

KEY SITE *cont.*

The Temple of Karnak at Luxor

anoint the statue, dress it and entertain it each day as they would the pharaoh himself. One relief shows a group of females playing musical instruments while others clap rhythmically. They are led by a woman who is identified by the hieroglyphs as 'the Hand of God'. Many scholars believe that the statue of Amun was shown in a state of sexual excitement grasping his erect penis and that the reliefs are picturing a ritual re-enactment of the original moment of creation induced by the rhythmic music and hand clapping. The central question here is whether the ritual was essentially a metaphorical act that happened in people's minds or whether it had some sort of physical reality enacted by the chief priest of the temple or by the pharaoh himself once a year.

Figure 8.4 *Entrance to the Temple of Karnak. The massive first pylons (gates) completely obscure the religious areas inside, while mythical creatures lining the approach signify the ritual nature of the site*

- http://www.memphis.edu/egypt/luxortm.htm
- Strudwick and Strudwick 1989
- http://www-ceg.ceg.uiuc.edu/~haggag/luxor.html

- Establishing rules and models of behaviour. Most religions put divine power behind definitions of what is right and wrong. They may tell believers the 'right' way to live. Religion can be used to enforce obedience to a ruler (e.g. medieval kings) or even to justify rebellion.
- The maintenance of social solidarity was seen as the primary function of religion by the sociologist Durkheim. His study of **totemism** (▶ p. 161) amongst Australian aboriginal societies suggested that what was being worshipped represented society and its values. By holding collective ceremonies people reinforce their sense of togetherness and social cohesion.
- Transmitting memory, especially in non-literate societies, by the learning of oral traditions and through repetitive rituals. The classic example of this is the telling of creation myths.

Myths are explanatory narratives that rationalise religious beliefs and practices. Myths invariably are full of accounts of the doings of various supernatural beings and hence serve to reinforce belief in them. The building of religious monuments can literally set collective memories in stone.

Detecting evidence of past beliefs and practices

When examining material evidence a standing joke amongst archaeologists has been the idea that anything that can't immediately be explained must be ritual. While there has been some overenthusiasm in what is still a relatively new area of archaeological interpretation, most studies are based on far more than an odd shaped building or one figurine. Egyptologists have the advantage of the Book of the Dead to draw on but for other cultures different approaches are required. Analogies drawn from ethnography have been particularly useful. Not for direct parallels so much as to demonstrate a range of possible options and influences and to prevent simplistic interpretation. It may appear common sense that a burial with many goods was that of a wealthy person, yet ethnography has provided examples where this is not the case. Studies have often focused on repeated patterns. These include symbols that recur in similar places or on specific types of artefact; non-random patterns of deposition of particular artefacts or animal remains and the distribution of deposits and monuments across the landscape. The treatment of boundaries in the past has also been a focus of many studies.

WHAT KINDS OF RELIGION WERE THERE?

Most known religions include a belief in supernatural beings and forces through whom appeals for aid may be directed. For convenience we may divide these into three categories: deities, ancestral spirits and nature spirits. While some societies have only believed in one of these categories, it has been common for belief in several or all of them to co-exist, for example belief in evil spirits in medieval Europe.

Major deities

Gods and goddesses are great and remote beings who are usually seen as controlling the universe. If several are recognised (**polytheistic**) each often

Figure 8.5 *Pharaoh as Horus at Edfu*

Kings were the earthly embodiment of the god Horus. Horus, the son of Isis was a protector god who destroyed evil. When a king died he became the god Osiris and the new king became Horus. As Horus he could mediate between men and gods. Note the double crown worn by the falcon is the same as the falcon-man in the background. All pharaohs had a 'Horus name' as part of their title, in order to identify them with the deity.

KEY STUDY

Copan

The acropolis of Copan in Honduras exemplifies the way in which religious beliefs can be embodied in material culture. The layout of the city reflects the cosmology of the Maya in a general sense. Some special buildings have more particular symbolic meaning. The temple pyramids symbolised mountains, the surface of the plaza the waters. Temple interiors were caves or magic portals to the world of the supernatural and **stelae** were symbolic world trees. **Glyphs** (carved reliefs), architecture, burial and iconography all help piece together the beliefs and rituals of the Maya.

For example, at the prominent structure 22, the entrance to the temple was carved to look like a mask of the earth monster. The fragments remaining include the stone fangs of the monster's lower jaw. Entering here, watched by his people below, the king symbolically died and was reborn when he emerged. He would be wearing an elaborate costume of feathers, jaguar fur and heavy ornaments of jade when he confronted the gods and his ancestors inside the temple. Weak from days of fasting and blood loss through sacrifices, he may well have been in an altered state of consciousness when he appeared before the inner portal. This has a row of stone skulls as its bottom step and above it arches a writhing two-headed serpent in whose coils swirl the figures of his ancestors and which is supported at each end by a skybearer god. Glyphs depict maize plants and remind us that stone, water and vegetation collectively suggest the other function of the temple as 'the mountain of sustenance'.

- Schele and Miller 1986

Figure 8.6 *View from the acropolis at Copan towards the ballcourt*

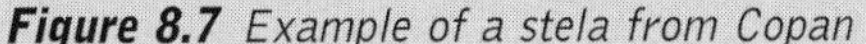

Figure 8.7 *Example of a stela from Copan*

Stelae were stone statues of the Kings but also symbolic world trees (◀ p. 155). They depicted the king bridging upper and lower worlds. The King's authority stemmed from his power to intercede with gods and ancestors on behalf of the people.

has charge of a particular part of the universe. Hinduism, the oldest major world religion, is around 6,000 years old and is polytheistic. Its contemporaries included the gods of Ancient Greece: Zeus was the lord of the sky, Poseidon was the ruler of the sea and Hades was the lord of the underworld and ruler of the dead. In addition to these three brothers there were many other deities of both sexes. Each embodied characteristics seen as typical of male and female roles; each was concerned with specific aspects of life and the workings of the world, or indeed universe. Pantheons or collections of gods and goddesses, such as those of the Greeks, were also common in non-western states such as Egypt or the Maya. Specific deities are identified from repeated images on buildings or artefacts ranging from mosaics to statues.

Belief in gods, goddesses or both, often seemed to parallel what we know of the gender relationships between men and women in everyday life. In societies where women have less power than men, the nature of 'god' is defined in masculine terms. This is commonest in societies where the economy is based upon herding animals or on intensive agriculture, which would have been largely male activities. In such societies men may often have been seen as rather distant authority figures to their children. Goddesses, on the other hand, appear more often in societies where women make the major contribution to the economy, enjoy some measure of equality with men and in which men are more involved in the lives of their children. Such societies often depend on horticulture or specialised craft production, which is done by women. Evidence from Catal Huyuk (Turkey) and Karanovo (Bulgaria) suggests that pioneer agricultural societies venerated female roles. The masculine god that replaced various goddess cults amongst the Hebrews during the late 2nd millennium BC may have helped establish gender relationships in which women have traditionally been expected to submit to the rule of men. This in turn shaped Jewish, Christian and Islamic society. Gimbutas (1991) took up this theme in her book *The Civilisation of the Goddess* and argued that world religions developed to legitimise the emergence of patriarchal, warlike societies in the Bronze Age.

Ancestral spirits

A belief in ancestral spirits has its origins in the widespread idea that human beings are made up of two parts: the body and some kind of vital spirit, which in Mesoamerica for example resides in the blood. For example the Maya Indians have always maintained that each person had a 'spirit-companion' that could leave the body and move around during sleep. The 'spirit-companion' was envisaged as an animal. One inscription tells us that 'the watery jaguar is the "way" of the Lord (King) of Seibal'. Given such a concept, it is only a small step to believe that the spirit could be freed by death from the body and have a continued existence. It has something in common with recent accounts of 'out of body experiences'.

Where people do believe in ancestral spirits, they are frequently seen as retaining an active interest and even membership in society. For example the 'ghost ancestors' of the Wape might either provide or withhold meat from their living descendants. Like living persons, ancestral spirits may be well or badly disposed towards the living, but they are often capricious and unpredictable, hence the need to appease them with offerings.

Whatever their involvement in particular past societies, belief in ancestral spirits provided a strong sense of continuity. These beliefs seem to have been particularly strong amongst early farming communities. Ancestors may have linked past, present and future generations and ownership of particular land.

Animism

One of the most common sets of beliefs about the supernatural world is usually referred to as animism. This centres on the idea that the living share the physical and spiritual world with all

KEY TERM

Propitiation

Making offerings or sacrifices to a spirit or deity. The widespread burials of human and animal remains in grain pits, as at Danebury, or Danish Bogs are usually interpreted as such offerings.

sorts of spirits. Animals, plants and people may all have their own individual spirits, as may springs, mountains, or other natural features.

People who believe in animism are inclined to see themselves as being part of nature rather than superior to it. This includes most hunter-gatherers, as well as those food-producing people who see little difference between a human life and that of any growing plant. Gods and goddesses may have created the world and perhaps provided the main physical fabric of that world but it is spirits to whom one turns for the ordinary needs of daily life and whom the ordinary hunter may meet during the hunt or while out roaming the woods. Many Native Americans subscribed to this view of the world and would pray to the spirits of their 'brothers and sisters' the animals for success in the hunt. They asked animals to give up their lives for the good of people and apologised to them when they were actually caught. The Hollywood version of this can be seen at the start of the film *Last of the Mohicans*.

Totemism is a label sometimes attached to animistic forms of religion. Here animals or plants with special powers may be worshipped or there may be complex rules about their treatment.

Animatism

Some societies believe in a supernatural power that exists independently of deities and spirits. The people of Melanesia, for example, believe that 'mana' exists as a force inherent in all objects. In itself it is not physical but it can be revealed through its physical effects. When a warrior experiences success in battle this will not be as a result of his own strength but directly attributable to the 'mana' carried with him in the form of an amulet that hangs around his neck. In much the same way, in farming societies an individual may know a great deal about the right way to treat plants, about soil conditions and the correct time for sowing and harvesting, but still be dependent on 'mana' for the success of his crop. He may build a simple altar for this power at the end of the field, as often seen in the rice fields of Bali. If the crop is good, it is a sign that the farmer has in some way acquired the necessary 'mana'. The possession of objects containing such power may provide the owner with confidence. For example, in going into battle. Confidence might then lead to fearlessness and victory. This would then 'prove' the power of the 'mana'. The Sioux followers of the Ghost Dance cult provide a less successful example. They believed their magical shirts would stop bullets in their final conflict with the US army in the late nineteenth century.

Belief in magic has some similarities with animatism. Magic involves individuals influencing events through potions or chanting. It can also involve divination, astrology and curses such as those found on the walls of Pompeii. The wearing of charms to bring good fortune and ward off evil combines elements of magic and animatism. It has survived in a watered down way in societies which have been Christian for many centuries.

- Havilland 1994

RELIGIOUS CHANGE

Comparative studies over long periods often reveal changes in the evidence for religion. This can be useful as the contrasts often suggest much about the nature of beliefs. The overlap between paganism and Christianity revealed in the changing grave goods and orientation of bodies from

Anglo-Saxon cemeteries such as Lechlade (▶ p. 282) are well known. Many Christian churches were deliberately built on earlier pagan sites, most spectacularly at Knowlton and La Hougue Bie on Jersey. The continuing power and importance of earlier beliefs can also be seen in the reuse of some religious sites. The nature of the religious changes of the reformation can be seen in the study of structural and decorative changes in churches. This is most evident when medieval wall-paintings are revealed under Puritan whitewash as at Baunton.

RITUAL ACTIVITY

Much of the value of religion comes from religious activities. These can range from daily rituals to great cyclical events from Easter to the Egyptian festivals of Opet or Sed. Participation in ceremonies enables people to relate to higher forces; it is religion in action. Ritual involves repeated performance of religious activities, usually at a particular place. It can reinforce the social bonds of a group and reduce tensions. Participants can feel a wave of reassurance, security and even ecstasy and a sense of closeness. Although the rituals and practices vary considerably, even those rites that seem to us the most bizarrely exotic can be shown to serve the same basic social and psychological function. Anthropologists have classified several different types of ritual, a major division being between **'rites of passage'** and **'rites of intensification'**.

Rites of passage

Rites of passage are ceremonies to mark crucial stages in the life cycle of the individual. These

Figure 8.8 *Scene from Agia Triada sarcophagus*

This painting on plaster covering a stone sarcophagus includes many aspects of Minoan funerary ritual. On the reverse a bull is strapped down for sacrifice by priestesses. Here a priestess pours liquid into a crater on an altar. This may be sacrificial blood or water or wine for lustration (bathing) of the altar or for purification rites. Another woman brings further liquid while a man plays a lyre. Birds wait for the gods, perhaps called by the lyre. To the right one of several men carries offerings of animals to a male priest.

might include birth, puberty, marriage, parenthood, and advancement to a higher class, occupational specialisation and death. Anthropological analysis of ceremonies, which help individuals through these potential crisis points, has often identified three stages: *separation*, *transition*, and *incorporation*. The individual would first be ritually removed from the society as a whole, then isolated for a **liminal** period and finally returned to society with a new status.

Van Gennep (1909) observed this pattern amongst Australian aborigines. When boys were to be initiated into manhood, elders led them to secret locations in the bush. Women cried and pretended to resist their removal while the boys pretended to be dead. In the bush the boys were taught the culture and stories of the tribe but also went through ceremonies including minor operations, such as circumcision, to teach them to bear pain. During this period the boys were 'dead' to the tribe. On returning they were welcomed with ceremonies, as though they had returned from the dead. The ceremony highlighted their new status as adults and reminded existing adults to act towards them in the appropriate ways. They skipped the ill-defined status of 'teenager', which causes problems in western society.

Similarly, female initiation rites prepared Mende girls in West Africa for womanhood. When they began to menstruate, they were removed from society to spend weeks, or even months in seclusion, usually on the grounds that their menstrual blood would 'contaminate' that with which it came into contact. There, they were trained by experienced women and change their appearance, setting aside the remnants of their childhood and undergoing surgery to remove their clitoris. They returned from their initiation as fully adult women in control of their sexuality and ready for marriage and childbearing.

Rites of intensification

Rites of intensification mark crises in the life of the group. Whatever the precise nature of the crisis (war, disease, etc) mass ceremonies are performed to mitigate the danger. Because these rites are carried out at a group rather than an individual level, the effect is to unite people in a common effort in such a way that fear or confusion are replaced by optimism and collective action and the natural balance is restored. The ancient Greeks routinely offered sacrifices before attempting hazardous undertakings, most famously the war against Troy. In regions where the seasons differ enough to force changes in human behaviour patterns, annual ceremonies develop. (Christmas replaced midwinter festivities dating back at least to the Iron Age.) Participation in such ceremonies cultivates the habit of reliance on supernatural forces through ritual activity, which can be activated in other stressful circumstances.

Funerary ceremonies

Funerals blur this neat distinction. The death of an individual can also be a crisis for an entire group, particularly if the group is small. The survivors must readjust, take up new roles and work out how to behave towards one another. They also need to reconcile themselves to the loss of someone to whom they were emotionally tied. This can take extreme forms. One of the **funerary rites** of the Melanesians was ritual cannibalism. This was felt to be a supreme act of reverence, love and devotion. Funerals offer the opportunity for outpourings of emotions without disrupting society. They can also emphasise that the values of the group outlive the individual. Burials are just one part of the funerary process but they are the most archaeologically visible. This does not mean they were the most important part.

Mortuary rituals

The treatment of the dead can overlap with funerals. The dead may be prepared in advance for funerals and their remains may need further ritual treatment afterwards. Much has been learnt from studying the treatment of the corpse, particularly its final disposal. This can take many forms:

Inhumation (burial) is a deliberate setting of the dead outside the world of the living. Where this occurs it may indicate attitudes to the dead. Christian cemeteries are placed apart from the living while some Upper Palaeolithic burials, as at Franchthi Cave, were kept close to the living. The orientation and position of the body – flexed, extended or contorted – may be significant. For example, foetal positions may indicate some belief in rebirth.

Cremation is more complex. Funeral pyres can leave several kilos of charred bones. The fire may destroy the body and release the spirit but these remains may have to be dealt with in a secondary ceremony. This can involve burial.

Excarnation is also likely to be part of a process. It involves exposing the body for scavengers and the decay process to clean the flesh from the bones. For example Parsees practise 'Sky burial' today. Cleaned bones may be used in other rites or stored in an ossuary.

Mummification is often an elaborate process, which can involve removing some parts of the body. It may be believed that the body can be used by the person's spirit in another world or the future. The use of certain types of coffin or funeral vaults that may slow down natural decay processes may reflect similar beliefs.

Sometimes the dead are hard to find. This may be because they are totally consumed. The Yanomano grind the cremated remains of their dead to a powder that they then drink. The dead thus remain in the living. There are also ethnographic examples of bones of ancestors being worn by their descendants.

Funerary monuments and grave goods

Both of these categories may tell us more about the mourners and society than they do about their

Figure 8.9 *Late Minoan sarcophagus*

These ceramic vessels, large enough to hold a crouched body, were used to bury wealthy Cretans. They are called 'bathtub style' and even include a plughole.

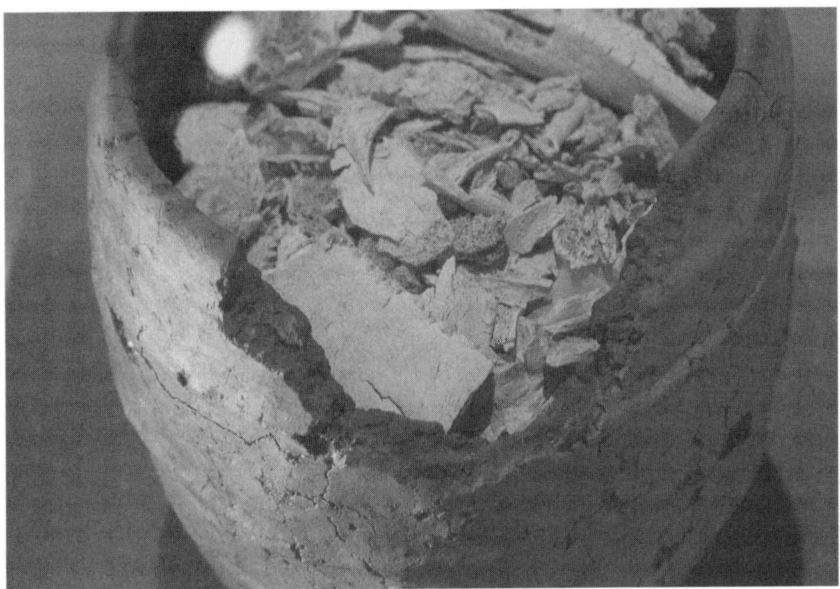

Figure 8.10 *Cremation in Bronze Age funerary urn*

Unlike modern crematoria, funeral pyres could not usually reach sufficient temperatures to reduce bodies to ash. The larger chunks of bone along with charred grave goods were often collected and placed in vessels for burial. Sufficient bone may survive to allow identification and even DNA testing.

Figure 8.11 *A pot being excavated from grave 5 at Empingham (◀ p. 32). Were grave goods such as these the possessions of the dead, offerings to them or the gods, or food for their journey to an afterworld?*

Figure 8.12 *The Pyramids. Probably the best known funerary monuments in the world*

religious beliefs (▶ Chapter 11). However, elaborately decorated tombs such as those in the Valley of the Kings or the reliefs carved on Maya tombs may provide detailed information about both beliefs and rituals.

Gravestones provide many insights for a variety of cultures, not least about the setting aside of respected areas for the dead. Goods buried with the body or which were consumed in a funeral pyre are suggestive of an afterlife but this is not necessarily the case. Goods may be placed in the grave by mourners as tokens of affection or because they belonged to the deceased and are considered unlucky or taboo. Tools used to prepare the dead, such as razors or tweezers, may fall into this category. There may also be important offerings of food or organic materials that have not survived. The absence of grave goods doesn't mean that there was no belief in an afterlife. It may suggest a belief in an afterlife where people are equal and provided for or it may reflect an idealised picture of society that masks differences in wealth.

IDENTIFYING RITUAL AND RITUAL SITES

Most essays on this topic rarely stray from Renfrew and Bahn's list of indicators. In most cases their key points – focus of attention, boundary zones, symbols or images of the deity, and participation and offerings – can be ticked off. Tombs and temples are obvious places but one can also apply the list to monuments such as shrines and ghats.

However, there may be exceptions. Their indicators work best for communal rather than individual ritual acts, many of which leave no traces. They also rely on there being a distinct area set aside. Even if it is in a dwelling special zones can be identified. For example, the altar or 'lararium' mounted on the wall of Roman houses. However, there are societies today where there is no clear demarcation between ritual and the everyday. The layout and structure of houses as far apart as Bali and the Amazon jungle are determined by religious beliefs. Their orientation, where

Figure 8.13 *Washing facilities at a mosque in Cyprus*

In many religions entry into religious sites is marked by ritual. This may mark a transition from the 'profane' everyday world to a 'sacred' enclosure or building. Ritual washing with its connotations of purity is a good example of this. This kind of categorisation into pure/impure and sacred/profane can sometimes be discerned through archaeology, for instance where special deposits are placed at thresholds or entrances.

Figure 8.14 *Ritual monuments such as Rievaulx Abbey are found throughout Britain. A visit provides a good opportunity to test out the indicators of ritual sites*

domestic activities occur and the direction particular people can move around them are all subject to religious rules.

Identification of objects with known religious links such as **votives** provides powerful clues. These have sometimes helped identify otherwise ordinary features such as wells or springs as being the focus of rituals. Objects cannot be seen as ritual simply because they are exotic. However, the form and find sites of particular artefacts have been used to suggest ritual objects for most periods. In some cases the material is important. Amber is associated with burials from the Mesolithic onwards. Its colour of blood and fire with slight magnetic properties perhaps marked it out. Pottery vessels with particular designs such as beakers or grooved ware are often seen as ritual artefacts. In some cases these have been repaired but not sufficiently to make them useable.

KEY TASK

Identifying ritual sites

This is a simple exercise designed to get you using and applying the terminology of ritual. List Renfrew and Bahn's (1991) indicators of ritual sites down one side of a piece of paper. Visit two different local centres of religion such as a church or mosque and see how well the indicators apply. Jot down what you find against each point. Next take studies of two archaeological sites from your area of study and apply the same test. You may find that this gives you almost enough material to support an essay on the subject.

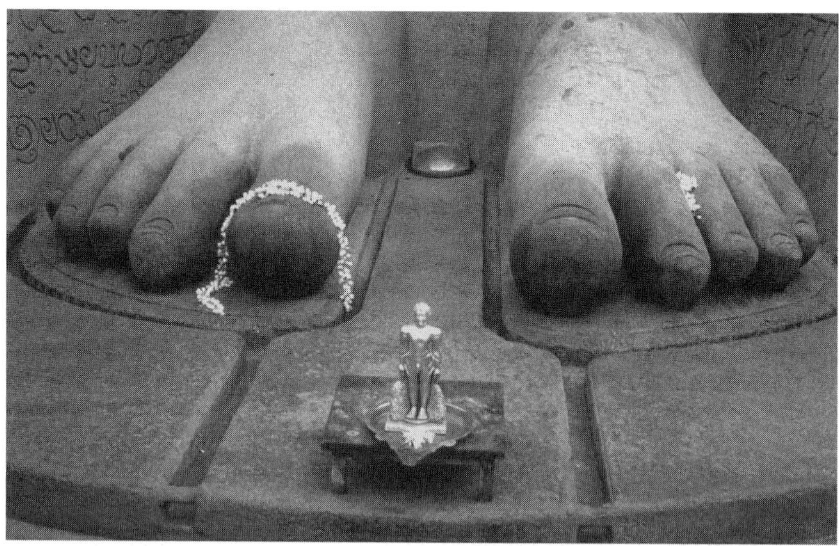

Figure 8.15 *Offerings to Lord Bahubali near Mysore*

The statue of Gomateshvara (Lord Bahubali) at Sravanabelagola is the worlds tallest Monolith, standing 17 metres high. Carved in 981 AD it commemorates a Jain ruler who gave up his kingdom to do penance in the forest for 1000 years. Visible for miles around, the statue is a major centre for Jain pilgrims, attracting over a million people to major events. The offerings and the extent of the pilgrimages would be very difficult to detect archaeologically. However, these activities are common in many religions and may have also occurred in prehistory.

Figurines and statues and non-functional artefacts such as copper axes are more ambiguous unless their context can link them with other indicators. Evidence of sacrifice – which literally means 'to make sacred' – might include deposits of valuable items, animals or even humans ritually murdered to invoke favours from deities.

Feasting falls into a similar category. The sharing of food is a powerful social unifier and is likely to feature in many rituals, but it can also be secular. The great halls of most castles were places of feasting for social rather than religious purposes. However, where there is other evidence, the remains of feasts can help identify ritual functions.

Evidence of other apparently waste material has also been used to suggest the embedding of ritual in the everyday. In particular Scottish and Danish middens (▶ p. 199) from the Mesolithic with their deposits of artefacts and human remains may not have been simply rubbish heaps.

Art and symbolism have also provided indications of ritual. Some, such as the example of Palenque are undoubtedly ritual, others are disputed. Palaeolithic cave art and Neolithic rock carvings have been particularly hotly debated. Other approaches to ritual symbolism have focused on repeated patterns including pairings such as left/right, male/female, in/out. This technique has been drawn from media and critical theory.

The sequential nature of the buildings at Palenque and Copan provides a good opportunity to study the continuity of ideas over time. Here one ritual structure would be ceremonially decommissioned and another structure, which was physically and iconographically related to its predecessor, would be built on top. The same rich

Figure 8.16 *Scene from the Yaxchilan Lintels*

This huge stone slab was originally placed above the entrance to a Mayan temple. It illustrates bloodletting or 'autosacrifice', an extreme form of participation in ritual. Blood, analogous with water, was vital for the fertility of crops and maintaining good relations with the gods. It repaid sacrifices made by the gods at the time of mankind's creation. Here Lady Xoc is perforating her tongue and Shield Jaguar is bleeding his penis. Blood is collected on paper to be burnt as an offering, smoke rising to the gods. They are rewarded by the appearance of an ancestor in the form of an armed warrior dressed as the 'vision serpent'.

symbolism in these temples is also found in graves below household patios, which connect commoners with the ancestors and the great cycle of heaven and earth.

LANDSCAPE RITUAL AND BELIEF

A combination of the development of landscape archaeology and a growing awareness from ethnography of the ritual significance of landscape has led archaeologists to look beyond burials and individual monuments. Studies from Australia, for example, reveal that to the aborigines the whole landscape had a mythical dimension and they in turn inscribed it with meaning, including the use of rock carvings.

RELIGIOUS SPECIALISTS

In all societies there are certain individuals especially skilled at contacting and influencing supernatural beings and manipulating supernatural

KEY STUDY

The Temple of the Inscriptions at Palenque

Figure 8.17 *The temple-pyramids at Palenque*

The stone temple-pyramids at Palenque, in north central Mexico advertised the special magical authority of the reigning king. The Temple of the Inscriptions has stucco figures on the outside showing the child king Chan-Bahlum (Snake-Jaguar) as a child inheriting power from his ancestors, including Pacal whose body lies in the tomb below. The child king has a prominent umbilical cord that links him to his famous ancestors and echoes another feature of the temple known as the 'psychoduct'. Other carvings show captives who were sacrificed when the new heir was presented to the people or later when the building itself was dedicated. The costumes worn by Pacal and his relatives are full of symbolic elements such as the net skirt that shows that Pacal personifies the 'First Father'.

Inside, a passage covered with inscriptions and a staircase lead down to the burial chamber of Pacal. The floor of the passage contains the remains of five sacrificial victims. The chamber is almost filled by a huge stone sarcophagus, decorated with portraits of Pacal's parents and ancestors. The body is dressed in exotic costume items, many of jade, which is associated with water and life, and maize, which represents rebirth. The central scene on the lid of the sarcophagus shows a similar scene to the Wakah Kan (◀ p. 155). Snaking into his coffin and extending all the way up the side of the staircase to the temple above is the 'psychoduct', a tube which allowed the king's spirit to travel abroad at night in the form of his 'spirit familiar', usually a jaguar. It also allowed the priests to communicate with Pacal now that he had joined the ancestors.

- http://www.virtualpalenque.com/

forces. They assist or lead other members of society in their ritual activities. Their qualification for this role may be certain distinctive personality traits or they may have undergone special training. A body of myths may help explain how and why they are different from those who lack such powers.

Priests and priestesses

Priests and priestesses are found mostly in complex societies that can afford to support full-time specialists of all kinds. He or she will be ceremonially initiated into a religious organisation and given a rank or office similar to those held before by others. They interpret their wishes or

Figure 8.18 *Temple complex of Srirangam at Triuchirappalli*

This is the largest temple complex in India and a major centre for Hindu worship of the god Vishnu. The huge gopurums (pyramidal entrance towers) are masterpieces of early modern Dravidian architecture. Their height dominates the town and ensures visibility at distance in the same way as European cathedrals

KEY TERM

Liminal

A boundary, space or time which is literally between two worlds. It may be between land and water as at Flag Fen or between the living and the dead. **Liminal** areas can be dangerous and therefore are likely to be marked by ritual. Most well known ritual sites have well defined boundaries. People, creatures and even time can be liminal – e.g. Halloween.

commands for other people but may also appeal to deities on behalf of believers. This may be for a fee or for payment in kind. The priest and recently the priestess are a familiar figure in western society. Priests may be recognised archaeologically through objects placed in burials, through special equipment and clothing, through literary and epigraphic evidence and through artistic evidence of persons involved in ritual activity such as Shield Jaguar and Lady Xoc at Yaxchilan. Their presence could also be inferred from the structure of monuments themselves. In most cases monuments physically divide people into those who are in and those who are out, those at the head of a procession and the followers.

Shamans

There have been societies without full-time occupational specialists for much longer than those in which one finds priests and priestesses. However, there have always been individuals who have individually acquired religious power. This often happens in isolation and may involve bodily deprivation, even self-torture, to try to induce shamanistic visions. It can also involve trances induced by hallucinogenic drugs or repetitive dancing and chanting. Through contact with a spirit or power, or visits to the land of the dead these persons acquire special gifts, such as healing or divination and the ability to deal with supernatural beings and powers. When they return to society they are frequently given another kind of religious role: that of the '**shaman**'. Faith healers and some evangelists in our own society are similar in some respects to this definition of the shaman.

Definitions of shamanism vary. Some writers reserve it for Siberian culture but it is widely applied, particularly to herding, hunter-gatherer and mobile **horticulturist** societies. Shamans are sometimes characterised as magicians rather than religious leaders. In some situations they may coexist. Unlike the priest or priestess who represents deities on earth the shaman is essentially a religious entrepreneur, who acts for their client. Sometimes shamans are paid in kind but usually the increased status that their activities bring is sufficient reward.

A shaman in action may put on something of a show. Frequently shamans enter a trance-like state in which they can see and interact with spirit beings (Lewis-Williams 1988). The shaman enters a dangerous contest to impose his or her will on those spirits, as in faith healing or exorcism. In many groups trancing is accompanied by conjuring tricks, including the use of elaborate masks (for example in the Pitt-Rivers Museum) and ventriloquism. Shamans know, of course, that they are tricking people, but at the same time most shamans really believe in their power to deal with supernatural powers and spirits.

The drama of the shaman's performance promotes a feeling of ecstasy and catharsis for the individual members of society. Psychological assurance is the key to the role of shamanism in society. The shaman may claim to be able to manipulate super-natural powers, and promise such things as protection from enemies, success in love, or a cure from some illness or mental affliction. This treatment may not be effective in any medical sense that we would acknowledge, but the

Figure 8.19 *A ritual artefact? This Neolithic flute carved from a human bone comes from the Trentino region of Italy (**▶ p. 202**). The anthropomorphic designs and the material itself suggest that it might have been used in shamanic rituals*

KEY STUDIES

Palaeolithic cave art

A common misconception is that Upper Palaeolithic cave art in Europe consists of 'hunting scenes' which we can interpret through our imagination and appreciate in our modern way as 'art for art's sake'. Nothing could be further from the truth. In most cases we cannot be sure which images on a particular wall were painted at the same time, never mind whether they 'go together' in any meaningful way. Images of animals predominate but not usually in proportion to their importance as a food source. Reindeer were often the most common prey species but not the most frequently painted. Images of human beings tend to vary hugely. They can be schematic at one end of the scale, as at Lascaux, or intensely realistic, as at La Marche. In addition to the main images there are also many 'signs', which have been interpreted literally as spears, nets, traps and houses. A new approach, pioneered by Lewis-Williams and Dowson (1988), sees these 'signs' as 'entoptic' or geometric shapes that are 'hard-wired' into our central nervous system as humans. We project them over the top of images from everyday life when in an altered state of consciousness such as a trance. These geometric shapes are shared by all modern peoples and therefore by the people of the Upper Palaeolithic. Similar analysis has been carried out on Neolithic rock art.

Ethnographic research has identified strong associations between entoptic art and shamanism. An image in Lascaux depicts a bison which appears to have its entrails hanging out and to be pierced by several feathery 'spears'. Both of these features could be interpreted in other ways. Opposite is a figure of a man with a staff below him topped with the image of a bird. On closer inspection the man is seen to have an erection. His hands and feet are rather like those of a bird with four toes, his face is elongated, ending in a beak and on top of his head is a crest. A recent interpretation of these images has suggested that the human figure is a shaman in a trance state.

San shamans from southern Africa often describe themselves as feeling weightless and elongated. They also record their visions and spirit travels as rock art. The image may be of a shaman transforming into his animal spirit companion. Such trancing may have involved the shaman dancing and imitating the movements and sounds of the bird as part of his performance,

Figure 8.20 *Palaeolithic images which may be of shamans transforming*

KEY STUDIES *cont.*

Palaeolithic cave art

perhaps dressed in a bird costume and carrying magical artefacts such as the staff. Rituals such as this were described among the native Americans of the north-west coast. Some of their elaborate masks and ritual equipment can be seen in the British Museum and Pitt-Rivers Museum. On the other hand, the staff may be a spear thrower.

The study of rock and cave art is a good example of the way archaeological interpretations change when new ideas are applied. Early analogies drawn from the Pacific or north America suggested the possibilities of totemism or 'sympathetic magic' designed to bring prey to the hunters. The inaccessibility of the galleries also raised the possibility that they were educational – to teach hunting and tracking skills, perhaps as a rite of passage. Research into links between shamanism and rock art across much of African and Eurasia suggests that cave art may be shamanistic in origin. It also may mean that we may even understand elements of ancient religion as far back as the last Ice Age.

Neolithic Art

Lozenge and zigzag rock art from Four Knocks tomb. This art like that of nearby Newgrange (◀ p. 147) bears a strong resemblance to entoptic images. Statistical analysis has established a significant correlation between these images and entoptic images produced during trancing. This may suggest that shamanism remained important into the Bronze Age.

Figure 8.21 *Lozenge rock art*

Figure 8.22 *Zigzag rock art*

state of mind induced in the patient may nevertheless play a large part in his recovery. The shaman may also help to maintain social control through the ability to detect and punish evildoers. This can backfire on the shaman. If they are believed to work evil as well as good, or are unsuccessful, shamans may be driven out of their group or even killed.

In societies without iconography shamans are most likely to be detected through burials (▶ p. 260). Siberian examples have been buried face down, tied up and covered with rocks.

Religion and ritual in later British Prehistory (4500BC–55BC): a brief outline

This will give you an introduction to the range of evidence and current interpretations. You need to be aware that in many respects, particularly monument type, there are regional differences that may be significant. Also that we only know about the mortuary practices for a tiny fraction of the population. They may not be typical. Excarnation or cremation before disposal in natural places (possibly rivers) may have always been the norm.

Earlier trends

Prior to the Neolithic, evidence of ritual practice from the British Isles is fragmentary. However, until the late Mesolithic, Britain was not an island. Its people adapted in similar ways to the environment as those in north-western Europe. It may be reasonable to draw inferences from the Ertebolle Culture (▶ p. 229) – the last Mesolithic people from Denmark and Southern Sweden – which has particularly well preserved remains.

Ertebolle burials including cemeteries suggest a reverence for the dead. Dogs were also buried in a similar way to humans. Grave goods emphasise natural materials including amber, red ochre, animal bone and antlers. Some of these have been associated with burials as far back as the upper Palaeolithic which may suggest some continuity of belief. Other human bones have been recovered from middens on settlement sites. The evidence points to beliefs in a spirit world perhaps with people seeing themselves as part of nature rather than in control of it. In Britain there is some evidence for excarnation in the nature and location of human bone remains. Middens in Scotland included human bone in what was appeared to be domestic rubbish. Perhaps middens (▶ p. 199) had some monumental significance as evidence of past collective activity or they provided as a symbolic resource. European cave art and finds of unusual artefacts including musical instruments from the Upper Palaeolithic have been used to argue the case for widespread shamanistic beliefs. The antler masks at Star Carr may be a rare example from the Mesolithic of similar practices.

The early to middle Neolithic c4500–c3000 BC

A number of major changes are apparent in the Neolithic. At one time this was put down to invasion by a new people. Increasingly archaeologists believe that in Northwest Europe, the indigenous Mesolithic people adopted aspects of Neolithic culture. DNA research shows that there has been no wholesale replacement of population since the last Ice Age. People's lives in the early Neolithic may have been similar to the later Mesolithic; herding rather than hunting but still seasonally mobile.

The most obvious changes in the archaeological record are:

- The building of circular enclosures, particularly on hill tops e.g. 'causeway camps'.
- The building of funerary monuments containing human remains such as long barrows or long cairns. These were sometimes in use for over 1000 years.
- Widespread evidence for excarnation and the association of human remains with manufactured artefacts (pottery, stone tools) and cattle bones.

- Structured deposition. Particular bones, and artefacts placed in particular places on sites.

A range of hypotheses have been put forward about the nature of the religion of the builders of the passage graves, cairns and long barrows of Western Europe. Although these monuments are similar in some ways there are significant differences in their contents. In long barrows there was a gradual change from individual articulated burials to collections of disarticulated bones as at Hazleton or re-sorted bones as at West Kennet. However, this pattern is not universal, which suggests some regional variety in beliefs. The tombs that hold the remains of the dead are often massive while remains of the settlements of the living are more fleeting. Neolithic people may have been mobile herders so this may not be surprising. Tilley (1996) suggests that monuments were sited in particular places in relation to important places in the natural landscape. Mountains, spurs and crossing points on pathways may have already been important.

The shape of the tombs may celebrate domestication in its widest sense: houses and control over the fertility of animals. Some writers (◀ p. 160) see the swollen mound of these monuments as evidence for worship of an earth or fertility

Figure 8.23 *A dolmen with stone ring from Carrowmore, Sligo*

There were once at least 60 tombs in the Carrowmore Cemetery and these have produced dates from 5000BC onwards, the earliest for the Neolithic in the British Isles. There is evidence of even earlier feature beneath some of them. This supports the idea that such tombs developed on the Atlantic seaboard during the transition from the Mesolithic. The monuments include early passage graves, cists and small stone rings. It is not clear whether the dolmen would have been covered by a cairn with the ring functioning as a kerb. Several monuments reference landscape features such as the hill of Knocknarea with its huge cairn. Others are aligned on the summer solstice. Cairns in the surrounding hills in turn reference Carrowmore. Most burials were cremations. Finds include early pottery and bone and stone pendants and flint scrapers.

goddess. The shape of passage graves with their narrow entrances suggests a womb from which the soul is reborn. For farmers, fertility is a crucial issue and reseeding Mother Earth with the bones of ancestors may have been a symbolic gesture to ensure good crops or plentiful livestock. Other archaeologists have noted the similarity between some of these monuments and the longhouses of the first farmers of central Europe. Some Neolithic monuments appear to have been sited at places which already had ancestral significance. Perhaps inscribing the landscape with permanent markers associated with their dead was to establish land rights. Mesolithic pits and post settings have been found underneath early long barrows and there are three huge Mesolithic post holes under the Stonehenge car park (◀ p. 131).

Figure 8.24 *A replica of the inside of a Neolithic tomb with disarticulated human remains*

There is nothing to stop modern visitors rearranging the bones. A modern example of taphonomy! (◀ p. 107)

Not all tombs had entrances. Amongst many that did, the disarticulated bones from different individuals were deliberately mixed and sometimes re-sorted. Perhaps this was to downplay individual differences and mask inequalities amongst the living. The dead became part of a shared group of ancestors rather than belonging to a particular family. The restricted entrance passages and evidence of the transformation of skeletons through sorting hints at the possibility of ritual specialists. Recent acoustic experiments (Watson 1997) suggest that the design of burial chambers may have enabled specialists, possibly shamans, to create atmospheres and illusions through the use of sound. Similar effects have been noted at later stone circles. The mortuary rituals in tombs may be linked to activities at other Neolithic sites. At some causewayed enclosures such as Hambledon Hill, human bones appear to have been subject to excarnation. Perhaps the spirits of the dead could not be released until flesh had been removed from bones. Some bones exposed at such sites may have later been transferred to tombs.

Around barrows there is often waste from feasting and some human bones. Ethnographic evidence from the Merina of Madagascar (Parker Pearson, 1997) has been used to suggest that the remains of the dead may have been removed from time to time to be involved in rituals. While they are radically different societies there are interesting parallels. The Merina use communal, chambered tombs, to emphasis community and kinship. Skeletons are wrapped in the tomb but are periodically taken out and re-wrapped. These rituals involved both the living and the ancestors.

Graslund (1994), in a comparative study of Scandinavian tombs from the Neolithic to Viking periods, concluded that settled societies share a belief in some sort of afterlife and in souls or spirits. He identified two models. The breath soul leaves the body with its last sigh and goes to join the ancestors. The free or dream soul is active when the body sleeps. After death it remains with the body until the flesh is gone. Graslund argued that the treatment of bodies after death reflected different soul beliefs. Where excarnation or disarticulation had occurred before placing in a tomb it suggested a breath soul. The tomb served as an ossuary. Where decomposition occurred inside the tomb it was a grave. The evidence for this is the presence of small bones that would have been lost during excarnation, skeletons in sitting

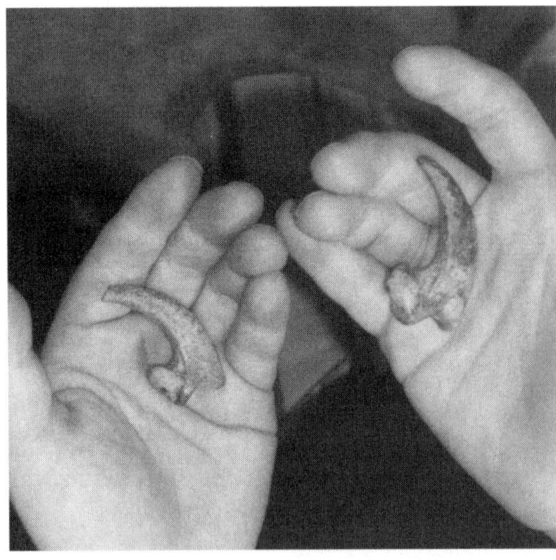

Figure 8.25 *Sea eagle talons from the Neolithic stalled cairn at Isbister*

Totemism has been used as an explanation for such finds in prehistoric tombs. Hedges noted that Isbister Tomb on Orkney contained the remains of at least eight massive sea eagles while nearby Cuween held the remains of 24 dogs and another tomb contained deer bones. Local tribal groups may have identified with particular animals. However, these may have been food or in some cases scavengers which entered the tombs independently or as part of the excarnation process. The tomb contained the jumbled remains of 342 people including rows of skulls on a shelf. Joints of lamb had been left in the tomb while outside was a pile of deliberately smashed pots and other remains of feasting.

positions and beads that may have come from clothing. There are also fatty deposits in the soil in some tombs. With dream soul beliefs the corpse would have to be cared for as if it were alive. This would also account for the presence of food remains and grave goods.

Evidence from the relatively small number of Neolithic houses that have been found suggests that these may not have been domestic at all. Many have odd, non-functional features and strange deposits or unusual artefacts and have been described as cult houses. The massive timber house at Balbridie appeared to have a screen just inside the door, which would have made the inside dark and restricted access. Another at Balfarg probably had no roof. It held finds of a beaker which contained possible traces of narcotic substances. Even apparently purely economic sites such as flint mines may have had some ritual functions. It seems that in the Neolithic there was no distinction between ritual and practical. Actions were informed by beliefs.

The later Neolithic and early Bronze Age c3000–2000 BC

The veneration of ancestors, communal rituals and belief in spirits continued into the third millennium BC but very gradually a number of changes occurred. The new elements included:

- The construction of a wider range of funerary monuments with significant regional variation. These included barrows, cairns, cists and megalithic tombs.
- A wider range of ritual monuments including cursus, timber circles, henges and standing stones (rows, circles and monoliths).
- Specific artefacts which are found in association with particular monuments. These include beakers with single burials and grooved ware pottery with timber enclosures and henges.
- The positioning or structuring of monuments to reference earlier monuments, rivers and/or solar alignments.
- Development of rock art across much of Britain and Ireland.

Amongst the significant developments here are the scale and type of monument and the symbolism of the alignment and positioning of monuments.

Many of the larger monuments would have required considerable organisation and millions of man-hours to build. Engineering skills were needed to transport and erect huge timbers and megaliths.

KEY SITE

Loughcrew passage graves

The 40 odd ritual monuments on three hills of the 4km long 'mountain of the witch' include chambered cairns, stone circles and date from 4000–3000BC. The complex dominates the landscape and may have been important as a territorial marker and meeting place as well as burial place. The name of the hills, 'Carnbane', means white cairn in Gaelic. It is thought this may indicate that the tombs were once covered in white quartz like the façade at Newgrange (◀ p. 147). A few rocks of quartz have been found on the hills.

Figure 8.26 *Cairn S*

This cairn, roughly 17m in diameter, illustrates the shape of the cairns and the distinctive ring of kerb stones. The antiquarian who emptied it reported an 18 inch layer of charred bone in the Y shaped chamber along with bone pins, flint and pot debris and a stone pendant.

Some passage graves are aligned so that the rising sun illuminates rock art panels at the back of the chambers at the spring and autumn equinoxes. Two large cairns provide focal points for many of the others. Unfortunately many of the tombs were opened by antiquarians and evidence about mortuary practice has been lost. Most human remains were either cremations or charred bones. Around the hills are clustered later monuments including a cursus, henge, standing stones and Bronze Age ring barrows. Recent airborne laser scanning has detected dozens more.

Figure 8.27 *Cairn H*

This view illustrates the passage and the cruciform shape of the chamber. The lintelled roof over the passage has been removed. The chamber would have been corbelled. Inside are carved panels with spiral designs and a basin stone thought to be used to receive cremations. Finds were similar to Cairn S plus a stone ball and amber beads. The cairn appeared to have been reoccupied in the Iron Age for bone artefact production.

KEY TERM

Megalith

Essentially it means 'big stone' and is applied both to standing stones and monuments constructed of large boulders. Increasingly 'megalithic' is used to describe other aspects of society such as art during the time when megaliths were erected – essentially the Neolithic and early to middle Bronze Age.

- http://www.megalithic.co.uk/index.php

Figure 8.28 *The standing stone of Clach An Truishal stands 6 metres above ground and is the largest megalith in Scotland. In France (and Asterix) it would be called a menhir.*

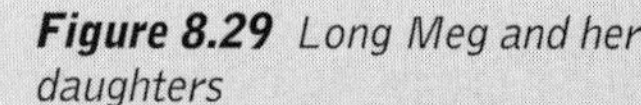

Figure 8.29 *Long Meg and her daughters*

In folk legend this was a coven of witches turned to stone. The 100 metre Bronze Age stone circle may have once been part of a larger group of monuments. Like many circles, several stones have been lost. Today only half of the granite survivors still stand. 'Meg' herself is a 4 metre block of sandstone engraved with rock art and stands 20 metres away.

Large, open monuments may represent a move to large scale rituals. Certainly there is evidence of extensive feasting at many, such as the slaughter of pigs and cattle at West Kennett timber enclosure. The architecture and use of space in the monuments also suggests that if they were not organised by ritual leaders, they may have created them. Linear alignments lend themselves to processions (someone always leads) while barriers, boundaries, elaborate entrances and series of concentric structures on some sites divide people into in/out. The circularity of monuments could symbolise many things. For example the horizons of their world as they could see it, the community or the sun. Some writers have suggested that monuments reflected the landscape. Henges often occur in river basins where long views are cut off.

The positioning of later monuments seems to be affected both by the landscape and earlier monuments. Loveday's (1998) work on Dorchester suggested that the cursus might have been aligned on a natural feature: a twin peaked hill known as Mother Dunche's Buttocks. Other monuments including cursuses are then aligned on it even after it went out of use. Its proximity to the Thames is surely also significant. Rivers, including their springs, do seem to be a focus for ritual activity from at least this period. Henges in particular are often associated with rivers. There are also many examples where monuments are aligned on earlier funerary monuments. The Dorset Cursus was aligned on a long barrow, the Giants Ring at Ballynahatty on a small passage grave. The new monuments are linked to earlier ancestral beliefs; perhaps to provide legitimacy. Many monuments are also aligned on solar or possibly lunar phenomena. The most famous is the reorientation of Stonehenge towards the midsummer or midwinter solstice. Equally significant are the 'lightboxes' on passage graves in Ireland and Orkney. These allow light to penetrate into burial chambers on the winter solstice. This linked ancestors to an annual cycle of death and rebirth.

Where large numbers of monuments cluster together, archaeologists have used the term ritual landscape. The idea that a whole block of land might have been dedicated to gods or spirits was first applied to Cranborne Chase where the 7-mile long cursus monument was the focus for burials over several thousand years. Analysis of field-walking finds revealed that higher than usual proportions of exotic artefacts and human remains were found close to the cursus with little sign of everyday activity (Green, 2000). Whether areas were set aside for gods or spirits the monuments affected the way people moved around the landscape and saw the world. They probably reinforced ideas about life, death and society. Some of the monuments may have been at points where people met during seasonal movements. The massive henge at Durrington Walls was the focus for a huge range of other monuments for hundreds of years. It may have been a place where herders crossed the Upper Avon and spread out into summer grazing lands in the spring. The site may have been important for seasonal rituals or festivals. Many monuments were remodelled several times perhaps reflecting changing beliefs. At Stanton Drew magnetometer surveys have revealed that the stone circles replaced earlier timber monuments. Recent work suggests that henges might be the final form enclosing ritual sites.

The study of sacred geography involves examining the relation between monuments and landscape and the ways in which the building of monuments affects the way in which people may have moved around or viewed the landscape. Amongst the range of techniques are studies of intervisibility, which examine whether monuments were sited in view of each other. This has been assisted by the use of GIS and has been particularly applied to rock art and barrows. Attempting to 'read' the way monuments structure experience of the landscape borrows from the sociological approach known as phenomenology and has been pioneered in case studies in Britain by Tilley (1994). This approach has led to a reappraisal of linear monuments. These clearly structure movement in a particular order and direction

Figure 8.30 *Achnabreck rock art (petroglyphs)*

This slab with its examples of classic 'cup and ring' marks, and 'stars and spirals', overlooks one of the approaches to the Kilmartin Valley, a significant ritual centre. Other examples have been found throughout north-western Europe on monuments such as Newgrange (◀ p. 147) and Long Meg (◀ p. 180). Analysis of the abstract images suggests that they comprise similar patterns to those recorded in research into hallucinogens and trancing. If this is the case then attaining altered states of consciousness through dancing, sound, drugs or fasting may have been a feature of rituals. Possibly the distinctive pottery (grooved ware and beakers) found in ritual deposits from this period may have held more than just refreshments. An alternative function may have been territorial markers (▶ p. 205).

but may themselves be permanent inscriptions of earlier movements or processions. Barnett's (1998) study of the stone rows on Dartmoor noted how many lead from the valleys onto the moors, perhaps marking a route for spirits or the dead. Similar suggestions have been made for Avebury and Stonehenge with pathways linking ritual areas for the living and those of the ancestors.

There is increasing evidence that dramatic events played an important part in ritual. Some monuments appear to have been built in stages over many years so that participation in the project may have been more important that the final product e.g. the Cleaven Dyke. Others were deliberately destroyed by what must have been spectacular fires. Often timber structures were repeatedly built and destroyed as at Dunragit and West Kennet. At the latter site Whittle's (1998) excavations revealed two massive but short-lived, egg-shaped enclosures. The large number of meat bones which had been discarded without being fully processed provided strong

Figure 8.31 *Cist at Nether Largie South Chambered Cairn*

This cist from the Kilmartin complex probably represents a secondary burial and contains rock art. The main cairn had been robbed and this may have been too. The excavator found scattered beaker sherds and human bones around it. Nearby cists contained crouched burials or cremations sometimes with beakers or other grave goods. Cists are generally found in the west of the British Isles and date from the Early Bronze Age. Like this one, most are rectangular stone boxes suited to a crouched inhumation or funerary urn.

evidence of feasting, as did large amounts of grooved ware. The enclosures were located very close to other monuments and the source of the Kennet. The concept of liminality was used to explain the special attention given to boundaries. In particular, deliberate deposits of grooved ware, bone and artefacts had been made around the entrances. This practice has been noted at other timber enclosures throughout Britain.

Beakers of course are best known from their place in a new tradition of single burials in graves and cists. As part of fairly standard assemblages range of grave goods (decorated beaker, arrowheads, dagger, wrist guard etc) they may represent a more individualised view of an afterlife as well as a more ranked society.

The Middle Bronze Age 2300 (or 1800) to 1200 BC

Once again, there is great continuity from the late Neolithic. This is most obvious in the elaboration of earlier monuments such as the remodelling of Stonehenge and the way new monuments continue to be linked to much earlier ones. Key features are:

- The building of thousands of round barrows or cairns.
- A variety of burial traditions including single and multiple burials, flat cemeteries and particularly cremations.
- The final phases of major monument building including major stone circles at Stonehenge and Avebury.

KEY STUDY

The Clava Cairns

This group of monuments near Inverness illustrates many of the different features of ritual sites.

This distinctive, regional complex comprising ring cairns, passage graves and standing stones had originally been thought to be Neolithic. Bradley's (2000a) re-excavation revealed that building had begun in the early Bronze Age around 2000BC. The complex was remodelled in the late Bronze Age and funerary deposits were also made in the Iron Age.

The passage graves are aligned on the midwinter sunset. When viewed from the passage of the north-eastern cairn the dying sun disappears over the south-western cairn, thus linking the event to the ancestors. The rays of the setting sun fall on reddish sandstone boulders while the rising sun would have sparkled on white quartz. This symbolism has been found in other monuments. On Arran red boulders were chosen to face the setting sun with white granite facing the rising sun. The colours red (blood, flesh, ochre and amber) and white (bone, semen and flint) are often associated in grave deposits.

A number of conventions were adhered to in building the monument. The kerbstones of the cairns were carefully graded in height from the south-west. From an engineering point of view this makes no sense but may have symbolised the passage of the sun . Rock carvings were included both inside and outside the cairns with the same 'cup and ring' designs as others in Britain and Ireland. However, these monuments seem to represent a change in ritual practice. Excavation revealed low platforms covered in seashells and flat stones surrounding the cairns. 'Rays' or ridges of stones led out through the platform to standing monoliths. Excavation showed that these were all integral to the cairns rather than later add-ons. These monuments seem to have been a transitional stage between passage graves, where the views of mortuary rituals would have been very restricted, to stone circles, where ritual may have been much more public and perhaps on a larger scale.

- Bradley 2000a

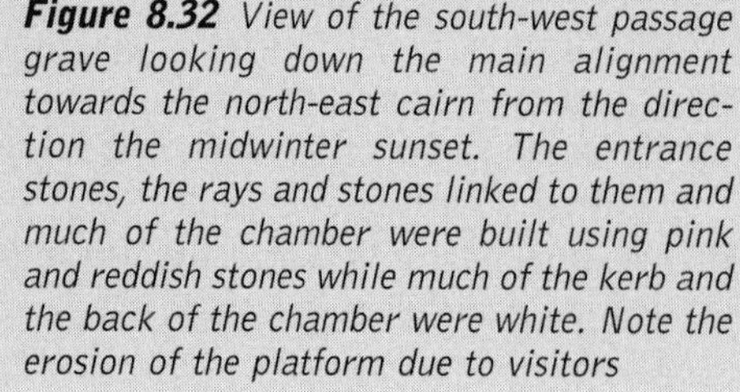

Figure 8.32 *View of the south-west passage grave looking down the main alignment towards the north-east cairn from the direction the midwinter sunset. The entrance stones, the rays and stones linked to them and much of the chamber were built using pink and reddish stones while much of the kerb and the back of the chamber were white. Note the erosion of the platform due to visitors*

Figure 8.33 *View of a relationship between the features of the monuments. Two standing stones on the left are linked by 'rays' to the central ring cairn. The child is standing on the first ray. This integral relationship could only be established by excavation. Note how small the kerbstones are on the back of the south-west cairn in the distance in comparison with the front ones*

- The importance of orientation for the entrance of enclosures and houses.

Individual burials occur throughout prehistory, but there seems to be a shift of emphasis in the Bronze Age. This is most marked in round barrows or cairns that were often constructed over a primary burial or cremation with satellite burials around it (and often later secondary burials). The development of a range of regional burial traditions could reflect changes in beliefs and society. The old way of life of semi-sedentary herding amongst roughly equal social groups was being replaced by a more unequal society based on control of the land. The new barrows and cairns cluster round earlier monuments, and in the case of some small circular monuments such as Cairnpapple, fill them. This surely represents high status individuals linking their families to 'the ancestors' and their rights and power. Some burials, particularly in Wessex, included rich and exotic grave goods. The 'Amesbury Archer' (◀ p. 79) and the Bush Barrow burial are the best known. The size of the burial mounds may also indicate the importance of individuals but could also be to provide platforms for funeral pyres. It is likely that the funerary rituals would have been more important at the time than the artefacts which archaeologists recover.

Perhaps reflecting the increasing importance of farming, the sun and seasons seem to become more important in the Bronze Age. Most of the circular enclosures, monuments and houses are aligned to the south-east or south-west. It may imply involve solar worship. The final phase at Stonehenge was constructed so that the midsummer sun shone along the processional 'avenue' into the heart of the monument. This strongly suggests a seasonal ritual involving large numbers. Alternatively the monument may be aligned on the midwinter sunset, linking the dying sun and year to the ancestors buried nearby. Stonehenge with its complex design, avenue and restricted interior provides a good indicator of organised religion and specialists. The nearby Upton Lovell burial (▶ p. 260) suggests a possible form.

The Late Bronze Age and Iron Age 1200–55BC

Some archaeologists have approached this period from later Roman accounts while others have traced developments in the archaeological record. While there is not full consensus, a number of patterns are clear.

- The abandonment of the monument building tradition.
- A move towards more extreme forms of propitiation (sacrifice) including that of people.
- The importance of deposition in natural places particularly water.
- Still relatively few burials. Most of the dead are missing.
- Evidence of ritual being part of everyday activity.
- Orientation remained important for houses and enclosures.

The impressive burials seen in museums such as the 'chariot burials' of Yorkshire and rich burials from Kent are exceptions. Most of the dead disappear. Excarnation seems to have been common with some cremation and possibly water burial. Bruck's (1995) study of human remains on sites from this period revealed that bones occurred in many locations not necessarily thought of as ritual, including huts and pits. Relatives may well have kept relics of their dead ancestors. Human bones along with animal remains were also used as deliberate deposits at entrances, boundaries, and in grain pits. 98 of the pits at Danebury contained some human remains. Studies of middens and rubbish pits have also shown that their fills were non-random. Rules structured their creation. Some domestic sites also had very patterned orientation. Hill's (1996) comparative study of Iron Age sites revealed a tendency for houses to face south-east. This may have been to do with light, although in Britain south would be the best direction to maximise daylight entering a hut. Light cannot have been a factor with enclosures. These tend to face south-west even when local topography and defensive considerations might suggest other directions. It may be that there was a 'right' direction from which to enter or perform activities. Ritual was a part of everyday life.

Society was now based on settled villages involved in mixed farming. Perhaps the domestication of religion reflects a less mobile society. The total abandonment of earlier beliefs appears to be evident in the way later Bronze Age field systems cut across earlier monuments whose faint traces had been respected for over a thousand years. Instead of monuments, natural places seem to have become significant. In addition to water and pits, deposits occur on hilltops, which may well have been wooded. The Romans mentioned druids lurking in oak groves! Symbolism was drawn from the natural world. Birds, particularly ducks, feature on some high status artefacts and bird bones are often found with human remains. The Romans also reported a number of taboos including against the eating of fish. Low amounts of marine carbon isotopes in skeletal remains may support this claim.

Some human deposits are likely to have been sacrifices, including some burials outside hillforts, which were previously thought to be battle casualties. Sacrifices may have been connected with fertility but also with rites of intensification. At Flag Fen the building of and maintenance of a huge structure for hundreds of years is associated with the sacrifice of dogs and of ritually smashed valuable artefacts into water. Flag Fen is one of several possible pilgrimage sites from this period. In Britain and Denmark bodies which had apparently been ritually killed have been recovered from bogs. Throughout north-western Europe large quantities of metalwork including the very finest, were deposited in rivers and lakes. Water sacrifices may be acts of propitiation, perhaps in appeals to a water or underground deity. It may also be the case that water was always important, but that it becomes archaeologically visible at this point. Alternately it may be a reaction to climatic deterioration and rising water levels which caused economic and social problems in this period.

Specialists remain elusive. The Mill Hill (Deal) burials (▶ p. 270) include a young man wearing what has been interpreted as a Druid's crown because of its similarity to Roman priests crowns.

***Figure 8.34** Welwyn burial*

This rich burial documents the influence of Rome in terms of burial goods if not religion. The cremation was buried with amphorae of wine, fine table ware, games and a variety of luxury items. This is not how most people in the Iron Age were buried.

The Birdlip burial (▶ p. 278) was classified as a woman's grave but some researchers have reinterpreted the grave goods as shamanistic. From the very end of the Iron Age a handful of possible temples have been identified. This may reflect a southern elite adopting continental customs along with imported goods in advance of the Roman invasion. The Romans also gave us some names of local deities such as Sulis at Bath and of the festivals which marked the Iron Age calendar including Samhain, the forerunner of Halloween. Some wooden carvings from bogs (◀ p. xxvii) and Roman reliefs (▶ p. 188) may represent Iron Age deities.

- Thomas 1991 Bradley 1998, Whittle 1996

A BRIEF INTRODUCTION TO ROMAN RELIGION AND RITUAL TO C.476AD

Roman religion encompassed a vast range of beliefs and practices much which we know from texts. This includes the state supported system of priests (flamen), temples, monuments and their pantheon of deities. However, archaeology

Figure 8.35 *One of three known temples of Mithras on Hadrian's Wall.*

This was home to one of the secretive and exotic 'mystery religions' of the Roman Empire. Only men were initiated into Mithraic rites. It was brought to Rome from the East by returning soldiers attracted by this heroic god. Images above the altar would have shown Mithras killing a sacred bull from whose body all the good things on earth were released. Other images included snakes, scorpions and a raven. It is thought that these represent constellations and that Mithraism involved astrology. The temples were windowless and often underground to represent the sacred cave of Mithras. Benches for the initiates lined the walls. In addition to sacrifices, rites involved ordeals and feasting. A virtual Mithraeum is at

- http://museums.ncl.ac.uk/archive/mithras/frames.htm

can contribute to understanding less well recorded aspects, particularly of everyday ritual practice.

Early Roman religion was animistic with worship of ancestors and spirits who inhabited or influenced particular everyday places, events and things. From the outset, Romans borrowed beliefs and practices from cultures around them starting with the deities of the Etruscans and Greeks. Roman deities had less developed personalities and mythologies than those of the Greeks. Their powers and relationships to each other were more important. The major deities including Jupiter, Mars and Quirinus had their own priesthoods, temples and festivals. As the empire expanded following the wars of the third century BC more exotic deities and cults were added including those of Isis and Mithras. Emperors also became divine.

Despite bad press for their treatment of Christians the Romans were generally tolerant of other cults. They usually dealt with new ideas through a process of 'syncretism' or equating native gods and their attributes with the nearest equivalent from their pantheon as in the famous example of Sulis Minerva at Bath. The first and second centuries AD saw growing intolerance with persecution of Christians amongst others. However, Christianity survived and from 391 was declared the state religion with many other temples being destroyed.

Temples were houses of the gods so the Romans built them on a grand scale and in prominent places. Temple layouts followed a defined plan which can be seen throughout the empire from the Temple of Apollo at Didyma (Turkey) to the Maison Carrée at Nimes (France). Each has a raised podium with access via a flight of steps, a large external altar, a temenos (boundary wall) and often ancilliary buildings for priests and pilgrims.

The priests of the various cults were all overseen by the high priest or 'Pontifex Maximus' who in imperial times was the emperor. Their responsibility for organising religion came from law codes found inscribed on metal and stone in local towns. Other specialists included 'augurs' and 'haruspices'. These diviners interpreted the meanings in natural phenomena and the livers of sacrificed animals. They were consulted before important decisions. Perhaps the most well known of Roman ritual specialists were the Vestal Virgins who tended the continually burning flame on the altar of the Temple of Vesta (the hearth goddess) in the Forum of Rome. Worship was not confined to temples. Rich people had their own shrine built into their houses while for ordinary people worship centred around a simple lararium or set of statues. There was also 'pietas', the sense of love, respect and duty towards both gods and their families, expressed through ordinary people's lives.

Figure 8.34 *Two of three Genii Cucullati from near Hadrian's Wall. Wearing their distinctive hooded cloaks, these Romano-Celtic gods symbolised healing and fertility*

A fundamental of Roman religion or 'superstitio' was establishing a contract between mortal and supernatural beings. One would make offerings to secure specific outcomes as in the practice

Figure 8.37 *Temple of Mercury at Uley*

Mercury, messenger of the gods, was the patron of travellers (and also thieves!). His popularity in Corinium and at the nearby cult temple at Uley is evidenced by statues, votives and lead 'curse' tablets. Mercury is often shown with sheep or goats (fertility) or a cockerel (herald of the day). The bones of these animals were found in considerable numbers at Uley. The complex with the standard temple design (right) also included shops and hostels for pilgrims which can be seen to the left of the aerial view.

of leaving 'defixiones' or curse tablets in watery places such as the spring at Bath. Offerings could hedge your bets when embarking on a new business venture, going on a journey or any potentially life changing event. Animal entrails were burnt, chickens sacrificed and the flight of birds consulted. Votive offerings were left at shrines in the spirit of 'do ut des', 'I give so that you may give'. This was a reciprocal bargain and the gods were expected to perform their side of the deal by using their power (numen) to influence events. 'Numen' was also embedded in particular places. This was later enshrined in temples and symbolised by statues of the 'genius loci' (spirit of the place) such as the many statues of the River Tyne found near Hadrian's Wall. The 'numinus' was everywhere in the Roman world from poems like Horace's *Fountain of Bandusia*, 'more glittering than glass. . .' to the end of a bar in Pompeii where one glanced across the top of a wine cup to see the household deities of the owner and the place, the Lares and Penates. Rather like our custom of leaving a mince pie and glass of sherry for Father Christmas, food and drink offerings would be left

Figure 8.38 *Triad of mother goddesses from Cirencester*

Roman Corinium appears to have been a focus for this cult. The goddesses, carrying bread or fruit symbolised fertility. Many such deities appear in threes since that was a magical number for many Iron Age peoples. There is a close correlation between finds of mother goddesses and genii cucullati.

• www.unc.edu/celtic/catalogue/triplism/#genii

at this 'altar'. Pompeii has provided much information about household religion. At the House of the Vettii two brothers had a very fine lararium on the wall, off the main atrium to the right, where a magical snake protected the household from evil forces outside. Phallic symbols performed much the same role outside many houses, including the town brothel with its massively endowed depiction of the god Priapus.

Initially the dominant mortuary rite was cremation. The ashes were placed into pottery or glass containers like those in the British Museum. In wealthy households marble chests usually covered with symbolism such as pomegranates, ox skulls, garlands and sphinxes were used instead. Families often visited the grave to feast beside the tomb. At Caerleon one cremation was served drinks through a spout which led down to the urn. Only neo-natal burials were allowed inside the 'pomerium' or town boundary. Cemeteries therefore were kept apart from settlement areas. In Rome burial could be in underground niches or 'loculi' but above ground tombstones were also very common. This was especially so in Britain due to the influence of the army.

By the second century AD inhumation became the norm across the whole empire. This may be associated with increasing worship of the sun god 'Sol Invictus'. At the same time cemeteries were laid out east–west and in neat rows.

Figure 8.39 *Altar from Cirencester*

This altar is dedicated to the Genus Loci of Corinium. In one hand he holds a cornucopia with a patera (an offering or sacrificial bowl) in the other.

Figure 8.40 *Tombstone of Sextus Valerius Genialis from Cirencester.*

This cavalryman and citizen of Corinium from 60AD is shown defeating a 'dying Gaul'. However, he was not from Rome but from Thrace. The Roman army was cosmopolitan. Soldiers posted to and often settling in Britain were as likely to have come from the Middle East or north of the Rhine as Rome itself.

Inhumations were usually in the extended position but it is also quite common for the head to be cut off and placed elsewhere in the grave, often between the knees. Grave goods include lamps, jewellery and shoes, usually surviving as sets of studded nails. One of the most spectacular graves is the 'Lady of Spitalfields'. Her unique collection of lead coffin, grave goods and high quality apparel is displayed in the Museum of London. One distinctive Roman religious organisation was the 'burial club' where people saved money to pay for their burial and tombstones. Such clubs were often affiliated to trade guilds with their own club room for meetings and dining – several of these have been identified at Ostia, the port of Rome. Unlike modern tombstones which tend to be conservative and modest their Roman counterparts often list in detail the good qualities and achievements of the deceased.

KEY SKILL

Developing an argument in longer pieces of writing

When faced with an open-ended question it is useful to break it down into manageable chunks. A title such as 'How far is it possible for archaeologists to identify ritual for your period of study?' provides a good example. First, you might want to distinguish between periods that have written sources and those that do not, although it is a good idea to ask about the reliability of sources. For the rest, you could subdivide using sub-questions based on the '4 Ws':

- *What*: can we identify the kind of ritual, which took place (for example, feasting, sacrifice)?
- *Where*: can we identify places where ritual took place, how, what evidence and examples?
- *Who*: can we identify who was involved (for example, individuals, groups of pilgrims)?
- *Why*: can we identify the purpose of the ritual (ancestor worship, rite of passage, etc.)?

In each case you will come up with an answer somewhere between yes and no depending on the techniques used and the quality and survival of evidence. This provides you with a structure and, taken together, the basis of an argument about the extent to which it is possible to detect ritual.

In writing up each section you need to argue. If your tutor keeps writing 'assertion' on your work then you are not doing this. You must support each point you make with evidence from relevant studies. There are several models or gambits for integrating supporting material:

- Using authorities to support statements: '. . . as Prior (1991) demonstrated at Flag Fen'.
- Cross-referencing: 'The possibility of the Dorset Cursus being used to structure movement was enhanced by Green's (1990) discovery of avenues of postholes leading from it to later round barrows. Analysis of the Stonehenge landscape by Parker Pearson (1998) also suggested movement along the avenue between the zones of the living and the ancestors.'
- Using evidence to choose between competing versions: 'Renfrew (1978) suggested that long barrows might have been territorial markers. Recent studies by Tilley (1998) and Barnett (1998) suggest otherwise. They found that . . .'
- Juxtaposing evidence to assess it: 'Deposits of cattle bones and smashed pottery near many entrances may suggest feasting but similar evidence inside is more ambivalent. Is it debris from feasting, gifts to the ancestors or the remnants of food the dead took with them?'

It is useful early on in your course to build up a vocabulary of *link words* and phrase such as 'however', 'for example', 'on the other hand'. These will prevent you from becoming repetitive and remind you to always back up your statements.

Finally you need to conclude. You should revisit the conclusions of each sub-question and see what the balance of your argument was. Use this to make a tentative judgement (try to avoid certainty) in response to the main question.

Chapter 9

The Archaeology of Settlement

YOUR GOALS

You need to

- know a range of case studies of different types of site, settlement and structure
- understand and appraise techniques archaeologists use to interpret the function and status of sites and structures
- understand methods used to study the relationship between people and the environment
- develop your use of case studies and plans to help you with essay writing.

WHAT DOES THE ARCHAEOLOGY OF SETTLEMENT COVER?

Whether you are studying a range of different cultures or following a thematic course, settlement is likely to be a central topic. However, the term itself can mean several things.

Today, when we think of settlements we usually mean cities, towns and villages. However, for most of human history none of these existed. For periods when the population was mobile rather than sedentary, humans created a range of temporary camps and sites for processing raw materials and food. Sometimes caves or rock shelters were repeatedly used for occupation and rich deposits remain. Other sites consist of scatters of flakes from stone tool making (debitage) or animal bone remains from a butchery site. It is likely that these people identified with an area of the landscape, through which they may have moved on a seasonal basis, rather than living in one fixed place as we do.

For many past societies, off-site areas that we sometimes detect as flint-scatters or field systems were as important as the 'sites' which archaeologists have tended to excavate. The work of Binford in particular demonstrates that individual sites can provide a rather biased picture of activity in the past and that there is a need to consider the whole settlement 'system'.

Settlement archaeology, therefore, includes the study of both permanent and temporary sites and the interaction of humans with their landscape in order to understand how they adapted to it. Human impact on the landscape from forest clearance to division by boundaries into territory is therefore a vital part of settlement study. Archaeologists also try to understand the ways in which people in the past understood their

Figure 9.1 *Mesolithic tent*

Relatively few settlements in the British Isles are known before the Bronze Age. Some degree of mobility, perhaps based on herding seems to have continued from the Mesolithic into the Neolithic. Instead of the foundations of houses, typical settlements from this period tend to be a series of small stakeholes and hearths. At Mount Sandal and Morton these were interpreted as the remains of skin covered 'benders' or tents as recreated here.

KEY TERM

Site

A broad definition is useful here. The term is applied to field monuments, such as round barrows, to concealed evidence, such as cropmarks on aerial photographs, and even to towns.

A **site** is any place where traces of human activity are found. Usually these traces include artefacts but depending on the period studied they might include remains of structures, faunal remains or modification of the landscape such as a quarry. Boundaries make it easier to define sites, but many sites appear as unenclosed scatters of material. The recent emphasis on the significance of natural places in the ritual life of past peoples in the works of Bradley (2000b) and Tilley (1994) stretches the definition still further. For this reason some writers have adopted the term 'locales' for less easily defined places. The duration of use of a site might range from a few hours for a hunting site to centuries for a village or town. A settlement is just one type of site. The specific forms of site will vary according to period: kill-site, barrow, motte, mill, etc.

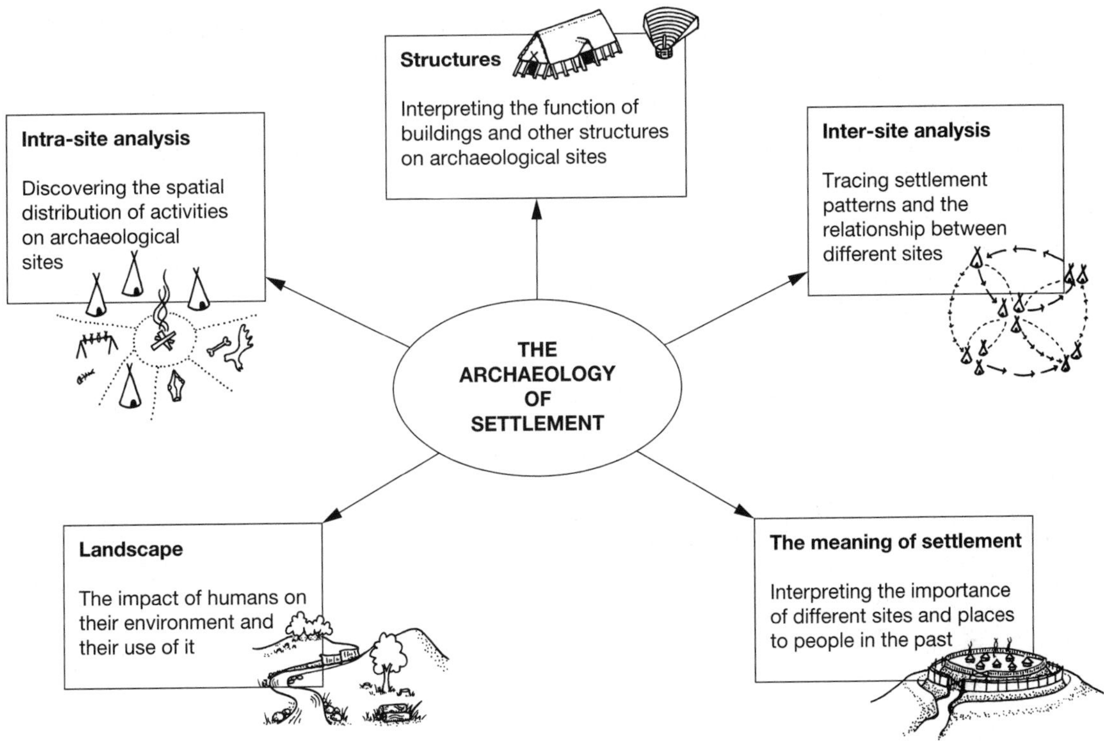

Figure 9.2 *The archaeology of settlement*

KEY TERM

Sedentary

Essentially **sedentary** means living in one place. It used to be thought that hunter-gatherers were mobile or nomadic and that people 'settled down' with the advent of farming. Evidence from archaeology and anthropology suggests that the reality is more complex. Many cultures have existed whose settlement pattern lies somewhere between the two poles of mobile and sedentary. A wealth of terms such as semi-sedentary, radiating or tethered mobility have been used to describe these patterns. Hodder argues that in the Neolithic people became 'entangled' with artefacts which they increasingly used to mediate between themselves and their environment or other people. Just as there is a truism that the longer you stay in one place the more 'stuff' you accumulate, the decisions Neolithic people made about 'things' led to accumulations of artefacts and permanent structures. These impeded movement and they became increasingly sedentary.

landscape through ideas such as ownership, territory and status. To do this they need to identify and explain the spatial distribution of past human activities. This might mean understanding the location of sites within a landscape or the placing of structures or other features within a settlement. At a micro level it includes studying activities within a room or living floor. The key questions asked usually revolve around identification of functions or the reasons for patterns in their distribution. Artefacts, ecofacts and features are the key evidence base in studying of distribution of ancient activities.

KEY STUDY

Nunamiut ethnoarchaeology

Binford's (1978) classic ethnoarchaeological research project amongst the Nunamiut Eskimo examined the dynamics of their settlement pattern through seasonal movement from an archaeological perspective. His studies revealed the huge range of territory covered and the variable factors that influenced the location and timing of campsites. Specialist camps were established for hunting, carcass processing and sexual liaisons while non-residential sites included caches of meat and deadfall traps. While careful not to draw direct parallels between Nunamiut and Palaeolithic hunters, Binford was able to argue convincingly that since humans do not confine their behaviour to identifiable sites, we should study sites as part of a wider context. Drawing an analogy with the parts of a car engine he showed that in order to understand the activities of a mobile society we need to fit all the parts of the system together to see the whole picture, from hunting stands to skinning sites. Within the sites he put great emphasis on the spatial relationship between lithic and bone evidence.

RECONSTRUCTING ANCIENT LANDSCAPES

Huge progress has been made in recent years in our ability to research and understand past landscapes. By attempting to reconstruct local environments, archaeologists hope to understand how sites developed and were abandoned, and how people adapted to their surroundings. To do this, archaeology uses intensive regional surveys that borrow from geology, biology and environmental science.

The land surface

Today's landscape has been shaped by human and natural activity on top of a geological base. Observing the morphology (shape) of the modern landscape is the starting point for research. Major investigations will also use GIS to produce digital maps and 3D models of past environments, for example that of Roman Wroxeter.

- www.arch-ant.bham.ac.uk/bufau/research/bt/

For the Palaeolithic and Mesolithic, understanding of geological changes is essential. For example, sea levels and the courses of rivers were often radically different. At Elveden in Suffolk geophysical survey was used to track ancient river channels running west-east through a series of narrow gorges. Today the land is flat and drains north-south.

For most periods, data on soils is essential both to understand the environment it may have supported in the past and to track changes in its composition due to human activity (◀ p. 86). For example, the soils of many upland areas, including Dartmoor, show that they were once wooded. Clearance and agriculture in the Bronze Age contributed to degradation of the soil and the formation of 'iron pans' which have prevented their use for crops since then. Studies of eroded layers of soil from the highlands of New Guinea around Kuk Swamp enabled Baylis-Smith (1996)

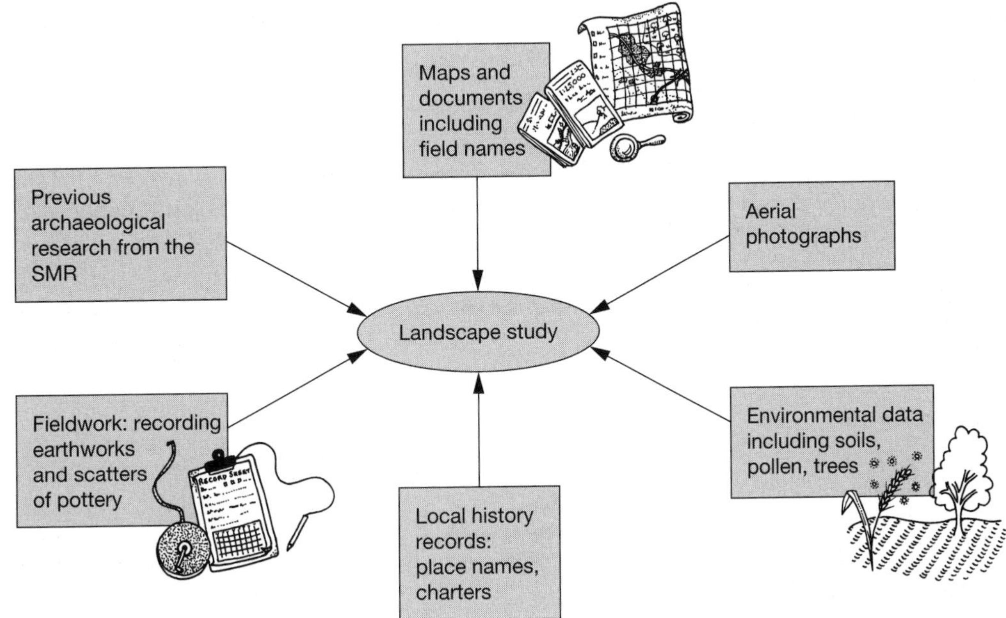

Figure 9.3 *Sources for reconstructing past landscapes*

to identify the start of slash and burn agriculture in the surrounding forests.

The environment

Climatic data can be obtained from international studies of deep-sea cores, varves and ice cores. These methods involve the examination of annual layers, which reflect climate at the time. In the case of sea cores the tiny organisms trapped in sediment were sensitive to contemporary oxygen levels. Strata of ice laid down at the poles reflect the temperature and salinity of the ocean at that time. Varves are layers of sediment at the bottom of lakes. Their thickness reflects the extent of annual thawing and the length of summer. Local climates can be inferred from ecofacts including animal bones, invertebrates and plant remains, especially pollen (◀ p. 84) The types of plants growing on specific soils can also provide evidence of past microclimates. For example, bluebells and oxlips indicate where ancient woodland stood. Consequently, landscape archaeology often begins with desktop research (◀ p. 6).

For more recent periods a wider range of evidence becomes available. The texts by Aston, Fleming and Muir in the bibliography provide a wealth of examples. Their research has revealed that earlier patterns of land use are often fossilised within today's pattern of fields and woods. Some boundaries may date back to at least Roman times and the hedges that mark some of them may be almost as old. Field names provide clues to what the land was used for. For example, assart refers to land cleared from woodland, while wick and chester refer to settlements.

Seasonality

People in the past often exploited different parts of the landscape at different times of the year. Ecofacts have been used on many transitory sites to identify periods of occupation. The activities around the Palaeolithic sites of Ambrona and

KEY SITE

Hayley Wood

Rackham's (1990) study drew on estate documents from the fourteenth century onwards and field-work to show how this ash and hazel woodland was managed as a renewable crop. Timbers were felled and replanted on a thirty-year cycle and coppiced on a seven-year rotation. His work demonstrates the range of evidence available to the woodland archaeologist including monuments, banks and the trees themselves. Coppiced and pollarded trees still remain from managed woodland.

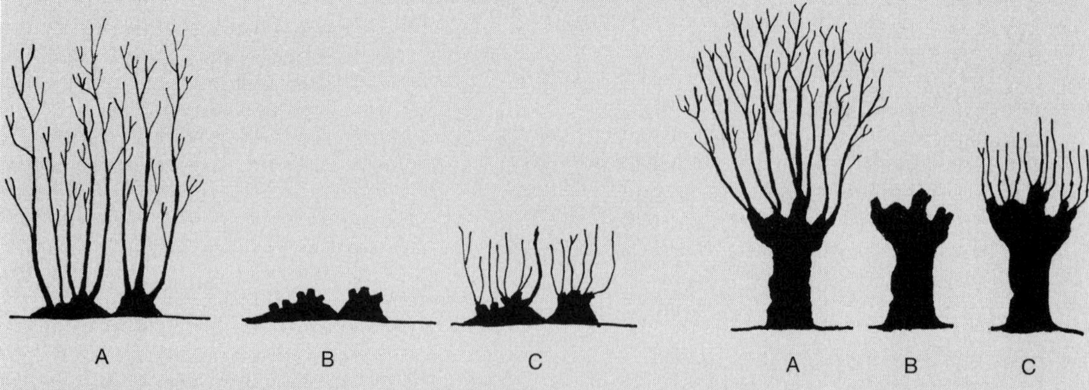

Figure 9.4 *Coppices and pollards (after Rackham)*

These are two of the easiest examples of woodland management to spot. Coppiced trees are repeatedly cut back to a stool. This encourages the growth of lots of long straight shoots suitable for fences, arrows and kindling. Where animals are present which might eat the shoots, pollards are used instead. The tree is repeatedly cut back to about a few metres height (a bolling). A, B and C show the process before and after harvest then after a year's new growth. Even when management has ceased and the tree has reached normal height, the distorted trunk or broad stool is a give-away.

Torralba were identified by the bones of migratory birds while occupation periods of the Mesolithic midden on Oronsay were estimated from the ear bones (or otoliths) of fish. These methods are not without controversy. The antlers found at Star Carr have been used to argue for the site's use in almost every season. Seasonal mobility is not limited to hunter-gatherers. Herders (pastoralists) often follow a yearly cycle, spreading out onto higher or cooler grazing areas during the early summer and then coming together in more sheltered areas for the winter. This pattern is called transhumance.

IDENTIFYING HUMAN USE OF THE LANDSCAPE

The term 'cultural ecology' has been used to describe the relationship between people and landscape. Humans are part of the ecosystem like other living organisms and climate, environment and natural food sources impose some limits on human populations and how they live. However, unlike that of other mammals, human movement around and use of the landscape cannot be explained solely in terms of biology and the physical environment. Humans adapt to their environment through the use of cultural technology. They

KEY STUDY

Early medieval settlement in the Cotswolds

Between the decline of Roman towns and villas and the emergence of known villages by the eleventh century, settlement patterns in the Cotswolds are hard to detect. The absence of dateable ceramics from the archaeological record means that fieldwalking has contributed little and there has been no major excavation of a village. Reece's ongoing study (1998) focuses on the possibility that hedgerows may be indicative of past settlement locations. They would have been used to separate arable land from pasture and trackways and would be expected to occur along tracks and within a doughnut shaped zone around settlement. The idea that there is a direct relationship between the number of species in a hedge and its age is well established. Hooper's hedgerow hypothesis held that the number of species in a 30 yard stretch equalled the age in centuries. It assumed diversity increase over time as new seeds take root. However this model only really works for the last 1000 years in certain conditions.

Through examination of the species in Cotswold hedges Reece found that periods in which hedge management lapsed led to domination by a few species and the elimination of slow growing species. This means that the Hooper method may underestimate the age of the oldest hedges. Reece found that combinations of certain key species such as wayfaring tree and guelder rose were better indicators of older hedges. Through comprehensive mapping of richer (older) hedges he hopes to identify lost settlements.

Figure 9.5 *One of the Culleenamore Middens on Ireland's west coast*

These huge mounds formed by the discarding of tons of oysters and other shells stand several metres high in places. Their builders were probably exploiting migrating salmon and pigs and plant foods from the surrounding woods. Middens are found from Portugal to the Baltic and represent repeated seasonal occupation by Mesolithic people to exploit marine resources. Although shells form the bulk of the finds, fish and animal bones, hazelnuts, tools and human burials are often present. Hearths and even the traces of dwellings are commonly found in middens. Middens are the first monuments in the British Isles.

can extend the range of resources and territory they exploit beyond their natural biological limits by, for example, harvesting sea fish through the development of boats, traps and nets during the Mesolithic (▶ p. 229) or using irrigation to farm arid areas. To understand the dynamics of human adaptation, archaeologists need to understand both the environment of the area studied and the technology available to the people living there. Humans can also modify their environment. Human fertility is not just determined by the carrying capacity of the land as the modern world demonstrates. However, the relationship is complex as archaeology can demonstrate. The collapse of the Mesopotamian civilisation at Mashkan Shapir provides a classic example. The city prospered in a desert area through the development of irrigation and the construction of a network of canals. At one time the city was also a port. Unfortunately irrigation contributed to the rapid salination of the soil. Crop yields collapsed and the civilisation crumbled. This process of human change provoking environmental change is referred to as feedback. Flannery (1976) identified an example of positive feedback in his study of the Oaxaca Valley in Mexico. His study showed how mobile foragers had encouraged the spread of a type of grass, which was to develop into maize. Maize flourished and as the average size of maize cobs grew, it became a major component of human diets. Maize was able to support a higher density and more sedentary human population than previously. Eventually this meant that there could not be a return to a foraging existence and dependency on maize agriculture increased.

- http://www2.learner.org/exhibits/collapse/mesopotamia.html

Site catchment analysis

In the 1970s archaeologists interested in understanding how humans exploited their environment and the extent of settlement 'territories' borrowed a range of analytical techniques from economic geography. Prominent amongst these was site catchment analysis. This assumes that settlements were not located randomly across the landscape, but were sited to maximise efficiency and minimise effort in gathering resources. By walking and analysing the area around a site, archaeologists tried to identify the resources its inhabitants would have been able to exploit and therefore understand its location. Ethnographic studies of site exploitation territories were used to determine the distance people might travel for subsistence resources. For instance, foragers such as the !Kung bushmen of the Kalahari rarely walk more than 10 kilometres (about 2 hours walk) from their base with a range of 20–30 kilometres to other sites with whom they traded and areas they occasionally visited, for example for building materials, clay or summer pasture. Studies of peasant farmers suggest that their normal limit is just 5 kilometres. Although models tend to feature circular territories around sites, in reality they would reflect local topography. This was the case with pioneering studies of early farmers in coastal Palestine.

Site catchment analysis can help understand the economic potential of a territory and perhaps generate ideas about population levels by estimating the carrying capacity of the land (▶ p. 280). It also provides a model, which can be compared with archaeological evidence such as food, remains, pollen and artefacts. Human remains can also provide some dietary information as to which resources were particularly exploited (◀ p. 80). Similar ideas can be used to understand settlements in the historic period. Mick Aston's study of Ashington in Somerset (1985) used the idea of site catchment to illuminate the way that medieval farmsteads organised their exploitation of the local environment. Resources needed on a daily basis were produced in or close to the settlement with less frequently needed resources located further out. He also demonstrated how the landscape could be used as a text to read off past activities and relationships.

Plants are good indicators of local environments because we know the conditions that the various species can tolerate. Analysis of plant samples from sites can provide insights into the 'catchment area' beyond the immediate locality with people bringing plants into the site which they gathered or harvested elsewhere (◀ p. 112). A good example of this sort of study was the analysis of weed seeds in the plant remains at Danebury. Weeds, like food crops, prefer specific soil conditions, such as wet lowland valleys or higher chalk pastures. From the types of weed present archaeologists were able to infer the soil conditions in which the main crops were grown before being brought into the hill fort. This information meant that the catchment area of Danebury in terms of agriculture was more clearly understood and future research could be focused on the soil types contributing to this overall assemblage.

However, site catchment analysis has limitations. It depends on accurate reconstruction of ancient landscapes, which is difficult since traces of changes in much of the flora and fauna may not have survived. It assumes that people in the past were aware of and could access the resources we can identify today. It also assumes that their behaviour was economically 'normal'. That is, they sought to maximise returns for the least effort. Finally, it is a rather deterministic model of human behaviour. It may well be that spiritual, cultural or political considerations were as important factors in decisions about site placement as economics. Kent's (1989) ethnoarchaeological study of modern sites in the Kalahari tested the importance of site catchment in determining difference in size, complexity and period of occupation between different settlements. She compared the camps of different groups of farmers and foragers to see whether ethnicity or a major source of subsistence was critical, and was able to talk to the people themselves about their behaviour. There was a marked variability of data but it could largely be explained by social factors, for example the layout and range of features was determined by how long people expected to remain at the site. Kent's work reminds us never to overlook human choice even when investigating environmental issues. Nevertheless, site catchment analysis remains widely used in exploring potential site use and in forming hypotheses to be tested against archaeological data.

Studying spatial distribution

The distribution pattern of sites and settlements across a landscape has the potential to tell us a great deal about the interaction between people and environment and the nature of social organisation. The first stage is to plot known sites of similar dates on a map and then add aerial and surface survey results if they are available. The distribution can then be analysed for signs of patterns, clustering, and relationships between larger and smaller sites. GIS is particularly useful here. Once the data is inputted, queries can relate sites to a wide range of factors including soils, water and intervisibility.

Describing the pattern is easier than explaining it. Various types of cluster analysis have been used to test archaeological site distribution against geographical models of distribution.

Central place theory (CPT) based on the modelling of Christaller assumes that as the landscape fills up, settlements will be spaced evenly throughout it. Where settlements are more or less of equal size this reflects a fairly equal society. Where there is considerable variation in size it reflects a hierarchical society and one where the larger places perform central functions and provide a wider range of goods on behalf of a cluster of smaller satellite settlements. These will also emerge at regular intervals across the landscape. The most efficient pattern of spacing is a hexagonal lattice so areas for each central place are modelled by drawing hexagons around them. A study of medieval English market towns found that they fitted this model quite well. Each town was 4–6 miles from its neighbours and served a cluster of satellite hamlets and farmsteads. **Thiessen polygons** have been used in similar ways. These are created by identifying the midpoints between settlements, and joining them to form irregular shaped zones of influence and exploitation.

KEY STUDY

Mesolithic hunters of the Trentino

Figure 9.6 *Replica of a rock shelter in use by a group of hunters*

Clark (2000) studied the connection between sites, environment and economic strategy in the mountains of Northern Italy. He was able to detect diachronic or gradual change over a long period in assemblages of animal bones (◀ p. 94) and lithic tools from well preserved deposits in valley rock shelters. By combining this data with comparative analysis of scattered assemblages at high altitude open air sites he traced changes in use of the landscape and hunting patterns. During the early Mesolithic, hunters went up into the mountains during the summer to kill ibex and chamois. To minimise the risk of wasted trips they developed arrow technology to maximise their chances of killing animals at well chosen ambush sites such as Colbricon. To facilitate this they had to acquire flint from quarry sites and bring it with them into the mountains. Ibex and chamois bone assemblages at the rock shelter sites suggest selected joints of meat were being brought down by the hunters.

In the later Mesolithic the high level intercept sites were abandoned and bone assemblages only comprised resources from the lower woods and river valleys. Lithics also changed in order to kill forest animals. Whole carcasses were now butchered at the shelters. This suggests that hunting territories were much smaller. These changes coincided with an extension of forest cover into the mountains. High level hunting became less reliable. To reduce risk new strategies, tools and landscape exploitation patterns were adopted.

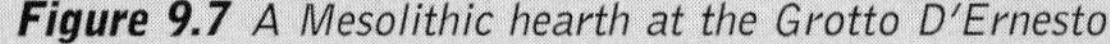

Figure 9.7 *A Mesolithic hearth at the Grotto D'Ernesto*

A hearth from the Grotto D'Ernesto rock shelter. The positioning of artefacts and ecofacts around the hearth provides clues about the size of the group and the activities they were involved in. Charcoal and bone collagen provided radio carbon dates around 8500 bp. Most of the bones were from young male animals which suggests very selective hunting. Upper leg bones were rarely found here but were found in larger shelters which suggest that this site was not a 'home base'.

KEY STUDY *cont.*

Mesolithic hunters of the Trentino

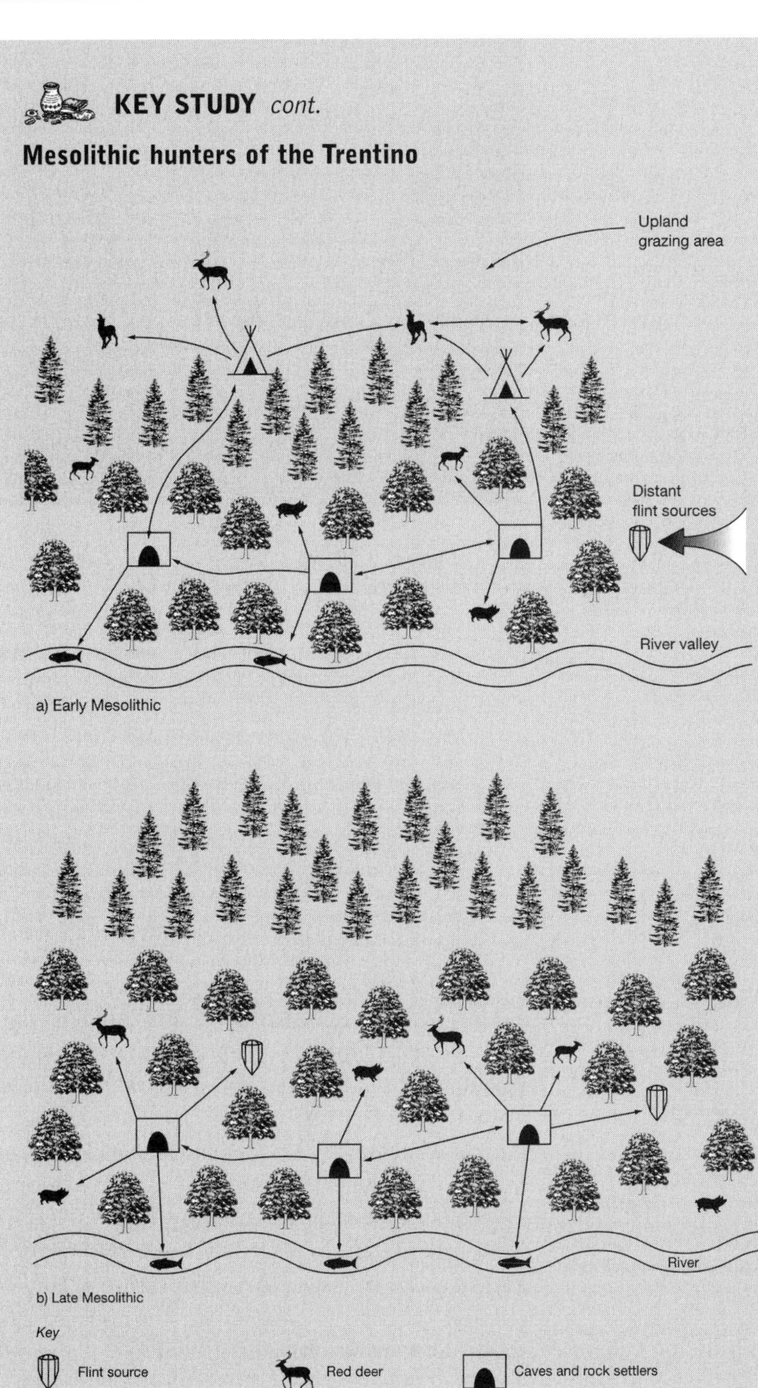

***Figure 9.8** Economic changes in the Trentino region during the Mesolithic*

During the early Mesolithic bone and lithic data from the valley rock shelters suggests that bands of hunters operated over wide areas, exploiting resources on a seasonal basis. Lithic evidence from high level sites suggests small groups from summer hunting camps ambushed ibex and red deer herds through intercept hunting strategies.

By the late Mesolithic, pollen evidence suggests that trees had colonised the high pastures, pushing herd animals and ibex beyond the reach of the hunters. Evidence from the valley rock shelters suggests a switch to broad spectrum foraging within a much more limited territory. Riverine resources increasingly supplemented forest animals killed through encounter hunting strategies.

a)

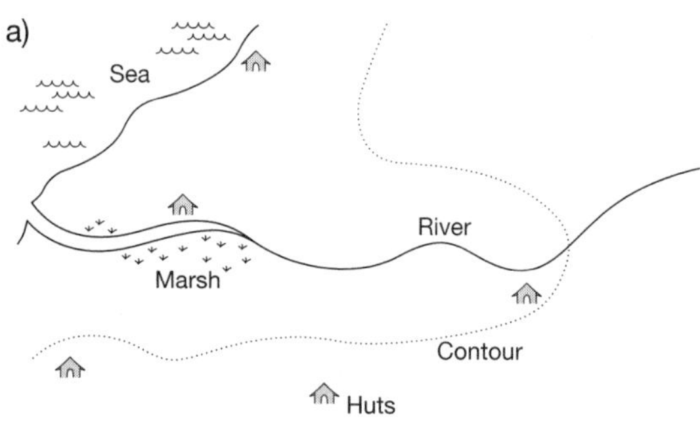

b)

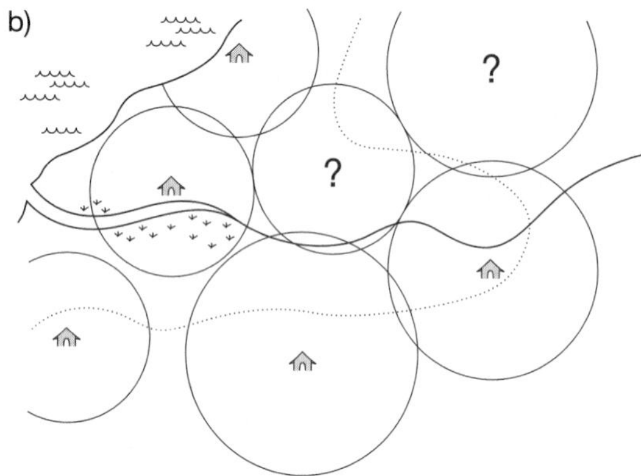

c)

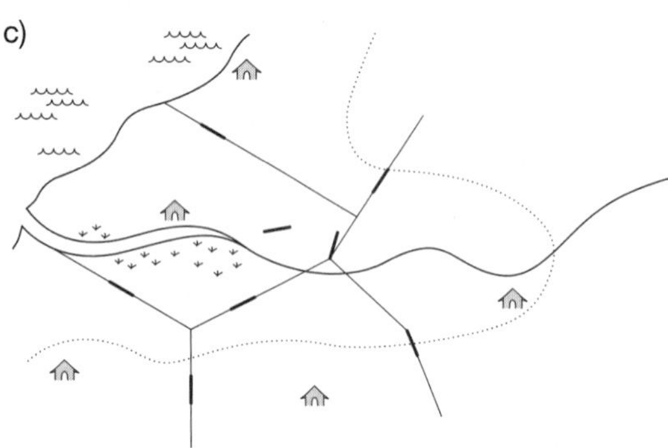

Figure 9.9 *Territorial models from Geography*

The effects of modelling with CPT (b) and Theissen polygons (c) on a prehistoric landscape (a).

These methods can be used to generate hypotheses to test ideas about territory or catchment. CPT could also be used to suggest where there might be undiscovered sites. Such models have been used in a variety of regional studies including predicting the influence of Roman

Figure 9.10 *Part of the Jupiter Column from Cirencester*

As the second largest Roman town in Britain Corinium had massive and extensive city walls and a range of public buildings including temples, basilica and an amphitheatre. Its high status is also suggested by the lavish mosaics and frescos the opulent townhouses. Proof of its political importance comes from this massive carving which stood in the forum or market place and included carvings of several deities. On a nearby inscription stone a general (Septimius) dedicated the column to Britannica Prima. This indicates that Corinium was the capital of the South Western province.

towns and changing social organisation in Iron Age Wessex. Cunliffe (1995) noted that a wide distribution of hill forts gave way to fewer, larger hill forts later in the first millennium. He interpreted this as representing a wider scale of social organisation with the development of tribal chiefdoms. A similar approach was used by Renfrew (1973) who interpreted the distribution of long barrows on Arran as reflecting the territories of groups of pioneer farmers. He found that the areas of land involved were similar to the holdings of modern crofts.

These idealised models tend to minimise the contribution of social and cultural influences and the influence of topography. CPT fits all known sites into one of the categories in a hierarchy of sites, which may not be realistic. A single pattern of settlement may be the physical expression of many different social systems. Belief, social relations and political considerations can be significant. For example, the distribution of Roman towns could reflect administrative areas for tax and law and order as well as the influence of markets. Some small sites may also have a social or ritual importance, which means they are of major importance in their region. One has to be confident that all the plotted features are related (for example contemporary) and also that no significant ones have been omitted. If not, the analysis is of the results of archaeological discoveries rather than of decisions made in the past. The key point is that these are models. Their primary function should be in helping generate questions and hypotheses that can be tested against archaeological data rather than fitting data to a model.

The social landscape: territory and boundaries

Of course, many social territories include many sites and are not obviously shaped by geography. Spatial distribution is of little use in explaining the British Empire of the nineteenth century although another geographical model, world systems theory, is useful in helping understand its workings. For state societies, written records often exist which help to identify centres and their territories. Roman inscriptions and the stone stelae of the Maya have both been used in this way. For some states the extent of political control is indicated by physical boundaries. Hadrian's Wall and the Great Wall of China are well known from the ancient world but during the twentieth century fortified borders became the norm for nation states. The ruins of France's Maginot Line and the 'Iron Curtain' dividing East and West Europe provide classic examples. Less certainty surrounds the purpose of early medieval earthworks such as Offa's Dyke or Wansdyke. Artefacts of administration also provide clues to territories and the influence of central authorities. These include clay seals (▶ p. 242), emblems, standard weights and measures and coinage. However, influence and territory are not identical. Well-recognised currencies were used in the past outside their area of issue just as the US dollar is today. The evidence

Figure 9.11 *Ormaig rock art panel, Kilmartin*

This recently discovered example is relatively unweathered and includes a unique rosette or dial motif. Like many other panels in the area it is located on poor agricultural soil near an entry point into the Kilmartin Valley. There are extensive views from the carvings but they cannot be seen from a distance. Similar arrangements of rock art have been noted on Ilkley Moor and around the Milfield Basin. Dating from the Neolithic or early Bronze Age there are several interpretations of their function. Waddington (1998) argues that they 'inscribed grazing areas'. In other words they identified secure upland pasture for particular groups which was used in summer as part of annual transhumance cycles. Bradley (1997) believes that intervisibility between the sites is more significant and that they may denote pathways through the landscape.

KEY SKILL

Using case studies effectively

Case studies are detailed examples that will provide the evidence that supports your answer. The key sites and key studies used throughout this book are case studies which indicate the amount of detail you might be expected to provide. To reach the higher levels in any mark scheme you must use case studies. They are usually the difference between getting grade D or grade B at A Level. You should build up a portfolio of case studies throughout your course, covering each of the major topics.

Finding case studies

Your teacher will provide you with a basic set of case studies but you should supplement this through your own research. Museums, television and archaeological magazines are all rich sources of case studies as well as the texts and websites we have listed. Select those which interest you and cover your course.

How to note case studies

Avoid copying down large chunks of information and keep in mind your purpose. You will find case studies as you research one piece of work, but need to consider what other questions you might be asked in the future which they could also help with. It is sensible to adopt a thematic approach as used in the Stellmoor example (▶ p. 227), breaking the study up into components. There are many ways to do this from simple highlighting of the original or sets of keywords and concepts to elaborate cross-referenced, illustrated and colour-coded separate notes. Use whichever system you find the most effective for retaining useable data. Experience has shown that the following work well:

- Condense the factual content to one third or less of the original, emphasising keywords and concepts. These will trigger recall of data in an examination situation.
- Extract phrases and quotations but keep them punchy and brief.
- Use illustrations and diagrams where possible. They can convey a concept more effectively than you could do with words.
- Use the 'list' or 'brainstorming' method to give consistency and information at a glance.
- Use highlighters sparingly in your own notes and never on the original!
- Use colour to code for methods and big themes. Limit yourself to six colours.

Managing case studies

As your folder grows it is easy to lose track of material. You should catalogue your studies by using a grid such as the one below. Enter the name of each site in the left-hand column and then indicate key aspects of the site which relate to the themes you are studying and which you may be examined upon. This grid is set up for A Level. It could serve as an index in your folder and help you to make links between themes. We have flagged up such links in many of the studies we have used.

KEY SKILL *cont.*

Study	Methods	Material culture	Economics	Settlement	Society
Gudme	Typology	Metal working	Exchange Manufacturing	Trade Ritual site	Status Specialists
Boxgrove	Box grid Use wear	Lithics	Hunting	Kill site	Band

may be contradictory in other ways. Zones of pottery and coin distribution have often not matched up. For early periods there may have been markers of territory which have not survived. These might have included totems or the appearance of peoples themselves.

On a local level, the landscape can also be used to explore power and status. The position of powerful social institutions such as churches and country houses are often prominent in the landscape. The traces of deserted villages on land cleared for sheep pasture in the later middle ages (◀ p. 23) or for deer parks in the eighteenth century provide insights into local control. Studies such as that at Shapwick (◀ p. 13) have revealed the way that the apparently natural distribution of villages nestling in the countryside was often a medieval creation. Powerful estate owners reorganised the landscape, creating nucleated villages from scattered farmsteads to maximise control and profitability. Modern field patterns strongly reflect the enclosure movement of the early nineteenth century, which was pursued for similar reasons.

- http://www.loki.stockton.edu/~ken/wharram/wharram.htm
- www.le.ac.uk/elh/whittlewood/index.htm

IDENTIFYING THE FUNCTION(S) OF ARCHAEOLOGICAL SITES

Archaeological sites are usually categorised by function. Generally this is a matter of determining the primary function since most sites have several. A castle is primarily defensive but may also have a domestic, economic and political function as well as being a status symbol. The same point could also be made about individual buildings. Archaeologists therefore try and identify what activities were carried out and whether there are any significant patterns in the evidence that might indicate that those particular spaces (areas, buildings or rooms) had specific functions. For example, was food preparation separated from storage? Taken together these enable the functions of the site to be described and assessed to determine their relative importance.

Evidence of human activities varies widely according to period, degree of preservation and the resources available to the excavators. If a site is from a historic period there may be written accounts, artistic depictions, plans and for the last few centuries maps, photographs, film and even living people! This is clearly not the case with much of prehistory. While there are cave sites and rock shelters with deep deposits of cultural

Figure 9.12 *City walls, Famagusta.*

Some city walls were meant to control trade but these massive examples from city walls in Cyprus clearly had a particular threat in mind. The 3 km long low, outer wall shields the main ramparts from artillery. Attackers then have to traverse a 46 m wide moat (which could be flooded) with vertical sides to reach the curtain wall. Projecting bastions provide a field of fire within the moat. The main ramparts are 8 m thick and 15 m high. Built by the Venetians, its 8000 defenders withstood a siege by a Turkish army of 200,000 for 10 months in 1570–1 before starvation led to surrender.

material that have been sheltered from erosion, these sites are not typical. Most Palaeolithic sites have been subject to the ravages of a full range of transformation processes (◀ p. 105) and any interpretation has to take these into account. The main evidence for most sites will come from the archaeological record resulting from excavation or reconnaissance survey. Archaeologists will then try to recognise and explain patterns in the data. This relies on the comprehensiveness and accuracy of excavation recording (◀ p. 45) for its validity.

How are different types of activity identified on archaeological sites?

Boundaries such as internal and external walls, fence alignments or ditches are usually intended to separate different activities. This applies equally to a room, a farm or a town. Clear demarcation with boundaries makes detecting patterns of finds or space and comparing finds and features in different areas easier than on open sites. Where boundaries are identified, their shape, size and orientation can provide indications to their use although analogies will be needed to interpret them. Certain shapes and patterns (for example 'four-posters' or 'church shapes') may occur frequently. This enables interpretation of features on new sites with reference to identified examples from known ones (for example, comparing Roman features with well-preserved examples from sites such as Pompeii). Shapes of buildings and patterns can also be detected from detailed aerial photographs or by remote sensing. Archaeologists use their experience and data from

KEY STUDIES

Interpreting Iron Age hillforts

Figure 9.13 *Aerial photograph of the massive ramparts of Badbury Rings Hillfort*

To us these concentric earthworks and complex entrances look defensive. Excavation of several hillforts has revealed military features including evidence of timber or stone facings to the ramparts and caches of slingshots.

Early studies of hill forts often started with classical sources and looked for evidence to support those historical accounts. Caesar had described chiefs and the warlike nature of the Celts. Evidence of violence at sites such as Hod Hill seemed to confirm this. Many had massive and complex earthworks which one might expect at the strongholds of powerful chiefs. Cunliffe's (1985) excavations at Danebury (◀ p. 112) seemed to support this view. The massive storage capacity might indicate foodstuffs being stockpiled by a chief for redistribution or exchange. Cunliffe interpreted Danebury as a central place occupied in part by a ruler, specialists and possibly a warrior aristocracy.

Maiden Castle had been seen as the archetypal military fort by early excavators and there was evidence that it may have been held unsuccessfully against the Romans. However, military use in such an emergency may have been atypical. Sharples (1991) found a more confusing picture. At times defences were built up, at others they were neglected as much of the hillfort was abandoned for long periods. Like Danebury there was massive storage capacity, firstly with four posters and later with pits. Like Danebury there was little difference in size or artefacts between the mass of huts concentrated inside its massive earthworks. The main signs of an organizing power were the ramparts and the reorganization of houses into rows during later phases. In many respects it was a giant farming village rather than a town. Outside there were few traces of the sort of farms which surround Danebury. This suggests that social organization might have been different at the two sites.

Hill (1996), in a series of attacks on Cunliffe's view of the Iron Age undertook statistical analysis of the ratios of finds per cubic metre of soil excavated on a range of Iron Age sites. While Danebury produced more finds of loom weights, spindle whorls, ornaments and metal horse fittings than smaller sites, more soil was trowelled to produce them than on other sites. Comparison of the ratio of finds to volume of spoil suggested that Danebury was unexceptional in its density of craft tools and fine goods. Several farmsteads such as Winnall Down produced higher densities of many finds and more evidence of iron working. These sites also had their own storage and similar sheep assemblages to Danebury. Hill also pointed out that the densely packed settlements on rich farmland in the Thames Valley (within a day's ride of Danebury) were undefended. This was hardly likely if hillforts were bases for raiding warbands. Hill used this kind of data to argue for a less hierarchical and warlike Iron Age.

KEY STUDIES
cont.

Interpreting Iron Age hillforts

Collis' (1996) work provides a further insight. He views hill forts principally as enclosures and sets them into a tradition of special hilltop enclosures in southern England stretching back to the early Neolithic. Many hillforts overlie earlier monuments and Danebury in particular has a large number of ritual burials and other deposits in its storage pits. Hill also discovered that just as most round houses and enclosures faced east or south east, most hillforts opened east or west regardless of defensive considerations. Nobody is suggesting that they were never used for defence and never occupied by a powerful leader, just that those may not have been their sole or principal functions. Ritual and seasonal gatherings may also have been important.

Figure 9.14 *Even today the ramparts of Barbury Castle look defensive. The height advantage to defenders using projectiles is clear from the relative positions of the students. Topped with a palisade and with a near vertical facing of stone or timber it would be virtually impregnable. However, this interpretation assumes warfare at the scale of armies. The defences seem excessive if raiding for cattle was the main problem.*

- Champion and Collis 1996
- Cunliffe 1995
- Hill 1996

excavation reports to identify connected groups of features. For example, a particular group of holes might be suggested as the postholes of a house from similarities in size, depth, fill, date and because the archaeologist recognises their pattern. Other evidence will be examined to see if the interpretation can be corroborated.

- www.silchester.rdg.ac.uk/

Association of artefacts and other finds with particular areas is the most common archaeological method. Detailed three-dimensional plotting of the distribution of finds across entire excavations enables patterns of activity to be identified. Examples include clusters of hide or bone working flints or the association of particular artefacts with particular features such as loom weights in a hut doorway. However, one has to be careful not to assign function on the basis of a few finds.

Computers make sophisticated density analysis possible such as comparing ratios of finds to area or volume of earth excavated. This can suggest which areas were most used for particular activi-

KEY TERM

Palimpsest

For the Palaeolithic, assemblages of artefacts and faunal remains are often the key to determining function. The 'living floors' of Olduvai Gorge and Koobi Fora in East Africa with their dense concentration of stone tools and animal bones have been much debated. Archaeologists who took these assemblages at face value tended to see these as kill sites or base home camps where groups of hunters butchered carcasses or shared meat from their prey. This idea has been challenged on the grounds that the 'sites' were unsafe for humans and that microscopic analysis of the bones suggests that humans scavenged the bones after other predators had processed them. Further studies have questioned whether we should consider these as 'sites' at all. Taphonomic studies of bone distributions from predator kills and experimental work on site formation processes affecting tools and bones in the region suggest that the sites might be **palimpsests**, that is, accumulations of material from different times caused by natural forces as well as human activity.

- Schick and Toth 1993
- Binford 1989

ties and may counter the bias created by large finds or raw numbers of finds. Similar analysis has been used on pits to suggest that they were not used solely for refuse disposal.

Areas with few finds present more of a challenge. The apparent deliberate clearing or 'purification' of an area can be a signature of ritual activity (for example the ditch at Avebury or the Zapotec temples of San Jose Mogote). However, absence of finds alone should not be taken as proof of ritual purification!

Analysis of soils or other environmental evidence has been used successfully on some sites to determine activity. Phosphate or heavy mineral analysis can indicate where animals have been penned and there is some suggestion that different animals may have different chemical 'signatures'. Other environmental data including the remains of invertebrates with specific habitats can also provide clues (◀ p. 87).

The immediate context of a site can also provide clues to its general function and the activities that may have occurred there. A site surrounded by arable fields is likely to have had areas for processing and storing crops while evidence of watercourses may help to identify the remains of a building as a mill. This is least easy to do in towns where a picture of overall patterns can only be built up over a long time through a series of 'keyhole' excavations.

There are, of course, limits to the conclusions that can be drawn about any site. Archaeologists are usually investigating at the end of lengthy post-depositional processes and need to understand the impact of these on the evidence. For example, is it a site or a palimpsest? Partial survival, partial recovery, accuracy of find identification and the quality of sampling will also influence what is there to be studied. For example not all excavations will have recovered environmental evidence. Beyond this there is the quality of the insights and interpretations of the archaeologists. Analogies can be drawn from experimental archaeology, ethnography and ethnoarchaeology (◀ p. 111). Studying patterns of deposition from known activities may reveal signatures, which can help unravel evidence from the past. Conclusions will also reflect the values and assumptions of the archaeologists as well as their skill and knowledge. This is even more significant if one hopes to identify areas associated with particular gender, status or age groups.

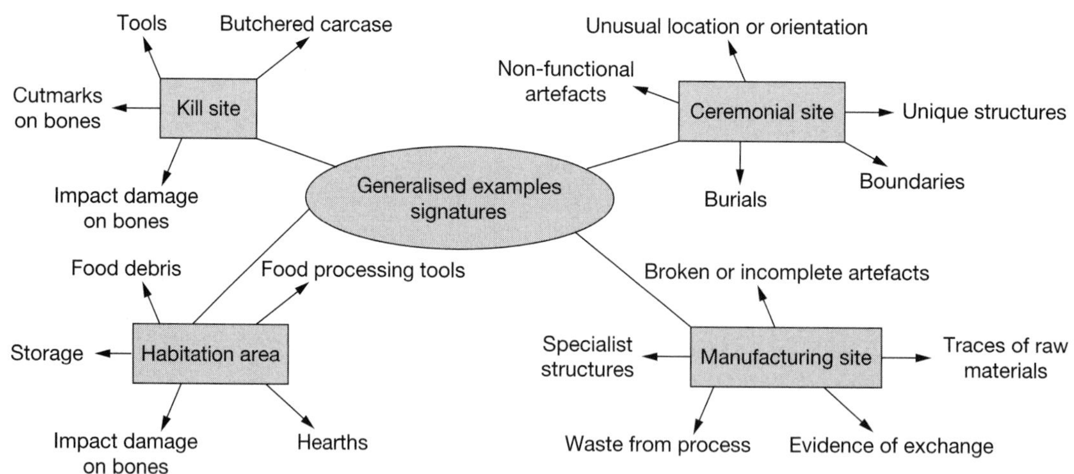

Figure 9.15 *The evidence from four different types of activities which could be used to develop a signature for each*

THE USE OF SPACE ON ARCHAEOLOGICAL SITES

The reasons why sites within the same area differ in their internal layout have been explored by archaeologists drawing on ethnoarchaeology. Binford's work with the Nunamiut (◀ p. 196) provided insights into the complex reasons for differences. He showed that it was wrong to expect the same group of people to produce homogeneous sites. Sites differed due to their role in the overall settlement system. For example, hunting and residential sites used space differently, but even hunting camps might differ widely. The site of a successful hunt might generate many additional activities to the site of an unsuccessful one.

Ethnoarchaeology has identified some of the problems that can occur if the distribution of artefacts and features on a site are interpreted as a direct record of economic decisions and activities. Site maintenance, the practice of disposing of rubbish, may create misleading patterns in the archaeological record. Different materials are treated differently, some being thrown aside while others are recycled or deliberately taken to dumps. Some activities are deliberately sited to be near heat and light while tasks that require a lot of space are rarely in areas where people socialise. In Clarke's (1972) study of Glastonbury Lake Village he used artefactual evidence in relation to spaces marked by boundaries to identify a series of zones which went beyond economic activity. Distinct compounds for carpentry, leather and iron working were identified and interpreted as male working areas while zones for spinning and baking were interpreted as female areas. Clarke also identified some differences in the value of artefacts in different huts, which he saw as evidence of a ranked society with differences in wealth.

The distribution of activities can be most clearly seen where buildings remain. Distinctive features such as ovens, drains and traces of fixings provide important clues. Decorative features, the size of the room and the nature of doors and windows provide hints to both function and status. Surviving buildings also enable greater exploration of the social use of space than on excavated sites. This involves analysis of what the use of space meant and how social relations were structured by the architecture. For example, the

KEY TASK

Linking signatures to sites

To familiarise yourself with the concepts and issues relating to identifying settlement function for the period(s) you are studying. Produce your own version of the signature diagram (Figure 9.15). This will provide a useful aide-memoir for when you write evaluative essays on this topic.

- Insert three or four additional, relevant categories in boxes, for example military site, port, extraction site and high status site.
- Enter one or two sites from your study in each of the boxes, for example Boxgrove as an example of a butchery site. You may find that some sites fit several categories.
- Around the boxes list types of evidence which could serve as indicators of activity on these sites.
- Finally, try to identify any problems you have encountered such as contradictory or ambivalent evidence. For example, some archaeologists have identified Neolithic houses as dwellings, others as ritual structures. It is possible that they had several functions.

household is the fundamental organisational unit for most known societies but there are exceptions where more extended social groups live under one roof. Physical space between clusters of huts may represent social distance while a building that physically dominates others may be the home of a social leader. For instance at Gurness (▶ p. 216) the architecture of the houses reflects this differentiation. This type of analysis has also been applied to investigations of gender relations. Gilchrist (1995) has suggested that the layout of domestic areas of medieval castles reflects and reinforces contemporary views on the differences between men and women. In the analysis of space, boundaries are of particular importance and archaeologists are careful not to see ditches and entrances as simply functional.

KEY STUDIES

The Mask site and Pincevent

Binford's observations of behaviour and the use of space around a hearth by Nunamiut caribou hunters at the Mask site have been particularly influential. He identified an irregular doughnut-shaped distribution of material. He divided this into drop and toss zones according to the way the hunters disposed of rubbish. For example, larger pieces of debris were thrown behind the hunters or across the fire. He was able to detect differences in distribution patterns caused by differing numbers of hunters. He also noted that hearths tended to be spread by people searching for food in the ashes and that when the wind changed direction, the hunters would turn around and start another hearth. Binford contrasted this behaviour with observations inside structures where hearths and resulting ash are usually surrounded by stones to prevent the spread of fire and to provide working surfaces. People also tend not to throw rubbish over their shoulders indoors.

Binford (1983) used these insights to challenge Leroi-Gourhan's (1978) interpretation of the Upper Palaeolithic site of Pincevent. Excavation here had revealed rings of stone associated with a number of hearths. Leroi-Gourhan had interpreted these as tents with the stones used to hold the edges of the tents down. Binford suggested that it was an open-air site with the stones used to hold down hides for working on. People built new hearths in response to changes in wind direction.

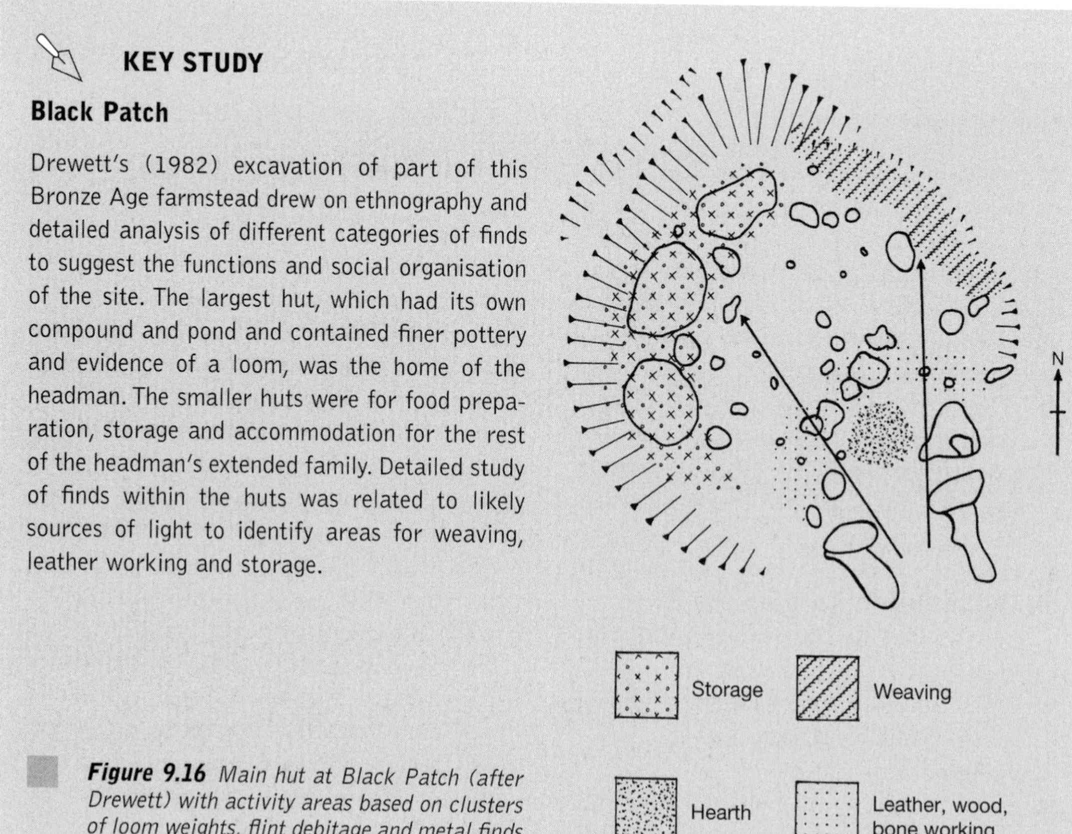

KEY STUDY

Black Patch

Drewett's (1982) excavation of part of this Bronze Age farmstead drew on ethnography and detailed analysis of different categories of finds to suggest the functions and social organisation of the site. The largest hut, which had its own compound and pond and contained finer pottery and evidence of a loom, was the home of the headman. The smaller huts were for food preparation, storage and accommodation for the rest of the headman's extended family. Detailed study of finds within the huts was related to likely sources of light to identify areas for weaving, leather working and storage.

Figure 9.16 *Main hut at Black Patch (after Drewett) with activity areas based on clusters of loom weights, flint debitage and metal finds*

On a larger scale the differing size and elaboration of buildings may suggest a stratified society while controlling elites might be inferred from settlements structured along gridlines or with fixed orientations. The layout of Teotihuacan in Mexico is an example where the existence of a directing elite can be substantiated from other evidence.

The status of different sites is also determined by examining patterns. Elite sites or buildings are expected to be larger and richer in finds and decoration than humbler versions. Key features such as unusually large storage facilities and exotic finds are also indicators of status. The Minoan capital Knossos (▶ p. 238) provides a good example of this.

UNDERSTANDING STRUCTURES

Many of the points made in relation to sites and features also apply to structures, but you also need to understand how archaeologists interpret structures from buried traces. Key questions revolve around why particular designs were selected and the technology and materials used to construct them. Structures range from traces of a windbreak around a hearth or stakeholes from a tent through to recent industrial or military buildings. Faced with pits, slots and postholes, archaeologists have to make imaginative leaps to reconstruct buildings from the past. Early examples reflected modern perceptions of people in the past or were drawn from ethnography.

KEY STUDY

Gurness

Brochs are double-walled, drystone tower houses surrounded by clusters of other buildings. Recent studies of this Iron Age broch on Orkney by Historic Scotland have challenged the idea that it was simply a defensive site. The great tower of the broch dominated the settlement and the smaller houses were ranged either side of the single passage leading into the broch itself.

The architecture controlled movement around the site and constantly drew attention to the tower. The broch provided a home to a chieftain and protection for his followers. However, it also made his dominance of the people and the area visible. In helping to build it and living under its shadow the local people accepted his authority.

- http://www.brad.ac.uk/acad/archsci/field_proj/scat/

Figure 9.17 *The broch at Gurness looking down the entrance corridor to the central tower. This was the only way in or out and the view would have been dominated by, and observed from, the tower*

Figure 9.18 *An example of a smaller building at Gurness*

Were these the houses of the clan members of a chieftain? Note how these building are all linked and cluster around the larger tower. They all open out onto the main corridor. These houses are similar to those at Skara Brae (▶ p. 273)

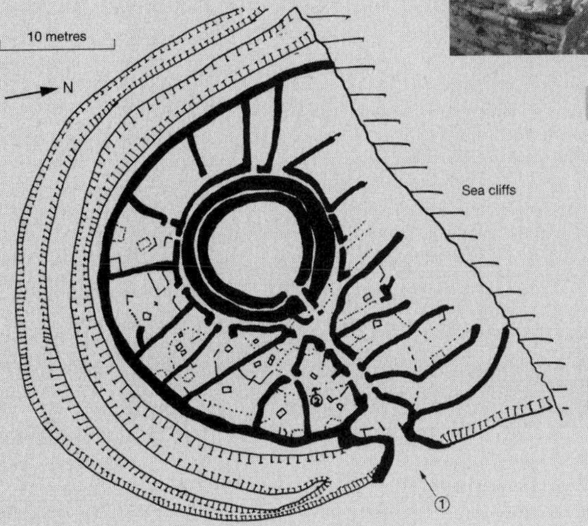

Figure 9.19 *Simplified plan of Gurness to show how the tower dominated the other buildings and the access route*

The places where Figures 9.17 and 9.18 were taken from are indicated.

Figure 9.20 *An Olympic village at Roman Salamis?*

A major commercial centre for 2000 years, most of the remains at Salamis are from the Roman period. This view illustrates some of the extensive public buildings. The re-erected columns would have supported a stoa or covered walkway. It surrounds the gymnasium square or palaestra. Adjoining it are hot and cold public bath houses and a 44 seat latrine. Nearby is an amphitheatre and theatre. Much of the construction is faced with marble. This indicates the wealth and importance of this centre.

Figure 9.21 *High status buildings may be marked by exotic or unusual features which would have required considerable expense to purchase or build. This beautiful Venus mosaic from Kingscote illustrates the status of the villa*

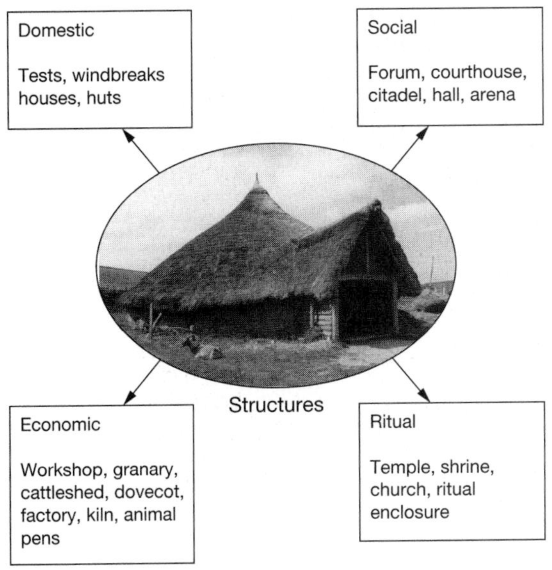

Figure 9.22 *Structures in archaeology*

The development of experimental archaeology has been particularly important in investigating structures from prehistoric and medieval times. While ground plans can be estimated from hearths and postholes or foundation trenches, the walls and roofs are problematic. However, we have developed an understanding of building and materials from sites with unusual preservation. Woodworking capabilities from the Mesolithic onwards have been informed by finds at waterlogged sites such as the Sweet Track in Somerset. They have provided insights into construction techniques, tools and the type of wood used and have hinted at the extent of woodland management. Experimental structures such as those at West Stow (◀ p. 148) and Butser Ancient Farm have used this information to test hypotheses about the design and materials used to make the walls and roofs and then about the use and function of the buildings. It is important to remember that while everyone refers to these buildings as reconstructions they cannot be reconstructions. We cannot be entirely sure what an Iron Age roof was like, so modern versions should properly be called constructs or models. Similarly we cannot know if the house was decorated or whether people slept on the ground or on platforms that lay across the roof beams. Experiment can only show what might have been and then test it to failure.

Experimental archaeology is, of course, weighted towards technological understanding. There may be social or religious reasons for particular designs and materials being used which reconstructions cannot directly address. Therefore other sources of analogy and analysis of the symbolism of designs are also studied. The predominant orientation of Bronze and Iron Age roundhouses and enclosures towards the south-east may be such a case. Experiment has shown that a southerly orientation would maximise light. The choice of south-east or west may reflect beliefs linked to the rising or setting sun.

Figure 9.23 *Model of a Minoan house*

This clay miniature is one of several models and illustrations which have provided much information about the construction of Minoan houses. In addition to windows and chimneys we know they were often two storey and used wood as well as stone and mud-brick in their construction.

Figure 9.24 *Reconstruction of Central European mammoth bone house*

A number of sites have been excavated in central Europe and the Ukraine dating from the Upper Palaeolithic with large quantities of carefully arranged mammoth bones. Although there is some controversy over the nature of possible structures, the dominant interpretation is that modern human hunters used the tusks, long bones and skulls of mammoths as substitutes for wood in constructing huts. Skins were probably tied over the bones to provide waterproof shelter. If accurate, this provides a classic example of human adaptability in harsh climatic conditions. It may also indicate a very specialised economy.

Where archaeologists are investigating standing buildings a wide range of insights can be gained into the technical skills, communications and prosperity of the societies and individuals that created them. For instance, petrological examination (◀ p. 65) to identify the sources of building stone used for Roman villas or medieval cathedrals tells us about contemporary geological knowledge and hints at the nature of markets for materials and the transport system necessary to move them.

KEY SKILL

Planning and writing successful archaeology essays

Today essays are generally marked according to 'levels-of-response mark schemes' (▶ p. 317). Generally, speaking, the first third of the levels are for descriptive accounts or essays that make assertions but provide no evidence. These are fails. The second third start to combine these two elements and are low to middling passes. For the upper third the same essential rules apply to essays in all subjects. Accurate statements and logical arguments which are well linked to the question and supported by relevant examples will score highly. It is more important in Archaeology than in subjects such as History to include detailed case study material at this level. The commonest reasons for underperformance are not supporting your statements and being irrelevant. To avoid this, most successful students plan their essays.

A plan can help you to:

- remain focused on what you need to do
- ensure you cover all key points
- prevent you wasting time on irrelevant points.

There are many different ways of planning. No one method is better than any others. During your course you should experiment with different methods and choose the one which suits you. The three most common models are:

A bullet point lists
B structured (p. 234) or tree diagrams (p. 221)
C brainstorms, mindmaps and spider diagrams (p. 314)

Often people will start with C to identify possible material and connections and then use A or B for finer planning. If you think of your essay as a body then the plan should enable you to reconstruct that body from its constituent parts:

Skeleton	Muscles	Flesh
Basic structure	Paragraph content	Depth and detail
Order of points	Major ideas	Content from case studies
Levels of importance	Links backward and forward	Theoretical concepts

Having planned what you need to include, you then need to choose a logical and appropriate structure. You should respond to the command words (▶ p. 319) in the title to identify the type of essay you are being asked to write. The most common are:

- List-type essays ask you to focus on a process or methods. For example, 'What can archaeologists learn from human soft tissue remains?' You need to detail a range of techniques with examples and try to assess their relative value.

KEY SKILL *cont.*

- Evaluative essays (p. 263), ask you to weigh up how far something can be supported by evidence. For example, **how far** is it possible to identify settlement in the Mesolithic? This is the most common kind.
- Comparative essays (p. 288) usually ask you to explore a theme in relation to two or more major case studies. You need to select examples that you know in depth which give you scope to discuss similarity and difference.
- Discursive essays (p. 293) ask you to explore all sides of an issue and reach a conclusion. They are often posed as a quotation followed by the instruction 'Discuss'. For example, 'Aerial photography has contributed more to our knowledge of Iron Age settlement patterns than excavation' **Discuss.** You can respond to these with an argument but you do need to consider other interpretations as well as your own.

While these require different structures in the body of the essay, they have common features, which you could use as a checklist.

1 Introduction

- Define terms mentioned in the title.
- Outline types of sources to be used.
- Make a statement about the issue in the question, even if it is pointing out that there are several dimensions to it.

2 Main body of the text

- Generalised answers are not appropriate and will not score high marks in essay questions. You must root your response firmly in archaeological contexts, selecting specific data and explaining how it is relevant to the original question.
- Link your answer to relevant theory.
- Do not be afraid to use anthropological or geographical terms and concepts where appropriate, for example Christaller, kinship, reciprocity.
- Explain conflicting or opposing theories which account for the same phenomenon where appropriate.
- Select the relevant parts of some of the bank of case studies you have at your disposal.
- It is usually better to use fewer case studies in depth than to attempt a broader approach, which runs the risk of being superficial.
- Length matters – it is difficult for your ideas to develop sufficiently or for the examiner to be able to reward you fully if your essays are very brief. You should aim for at least three sides of A4 for a formal essay.

3 Conclusion

- Don't just repeat what you have already said.
- Sum up your main arguments.

KEY SKILL *cont.*

- Express a view where appropriate.
- Answer each part of the question. It is acceptable to give different responses to different aspects of a question. Most conclusions will be a variation of 'to some extent'.

Example using a list-type essay

'How can archaeologists differentiate between attached and independent craftsmen?'

Introduction Define attached and independent craftsmen (p. 256) and provide an example for each. Hint at the range of possible evidence and techniques. If you are going to limit yourself to 2 or 3 case studies then say so.

Body Text each point could be a paragraph.

- What kind of societies and economies are associated with each type.
- The emergence of specialists – Upton Lovell
- Patronage and kinship at Copan (▶ p. 258)
- Palace workshops at Knossos
- Craft areas in towns – Yorvik
- Shipwrights and social change
- Metalworkers and the Gundestrup Cauldron.
- Other sources including art.

Conclusion: Focus on qualifying judgements:

- Is one sort easier to spot than another
- Does it depend on society, materials used
- Is some evidence more reliable than others

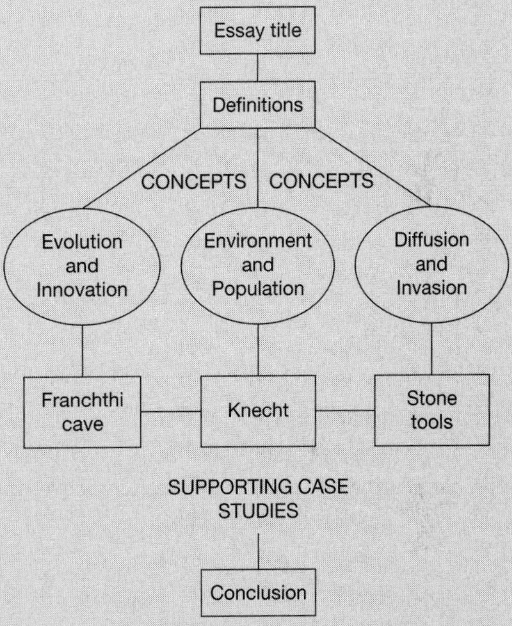

Figure 9.25 *Tree diagram for the question 'How does material culture change over time?'*

Chapter 10

Material Culture and Economics

YOUR GOALS

You need to

- understand, define and use the key concepts associated with these themes
- be familiar with a range of relevant case studies for your period which each cover several topics
- be able to synthesise ideas and data from case studies to respond to a variety of types of questions
- write well-structured and relevant essays.

Although material culture and economics are different themes, there is considerable overlap in relevant case studies. Economics is concerned with how people manage the cultural and natural resources available to them. Material culture is concerned with the things (in their broadest sense) that people made and what they signified.

Material learnt for one theme can usually be applied to the other. This chapter should be read in conjunction with Chapter 3. A grasp of analytical methods helps you understand and evaluate case studies. Other major links include interpretation (Chapter 5), particularly the use of ethnographic and experimental analogies, and the use of geographic models to interpret distribution patterns and site function (◀ p. 204).

SUBSISTENCE: HOW DID PEOPLE IN THE PAST FEED THEMSELVES?

This is a fundamental question in most periods. Many writers have assumed that the type of economic system used largely determines the nature of society. Indeed, archaeologists define many societies according to how they acquired their food. This is because there seems to be a relationship between the type of economy and the kind of society it supports. For example, hunting and gathering economies seems to support fairly egalitarian, small scale societies (▶ p. 265). Their rituals and rules focus on the group and their relationship with their environment. Agricultural societies which produce a food surplus seem to develop marked social hierarchies and laws and rituals which promote the interests of the elite.

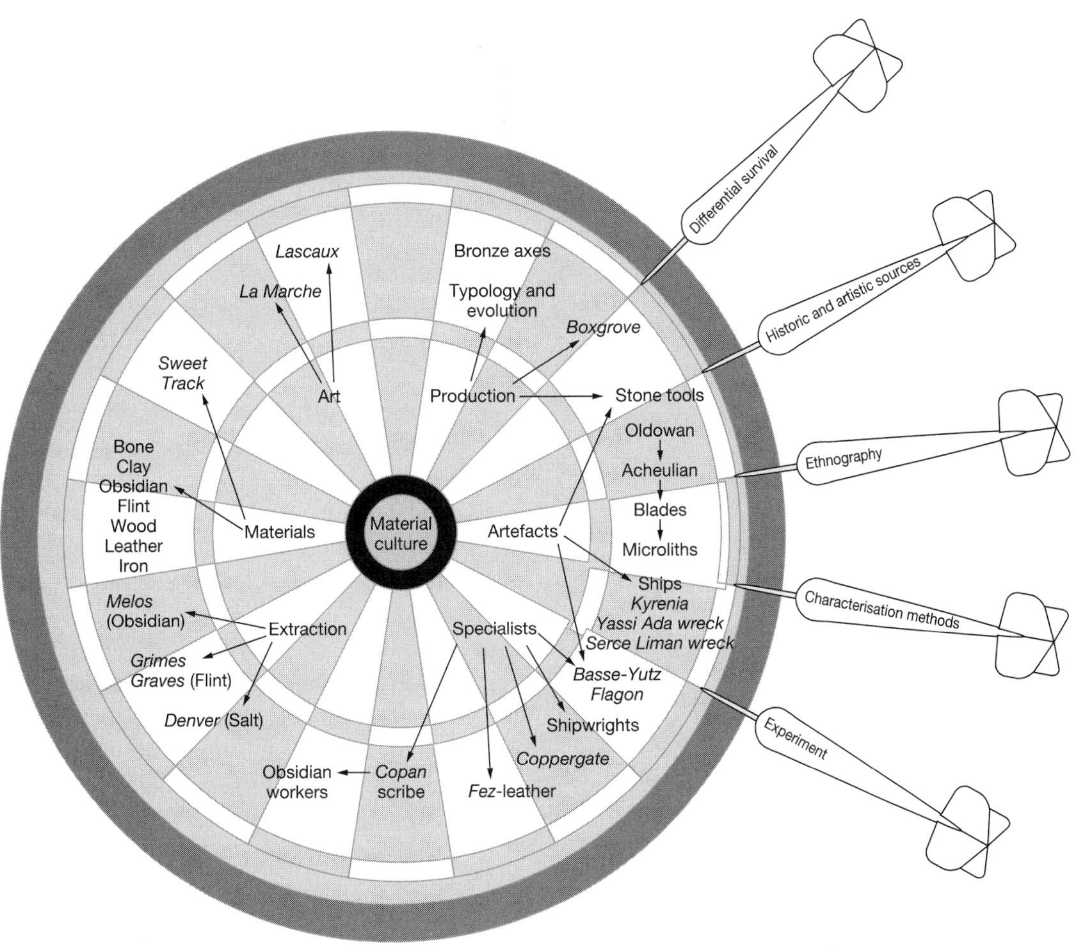

Figure 10.1 *Target diagram*

This is a way of gaining a synoptic view of this theme. This could be a revision exercise but here it summarises the content of the Material Culture chapter. The inner ring holds the topics while the outer ring has our examples of case studies. Arrows provide connections and show how one example can be used for several topics. Darts are points from earlier chapters which you can use to evaluate sites and ideas.

Faced with different environmental challenges humans have always adapted to minimise the risk of starvation. Archaeologists try to identify the strategies they adopt and the reasons for those choices. If your course is thematic, you need to ensure that you have case studies from a range of societies. **'Hunter-gatherer'** is a label used to cover a wide range of societies across over 90 per cent of human history. For the earliest period humans were not hunters at all but forages and scavengers. Hunting developed following a lengthy period of scavenging and gathering. Archaeologists are divided about when hominids began proper hunting. Estimates have ranged from over 1 million years ago to about 100,000 years ago. The Mesolithic saw diversification into a broad range of animals, fish and marine foods. In most parts of the world this was followed by agriculture which provided the economic basis for life up to the Industrial Revolution. Societies that herd animals are called **pastoralists**. Rearing animals for food is also known as animal husbandry. Sedentary *farmers* are usually associated with societies from the last 10,000 years. In some regions they were preceded by mobile *horticulturists* whose pattern of farming was very different to those of **arable** (crop) agriculturists of historic times.

Direct human exploitation of animals takes many forms. *Hunting* may be random (you kill the first animal you encounter) or selective (you take only young males or old females, leaving breeding age females and hence maintain the effective breeding population). Intensive hunting may also include human manipulation of the vegetation environment to make conditions more favourable for a particular species. Pastoralists may herd the animals and exercise some control over reproduction by selective culling of the stock. Finally, they may control all aspects of an animal's life, dictating where it feeds (by the creation of fields), dictating its mate (by creating single sex herds) and so on. Wherever an economy lies between hunting and *stock rearing* it will leave slightly different signatures in the archaeological record (◀ p. 117). Interpretation of this will depend on an understanding of local taphonomic processes.

Identifying the nature of exploitation

The interpretation of the contribution of animals to the economy of a site is dependent upon the recovery of a sufficiently representative sample of the animal population and the identification of its age and sex structure (◀ p. 74). Kill ratios are indicative of particular strategies. **Catastrophic profiles** of the age and sex of dead animals, where whole herds were killed, suggests unselective hunting, for example using stampedes. Over-representation of particular animals provides evidence of more selective hunting. The type of damage caused to animal bones by hunting tools can help corroborate this. Natural predators tend to pick off the old, young and sick and early human hunters were probably similar. This does not endanger the survival of the herd and creates an **attritional bone profile.** More sophisticated hunters will manage herds, producing indistinguishable patterns of kills to many farmers. For instance culling young males but not the females needed to reproduce the herds. The presence of very young or migratory animals provides clues to seasonal patterns of exploitation.

Bone assemblages also provide insights into preferred food sources, although the archaeological record has a preservation bias towards larger bones. Assessing the use of invertebrates, with the exception of molluscs is much harder. Inferences about the importance of fish and birds can be made from the remains of fish traps, specialist fowling tools or even art, as in Egyptian tomb paintings. **Isotope analysis** of human bones and teeth can indicate the proportion of diet from animal, marine and plant sources. Modern excavation techniques have also added to our knowledge. Animal fats have been recovered from Upper Palaeolithic cave sites and phosphate analysis has been used to identify stalls and paddocks. Tools, once they have been interpreted, are used to make inferences about hunting and processing animals. Use wear marks (◀ p. 68) and traces of blood on tools can also be examined. Experimental archaeology can show the capability of tools and provide insights into the ways that they might have been used. It can also indicate how the animal was processed through comparison with modern butchery practice and experimental observation of scavenged carcasses. Cut-marks near the joints may indicate butchery for meat while smashing the mid-section of long bones suggests marrow extraction. Similarly, angled cut-marks on animal skulls may indicate skinning. Assemblages comprised of particular meat bearing bones possibly indicate storage. Their absence from kill sites suggests that consumption occurred at a home base.

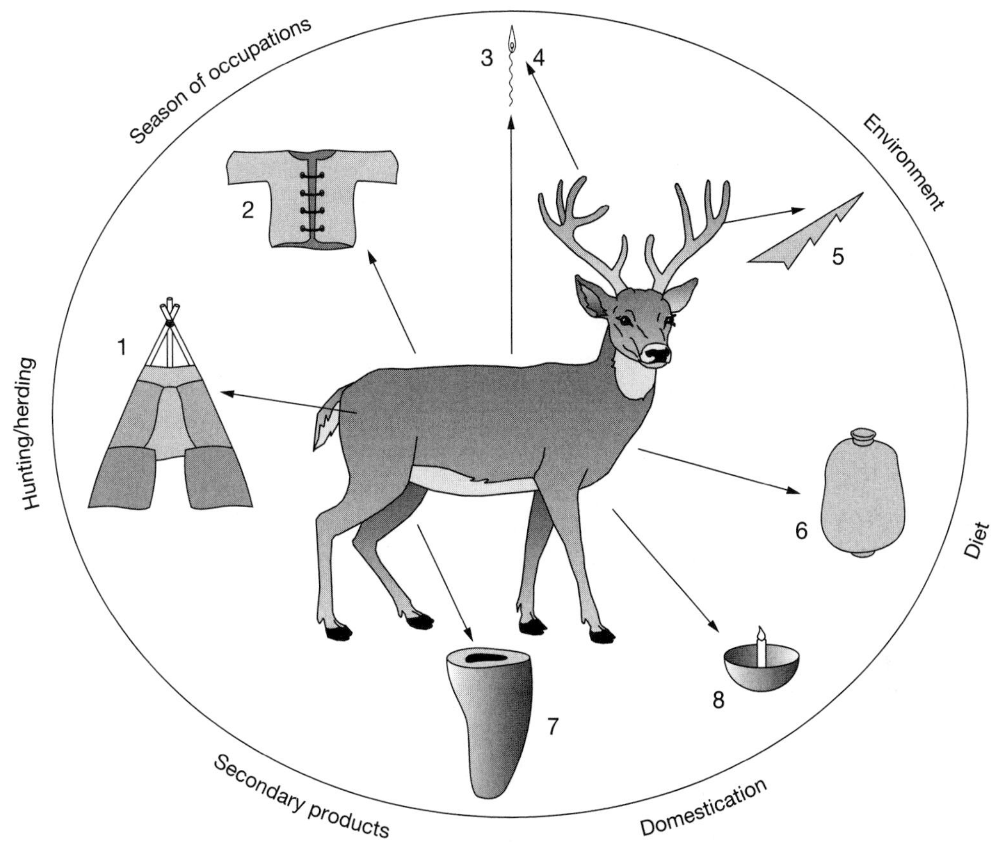

Human exploitation of animals and areas which archaeologists can explore using surviving evidence

Key to primary use of animal

1. skin for tent
2. skin for clothes
3. sinew for thread
4. bone for needle
5. antler for harpoon
6. intestine for water container
7. meat
8. fat for fuel or lamps

Figure 10.2 *Human exploitation of animals and topics that animal remains contribute to*

The direct contribution of animals to human economy takes four main forms:

- as a source of food products such as meat, blubber, fat or marrow
- as a source of secondary food products such as blood, milk, cheese, butter
- as a source of raw materials for artefact manufacture, light and fuel including antler, bone, skins, grease, dung, hair and wool
- as a source of traction, haulage and transport.

Primary products are all those which require the killing and butchery of animals such as meat or bone. **Secondary products** include all those that involve utilising the products of living animals such as dung and wool.

Tracing developments in human exploitation of animals

Hunting or scavenging?

There has been continued debate amongst archaeologists about when hunting began. Evidence from hominid bones suggests that more protein was needed as brains enlarged. On the other hand, the long digestive tract in humans is not suited to meat processing and we are slow and lack cutting teeth. This does not point to a biological adaptation to hunting. Clues to humans consuming meat include bones and tools found next to each other on 'living floors' (◀ p. 41). Yet even when the site is not a palimpsest, association does not prove whether humans were hunters or scavengers. Marks from human butchery are distinctly 'V' shaped when compared to the 'U' shaped irregular scratches of carnivores. Analysis can show who got to the bone first. Analysis of the bones from Olduvai Gorge suggested that hominids began as scavengers.

A growing body of evidence supports unselective hunting by the Middle Palaeolithic. During that period the sea cliff above what was then a plain at La Cotte de St Brelade on Jersey had a deep cleft in it. At the foot of the 30 metre drop were the butchered remains of large herbivores, mainly mammoths and woolly rhinos and thousands of stone artefacts. The catastrophic bone profile (◀ p. 74) suggested stampeding or other form of mass slaughter. Some shoulder blades appeared to have been deliberately arranged against the wall of a small gully in at least two separate episodes. Amongst these remains were stone tools and several Neanderthal teeth.

The site was interpreted as a 'drive site' for hunting. The animals would have been carefully herded into position on the slope leading to the cliff and then stampeded to their deaths in the gully below. There they could be butchered at leisure. There is a considerable body of ethnographic evidence for similar practices involving bison in North America such as at 'Head smashed in'. This suggests a very organised and concerted group effort perhaps using firebrands to frighten the animals and groups of people or stones as guide lanes to steer them towards the cliff. The end result would have been large quantities of meat to be processed and the arrangements of large parts of skeletons against the gully wall may suggest storage practice in the form of a cache.

Figure 10.3 *What a mammoth trap might have looked like. If only . . .*

KEY SITE

Stellmoor

This site on the North German Plain dates from the last Ice Age of 9000BC and illustrates the development of selective hunting. First excavated by Rust in the 1930s, the site lay in a peat deposit near a lake and had excellent organic preservation. Wells were bored to help drain the site and a huge area opened up for excavation. An occupation layer around half a metre deep was uncovered. Thousands of tanged points (arrow heads) were recovered along with axes, harpoons and 105 long, pine arrow shafts. Bones of elk, horse, wolf, marten and water-birds were found but the main prey were reindeer. 1300 antlers were recovered, mostly from male animals. Reindeer on their summer migration to the northern tundra passed through a 'tunnel valley' where hunters used bows to kill selected animals. This is known as an intercept strategy (◀ p. 202). The survival of a pine post suggested that fences may have been used to direct animals towards an ambush – a technique also used by Native Americans. Some complete animals had been weighted down in the lake with stones. Were these offerings?

Bratlund's (1991) analysis of the lesions (impact damage) on the bones was able to determine the angle and velocity of the arrows. The hunters predominantly used head shots or shots towards vital organs, avoiding the ribs. These targets were used to maximize damage and blood loss. It appeared that animals passed in front of hunters and were driven into the lake so that selected

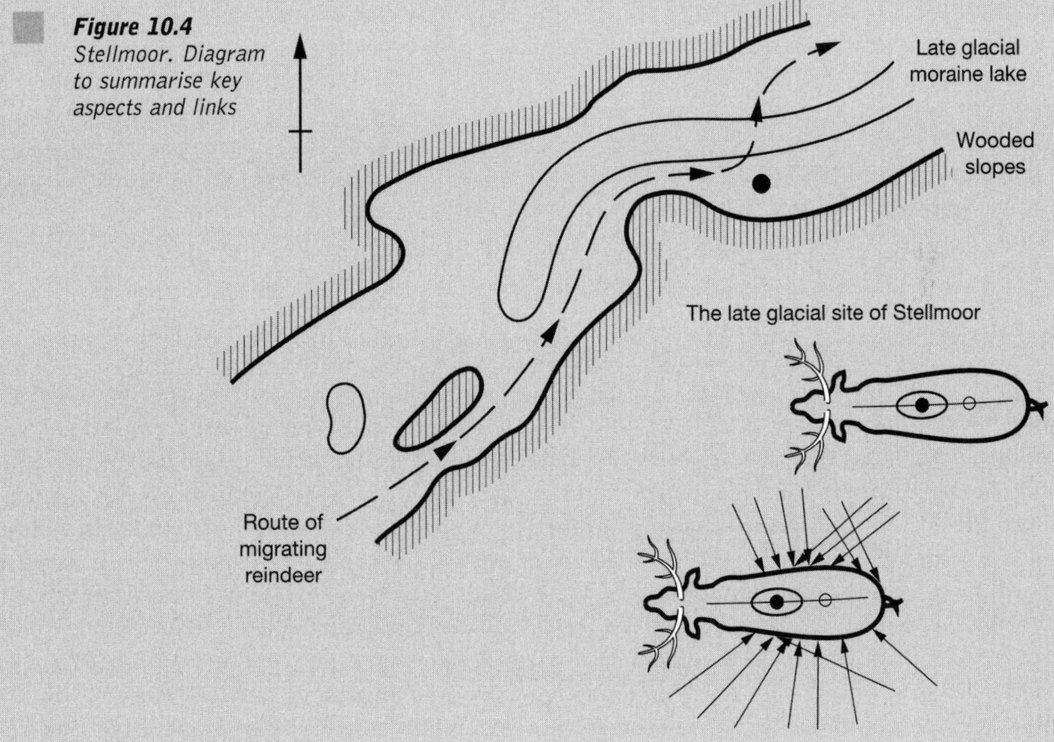

Figure 10.4
Stellmoor. Diagram to summarise key aspects and links

KEY SITE *cont.*

Stellmoor

individuals could be picked off. Analysis of the sex and age of kills provided evidence for selective culling of young males. This indicates a very purposeful and organised approach to hunting in this period, and knowledge of the animals' behaviour that is perhaps to be viewed as a stepping stone towards domestication. The huge quantities of bone dumped in a nearby lake margin suggest the hunters were processing more meat than they could consume. Ethnographic analogy suggests storage practices could have included caching, drying or making pemmican.

Figure 10.5 *Part of a mammoth ivory atlatl*

Humans adapted to challenging environments using their conceptual abilities and technology. Their material culture transformed their position in the food chain to dominant predator. Knecht's (1994) study of the evolution of projectile points during the Upper Palaeolithic helps explain how they did this. She demonstrated how people used an understanding of design and the physical properties of raw materials to produce increasingly efficient and flexible spears which were easy to repair. Her experiments with a goat carcass confirm the accuracy and penetrative power of spears thrown by hand or by spear-thrower or atlatl. Technology enables humans to hunt large, dangerous prey effectively and from a safer distance than previously possible. As with much innovative technology, tools could also be art as this beautifully carved Palaeolithic spear thrower illustrates. Mesolithic arrows developed in response to smaller, fast moving prey in thickly wooded environments.

Selective hunting

Modern human hunts are more persistent than the charges of predators and involve human culture. Hunters often work together, exchange information and share food in base camps. Knowledge is needed, for example how to create balanced, aerodynamic spears and where to penetrate large animals to kill them. This requires communication and the debate about modern hunting is closely linked to debates about when human social attributes developed. The evidence for selective hunting includes **specialisation**. On some Upper Palaeolithic sites in the Dordogne 99 per cent of the bones are from reindeer. The kill profile is attritional while specialised artefacts indicate sophisticated hunting technology. Spear throwers, blades, bows and a variety of traps for fish were all developed during this period. Some aspects of this may be reflected in their art (◀ p. 173). Sadly, no mammoth traps of the type pictured in children's archaeology books have ever been found.

KEY STUDIES

Baltic foragers of the late Mesolithic

Sites in Denmark and Scania (southern Sweden) have produced remarkably well-preserved evidence of foraging peoples. Continuity in flint technology and skeletal shape suggests stable populations, while site density and the absence of much disease from human bones suggest that they were well nourished. Their 'broad spectrum' foraging economy drew on many different resources. Quantities of nuts and water chestnuts and residues of porridge made from seeds testify to the importance of plant food. However, isotopic evidence from human bone and a range of specialised equipment suggests an **intensification** focusing on marine foods.

Fishing equipment included hooks, nets, harpoons and weirs. Remains of whales and sharks in coastal middens may indicate offshore fishing although they could represent strandings. The faunal assemblages on some sites suggest some specialisation, possibly on a seasonal basis. They may have

Figure 10.6 *Reconstruction of life at a lagoon site such as Tybrind Vig*

The inhabitants of the site literally built fences in the sea. This illustrates passive hunting taking advantage of tidal movements of fish through fish traps and nets as well as the use of hooks and lines. The canoe has a hearth at the stern, possibly to attract eels at night. Special eel spears called leinsters which pierced and grasped the fish have been found on nearby sites. Tybrind Vig (Andersen 1985) like many Danish sites was submerged by rising sea levels. This preserved many organic artefacts including knotted string, baskets and beautifully carved paddles such as the one illustrated. Under normal conditions most of the features in the drawing would have been archaeologically invisible.

KEY STUDIES *cont.*

Baltic foragers of the late Mesolithic

hunted seals for their fat. Large numbers were killed and sites often had exotic artefacts that may have been traded for seal oil. Contemporary sites such as Ringkloster included the processed bones of fur-bearing animals such as pine martens. Some skulls were marked in a way which suggested the animals had been caught in traps. Analysis of faunal assemblages indicates selective hunting of deer, pig and aurochs, possibly even herd management of smaller species.

Danish data was sufficient for Mithen (1990) to use computer analysis to compare real assemblages with predicted assemblages based on different models of hunting behaviour. His research suggested that hunters were being highly selective in animals they stalked and killed and were under little pressure to bring back meat from every trip. The key sites such as Ertebolle, Vedbaek and Skateholm had hearths, pits, various structures and their own distinctive pottery. Some even had cemeteries. They could afford to become semi-sedentary and develop a rich culture because their subsistence strategy was so successful.

Figure 10.7 *Semi-sedentism in the Baltic*

Mobility is a strategy to reduce risk. However, rich coastal environments and technological innovation allowed Ertebolle foragers to become almost sedentary. This has been called tethered or radiating mobility where a band has main site but task groups might go on seasonal foraging trips for short periods. This might be to outer islands to exploit seabirds and seals in the spring or inland lakes for migratory waterfowl in the winter. The increase in investment in a site through burials and the building of traps and other structures might eventually lead to a mobility pattern paralleling that of early farmers.

KEY SITE

Tell Abu Hureyra

A tell is an artificial mound up to 60 metres in height composed of mudbricks from generations of houses combined with domestic rubbish. Their extremely long period of occupation produces a very deep stratigraphy and make them particularly valuable for archaeologists studying long term changes.

Figure 10.8 *Tell es Sa'idiyeh*

This huge tell, site of the biblical city of Zarathan, sits at a crossroads of trade and dominates the fertile land of Canaan east of the Jordan River. Occupied from the third millennium to the 7th century AD, it began as a village of Neolithic transhumance farmers. By 2900 it was a large planned city falling under the influence of several empires, particularly the Egyptians. Despite such changes it provides evidence of long term Canaanite cultural continuity.

Faunal remains from the lowest level of Tell Abu Hureyra were dominated by Gazelle. After several thousand years the numbers of gazelle being caught fell dramatically. Sheep and goats took their place. These two species are often lumped together and referred to as 'ovicaprids' since it is difficult to distinguish between their bones at this early stage of domestication. Later morphological changes such as horns changing from curved to curly make the distinction much easier. The change in bone assemblages coincides with a period known by archaeologists in the region as PPNA (▶ p. 232). Similar changes are evident in plant foods with a wide range of wild food being replaced with a few cereals and increasing finds of grain processing artefacts (▶ p. 232). Initially the inhabitants of the tell were specialised hunters who ambushed the Persian gazelle that migrates in herds along predictable routes. They were herded into 'desert kites', landscape features used as traps, and then killed with spears. However, the gazelle could never have been domesticated because they lacked traits of behaviour which made the ovicaprids more manageable. Gradually, in line with other local settlements the inhabitants switched to pastoral agriculture and then mixed farming.

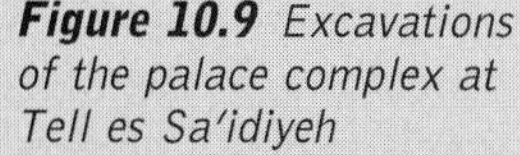

Figure 10.9 *Excavations of the palace complex at Tell es Sa'idiyeh*

The great depth and the complexity of the stratigraphy is evident in this excavation by an international team of archaeologists working with Jordanians in the palace area. They revealed evidence of production on an industrial scale of wine, textile and pottery as well as extensive storage.

KEY TERM

Neolithic

Archaeologists first divided human prehistory according to changes in materials used such as bronze and iron. A further refinement has been the breaking down of the Stone Age in relation to other changes. The Neolithic or 'new Stone Age' was originally associated with domestication and farming. It was identified from a 'package' of changes including domesticated crops and animals, sedentary 'village life', agricultural tools such as grinding stones and polished stone axes, and pottery. However, reality is rarely clear. At Near East sites such as Jericho layers revealed settled villages with domesticated animals but no pottery – hence the term Pre-Pottery Neolithic Age (PPNA). Baltic forager sites (◀ p. 229) had some 'Neolithic' artefacts but not domesticates.

Figure 10.10 *Saucer Quern*

The processing of grains to produce flour led to the adoption of grinding tools which are one of the first artefactual indicators of settled agriculture. Grain rubbers or quern stones were quarried from very hard stone and became an early trade item. The effort involved to process flour was considerable. At Tell Abu Hureyra female skeletons had worn and arthritic toes, knees and lower backs. This damage had been caused by kneeling with the big toe curled under as a lever and repeatedly pushing and pulling the quern for long periods. It also illustrates division of labour based on gender and possibly age.

Broad spectrum foraging

Humans have been hunter-gatherers for most of their existence. Today this part of our history is rarely studied and almost never below university level. In the 1960s attempts were made to explore prehistoric hunting through ethnography. One surprising finding was that even in hostile environments, hunter-gatherers spent much less time working than did farmers. Although some have questioned the romantic view of hunter-gatherers as the original affluent society (they were time-rich whereas we are rich in consumer goods), sites with good organic preservation have revealed that they often had rich diets and rich cultures. A second finding was that in most societies, the bulk of the food came from gathering. Where a diverse range of food resources were exploited, many archaeologists now use the term **foragers** to describe the economic strategy. Foragers are not usually nomadic but often move around an area during an annual cycle. This is rarely random. It is a strategy to exploit a series of environments in turn and minimise seasonal shortages. However, not all foragers need this mobility.

Herding and the domestication of animals

It used to be thought that domestication could be identified from morphological (shape) changes in animals such as smaller horns. Domesticated animals were also smaller and their bones less thick than their wild ancestors. However, climate can produce similar changes and in any case the changes take place slowly. Where archaeologists have dated domestication from changes in the size of animals or certain features such as horns, they may have underestimated the date at which farming began. Herding was probably the end point of a long period of parasitic herd management during which humans acquired knowledge of animal behaviour.

For areas where domesticated species were not native the dating of farming practices is easier. However, care has to be taken that a few exotic food or sacrificial imports are not mistaken for farming. The same applies to cereal grains.

Post-domestication studies focus on what purpose the animals were exploited for. The 'secondary products revolution' is used to refer to rearing animals primarily for purposes other than food. This can be difficult to detect even in the bone record. Fleece, for example, rarely survives and leaves no physical trace on the skeleton. Deformity from use in traction can provide a useful indicator, but not always.

Figure 10.11 *Loom weights*

Clay or stone loom weights and spindle whorls (◀ p. 105) are almost universal finds on Iron Age sites and provide evidence of widespread production of woollen cloth at a household level. We understand the operation of such looms from ethnography and reconstruction. Typically only the loom weights and weaving combs survive. Further evidence of rearing sheep primarily for wool rather than meat or milk comes from bone assemblages and landscape evidence. Prior's (1991) investigations of the area around Peterborough have revealed a mass of fields, pens and trackways which typify animal husbandry.

Identifying human exploitation of plants

For foraging peoples, research has focused on identifying which plants they used from plant remains and specialised artefacts such as digging sticks and grinding stones. Site catchment analysis has been used in conjunction with environmental data to suggest possible resources. Glimpses of the range of non-food uses of plants have been obtained from sites with exceptional preservation. Nets, boats and clothes (Otzi the Ice Man's grass cape) have been recovered from later prehistory and probably represent only a fraction of plant uses. With the development of pottery, twisted cord was used for decoration, suggesting that the use of rope was well known. In the historic period, the economic importance of agricultural produce means that there is considerable historical documentation of various sorts and artistic sources that provide information on techniques, organisation and productivity.

Most attention has centred on the transition to agriculture because of the impact it has had on social development. Almost all civilisations have been based on wheat, barley, millet, rice, maize or potato.

Identifying the change to food production

Much early research on farming tried to identify where the first domesticates appeared. The Near East is generally acknowledged to have been the first, with wheat, barley, goats/sheep and cattle as its staples. However, it seems that a number of 'hearths' appeared in different parts of the world based on a different range of crops including maize in Mesoamerica and rice in East Asia. Horticulture involves modifying the growth cycles of plants, most simply by weeding, to increase productivity and usefulness. Arable agriculture is associated with a specialised and systematic approach to crop production, ultimately including fields. However, in its early stages agriculture involved minimal changes in the toolkit of late Mesolithic peoples, which makes its detection difficult. Most of the evidence comes from seed crops, which can give a somewhat distorted view. Cereals are genetically malleable and domestic varieties eventually became morphologically different from wild varieties. For example, domestic maize cannot disperse its seeds. The way they were processed meant there was more chance of grains being preserved through carbonisation than other plant foods. Furthermore, other crops such as legumes (peas and beans) seem to have changed more slowly while root crops are almost archaeologically invisible. The spread of arable farming is easiest to track in regions where the species were not native as long as original distributions are known.

In Britain but not Ireland there was a lag of hundreds of years between the appearance of the first sign of arable crops and evidence of

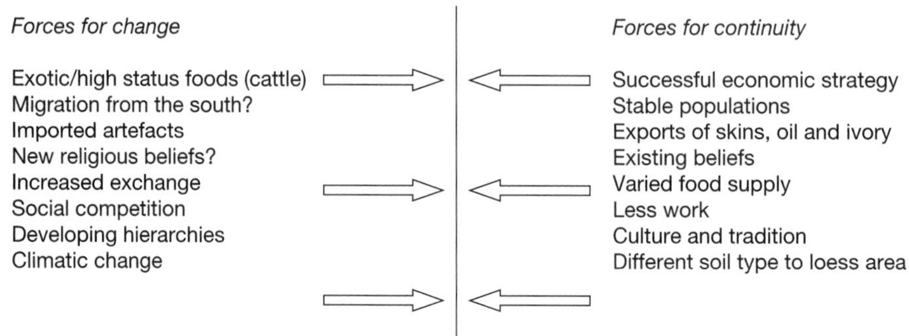

Figure 10.12 *A force field diagram to illustrate the different pressures and motives which influenced the 'Neolithic standstill' in the Baltic. A shift in the strength of some of these eventually led to a very rapid conversion*

KEY TASK

Contextualising the domestication debate

It is over 70 years since Childe identified the 'Neolithic Revolution' as the single most significant change in the way humans lived. Since then archaeologists have competed to explain the development of agriculture. Most theories seem plausible but all have their limits and exceptions to their rules.

1. Take each of the seven explanations below.
2. List them in the first column of a three-column table.
3. For your area of study insert evidence that supports each theory next to it in the second column and evidence that contradicts it in the third.
4. Use this to rank the explanations for your area.
5. Your analysis and evaluation would provide a skeleton for an essay on this topic. A problem with each argument appears in italics.

Agriculture developed:

a) when climatic changes led to humans and future domesticates being concentrated in particular areas. *Climatic data does not support this idea*
b) as increasing knowledge of plants and animals led via a series of stages to domestication. *This doesn't explain why it happened in some areas and not in others*
c) in areas that were rich in the right resources where people had time to innovate. *This doesn't explain why it didn't happen in all the 'right' areas or, if wild resources were so good, why people should bother with farming*
d) in areas where there was population pressure and less wild food. Farming develops to minimise risk. *Population levels do not appear to have been high enough to force this*
e) in areas where foragers had been successful and become less mobile. Agriculture and storage are developed to reduce risk in lean periods. *Again, this does not happen in all successful areas*
f) when successful broad-spectrum foragers in good areas spread into more marginal regions. Food production began in these regions to supplement foraging. As population levels were raised farming spread. Eventually the environment was changed so that there could be no return to foraging. *This positive feedback model works best with maize and beans in Mesoamerica but is more difficult to fit with evidence elsewhere*
g) when hierarchies developed in successful foraging societies. They turned to agriculture to produce surpluses for trading and prestige reasons. *This may work best with the adoption of agriculture rather than its initial development*

widespread farming. Most of the early finds of cereals and cattle come from ceremonial sites, (◀ p. 175) suggesting that economics may not have been the main reason for importing them. Relatively few settlement sites have been excavated before the Middle Bronze Age which has led many writers to suggest that the population was mobile rather than sedentary and that wild resources were still important.

Once arable agriculture was established, its traces are relatively easy to detect archaeologically, particularly through changes in pollen sequences. Field and irrigation systems, storage pits and specialist equipment from ploughs to sickles become common from the late Bronze Age. Interest then shifts to the productivity and use of agricultural products. For classical civilisations, art and written sources have provided data on consumption and types of crops. For other areas, experimental archaeology has been valuable. Butser Ancient Farm has demonstrated the kinds of yield possible with ancient crops and explored their response to a range of growing conditions. Detailed analysis of plant assemblages to examine weed types and ratios of weeds to grain and grain to chaff enable archaeologists to identify whether crops were grown and processed on-site and suggest where the fields were (◀ p. 84).

Most early works on the origins of agriculture assumed that a sedentary, farming life was superior to foraging. Certainly the wave of pioneer farming which spread (diffused) through south-eastern and central Europe at a steady rate seems to support this view. However, recent work on successful foragers (◀ p. 229) provides an opposing view. For up to a thousand years the Mesolithic peoples of north-west Europe did not adopt farming in what is termed the 'Neolithic standstill'. There were farmers to the south with whom they occasionally traded so the ideas and crops were available, but they chose not to adopt them. Why should people give up economic

Figure 10.13 *Roundhouse from Archaeolink*

Although the first farmers in central Europe lived in massive rectangular longhouses, the preference in Britain when arable farming became common during the Bronze Age was usually for roundhouses. These are the commonest large structure on sites up to the Roman period. Their universality suggests that similar sized groups of extended familes were the basic building block of society and probably of production and consumption too.

strategies that produced a wide variety of foodstuffs and other resources and may have provided surpluses? Farming is hard work and would have produced a monotonous diet.

Eventually agriculture did spread and this raises another question, why then? Theories include environmental change, the prestige attached to cattle and grain and the possibility of conversion. What is clear is that the transition to farming was not a simple process and that a variety of economic strategies were selected by people according to social requirements as well as ecological pressures. Increasingly, archaeological studies have examined the social significance of different models of food acquisition including gender relations and social structure.

STORAGE

Storage is an economic strategy. It may be used to overcome fluctuations in supply or to collect a surplus to use in exchange. Storage can be linked to social power (▶ p. 247) perhaps used by an elite to control the distribution of resources to gain prestige or power. The concept of storage can be used to include energy, information, and even the dead. Archaeologists study both the methods of storage and the social and economic reasons for it.

Direct evidence of storage comes from the containers or other features used to hold produce. Many ancient civilisations developed central storage facilities (▶ p. 238) to hold food and other agricultural produce. At the Inca site of Huanuco Pampa, circular, ventilated warehouses which were once used for freeze-dried potatoes still survive. The same is true of many medieval tithe barns. Sometimes they contain traces of their former contents or illustrations on their walls. Dumps of raw inorganic materials such as coal or stone will also leave at least small traces of minerals in the topsoil. Similarly, features such as pits or silos of arable farming communities are frequently

Figure 10.14 *Roman granary from Corbridge*

Built to similar plans, military granaries were raised to reduce damp and allow dogs to hunt rats underneath. They testify to the economic organisation of the Roman Army who did not just rely on local food sources. Grain surpluses were transported to bases and stored to ensure a constant supply for the troops. This is a good example of redistribution (▶ p. 247).

KEY SITE

Knossos and the Minoan palaces

Europe's first civilization developed in early Bronze Age Crete around 2000BC. It was centred on large 'palaces' of which Knossos is the most famous. Palaces were complex groups of buildings often two or more stories high. The public areas include a large central courtyard and often huge stepped areas that may have been for ceremonies. The west wings of the palaces were high status areas. Some had wall paintings, columns, bathing or ritual pools and light-wells which brought sunlight down through the building. Exotic artefacts including fine pottery (◀ p. 64), jewellery (▶ p. 256) and imported Syrian seals and Egyptian scarabs were also found in these areas. There were also magazines or storerooms. Some held huge ceramic jars called pithoi, others had lined vats in the floor. Elsewhere at Knossos were huge silos which may have been granaries. This huge storage capacity identifies the palaces as redistributive centres. Their fertile hinterlands provided a surplus including grain, wool, olive oil and wine. Palace accountants used Europe's first written language – Linear A to record stores and transactions. Palace workshops produced fine pottery, metal and stone artefacts often using imported materials such as ivory and copper. Cult rooms housing ritual artefacts and figurines provide evidence of other specialists. Clustered around the central buildings were more ordinary dwellings. Populations in these 'proto towns' were quite high. Estimates for Knossos reach 20,000.

The nature of the social organisation which ran the palaces is less clear. Elite rooms, exotic goods and some of the paintings suggest a ruling class, perhaps an aristocracy. Ritual evidence, images and the repeated symbolism of bulls and the double headed axe or labrys suggests a priesthood, possibly dominated by priestesses. While weapons have been found there is no sign of defences. Perhaps the population was controlled through ideology or perhaps the elite were genuinely benign – distributing good in times of hardship. In the countryside around each palace were villas: rich houses which also had storage areas. Perhaps a local elite controlled the farms and supplied the palaces with their craftsmen, architects, masons and administrators.

Figure 10.15 *Reconstructed three storey buildings at Knossos*

KEY SITE *cont.*

Knossos and the Minoan palaces

The reason for the emergence of the civilisation is also unclear. Apart from the myth of the Minotaur and labyrinth (probably a palace) the Minoans were unknown till archaeologists discovered them. Possibly ideas spread from Syria or Egypt but it is not impossible for indigenous development to have occurred. The introduction of crops such as vines or olives created regional diversity and may have encouraged redistribution. The long term investment in such crops or the development of craft skills may have led to inequalities in land holding or wealth. Continuity of tomb use and of sites such as Knossos suggest that these 'early states' emerged from pre-palace society rather than arrived from outside. Increased archaeological focus on rural settlements rather than palaces may help answer this in time.

Once established, the palaces established links all over the eastern Mediterranean. Fine Minoan pottery has been found from Egypt to Greece and luxury items and raw materials from those societies flowed into Crete. Shipwrecks such as the Ulu Burun (▶ p. 252) provide further evidence of these exchanges while the discovery of a Minoan port at Kommos tells us something of the scale of trade.

Figure 10.16 *Storage magazine at Knossos with pithoi and lined vats*

Figure 10.17 *Entrance to palace complex from central courtyard at Phaistos. The columns, facings of gypsum and construction from ashlar (sawn stone) blocks indicate a prestigious building*

recognised and contain pollen or carbonised grain which indicate their uses. On a smaller scale, storage vessels including pottery and glass can be examined in the same way for external decoration or residues of former contents (◀ p. 67). There may also be written or artistic sources that illustrate storage, including tax records and tomb paintings. Other traces of storage need greater interpretation. Drying racks and off-ground structures will only be represented in the archaeological record by postholes.

Landscape features may represent very different types of storage. Millponds, for example, may be stores of power, fish and water. Dense clusters of posts or ditches may represent corrals or stockyards for storing food on the hoof. Phosphate analysis is useful in confirming their function (◀ p. 15). Herds of animals are a form of storage in themselves. It is important to remember this because there is a tendency to associate storage with sedentary societies, yet ethnography has shown many examples of storage practised by mobile pastoralists.

Other forms of storage leave only indirect evidence. Salting is often traced through distinctive containers, known as briquetage, used to

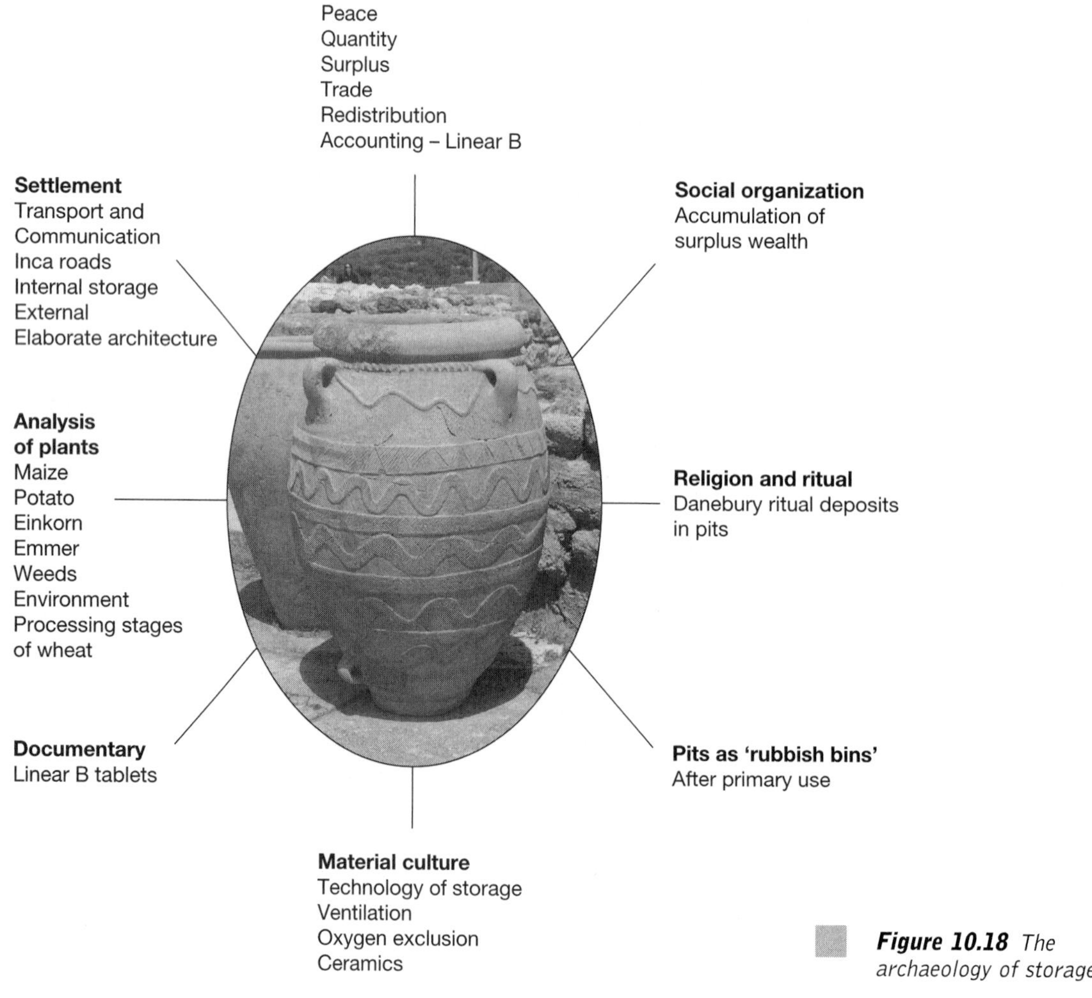

Figure 10.18 *The archaeology of storage*

KEY STUDIES

Early writing systems

Figure 10.19 *The sedge (plant) and bee represented the Nile Delta and Upper Egypt respectively. Shown above the two original mounds of land these hieroglyphics announced the Pharaoh as ruler of both kingdoms of Egypt*

The first writing dates from the 5th millennium BC in the Balkans and has proved impossible to decipher. The earliest writing systems were pictographic. This is where ideas are transmitted through images. We use pictographs today to sign toilet doors. The most well known pictographic system was Cuneiform which emerged in Mesopotamia after 4000BC. It was inscribed on clay tablets using a wedge (Latin – cuneus) shaped stylus. An ideographic or logographic system developed from this, using an abstract symbol to signify a word. For example 4 symbolises 'four'. Early Egyptian hieroglyphics were ideographs but from about 2000 BC other characters began to be used which represented the phonetic sounds of an alphabet. Modern European alphabets from the Romans onwards are based on the Greek alphabet. That in turn can be linked back via the Phoenicians to the Semitic language of the Egyptian alphabet. Greek included vowel sounds and from 1500BC used a linear writing style – Linear B. The Mayan writing system used glyphs as both ideographs and to represent phonetic sounds. It developed in parallel to Eurasian writing systems.

Egyptian tablets and inscriptions potentially offered a vast amount of information to scholars. The problem was that nobody could read them. The breakthrough came in 1799 when Napoleonic soldiers found a stone with inscriptions built into a wall in Rosetta in Egypt. The Rosetta Stone dates from 196BC when the Greek dynasty of the Ptolemies were the ruling Pharaohs. It was written by priests to praise the Pharaoh in three scripts:

- Egyptian hieroglyphs – the script of the priesthood
- Egyptian demotic – the linear script used by ordinary people
- Greek

Since they all said the same thing it was possible for the French scholar Champollion to eventually work out how hieroglyphics worked and decode what they said. Unfortunately we cannot be sure of Egyptian vowels, which is why there are alternative spellings for many words and names. For instance Imen/Amen/Amun.

Not all languages have been deciphered. The clay tablet in Figure 10.20 is in Linear A, the writing used by the Minoans. Although it has not been decoded there is sufficient similarity between it and the later Linear B (the writing of the Myceneans) to establish that it was used by palace accountants to record agricultural produce entering and leaving the storerooms. The tablet is an example of preservation by fire. The tablets were soft clay and could be reuse. Normally they would decay over time. However, when the Palace of Zakros (▶ p. 274) burnt down, hundreds of tablets were fired and thus able to survive.

KEY STUDIES *cont.*

Early writing systems

When explorers discovered the ruins of Maya cities in the jungle in the mid 19th century they realised that the glyphs which covered the monuments were the remnants of a lost language. Until recently little progress was made with the translation. It was assumed from the little that could be read that the Maya were a society of peace-loving astronomers with an obsession with mathematics and a complex calendar. Recent breakthroughs have allowed most glyphs to be translated. Unfortunately few Mayan texts survive because Spanish priests burnt them. However the carvings survive and the stories of gods, wars and rulers such as Pacal at Palenque (◀ p. 170) and the kings of Copan (◀ p. 159) can be read. The glyphs provide us with information about real, named people. This is impossible for periods without writing.

Writing probably developed due to trade. Merchants needed to ensure their goods arrived at distant destinations. They made tokens shaped like each of their goods such as cattle or jars of oil. These were enclosed in a hollow ball of clay which was sealed using their unique cylinder seal. The recipient could be sure who had sent the shipment from the seal. The tokens inside would tell them how many of each item should have arrived. Writing developed from the tokens and the symbols on the seals.

- http://www.omniglot.com/

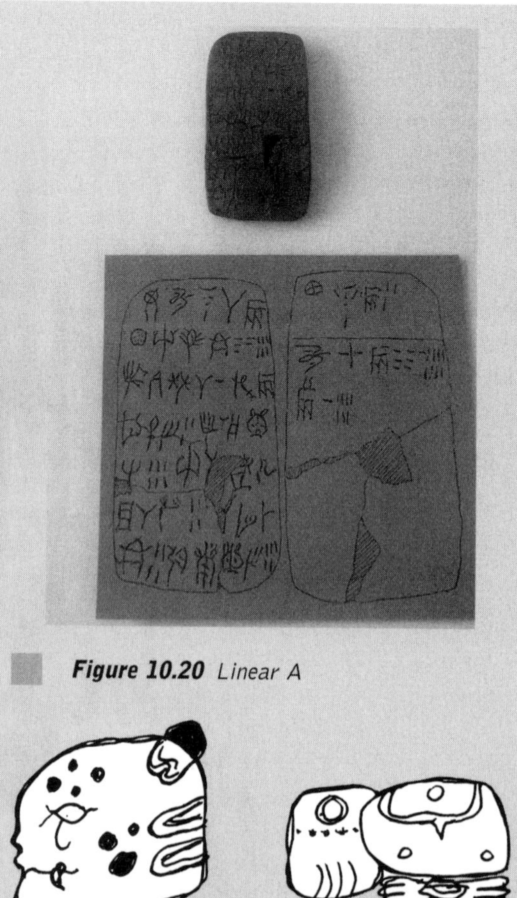

Figure 10.20 *Linear A*

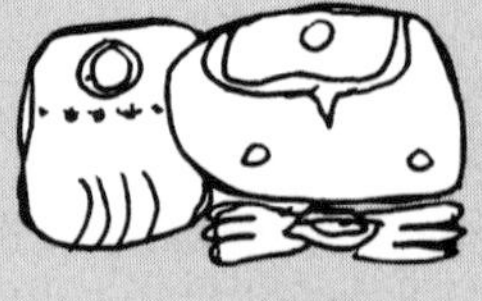

Figure 10.21 *'Jaguar' in Mayan glyphs*

Figure 10.22 *This merchant's cylinder seal from Crete had been rolled on wax to display the inscription. Cylinder seals themselves provide strong evidence of trading systems*

transport it. On some sites inferences can be drawn from the nature of the food remains. The restricted range of bone types at La Cotte de St Brelade suggested the 'caching' of meat. At Stellmoor the sheer quantity of meat was indicative of pemmican making. Insects associated with particular foodstuffs also provide clues, for example grain beetles from Roman York.

Finally there are forms of storage which leave no trace. Woodpiles constitute one of the commonest types of stores but are usually archaeologically invisible. Organic containers such as baskets and skins only survive in exceptional circumstances. The same is true of some agricultural produce, particularly tubers.

Symbolic or abstract forms of storage are visible in the archaeological record from later prehistory. Instead of raw materials themselves being stored, they are exchanged for something which is widely accepted as symbolising a value in those materials. Coins are a particularly sophisticated method of symbolically storing value. They can be converted into goods at a later date. They have the advantage of being easily transported and concealed. Jewellery, cattle, carpets and cowrie shells have been used in a similar way. The concept of **social storage** should also be considered under this heading although it is much more difficult to recognise archaeologically. This is where one person stores value in others. In simple terms, if I give you a gift of a cow, at some point in the future you will give me something of at least equal value. (▶ p. 246) In practice, social storage is often highly complex and can encompass marriages, feasting and military alliances. Social storage blurs economics with social and political affairs. However, for most of human history these areas have probably been inextricably linked.

INTENSIFICATION

In a general sense intensification can describe any strategy which re-organises economic activity to increase production. It could be applied to the development of traps and weirs for fishing or the use of two-piece moulds to speed up the manufacture of bronze axes. The greatest physical impact of intensification can be seen in evidence for increasing control over the productive capacity of the land. It is often associated with population pressure or social control.

The first traces of intensification of the landscape can be detected from the soil and pollen evidence for forest clearance and pioneer farming. The intensification of production including the exploitation of stock animals resulted in the construction of elaborate field systems and land divisions such as the Dartmoor 'reaves'. Environmental evidence can often establish the ebb and flow of human impact. For example, around Avebury cycles of forest clearance and later regeneration in association with fluctuations in the intensity of agricultural exploitation have been traced. Medieval attempts to intensify production by extending the area of arable land can be identifed through place names and earthworks such as strip lynchets where hillsides were ploughed. Manuring to increase yields is generally recognised from the halo of pottery scattered in the fields around settlements (◀ p. 14). The countryside has also been the scene of other forms of intensification, particularly extraction. Traces of quarrying, smelting and mining can often be seen, particularly in upland areas.

Some of the most dramatic evidence of intensification comes from areas of the world where artificial ways of supplying rainfall to crops were needed to raise yields. Tomb paintings supplement the archaeological evidence for irrigation schemes in Ancient Egypt. Here, canals had been used to extend the area watered by the annual floods of the Nile and so intensify production. Records survive of the technology developed to lift water from canals to fields including the shaduf and later the Archimedes' screw, an early bronze version of which may have been used to water the famous 'Hanging Gardens of Babylon'. In the Oaxaca valley of Mexico, field survey at Arroyo Lencho Diego located 20 metres of sediment which had accumulated behind a vanished dam. The inhabitants had used the dam to irrigate the whole of the valley in an area of otherwise unpredictable water availability. The canals and terraces that watered the fields supplying the major town of Monte Alban still survive as landscape features. Else-where in Mexico the Aztecs developed in intensive system of agriculture based on floating gardens or 'chinampas'. Rafts were covered in weeds and mud and anchored in rows. Over time more mud was added and the root systems of trees bound the rafts together as fertile islands. They could be cropped two to three times a year. The Aztec capital Tenochtitlan received most of its food from chinampas. Sometimes irrigation schemes are not immediately visible. In the third millennium BC a network of canals supplied water from the rivers Tigris and Euphrates to the fields and the port of the Mesopotamian desert city of Mashkan Shapir. Today they are buried under sand but were detected by satellite imaging (◀ p. 25). In other instances there was too much water for successful cultivation. At Kuk Swamp in New Guinea a huge network of drainage ditches was first revealed by aerial photography, showing as lines several kilometres long in modern tea plantations. Excavation revealed that early farmers had built them to drain the swamp in order to intensively cultivate the fertile soil and grow taro and other crops. (Bayliss-Smith 1996)

Figure 10.23 *Sail-wing windmill from Crete*

Windmill technology arrived in Europe by way of Persia in the twelfth century. Unlike their Islamic predecessors, European mills had a horizontal axis. This may have been because that was used in existing watermills. Mills such as this were used to pump irrigation water and grind corn.

Communications

One aspect of economies, which generally develops in conjunction with intensification, is transport. The remains of permanent tracks and roads such as the Sweet Track or Roman and Inca road systems can indicate increasing traffic on routes. Intense use of these features can sometimes be inferred from wear such as rutting and evidence of frequent repairing.

The development of vehicles can be traced from burials, such as the four-wheeled carts in burials at Ur or the 'chariots' from Garton Slack, and through art and figurines. Evidence for the use of animals for riding and draught purposes can sometimes be determined by bit-wear marks on teeth or artefacts associated with harnesses. Artistic sources and shipwreck evidence (▶ p. 252) provide evidence of the evolution of shipping.

TRADE AND EXCHANGE

Early archaeological studies tended to largely interpret the movement of artefacts and materials as trade or the movement of peoples. Ethnographic examples have provided a much wider range of options with which to interpret archaeological evidence. There has also been recognition that exchange does not just involve goods and that its aims are often social rather than economic. Often the relationship is of more value than what is exchanged, as with modern Christmas cards. The exchange may involve social obligations which help bind society together.

Exchange in its widest sense includes any transaction between people. This can include exchange of information, services and people. For instance, the spread of bell beakers throughout Europe and North Africa in the third millennium BC was due to exchange. Archaeologists have been divided over the mechanism for this exchange,

Figure 10.24 *Relief from Rievaulx (◀ p. 167)*

This carving encapsulates several key economic elements. Market trade in wool from the extensive sheep farms of the Cistercian monks helped pay for the great monastic establishments of the Middle Ages. Bulk goods such as wool were transported to river ports by packhorses. The windmill represents the intensification of energy production. Human and animal muscle was replaced by machinery harnessing wind power. In this case probably to grind grain for flour. The contrast with grain rubbers (◀ p. 232) is stark.

- http://www.windmillworld.com/windmills/history.htm

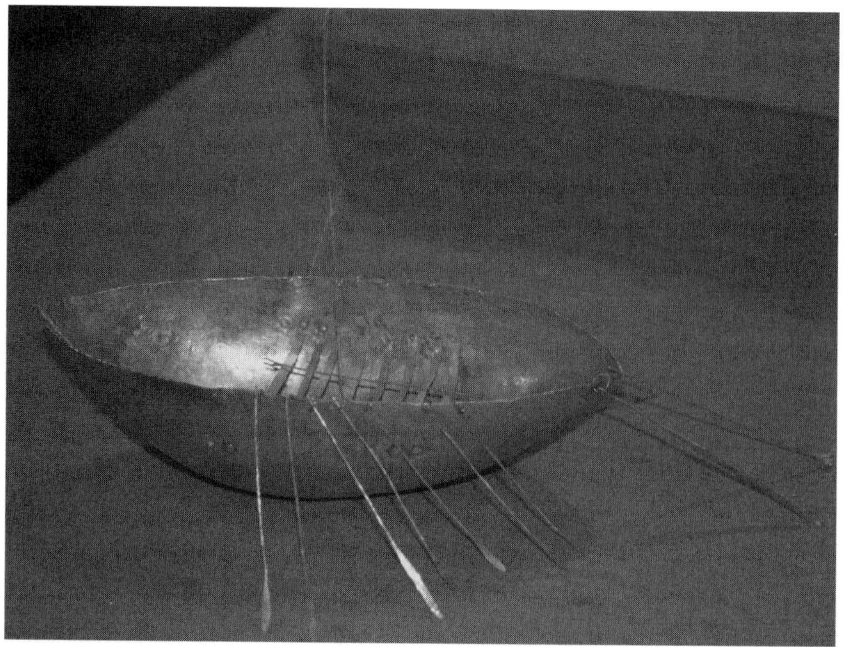

Figure 10.25 *Gold ship from the Broighter hoard*

This model ship was one of seven gold ornaments from the first century BC buried near the entrance to Lough Foyle and uncovered through deep ploughing. It provides evidence about early boats in Ireland.

whether it was through movement of people or the spread of ideas, drinking culture or religion. Trade is just one form of exchange.

Three main categories of exchange have been adopted by archaeology from economics. These are **reciprocity, redistribution** and **market exchange**.

Reciprocity

This involves transactions where a gift from one person creates an obligation to return something at a later date. We do this when we buy a round of drinks. Many societies have used it as the basis for social stability. In some cultures marriage involves payment of bridewealth from the husband's family to the bride's family. This is to compensate for their loss of a fertile worker. Payments may be in goods and may take place over time. Such exchange also cements the relationship between the two families. Feasting and the sharing of food with others are often a powerful example of reciprocity. It creates an obligation to return the favour at a later point. It can also be seen as an exchange of food for social prestige. A popular example for archaeologists has been the Big Man feasts of highland New Guinea where status is acquired by throwing huge feasts at which party-goers are given generous gifts of meat or livestock. A related concept is social storage. Here a gift or favour is given which stores up future gifts or assistance for times when they will be needed. Extreme examples of this are provided by ethnographic accounts of the Potlatch and Kula Ring (Orme 1981). Reciprocity can involve an equal exchange (balanced reciprocity) but can also be positive or negative if one partner does better. Ethnography once again warns against imposing our values on the evidence. Islanders on Yap in the Caroline Islands used to gain prestige

Figure 10.26 *'Agia Triada' market*

A market place would seem to be the clearest evidence for a market economy. While some are easily recognisable, the evidence for others is ambivalent. In this example there appear to be shops and storage containers with a public area between. It is also situated between the town and the high status buildings which might have controlled trade. However, the same evidence can be used to argue that it is another variation on Minoan central storage depots (◀ p. 238).

by spending their savings on huge stone discs, which they then buried under their homes.

Historical sources such as Homer and Egyptian tomb paintings have provided insights into prestige goods exchange. High status individuals established and cemented relationships through reciprocal exchanges. This continues at a symbolic level amongst leaders of state today. These exchanges used to involve marriage partners and exotic goods or creatures. Archaeologically this sort of exchange may be recognised where special artefacts such as gems, amber, jade and ivory move long distances. In these cases archaeologists have talked of '**prestige goods chains**'. A classic example is the movement of amber from the Baltic to Mycenae during the Bronze Age and some of the fine metalwork that travelled in the opposite direction from central Europe. Grave goods and special votive deposits have often been the source of such material for archaeologists. The rich graves at Varna (see front cover) contained bracelets of spondylus, a Mediterranean shellfish. One interpretation is that these were exchanged for gold from sources close to Varna. However, some prestige goods such as furs, slaves, silk and feathers may be archaeologically invisible.

Redistribution

This model involves a central authority collecting together resources and then redistributing them. Our welfare state is a giant version of this, while harvest festivals symbolise it. In the past redistribution tended to be operated by individual rulers

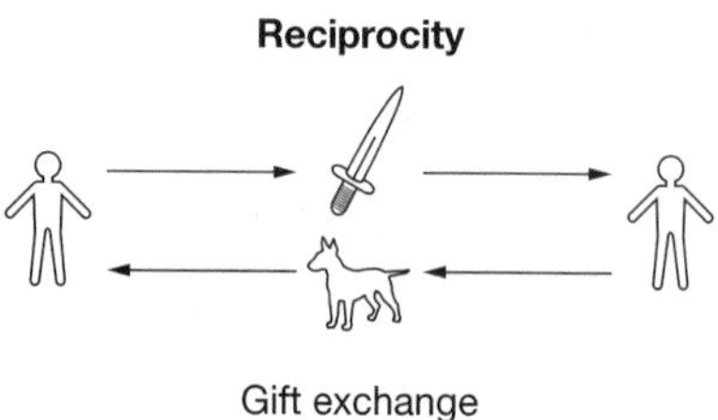

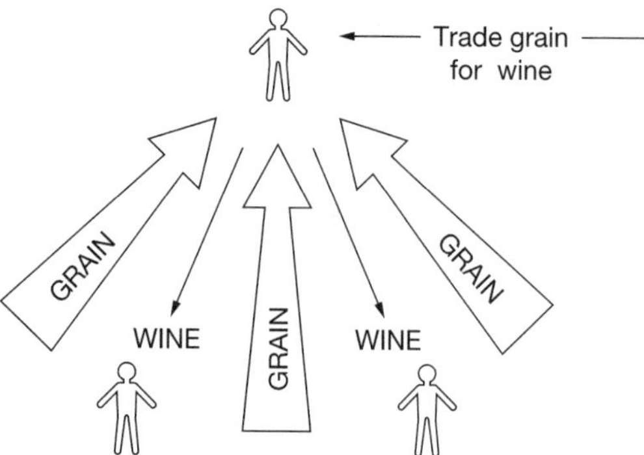

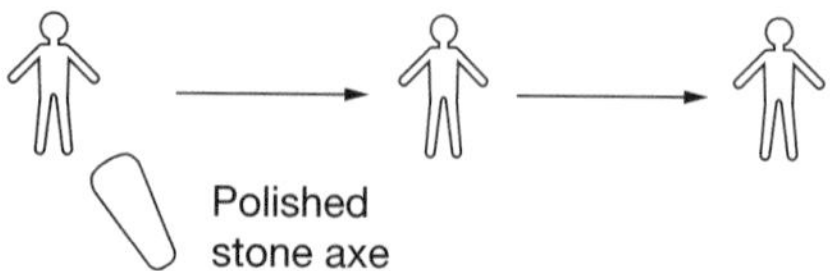

Figure 10.27 *Some types of exchange identified by archaeologists*

to whom it gave both prestige and legitimacy. Ethnographic studies have tended to emphasise this as a feature of chiefdoms, particularly in areas of economic diversity. Redistribution shares out particular resources to areas that lack them, for example fish to farmers and crops to fishers. Historic accounts such as Celtic histories suggest that rulers would use redistribution to reward their followers with weapons, cattle and exotic goods in order to secure their loyalty. As with reciprocity, the social aspects of the exchange may be important and as before, feasting may be the vehicle for the exchange.

Archaeological evidence includes sites with central stores as at Knossos. Some interpretations of hill forts such as Danebury (◄ p. 114) have reached similar conclusions although there is less agreement on this. Patterns of distribution where valuable goods have been widely distributed are also potential evidence of redistribution to local leaders from a central chief. The distribution of Bronze Age swords may be such a case. The clearest evidence comes from those sites where records have been recovered as at Vindolanda and Pylos.

Market exchange

In its simplest sense 'a market' suggests a recognised place where bargaining takes place. The easiest to identify are those where defined areas or

Figure 10.28 *Late Minoan marine style stirrup jar*

Cretan potters made some of the best ceramics in the early Bronze Age. Eggshell thin Kamares wear and fine Marine style vessels with their entire surface covered in sea creatures have been found across the eastern Mediterranean and as far up the Nile as Aswan. They provide evidence of widespread trade in luxuries.

buildings exist. The agora of Greek towns is an example. Another signature is the development of mechanisms to regulate amounts or to make exchange flexible such as weights and coinage. Of course, not all market exchange happens in a fixed place and not all currencies are archaeologically visible. Blankets and carpets have been used as standards against which value can be measured. Identifying these instances of trade in perishable goods is difficult. The well-preserved Pazyryk 'Ice Maiden' from the Altai Mountains provided such a clue. Pazyryk tribes were known to have trade links with China. When silk in her clothes was analysed it was expected to have been made of yarn from cultivated Chinese silkworms. To the experts' surprise it turned out to be characteristic of wild Indian silk. This indicated that the Pazyryk traded to the south as well as in China.

Concentrations of artefacts from many areas would be expected at a port or market. The Iron Age settlement at Hengistbury Head, with its modified harbour and apparently defensive wall, may be such an example. Finds included imported pottery, glass and figs, with evidence of metals and perhaps hides and corn being exported. However, in some cases the pattern of finds could equally represent a religious or high status site. The many interpretations of Neolithic causewayed enclosures typify this sort of ambivalent evidence. Although markets today are almost entirely about buying and selling, they too have had social functions. Ethnographic studies have noted their role in information exchange, tax collection and as places for social gatherings. Historic and artistic sources are again useful. Spanish accounts of the use of quetzal feathers and cacao beans in Mexico are supported by the images of merchants and their backpacks from the rather earlier site of Cacaxtla.

Identifying the signatures of different modes of exchange

The origins of materials used in exchange are tracked using characterisation studies (◀ p. 64). For example. Roman documentary sources tell us very little about trade, but amphorae are very common finds on excavations and in shipwrecks. The fabrics of the millions of Roman amphorae that were traded all over the Empire have responded particularly well to petrology, with the result that we now know where most types were manufactured. As a result it is possible to study the sources and distributions of important agricultural products such as Italian wine, Spanish fish sauce or North African olive oil. Seals or other marks on the objects themselves may indicate their place of manufacture. For example, many Roman amphorae have potters' stamps and some even have handwritten inscriptions, written in black ink, giving details of their contents and origin. Artistic sources can provide considerable detail. Some Egyptian tombs from the second millennium have pictures of Minoans bearing goods from Crete.

Distribution patterns of artefacts from their place of origin are plotted on maps to see whether they match models for particular types of exchange. For example, clusters of Lava quernstones at centres of manufacture and ports such as Dorestadt and Ipswich have enabled the trade to be traced.

Trend surface analysis turns plots of finds on a map into contours to smooth out distortion caused by chance finds. This has been used to map the distribution of Neolithic stone axes from their source.

Fall-off analysis is used to examine the rate at which finds diminish the further one gets from the place of manufacture. A sharp fall suggests very local exchange, a smooth decline suggests 'down the line' trade while a pattern with several blips in the curve indicates secondary trading or exchange centres. This technique has been used to identify the nature of trade in copper, obsidian and pottery.

The context in which particular artefacts are found provides some clues. Shipwrecks provide insights into the nature and scale of exchange and who was trading what. **Hoards** may also provide such evidence although the motives for deposition could be more varied. A deposit of axe heads could be a votive offering, a store of scrap for manufacturing or a cache of trade goods.

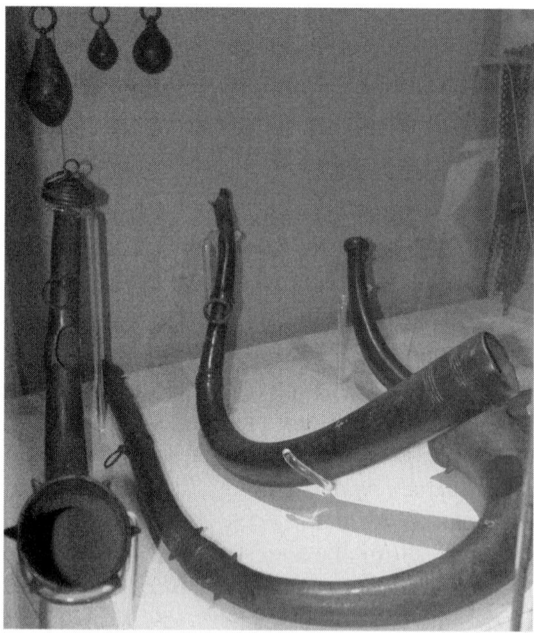

Figure 10.29 *Loughnashade trumpet*

Hoards present particular problems of interpretation. Initially it was supposed that burying objects or metals was a form of storage ('tinkers' hoards') or to hide things from attackers. This is the sole survivor of a hoard of four bronze trumpets found in a bog near the hillfort of Navan. It required a high level of craftsmanship to make and repair and was designed for use in ceremonies, possibly before battles. Similar deposits occur elsewhere in Northern Europe which often include feasting equipment and weapons. The lake where this was found contained human skulls while an artificial pond nearby contained another skull and the bones of sacrificed dogs and deer. Increasingly it has been recognised that fine objects were often consumed by destruction or deposition during rituals (◀ p. 185). The trumpet became a high status ritual offering.

Problems with exchange

Despite all these tools the nature of the movement of artefacts or exchange is not always clear. Not all of the possible types of transaction leave clear traces in the archaeological record and different processes can look remarkably similar in their spatial distribution. Sometimes only one side of an exchange can be found. The fourth-century site at Gudme in Denmark has revealed many hoards of gold which originated in the Roman Empire. Whether these represent tribute, booty, mercenary pay or religious offerings is unclear. There

KEY TERM

Material culture

This term is used in a general sense to mean the artefacts and structures produced by a given people. There are two major approaches to studying them. A 'biographical approach' is the most familiar. This might involve asking what raw materials were used, how they were obtained and worked and how the finished products were used. The second approach involves 'reading' the symbolic meanings embedded in artefacts and structures. This is based on the idea that the beliefs and values of a culture are expressed to some extent in the material things it produces. People's actions are 'structured' by the beliefs, ideas and knowledge of their culture. These actions in turn shape the things they create.

To 'read' artefacts as texts, archaeologists study artefacts and the contexts in which they are found and look for repeated patterns. They also explore the way that material things symbolised values and in turn structured the way in which people thought about and interpreted their world. For instance certain artefacts (for example beakers) may have been used to express social identity.

are also cases where there was no exchange. In some cases people moved, taking artefacts with them. More commonly, people collected local materials themselves. This is thought to be the case with the movement of obsidian from Melos, which has been found in nearby settlements.

STUDYING MATERIALS

Many of the methods used in studying materials have been discussed in Chapter 3 and they should be referred to for further detail. This section provides some additional pointers for various stages in the use of material. You need to be familiar with a range of materials, particularly metals, ceramics and stone, and how they were used for the periods you are studying. This should include at least one example of **diachronic change** and the development of technology. For example, the gradual improvement in the efficiency of stone tools from Oldowan pebble tools through Acheulean and Mousterian types to the 'creative explosion' of the Upper Palaeolithic and blade technology.

Acquisition of materials

Extraction of clay, stone and metal ores up to the point where the material is ready to be used are most frequently studied. Aside from sourcing materials the remains of extraction sites such as mines and quarries provide insights into technology and scale of production. Waste material also provides a signature for particular processes

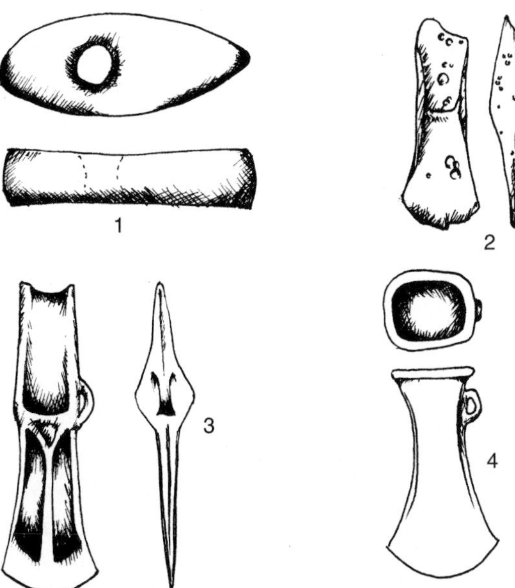

Figure 10.30 *Diachronic change: the development of axes*

Lithic axes evolved to polished stone axes such as (1). The first metal axes were flat copper (◀ p. 66). Later developments included a stopridge (2), flanges (3) and sockets and loops (4).

Figure 10.31 *The unfinished obelisk, Aswan*

Lying in the quarry where it was abandoned thousands of years ago, this monstrous chunk of red granite has contributed much to our understanding of stone working in ancient Egypt. Tools left with the obelisk and markings on the stone enable an understanding of the technology used. At around 1200 tonnes and 40m in length it would have been the largest obelisk erected. However a crack in the rock led to work being stopped.

KEY SITES

Four Mediterranean shipwrecks

Four wrecks excavated near to Turkey by teams led by George Bass over the last forty years provide a glimpse of developing trade patterns in the ancient world. They also document changes in shipbuilding techniques over time in response to social and environmental factors. In each case the ship is named for where it was found.

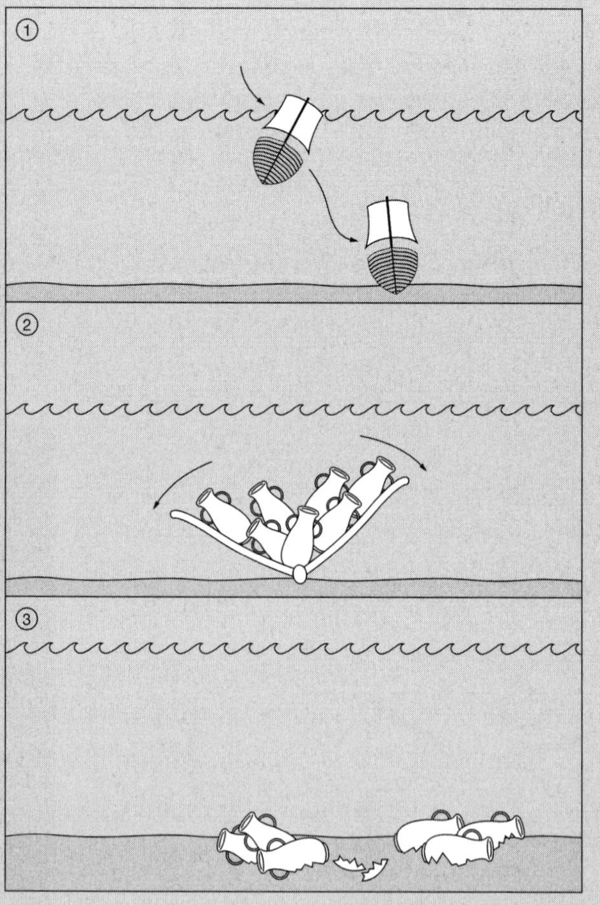

Figure 10.32 *The decay of the Kyrenia wreck*

Ulu Burun, Turkey c. 1400BC

The oldest sea-going ship in the world was 50m long with a short mast and square sail. It was a slow, heavy vessel similar to those depicted on Egyptian reliefs with at least 15 tons of goods onboard. These were painstakingly excavated and raised in it by lifting balloons and nets. Cargo included a 'sumptuary' range of exotic goods from across the eastern Mediterranean. The wreck was dated from Egyptian rings and seals. Also from Egypt were scarabs, gold artefacts and elephant tusks along with seals (◀ p. 242) from Mycenae and Mesopotamia, 6000 Canaanite and Mycenean swords and Baltic amber. Hundreds of copper oxhide ingots (◀ p. 66) were sourced by lead isotope analysis to Cyprus while tin ingots probably came from Turkey or even Afghanistan. Amongst organic finds were African ebony logs, pistachios, almonds, figs, olives, spices and grain. Most of the 130 amphorae contained terebrinth resin used to make perfume. Fine pottery came from Canaan, Cyprus, Mycenae and Syria and there were murex shells (used to make purple dye) and thousands of glass beads. A wooded, wax-covered writing table and balance weights suggested someone on board kept records. The personal effects suggested a Greek or Canaanite crew. Bass interpreted this as a royal cargo. Contemporary inscriptions and tablets document gifts sent as tribute, dowries or to seal alliances between rulers. On route the ship had put in to many ports and bought, and probably sold, different goods. This wreck demonstrates how long-distance trade could have developed on the back of reciprocal exchanges.

KEY SITES *cont.*

Kyrenia, Cyprus c. 300 BC

This wreck was a small merchant vessel with a cargo of 400 amphorae from the island of Rhodes, identifiable by their seal stamps, and millstones. There were very few personal possessions, only a few bone eyelets from a sandal and some fig seeds. Underneath the hull a collection of concretions were recovered. When opened and used to produce resin casts they proved to be iron javelins, some of them bent from impact on the hull. Since there are no natural hazards in the area, this evidence led the excavators to believe that pirates may have sunk the Kyrenia. The vessel had settled down onto the ocean bed, and gradually became covered in silt. As its mast and rigging rotted away, the lower part of the hull was forced outwards by the weight of the cargo and broke apart. Protected by the silt, which choked off oxygen and killed the marine worms that infested it, the remains of the hull were preserved. The ship was built in the traditional way of the classical Greeks, which is 'hull first'. Planks are carved by eye to fit along a keel, with timber selected for its natural curvature as appropriate to different parts of the vessel. The sculpted planks were held together along their edges by thousands of mortise and tenon joints which gave a very strong hull braced only with frames at a later stage. The pine frames were clenched together with treenails, fastened with copper nails. This process wasted 70–80 per cent of the wood used and required a high standard of craftsmanship from the shipwright. It would only be possible in a society which valued craftsmanship, where raw materials were abundant and where time was no problem. The man who built the Kyrenia ship was probably a slave and his time was his master's. Over its life, the 90 year old vessel had been much repaired and partly sheathed in lead to remain watertight. It was engaged in what has been called 'tramping': sailing (usually within sight of land) between ports on a long circuit of the region, taking on and selling cargoes as she went.

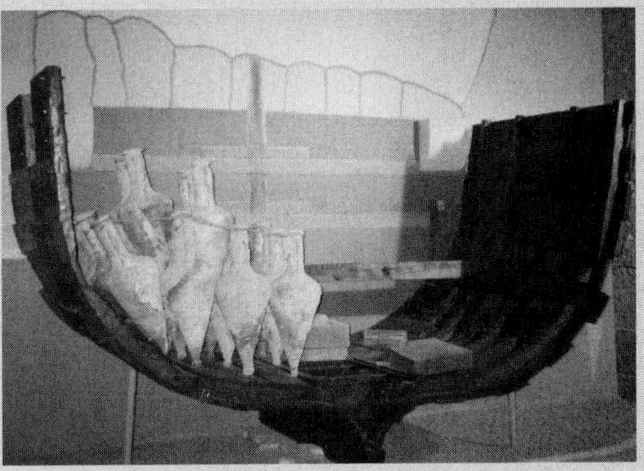

Figure 10.33 *Cargo of the Kyrenia wreck*

This partial reconstruction shows the Amphorae densely packed in the bottom of the vessel. It is not clear if it had a deck over the hold but the pottery was probably packed in thorn branches to protect it. The millstones are also visible. There may have been textiles on top but no trace of them could survive.

Figure 10.34 *Construction of the Kyrenia*

The freeze dried hull of the ship reveals structural elements and construction techniques. The degree of carpentry skills which went into building the vessel is clear.

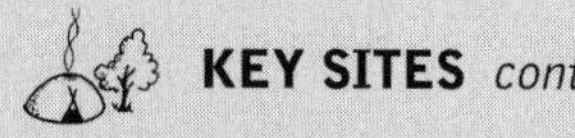

KEY SITES *cont.*

Yassi Ada, Turkey *c.* AD 625

This wreck was dated by coins recovered from the wreck to the reign of the Byzantine Emperor Heraclius. An elaborate 'steelyard' with the head of a boar at one end and a sliding bust of Athena at the other declared itself to be the property of 'George senior, sea-captain'. Historical documents suggest he was one of a growing class of merchants who financed their own ventures and often captained their own ship. The vessel itself was partly constructed in the old classical 'hull-first' style, with logs sculpted to fit. However, this time the mortise and tenon joints were less carefully executed. They were fewer in number and often nails were driven through them once the plank was located. The upper section of the hull was built by the new 'frame-first' method. Many flat planks were cut from a log and twisted against internal frames as they moved forward along the hull. This more economical use of materials and time suggests that social conditions had changed from the time that the *Kyrenia* was built. The Byzantine shipwright was a free man contracted to do the job. His employer would have been concerned to save time and timber and therefore money. The skeleton first building is a shift to a more modern approach and meant that much of the vessel could be built by semi-skilled workers rather than expensive specialists. Byzantine society still used slaves but only in the household and not in an industrial context. In seas full of pirates, this freighter was built for speed. With its varied cargo of 9000 old amphorae full of low grade wine, olives and lentils it may have been a supply ship for the Byzantine Army.

Serce Limani, Turkey *c.* AD 1024

This medieval Arab merchant vessel was found to contain a cargo of glass. Eighty intact pieces from the ends of the ship possibly represented personal possessions or items of merchandise but the centre of the ship held several tonnes of raw and broken glass. The raw glass or 'cullet' would have been added to new batches to improve quality and the broken glass seems to represent the sweepings from a glass factory. Many of the pieces were twisted or malformed in the process of blowing or moulding and had been discarded. The excavators classified the millions of pieces of glass by sorting them according to attributes such as colour, pattern and location on original vessels, for example rim sherds. By following this process meticulously a large number of pieces were eventually re-assembled. The cargo demonstrates craft specialisation and the technology of production, but the fabric of the ship itself is equally rewarding. The Serce Limani ship was built entirely by the 'frame-first' technique. First the keel was laid down. Frames were attached to it and planks bent around the frame to form the hull. The technique is still used in shipyards around the Mediterranean and gives a strong hull while being economical in use of wood. Many hull planks can be cut from a single log. This development clearly happened between the building of the Yassi Ada and the Serce Limani wrecks in the early medieval period when historical scholars tell us that there was considerable conflict between the expanding Arab world and the Byzantine Empire. Historical records describe massive losses of ships through warfare. It is easy to visualise a cycle of forest clearance to feed an ever-increasing demand for ships creating a situation where there was pressure to budget-build new ships. The Serce Limani vessel shows signs of compromise on quality but it was also 'armed to the teeth'. In addition to the glass, large numbers of spears and a cache of fine swords were discovered. These wrecks demonstrate diachronic change in technology over a thousand-year period, the evolution of trade and a range of economic specialisation (▶ p. 257).

- http://www.diveturkey.com/inaturkey/projects.htm

KEY SITE

The Sweet Track

The only areas of higher ground on the area of peat wetland known as the Somerset Levels are slight sandy knolls. These have been used for settlement since the Neolithic. Prehistoric people faced the problem of ensuring effective communication between settlements and they solved it by constructing sophisticated trackways. They invested considerable communal effort into ventures that in some cases lasted only a few years. The 'Sweet Track' has been dated by dendrochronology to the Neolithic period around 4000 BC, which makes it earlier than most of the megalithic monuments. Its construction reveals considerable woodworking skill and woodland management. The planks of the walkway were split from tree trunks using wedges, and other components were made from coppiced wood from oak, hazel and alder. This implies sustainable management strategies and forward planning. Items found alongside the track, such as jadeite axes from Europe, suggest far-reaching exchange contacts. Environmental evidence such as spiders and rodent-gnawed hazelnuts provided much detail about the surrounding wetland. Precise dating of the timbers suggests that the Sweet Track was built fairly quickly and only lasted some eleven years before going out of use.

- Coles and Coles 1976

Figure 10.35 *A replica of part of the Sweet Track at the Peat Moors Visitor Centre. The various construction methods are clearly visible*

whether it is chippings from roughly dressed stone or slag from smelting iron. Waste can be subject to microscopic and analytical procedures similar to those for artefacts. The distance materials have travelled can be significant. Materials which have travelled far from their source and which are relatively rare in the context where they are found are referred to as 'exotics'. This term also often implies a high 'value' for the material in the eyes of the people using it and consequently its possession may suggest high status. Such materials include gold in burials, for example Bush Barrow or Roman amphorae in Late Iron Age burials. Exotic materials often have their own inherent symbolism.

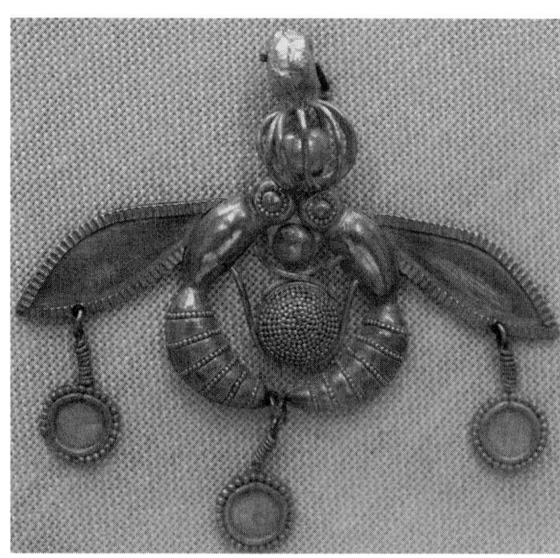

Figure 10.36 *Malia bee pendant*

This exquisite gold pendant from a burial at Malia is evidence of professional metalworking. A new technique – granulation – had been developed by Cretan goldsmiths in order to produce realistic images such as these bees on a comb of honey. It is evidence of sufficient food surplus to support craftsmen since it would take years of training to develop the skill required here. It also suggests an elite who wanted such artefacts. Palace workshops suggest that the goldsmiths were attached craftsmen with raw materials provided by their masters.

Manufacture

Analysis of materials and finds of tools and processing features such as kilns are vital in understanding production. Our understanding of Bronze Age metallurgy combines chemical and physical analysis of ores, interpretation of moulds and finished artefacts, and analogies drawn from ethnography and experimental archaeology. Similar approaches have been applied to stone tool manufacture and ceramics production. For example ethnographic studies of discard patterns, experimental knapping and refitting have been used to interpret lithic scatters from the Palaeolithic. These insights have to be balanced against awareness of the impact of differential survival of materials.

Our knowledge of ancient woodworking, for instance, largely comes from exceptional wet sites.

SPECIALISATION

Specialisation is often used as an indicator of social complexity. It demonstrates a degree of interdependence within a society and often between that society and others. The more complex a society becomes the more interdependent its members become. If the production of artefacts is concentrated in the hands of a few people it also implies skills are not available to all members of society. It may indicate age and gender differentiation. There are two main types of specialisation:

- *Attached specialists* are craftsmen who live in close proximity to a high status person. They may be part of their extended family and related by birth or marriage.
- *Independent specialists* produce goods to market for their own profit. They are not controlled by anyone else but may still be interdependent.

KEY SKILL

Improve your essay writing style

A comment frequently seen on student reports and returned work is 'your style could be improved'. It is often difficult to work out what this means and harder still to do something in response. Sometimes the comment actually refers to structure and sometimes to written English. Generally speaking it is about how you knit the essay together. Here are three mechanical things you can do to help yourself in your next piece of work:

1 Use words and phrases which lead you to consider several pieces of evidence and reach judgements

Include all of the following at least once:

for example	however	therefore	an alternative
potentially	extent	on the other hand	nevertheless

2 Gobbets and gambits

One way of looking at your notes is that they represent lots of chunks of knowledge. These are your gobbets. In responding to a question you need to join these together as seamlessly as possible. The linking phrases which join up explanations or examples are gambits. (◀ p. 192.)

3 Vary your sentence length

At secondary school you may have been encouraged to use longer words and more complex sentences. Sometimes this can lead to rather turgid writing. To make your work more 'punchy', experiment with alternating sentence length. Short sentences can give your work more impact and are often clearer. Never use a complex word if a simpler one does the job just as well.

IDENTIFYING SPECIALISTS IN THE ARCHAEOLOGICAL RECORD

Very often archaeology concentrates on the finished products as evidence of craftwork, for example mosaics, figurines, swords or ships. However, manufacturing debris can be important, as can the very names of locations where craft workers concentrated, which may have survived, albeit in altered form, over time. Both of these sources are illustrated in Viking York where there is much waste material from leather working and trial pieces for carving in bone, together with the name of the most famous excavation site in York – 'Coppergate' – which comes from the Old Norse for 'Street of the Barrel-Makers'. Burial evidence has often been interpreted as evidence of specialisation, where particular tools are found in graves. The Sutton Hoo burial contains several examples of craftsmanship from all over the Anglo-Saxon world, in particular a tiny pyramidal jewel that had been originally attached to a sword hilt. Each face is a plate of gold with tiny 'cells' built up on it with gold wire in the technique known as *cloisonné*. Each cell is fitted with its own individually cut prisms of garnet and some

KEY STUDY

Copan

Close to the House of the Bacabs in the elite residential area of the city a stone built room with a stone bench along one wall was discovered. The room had been buried quickly by an earthquake leaving artefacts where they had been used. Ceramic vessels on the bench contained tools. Some were wrapped in a leather 'quiver' rather like a chef's knife holder. Tools included antler drills which would have been used with sand and water to perforate bone and antler (◀ p. 118). They also drilled the teeth of nobles so that prestigious jade inserts could be set in the teeth. Obsidian blades were used for cutting material. Although obsidian is as strong as surgical steel it is very brittle so the blades would have been glued into wooden handles for support. Evidence of their use came from a flat cutting stone scored from the action of blades and saws. The workshop was littered with exotic raw materials and with incomplete artefacts. One outstanding find was a 'star gorget' made from conch shell similar to examples worn by statues of the Bacabs – the gods who held up the sky. This prestige item was probably made for a high status person, possibly the owner of the elite residence in whose compound the workshop stood.

So who were these craftsmen and what was their status? As in most early societies the very existence of craft specialists indicates an economic surplus can support people who are not engaged in food production. The fertile Copan Valley provided a huge quantities of maize and other crops. In the essentially closed economic system of the Maya, these resources were not used for large-scale trade, but rather to enhance the prestige of the elite by allowing them to support an ever-growing number of 'retainers'. Many of these people would have been close relatives, members of the elites themselves. These people could not be expected to carry out menial tasks but seem to have become specialists including scribes and priests. They also included craftsmen who produced jade, jewellery, featherwork and other exotic items for their lord and relative. Archaeologists call this 'attached *specialism*' as their output was devoted to their master rather than being sold or exchanged. Confirmation of these ideas came from underneath the floor of the workshop itself where several skeletons were discovered in stone cists. One of these bore the telltale signs of elite status. The Maya used

Figure 10.37 *Ritual staircase from structure 26 at Copan, carved with hieroglyphics*

KEY STUDY *cont.*

Copan

cranial deformation to distinguish elite children. This left them with a high-domed head and flat forehead.

The elite position of craftsmen is corroborated by a burial behind the staircase in Figure 10.37. A body lay in an elaborately decorated chamber at the heart of the acropolis. The floor of the tomb was littered with decomposed pieces of bark codices – the books of the Maya. Rich grave goods and the sacrificed body of a young slave had also been provided. It was clearly a royal burial but whose was it? The ages at death of the kings of the time did not match the skeleton. Ceramics in the tomb provided clues. Some of them were clearly associated with painting. Indeed one carried a human portrait of a man wearing a special monkey headdress and with scribes' brushes in his mouth. He represented the patron god of scribes. The body was probably a son of King Smoke-Imix , a royal scribe whose duty was to paint the books containing the history and mythology of his dynasty, and who performed a vital role in sustaining his family's power and status. In another link the façade of the houses of the Bacabs includes figures of scribes holding conch 'ink pots'.

Schele and Miller 1986

are provided with chequered metal foil underneath to enhance the glitter of the stones. The precision and exquisite craftsmanship of the worker at such a small scale is breathtaking. That so much time and effort was lavished on what is really a tiny detail of the king's burial goods is also a testament to his status.

ART

This term is applied to images and objects which show appreciation of aesthetic qualities. It may include decoration on functional objects or decoration that forms part of a system of **iconography**. The *meaning* of art is culturally embedded and may prove difficult to access. Meaning is usually studied as part of the archaeology of religion or society. Studies of art under material culture should concentrate on the technology of their execution rather than on interpretation. Thus if the context of study is Palaeolithic cave art, the focus should be on skills of draughtsmanship, paints used and the techniques of painting.

While there is debate about the meaning of cave art (◀ p. 173) we can be more certain about the techniques. Research has discovered the use of ferrous and manganese oxide for paint, chewed twigs and fingers as brushes and stone lamps with animal grease or pine torches for light. Experiments have established that paint was blown through leather stencils to create handprints. Examples can be seen at the Chauvet website.

- http://www.culture.gouv.fr/rhone-alpes/chauvet/anglais/lettre3/indexes.htm

Higher levels of study will require you to grapple with definitions of art and material culture. Pottery provides a good example of the sort of issues you might want to consider. Ethnographic studies suggest that both the production and the form of pottery are often determined by cultural rather than purely material considerations. A pot can be functional in terms of its ability to hold its contents and withstand heat but other aspects are more to do with its social use than its functionality, particularly decoration and colour. Beliefs and

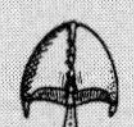 

KEY SITE

Upton Lovell

An early Bronze Age bowl barrow excavated by antiquarians in 1802 is possibly one of the earliest examples of a specialist in Britain. Whether he was a shaman, goldsmith or both is unclear. Across his chest and by his feet were rows of drilled bone points. He also had several boars tusks and bone buttons or toggles. These have been interpreted as decoration or fastenings on his clothes. These were unusual in themselves, but the stone artefacts were even more fascinating. On the chest of the extended skeleton was a large highly polished flat round stone and a high quality stone battle axe. At his feet was an array of different stone artefacts.

The exotic battle axe suggested the man may have taken part in ceremonies where his bone-tasselled clothes would have been very distinctive. The polished stone was also unique. Some shamanic cultures use polished, reflective surfaces as an aid to divination. (As with a crystal ball.)

The other stone tools were more of a puzzle. An A level student who happened to be an amateur goldsmith commented on the similarity of the burial assemblage to his own tools. He was able to suggest how each of the smooth stones

Figure 10.38 *Artefacts from Upton Lovell*

To the left are 3 stone axes in front of 3 hollow flints with a fine stone axehead at the back. To the right are whetstones in front of smoothing stones and hammers.

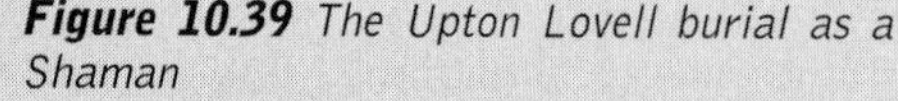

Figure 10.39 *The Upton Lovell burial as a Shaman*

This interpretation at the excellent Devizes Museum where the artefacts are displayed explains the possible use of the bone artefacts, the battle axe and polished stone. The significance of the latter two is enhanced because they were placed on his chest.

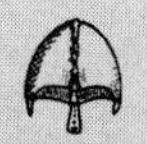 

KEY SITE *cont.*

Upton Lovell

might be used to produce the hammered gold trinkets visible in several of the other cabinets. The flint nodules could be tiny crucibles. The only thing missing is the gold. Historically gold workers have often not owned gold. It has either been supplied by their patron or in the case of independent specialists, by the person commissioning an artefact.

It is possible that the man was both goldsmith and shaman. In many cultures, metalworkers ability to magically transform material has classed them with other 'liminal' roles such as midwives, musicians and diviners. Metallurgical analysis of the tools in 2004 did find traces of gold. The resuls of the re-excavation of the barrow in 2000 are awaited with interest.

Figure 10.40 *Modern gold worker's toolkit*

As with the grave goods an array of hammers and tiny anvils is used to produce sheets, cones and circular artefacts from gold.

values determine the 'right way' for things to look even when that way is not the most functional. In Middle Saxon Southampton, imported pitchers became popular. They were more functional for pouring liquids than existing pots, yet local potters did not copy them. Instead they continued to turn out traditional vessels. Another instance where symbolism may have outweighed practicality was the use of flint as temper in some prehistoric pottery. There are usually alternative tempers available and flint would be painful to work in.

KEY STUDY

The Basse-Yutz flagons

A pair of bronze flagons, now in the British Museum but originally from Alsace, illustrate a number of points about the nature and role of craft specialists. They are from the Iron Age and yet they are made of bronze in common with most decorative objects from that period. They were decorated with inlaid enamel and coral that must have come from the Red Sea. While the wolf handle is a classical idea, the artist linked Celtic mythology with classical ideas in the iconography of the pieces. He also had a sense of humour. Ducks appear to swim down the stream of liquid as it is poured from the spout. These jugs were almost certainly used to serve wine, a novel drink in central Europe at this period, which was imported from the classical world to the south. Although the grave they were found in was not properly recorded we know that two Etruscan wine-mixing vessels were also found there. The mixture of native and classical ideas in the art shows clearly that classical culture was having a great impact on the Celtic world long before the Roman conquests. The Celtic craftsman exploited exotic materials and iconography to enhance a vessel used to serve an exotic drink at an institution which classical writers tell us was central to Celtic society – the feast. We have to imagine the gleam of polished bronze, lifted high to pour the dark red wine in a glittering stream into the goblets of rival chieftains. The ability to procure the fashionable wine and outface others who still relied on the old beer or honey mead was a powerful way to mark status.

Figure 10.41 *Close up of the spout of a Basse-Yutz flagon*

KEY STUDY *cont.*

The Basse-Yutz flagons

In Celtic society craftsmen were regarded as part of the elite. They were on a par with bards and druids, in view of the 'magical' processes that they controlled, turning dull ores into functional objects like chariot fittings or superb works of art like these flagons. They had a much wider social role than the purely functional at a time when kings began to advertise themselves through coinage and the iconography it carried.

KEY SKILL

Writing evaluative essays on concepts

These are often the types of essay which students find hardest. Questions on this theme often take the form 'To what extent can archaeologists recognise X?' X could be status, gender, chiefdoms or war. Whichever it is, you need to deploy several relevant case studies to explore the concept and its archaeological visibility. The nature of the topic means you need to be very aware of bias in interpretation and of the strengths and weaknesses of models, particularly ethnographic ones, which archaeologists have employed. You need to be comfortable with the terminology and to construct a coherent argument.

The following exercise includes examples from different periods. Try producing your own version, using examples from your studies.

Q: To what extent can archaeologists recognise territoriality?

1 Discuss what territory is. Is it the same as site catchment or the hunting ranges of Mesolithic foragers?
2 Discuss the modern idea of territory, as static and rooted in ideas of the sovereignty of nation states. It is marked by physical borders, coinage distribution, flags and other symbols.
3 Discuss some possible archaeological examples of territory:

- *Bronze Age:* land divisions on Dartmoor or Fengate – territories, or ranches?
- *Iron Age:* distribution of hill forts, coin distribution, Roman accounts of tribal areas
- *Roman period:* coinage, public buildings, Hadrian's Wall (a border?)
- *Medieval period:* boundaries (for example Wansdyke), coinage, charters, siting of castles

4 Discussion: does Territory mean the same thing in all periods? Is it a dynamic or static concept? What types of evidence are the most/least persuasive? What are their strengths and limitations?
5 Conclusion: which of your examples provides the strongest evidence and why? Is this because there is more likely to have been territory in those examples or is it to do with survival of evidence? Use these points to explicitly address the 'how far' element in the question.

Chapter 11

Social Archaeology

YOUR GOALS

You need to

- understand the main concepts used
- use case studies to apply and test the key concepts
- grasp the strengths and weaknesses of the techniques used by archaeologists to reconstruct society from physical evidence
- develop your ability to write evaluative essays.

Hawkes (◀ p. 154) identified the archaeology of past social systems as a difficult topic for archaeologists. Despite this, most archaeologists have written with confidence on the societies they have studied and used a wide range of models (particularly from ethnography) to help interpret their sources.

When studying this topic, an anthropological or sociological textbook (for example Giddens 1989) is a useful source of help with terms. Since this is the last thematic chapter of this coursebook there is danger of repetition. Where possible, we have cross-referenced issues here to studies in earlier chapters. We have also tried to include critical points in each subsection to help you write evaluative essays.

WHAT IS SOCIAL ARCHAEOLOGY?

Social archaeology can usefully be divided into three main subsections: How societies organise themselves ranges from the basic units of family, **kin** and **bands** to the political organisation of states: Divisions within society include different treatment based on age or gender and also stratification according to wealth, power or status. Social action and change includes phenomena like warfare, immigration, and how and why societies transformed themselves.

For non-literate societies, archaeologists have relied heavily on evidence from burials to understand social organisation. Burial evidence has also supplemented historical records for the classical period. In addition, information has been drawn from settlement patterns, artefacts and art. Since the strengths and weaknesses of these sources are

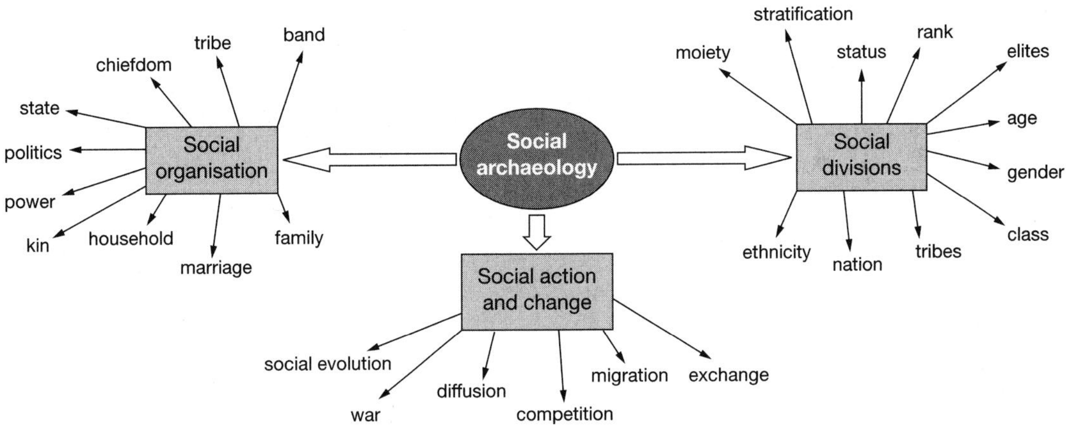

Figure 11.1 *What is social archaeology?: some key topics*

similar for each topic, we have tackled them more fully for status and gender and avoided repetition on the other topics. Where you are writing evaluative pieces you should ensure that you refer to status and gender in your reading.

FORMS OF SOCIAL AND POLITICAL ORGANISATION

Archaeology developed in the early twentieth century when evolutionary ideas were being applied in the social sciences and when much of the world was directly ruled by colonial powers. It is understandable then that evolutionary models of social development were applied to the past. As societies became increasingly 'advanced' and 'civilised' they were expected to develop along similar paths. Much archaeological research sought to trace this development and identify reasons for particular regions being more advanced than others. Although western ideas of superiority have been challenged in recent decades, what are now termed neo-evolutionary models of social development are still commonplace.

All of the terms used to classify social organisation conceal considerable variation. However, we need to use such concepts as our starting point when comparing and contrasting social groups and talking about them. Households or families are the basic building blocks of all human societies. This is not to say that any particular model such as the nuclear family always existed in the past. However, from the point that humans began sitting round campsites or living in tents or huts, evidence about the form of early family groups accumulated. Perhaps the most significant social aspect of a house is that it defines the living arrangements of one group by excluding others. Any internal divisions tell us something about differences within this basic group (▶ p. 273).

Kinship is also important in most societies although the significance attached to blood or marriage ties varies widely. In the past they may have been the most important form of social organisation, for example the Scottish clan system. Although their relevance in modern western society has declined there are still exceptions, notably the Mafia. Other divisions, which may cut across simple group definitions, are age or moiety-based groups. Their existence means that individuals may have several different affiliations.

Bands are self-sufficient groups of a few families numbering up to 50 individuals. They are linked through kinship or marriage. To some writers bands looked like an egalitarian society although ethnographic research has shown that inequalities exist in many modern bands. Leaders are likely to have emerged because of experience

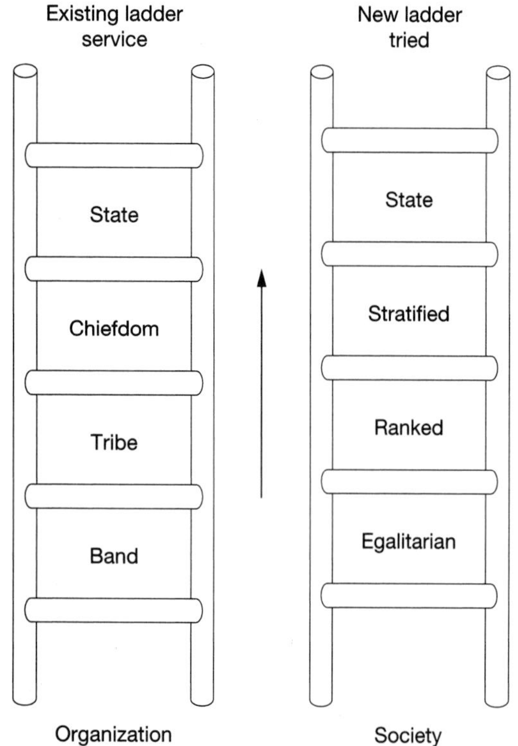

Figure 11.2 *Two social evolutionary ladders*

These model the linear development of society. One focuses on organisation (Service, 1971) the other on social relations (Fried, 1978). There is a close match but some overlap.

or personal qualities but may have been temporary. Bands were probably fluid, with families or individuals moving to join other groups. They may also have only lived together during particular seasons. The term is most frequently used in archaeology for the Upper Palaeolithic and Mesolithic.

Tribes are larger than bands but with kinship still linking the group together. Numbers can range between a few hundred to thousand or several bands. Tribes often have activity leaders who are recognised as having skill and authority in particular areas such as hunting or ritual. Potentially most adults may achieve leadership in some areas and therefore none may stand out overall. Of the models of political organisation and leadership that have been borrowed from anthropology for tribes, the most influential has been the **Bigmen** of New Guinea. These are individuals who rise to prominence through their skill in key areas of economic and social life such as herding or hunting. Their position as Bigmen allows them to conduct trade and alliances on behalf of their group of several hundred people. Their position is cemented by their ability to provide generously for their followers. They accumulate wealth, usually pigs or another food source, and redistribute it at major feasts. The position is not hereditary and others who are better placed to dispense generously often replace Bigmen.

Both bands and tribes are sometimes referred to as **segmentary societies**. This is where society is made up of lots of similarly sized groups with little difference in wealth, status or power between individuals. This contrasts with the more ranked and unequal chiefdoms and states. Tribes are usually associated with horticulturalists or pastoralists rather than foragers.

Chiefdoms are more formally organised and ranked than tribes. Within ethnographic literature there is a huge range of different forms of chiefdom with numbers of followers ranging from around 1,000 to 10,000, so we must assume the same is true of the past. Chiefdoms are usually hereditary, with an individual holding some central power over the group although the role may alternate between a group of families rather

Figure 11.3 *Segmentary social divisions. These are some of many ways of organising society horizontally which don't necessarily result in a permanent hierarchy*

than remain in just one. As a result usually chiefs and their relatives are viewed as different from the rest of the social group. They usually have an important ritual role as well as redistribution, law giving and organizing labour. Their permanent position and high status may result in other differences including more marriage partners and more or different possessions. Social hierarchies in chiefdoms can be very elaborate and at least one of their settlements is likely to be a ceremonial centre.

Kings can differ from chiefs simply in terms of scale. Kings will usually preside over several social groups, each with their own sub-king or chief. The term was used for nineteenth-century Africa as well as for the classical and medieval worlds so variation is considerable. The position is hereditary with some, although not all, being seen as divine. They are likely to have a larger than usual household and may have permanent social and economic organisations based close to them, for example a permanent guard. Their need to display their position through exotic goods and provide gifts to supporters may mean that their household includes attached specialists.

Figure 11.4 *Hermitage Castle*

Built in Liddesdale to dominate what has been called the 'bloodiest valley in Britain' Hermitage Castle represents a struggle between states and allegiances rooted in kinship which is still familiar today. In the late Middle Ages the English–Scottish border zone suffered frequent invasions and rival kings encouraged local clan groups to raid across it. By the thirteenth century, raiding in these 'debatable lands' had become endemic. The exploits of the closely knit 'reiver' families (so significant that they gave us the word 'bereave') are well known from songs and stories. At times their action provoked military action in reprisal. To attempt to control Liddesdale and prevent war with England a Royal Warden was appointed and Hermitage was built first in wood then in stone. The earthworks are ruined but the main building survives. It contains a prison tower and would have had wooden fighting platforms around the upper walls. Ultimately Hermitage was unsuccessful. Reiving continued until the Union of the Crowns in 1603. With the border gone, James I used arbitrary execution and exile to impose his will on the Armstrongs of Liddesdale and their neighbours.

States are political systems where permanent institutions develop independent of individual leaders. Central authority is likely to include formal laws, weights and measures and specialists associated with justice, warfare and taxation. All modern societies are nation states. Key features are likely to include permanent borders, currencies, armies and centralised beaucracy. Developed states are very complex with a tendency to increasing specialisation. In some states kinship remains important, particularly those kingships which are also states, but this need not be the case. State societies are hierarchical with ethnicity, wealth and class some of the common divisions. States are associated with large urban populations supplied by agricultural surpluses collected from the countryside. States first emerged in the Bronze Age.

KEY TERM

Moiety

A division of society into two halves (or moieties) which was common in North America. People are born or are inducted into one or the other. Depending upon the society rules they must either marry within the moiety or marry someone from the opposite moiety.

Figure 11.5 *Keep of Norham Castle*

Defensive borders are a common feature of states. This royal castle on a natural strongpoint high above the River Tweed formed part of a chain of strongpoints defending the northern borders of England against Scottish invasion. The scale of the defences and size of the bailey indicate that it was designed to hold a large garrison and hold off an army. This contrasts with the many smaller castles in the area which were designed for protection against raiding (▶ p. 267). Norham repeatedly did its job, only falling to James IV's guns in 1513, days before the decisive battle of Flodden (▶ p. 287).

KEY STUDY

The Palette of Narmer

This cosmetic artefact excavated at the Egyptian city of Hierakonpolis dates from 3000 BC, the period just before the First Dynasty when the rules and icons of kingship were being established. It is considered a classic example of the manipulation of iconography in support of an individual's status. It is also one of the first examples of hieroglyphics (◀ p. 241).

The king's name is written at the top, surrounded by a frame which is reminiscent of the architecture of the royal palace. The catfish (Nar) and chisel (mer) spell out the Horus name (◀ p. 158) of the king, Narmer. The king stands, left hand clasping the topknot of a kneeling captive, with a mace in his right hand. The hieroglyphs tell us that the prisoner's name is 'Wash'. The design immediately above him shows a falcon on papyrus plants pulling back the head of a figure who looks remarkably like Wash and the location is the Nile delta. The main figure is wearing the white crown of Upper Egypt and a flywhisk, early symbols of kingship. Below are defeated enemies and a sign that represents a fortified town. We are clearly being told that the king has won a victory over an enemy in the north, the delta.

On the right-hand side of the palette the king, carrying the mace and flail, and this time wearing the red crown of Lower Egypt, is explicitly labelled and accompanied by standard bearers called 'The Followers of Horus'. They march within a panel that represents the gate of the royal palace, towards two rows of bound and decapitated prisoners. The dead prisoners are now powerless and reduced to order, compared with the figures on the other side who have spread-eagled limbs. This may be symbolic of the Egyptian concept of order. In the central panel are two mythological beasts with their long necks entwined to symbolise harmony and perhaps the unification of the two lands of Egypt. This is echoed by the two crowns, which would later be incorporated into the 'Double Crown', indicating that the pharaoh was 'The Lord of the Two Lands'. At the bottom right is a raging bull, representing the king's anger, trampling a man and a walled city. There is a balance in the composition, with harmony offsetting the violence, but the message is abundantly clear. The enemies of Narmer can have been in no doubt as to what lay in store for those who defied him.

Figure 11.6 *Smiting scene from Edfu*

In a strikingly similar scene, Pharoah Ptolemy XII (c80–51 BC) is shown about to dash out his prisoners brains with a mace. In fact he is not known to have fought a war. The iconography for depicting a powerful ruler had become standardised over 3000 years.

- www.ancient-egypt.org/kings/0101_narmer/palette.html

Some writers add Empires as a fifth evolutionary stage where one state becomes dominant over several others. It is worth noting that bands, tribes and chiefdoms still exist today in many parts of the world.

POWER AND SOCIAL CONTROL

Power, the ability to make others do what you want, can be approached via status or via evidence of social control. This can be inferred, but not proved, from the apparent organisation of labour for large communal monuments such as the henges of Neolithic Wessex. In some cases such as Egypt or the Maya the religious control exerted by the Pharaohs or Maya shaman-kings is illustrated in art on artefacts and temple walls.

Typically the more powerful figures are larger and wear more elaborate costumes. Their subjects, or those they have defeated, are smaller and sometimes depicted naked and bowed or lying face down.

THE ARCHAEOLOGY OF RANK AND STATUS

These terms are often used interchangeably but do have slightly different meanings. Status is associated with social prestige; rank implies a position within a hierarchy. Both status and rank may be inherited or acquired during life by an individual. **Ascribed status** is where an individual inherits social position, usually at birth, for example being born into royalty. **Achieved status** is where the

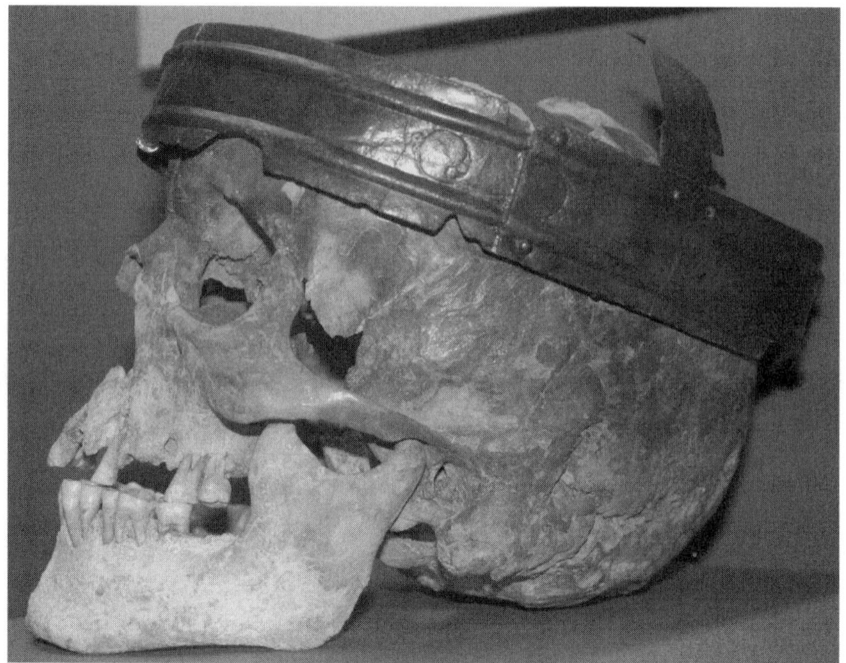

Figure 11.7 *Skull and crown from Deal Iron Age cemetery*

This discovery of a young man wearing a crown has been interpreted as evidence of royal families. It is unlikely a man would have achieved kingship by around twenty so it is more likely that the role was inherited. However, the crown bears an uncanny resemblance to the headgear of later Romano-British priests. This raises the possibility that the young man might be a priest or druid.

individual earns or obtains position due to their own efforts, for example qualifying as a doctor. Rich burials of children are often interpreted as evidence of ascribed status.

Evidence of societies based on ascribed status is usually easier to find partly for this reason. In societies where status is more fleeting, evidence may not enter the archaeological record. In bigman societies fame is achieved by giving away wealth. A successful bigman might be buried with very little. Not all marks of status are easily preserved. Clothing, tattoos and tribal scars would have been very significant in life but are usually invisible to archaeologists.

Archaeologists employ a number of sources of evidence in their attempts to recognise status in past societies. In a few cases such studies are text-aided but in general they have to rely on material culture to provide answers. All of the main approaches try to isolate particular variables that will allow differentiation between sectors of a society and between individuals:

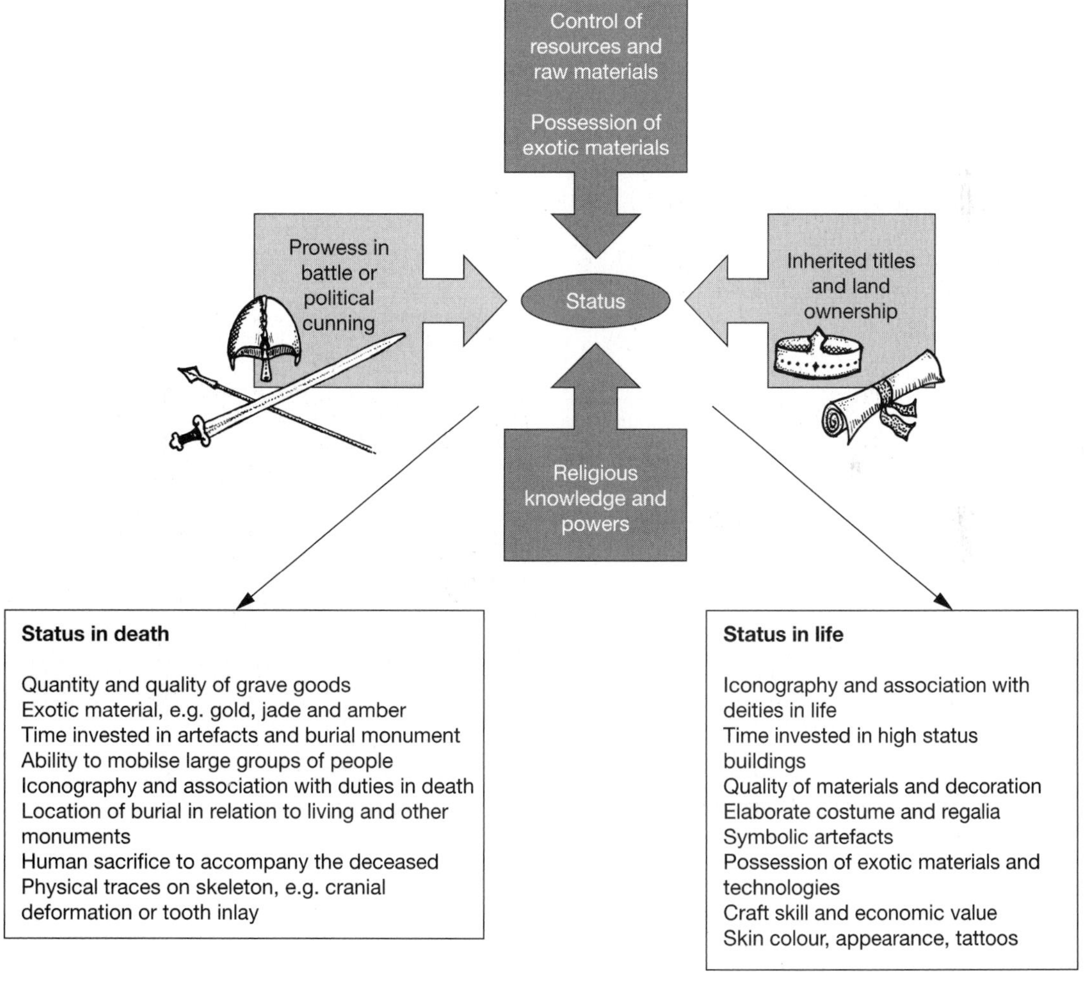

Figure 11.8 *Status and the archaeological evidence for it*

Burial evidence

Personal status is often suggested on the basis of grave goods. Rich burials such as those at Sutton Hoo, Varna and the 'Amesbury Archer' are usually interpreted as being the graves of high status individuals. Sometimes there is additional evidence to confirm this, as in the cases of Tutankhamun and the royal scribe burial at Copan (◀ p. 258).

In the Royal Cemetery at Ur, mortuary practice involved the sacrifice of attendants with royalty. The grave of Pu-abi included a 40-year-old woman who is identified as a queen on a seal-stone buried with her. She was accompanied by exotic objects, including a lyre with a golden bull's head decoration, gold and silver vessels, a magnificent headdress of golden leaves and rosettes and twenty-three of her courtiers. These 'victims' seem to have gone to their deaths willingly as there was no sign of coercion. Human sacrifice to accompany the dead may be aimed at establishing the power and status of an individual. Equally there are many instances where such behaviour is a ritual full of meaning for the whole community in terms of the fertility of the earth or the continuity of cyclical events.

However, we need to take care that we don't impose our values and assume that certain materials held the same value and prestige in past societies as in our own. In some cases symbolic associations may be an equally important factor in the choice of raw material, such as jade in Mesoamerica. Even the gold at Varna (see cover)

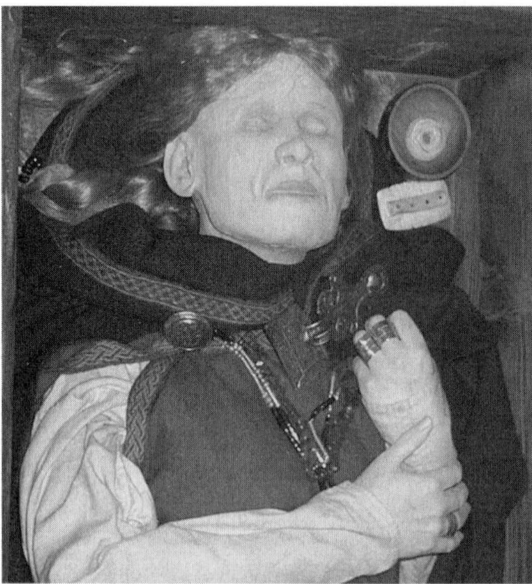

Figure 11.9 *'Mrs Getty'*

This 6th century burial of a woman aged 25–30 from the Lechlade cemetery (▶ p. 283) got her nickname from her exceptional grave goods which included 500 beads. Unlike most, she had a wooden coffin concealed under stone packing. Inside, her possessions came from far beyond the Anglo Saxon world. Along with Baltic amber and metal bowls from the Rhineland were cowries from the Red Sea, garnets from India, Spanish glass and an ivory purse mouth. Her bronze brooches and silver spiral rings were also rare. Despite the humble spindle whorl in her coffin she was a woman of high status. Forensic reconstruction of her face along with detailed excavation records has enabled the Corinium Museum to present her as she looked at her funeral.

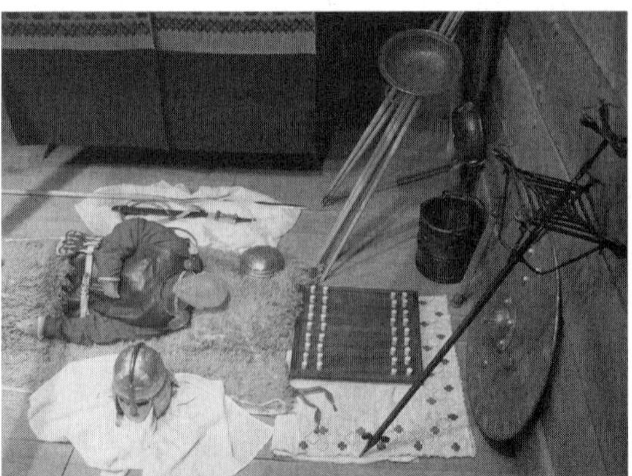

Figure 11.10 *Sutton Hoo*

This recreation of the burial inside a ship allows one to see the paraphernalia of status in its context. The carefully laid assemblage of rare, symbolic and everyday artefacts provides an insight into the reality and the image of early medieval kingship. Compare these artefacts in terms of craftsmanship and the distance items travelled with those from ordinary Anglo-Saxon graves.

KEY STUDY

Branc

Shennan's (1975) study of over 300 rectangular pit graves in a Bronze Age cemetery in Czechoslovakia adopted a systematic approach to evaluating the social significance of grave goods.

Gender differences were evident in the way bodies had been laid out. Males lay on their right sides and females on their left. In addition, some individuals had more valuable assemblages than others. The interpretation was that wealth and status was inherited (ascribed).

Instead of assuming that what we might value, for example gold, was of most value in the past she used other measures. The key one was energy expenditure. In other words, artefacts that required more skill, effort and resources from long distances were likely to have been most prized.

may not be what it seems. Some of the richest graves there are empty 'cenotaphs'. It may be that the gold represents offerings from the living rather than the belongings of the deceased. A further complication occurs with vessels such as beakers. Their contents may have been the material of greatest value rather than the pottery. Other organic materials such as textiles, food or wood may have been placed in what to us appear to have been 'poor' graves, but these rarely survive.

- Parker-Pearson 1999

Status is only likely to be represented *in* death where the person held that status *at* death. In cases where status or rank did not stay with the individual for their whole life it may not be visible. Similarly, where beliefs dictate that people should appear equal in death (as in Christian burial), indicators of status may be absent. In general, ascribed status is more likely to be visible than achieved status. The position of burials, their orientation and any funerary monument associated with them can also be used to examine status.

Settlement evidence

Status can also be inferred from settlement evidence. Segmentary societies are associated with lots of small, scattered, similar settlements. A mix of small and very large settlements suggest a more unequal society with large settlements expected to be the residence of powerful individuals. The palaces at Knossos and the hill fort at Danebury have both been interpreted in this way. High status individuals might be expected to have different houses from other people. The energy

Figure 11.11 *Skara Brae*

This late Neolithic settlement from Orkney may provide architectural evidence of an egalitarian society. The cellular houses are roughly the same size and linked by a covered passage. Inside they share very similar features which may be dressers, box beads and storage containers. Finds were similar too. The real division is between the band inside and those outside, separated by thick walls and a build up of midden material.

KEY TASK

Investigating status and rank in your settlement

Identify some useful criteria for identifying status and rank in your community. House prices may be one guide; local information on occupation and earnings by electoral ward may also be available. Focusing on the built environment (houses, gardens, enclosures, not cars), use observation to compare different areas. Identify whether there are visible indicators of rank and status and what they are. Present this in diagrammatic form.

expenditure model can be applied here too. Houses may simply be bigger because the inhabitants have more to store or may have larger household units. They may also occupy a prominent position. Eighteenth-century landowners chose to build in prominent positions in the landscape to emphasise control over land. Rich merchants in earlier periods clustered in central positions in towns. In many cases their houses will be larger, more elaborate and built of better quality materials – part of a general display of wealth and status, which might also include dress and visible forms of consumption. Romano-British villas, for example Chedworth, and palaces, for example Fishbourne, can be compared to see the relative differences in status between them. The layout of a site may reveal individual

Figure 11.12 *View of Zakros palace from the north*

Looking from the town area the central courtyard is top left. To the right is a colonnaded ceremonial hall and behind that archive rooms, 'lustral basins' for ritual purification, treasury and shrines. Bottom right are the storage magazines while top right are the craft workshops with more to the south of the courtyard. Immediately left of the courtyard are the 'royal' apartments or megarons backing onto a hall with a cistern and other water related rooms. Off to the left are more courtyards and some industrial buildings on the road to the port. The ashlar walls cut into blocks with two-man saws indicate the scale and size of the buildings. Attached workshops included stone cutters, perfume making and ivory carving. The palace was destroyed by fire but the boxes of clay archives (◀ p. 243) on shelves survived as a result.

status through the control of space and therefore the way people relate to each other. Higher status people are also more likely to enclose their property in a more visible way than are others. These aspects and the control of space and access can clearly be traced in medieval castles and monasteries and in earlier sites such as brochs (◀ p. 216).

The development of large ceremonial and defensive sites from the Bronze Age has been seen by many archaeologists as evidence of the emergence of chiefdoms in the British Isles. Grogan's (1999) regional level study of Irish hilltop enclosures showed that these very visible, although not always defensive, sites were established at regular intervals across the landscape. Finds from these enclosures (◀ p. 250) suggest they were of high status. Certainly the Bronze Age saw increasing control over land in many areas such as Dartmoor (Fleming, 1988). The intensification and extension of farming coincides with evidence of prestige goods (◀ p. 247) exchange over long distances. This suggests that powerful individuals were amassing surpluses to trade on behalf of their communities. At the far end of the European gift chain was Ancient Greece. Homer's epics were based in this period and feature heroes who 'spent' the agricultural wealth of their communities on gifts of fine weapons and feasts for their followers. Perhaps similar warbands developed elsewhere in Europe.

Figure 11.13 *Battersea cauldron*

Large and elaborate items of feasting equipment suggest feasts and elites capable of supplying such hospitality. We know from classical and medieval literature of the crucial importance of feasting as a way of binding leaders and followers together. Rewarding followers through redistribution seems to have been a key element in the emergence of chiefdoms from the late Bronze Age. Food and drink were dispensed (with the order of serving reflecting rank) along with gifts of weapons, animals and exotic artefacts in return for loyalty. This may explain why fine goods, harness equipment and swords are often found across many sites rather than concentrated in places where one might have expected rulers to live.

Artefactual evidence

Concentrations of valuable finds can be used to suggest locations used by important individuals. Evidence of long-distance trade in exotic or prestige goods or of the craft workshops of attached specialists can also be important. Their skill and effort is not easily duplicated and means such artefacts are rare and thus valuable. Sherratt's (1997) interpreted bell beakers (◀ p. 62) as part of a drinking culture, perhaps in imitation of the metal drinking and feasting vessels of classical Greece. The association of elite warriors and feasting has echoes in the archaeological record of the Iron Age, the Saxon and Viking period and until well into the Middle Ages.

Of course value does not only come from the skill of the craftsmen and the rarity of the materials. Objects gain prestige from their own histories. A relatively ordinary sword associated with a great hero becomes an object of value. Tolkien was well aware of the biographical value of objects when he wrote *The Lord of the Rings*. This aspect is difficult for archaeologists to recover.

THE ARCHAEOLOGY OF GENDER

Archaeologists usually distinguish between sex, which is biologically determined, and gender, which is regarded as a social construct. Gender is the identity assigned to different sexes. In any human society there is at the very least some difference between the roles of men and women. This stems from the fact that women give birth and that there are obvious anatomical differences between male and female. Gender explains these differences and specifies what is to be done about them. There is tremendous variation from one society to another. In the early stages of hominid development, males were up to twice the size of females but this distinction had largely disappeared by the time modern humans emerged. Paradoxically, gender differences were far more extreme in late nineteenth- and early twentieth-century West European societies, than they were among historically known food-foraging peoples.

Assumptions about 'natural' roles and their significance profoundly influenced the development of archaeology up to the 1970s. In particular, males were portrayed as the active sex in human evolution. For example, hunting was seen as the key humanising activity in evolution. Since then the importance of scavenging and the likely role of women in the transition from gathering to horticulture has been recognised. Even among the !Kung bushmen, often seen as archetypal hunters, women actually contributed more protein to the daily intake of the group than did the men. Hunting was very hit and miss, while gathering of wild plant foods made up 60–80 per cent of the !Kung diet.

As with most areas of archaeology, ethnographic study has been employed to gain insights into task differentiation between males and females. One weakness in this approach has been that most anthropologists have been male. This has led to criticism that they are more interested in male activities and have failed to observe female tasks and behaviour. If this is true then we need to be particularly cautious in transferring such observations to archaeological material. A further point to be borne in mind is that gender is rarely just two opposite identities. If we are to avoid stereotypical responses we should treat gender as a continuum – a curve along which individuals are

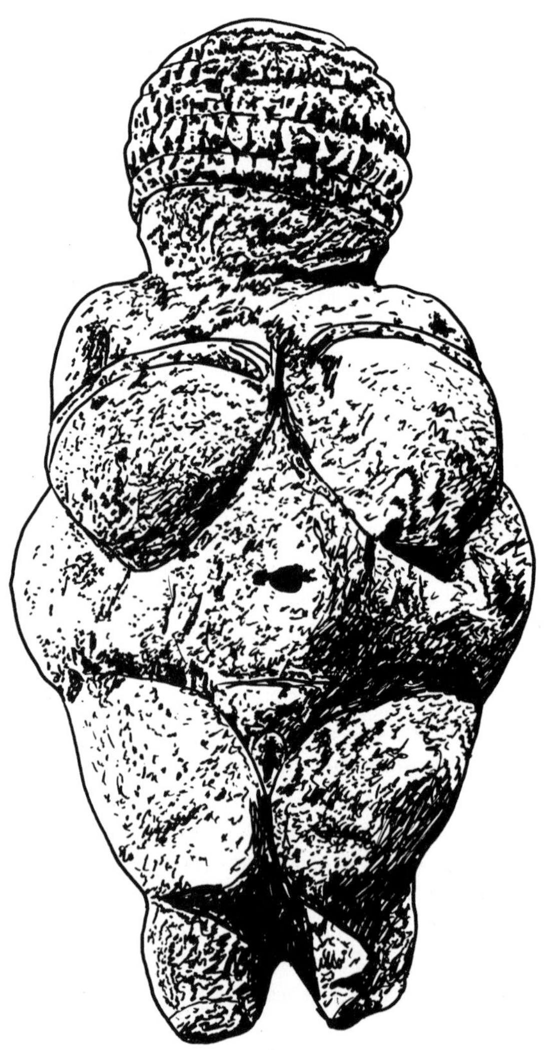

Figure 11.14 *Drawing of 'Venus' figurine from Dolni Vestonice*

Upper Palaeolithic carvings of pregnant female figures have been found across Europe and are fairly uniform in character and style. Most appear to be associated with hearths and home bases. They are made from a range of materials including baked clay (Dolni Vestonice), mammoth ivory (Lespugue) and limestone (Willendorf).They have widely been interpreted as evidence of veneration of a mother goddess deity by the first modern humans in Europe. Others see them as fertility symbols or primitive pornography. Either way they provide insights into Ice Age hairstyles.

- http://www.arthistory.sbc.edu/imageswomen/

placed from female to male, according to the norms of particular societies.

Studies of gender have relied heavily on burial evidence including human remains and grave goods. Settlement and architectural analysis and artistic sources, where they survive, have supplemented this.

Human remains

Differential evidence of disease can be used to identify gendered patterns of activity or consumption. Canadian Inuit hunter-gatherers from the 1890s show osteoarthritis in the right hand and jaw of women, combined with tooth loss. These women spent considerable time preparing skins and sewing. They made the thread by rolling sinews against their cheeks. Areas most pressured by this activity reveal damage. The men hunted with harpoons, which sometimes caused disease of the right shoulder and elbow, while kayak paddling also resulted in distinctive wear of the bones. Other studies of damage and wear have identified gender-specific activities as diverse as basket-making, fighting and grinding corn.

These patterns are echoed in the skeletons from Tell Abu Hureyra (◀ p. 231). Wear grooves in the sides of women's teeth were caused by drawing fibres through them to work and soften them as a prelude to making baskets. Male skeletons had lesions and strain injuries to their arms as might be associated with spear throwing. This fits with faunal evidence for hunting gazelles.

The quantity and quality of food consumed may relate to status. Chemical analysis of prehistoric Native American skeletons show that women have a higher strontium:calcium ratio than men in the same community. This may indicate that they ate a smaller share of the available meat. However, strontium levels also alter when a woman is pregnant or breast-feeding. Differential care and nutrition of female and male children might also show up in X-ray analysis of bones. Lines of increased bone density, known as Harris lines, reflect periods of malnutrition during growth.

Graves and grave goods

The association of male and female burials with different ranges of grave goods has been noted in many cultures. At Tell Abu Hureyra women were most often buried under the floor of the house, suggesting strongly that this was their area of activity and their domain in life. From the Neolithic onwards arrowheads, daggers and other weapons are frequently found in male and not female burials, which seems to confirm that these activities were male-dominated even by the prehistoric period. From the Bronze Age women were regularly buried with a variety of ornaments and jewellery such as pins, necklaces and bracelets. While this may indicate different roles in life there are problems with this analysis. Until recently, sexing of burials often relied on the grave goods. Jewellery without weapons was expected in female graves so these finds were used to define female burials. Today there is less confidence in

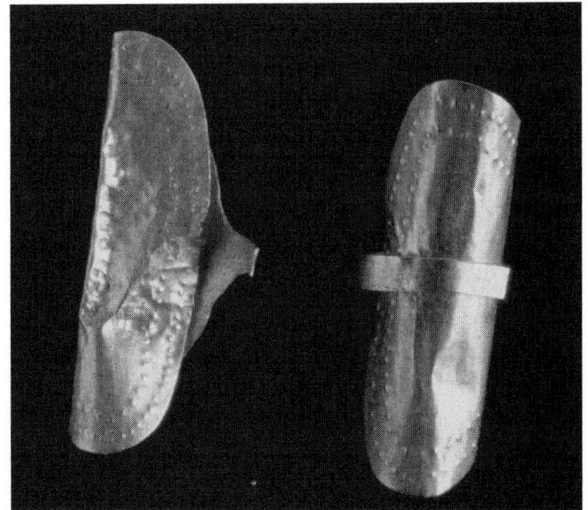

Figure 11.15 *Gold hair rings from the Amesbury Archer burial*

These golden baskets were long interpreted as earrings and associated with female graves. Perhaps with changes in our views on masculinity as well as experimentation and improved sexing of remains they are seen as hair rings worn by males. Similar examples were worn by leading male characters in the movie *Troy*.

this interpretation. DNA analysis at West Heslerton (▶ p. 283) showed that some females were buried with weapons and some men with jewellery. Many museums are currently reviewing their labelling of burials. Whether beautiful objects are just jewellery and whether daggers are always indicative of fighting has also been questioned. Spear-throwers have been found in some female burials of the mid-western Indian Knoll culture of the third millennium BC. Were they just ceremonial or to do with inheritance, or did women as well as men hunt?

Rich male graves are often interpreted in terms of what *he* earned or won, whereas when a woman is found with elaborate grave goods they are often attributed to her husband or father. For example, if women over a certain age have certain grave goods and younger ones do not, it may be argued that these represent goods transferred at marriage. The possibility that women have achieved their own wealth is rarely considered. Examples of high status Iron Age female burials include those at Wetwang Slack, which features a 'chariot' burial surrounded by rich grave goods, and the Vix Burial at Saone, which has a gold torc, huge Greek bronze krater (wine-mixing vessel) and decorated metal bowls. A different kind of status may be visible in the female graves at Khok Phanom Di where craft specialisation seems to have played a role in achieving higher social ranking. The Pazyryk 'Ice Maiden' also suggests high status based on a particular talent.

• www.pbs.org/wgbh/nova/icemummies/

Differential survival can be an issue when studying gender differences. In the Mesolithic period men, and especially older men, appeared to receive

KEY STUDY

The Birdlip princess

This rich Iron Age burial from the middle of three barrows contained a mirror, a range of jewellery including amber and shale objects, and some bronze bowls. It was interpreted as a rich woman's grave and some speculated that it might even be that of Boudicca. However, recent examination of the skull has shown that it has masculine traits. The assemblage is also notable in that the artefacts have all been broken and one of the vessels was placed over the face of the skeleton. Could it be the burial of a male shaman rather than a princess? Another burial was discovered in 1999 in the Scilly Isles with similar characteristics.

• www.glos-city.gov.uk/libraries/templates/page.asp?URN=1279

KEY STUDY

The Omaha

O'Shea (1981) was able to compare eighteenth- and nineteenth-century ethnographic descriptions of the Omaha by European explorers with burial evidence to test the visibility of status and social grouping in mortuary data. Where social divisions were vertical or ranked, there tended to be evidence in the grave goods. In addition, while rank was concentrated in particular age and sex groups in the population it was more archaeologically visible than horizontal divisions which were more equally distributed. Horizontal social divisions based on clan, moiety and age tended to be archaeologically invisible. From the historic accounts it was clear that some of these identities had been celebrated during the funerary rituals while a person's ranking had not been emphasised. This may indicate that the horizontal divisions were more significant in life. It also tells us that we cannot hope to read all status from burials.

special treatment, being buried with ochre, antlers or stone artefacts. However, if women had grave goods of organic materials, perhaps offerings of plant foods and medicinal herbs rather than joints of meat, and tools or ornaments of wood, these would not have survived.

Settlement evidence

Studies which have used differential distribution of artefacts to identify male and female activity areas, such as Clarke (1972) at Glastonbury or Flannery and Marcus at Guila Naquitz, could be criticised for making assumptions about gendered tasks. For example, the complete absence of men's large fingerprints on pottery at Khok Phanom Di might argue against the involvement of adult men in potting. However, while small fingerprints could have belonged to women potters they could also be those of young assistants. More recently, studies of architecture have been used to explore the way in which societies structured gender in the past. Gilchrist's (1995) study of the relationship between ideas of chivalry, gender roles and the different zones of medieval castles is a good example.

Artistic sources

Depictions of males and females in scenes on pottery, reliefs, wall paintings and metal artefacts have been quarried for information about gender roles. Some appear fairly straightforward and provide evidence for a division of labour. Pottery from Sopron, Hungary, from the sixth century BC shows figures which seem to be women engaged in weaving and spinning: one is dancing or praying while another figure, which may also be female, is playing a lyre. Men in comparison are riding horses, herding animals and leading horse-drawn wagons. Other material is more ambivalent. A depiction of a person gathering wild honey from a tree at Bicorp, in Spain, from 7000–4000 BC has been interpreted as both male and female by different commentators. The majority have

Figure 11.16 *Male and female images from a Classical Greek vase*

assumed it is a woman due to the size of the buttocks and the flowing hair.

Even where artistic images are clearly of females or males, they cannot always be taken at face value.

However, representation cannot in itself be taken as evidence of high status, nor can we assume that the women depicted are typical. Until recently, sexuality in the past was rarely considered by archaeologists. Indeed, in several countries collections of artefacts with sexual imagery are often kept from public view. In 1999 the British Museum faced a dilemma over whether to display a rare Roman vase that depicted homosexual sex. A survey of sexuality in the archaeological record appears in Taylor (1997).

POPULATION AND ETHNICITY

Demographic information about past populations is largely obtained from human remains. Where there are large collections from cemeteries they can reveal information about the age and sex

Figure 11.17 *Minoan procession*

At Knossos (◀ p. 238) a series of figurines of bare-breasted women with full length skirts have been found. They frequently have snakes twined round their arms. There are also frescoes which show women and men involved in various activities. They are easily distinguished as the Minoans adopted the convention of painting the skins of women white while those of men are painted brown. Women are depicted more commonly than men. Taken at face value it seems that elite women may have had more status and the right to participate in a wider range of activities than women in many other societies. Some writers have gone further. These images and an absence of fortifications, male statues, temples to gods or boastful inscriptions might be evidence of a matriarchal (headed by women) society. This fresco (produced by painting with plant and shellfish dyes onto wet plaster) apparently shows young men processing towards a priestess.

structure of the population, average height and life expectancy of adults as well as common illnesses and injuries. DNA offers the opportunity to explore relationships between people and to determine how homogenous any population was. It has also been critical in tracing the evolution of humans. Artistic sources and preserved bodies can fill in details of appearance. For periods where burial evidence is sparse, including most of prehistory, population estimates are based on the carrying capacity of the land. This method was originally used to work out likely population levels of animal species within a given environment. It relies on accurate reconstruction of past ecosystems. Archaeologists model different strategies such as foraging or horticulture to work out what maximum density of human population could have been sustained.

Ethnicity and race have the same relationship as sex and gender. One of each pair is in our DNA, the other is in our heads. Racially we are all Homo Sapiens but ethnicity consists of cultural norms and values that differentiate one social group from another. Physical differences are sometimes, but not always, used to distinguish different ethnic groups.

Until the later twentieth century cultural approaches to archaeology tended to dominate interpretations. In some cases they were used to support racist political ideas, such as Nazi archaeology (◀ p. 138). Such approaches also led to a diffusionist 'invasions model' of social change in Britain with successive waves of invaders bringing developments and their own special pottery, for example, Windmill Hill Folk or Beaker People. This idea fitted with colonial experience of

KEY SITES

Pompeii and Herculaneum

Recent developments at these two Roman towns, destroyed by Mount Vesuvius in AD 79, provide an insight into the way archaeology has developed. The first excavations in 1748 were a search for treasure to adorn royal palaces. Today the material evidence is painstakingly studied to try and bring an ancient culture to life.

Classical accounts, particularly Pliny's letters, led to a view of a cosmopolitan population being entombed in ash at Pompeii or engulfed in mud at Herculaneum by the sudden eruption. The ghoulish plaster casts of victims have been used in conjunction with the range of good-looking people on the wall paintings to illustrate this view. Vulcanologists have now shown that the eruption did not happen without warning. Evidence for grand villas being taken over by squatters who hung agricultural implements over grand wall paintings suggests that many of those who could had left. Statistical analysis of the piles of disarticulated bones in the basements of Pompeii has yielded a picture of the 'average Pompeian'. Skull deformities suggest a group of closely related people and a high proportion of older women. This suggests that ideas about Roman lifespans may be wrong. If women survived childbirth then they had a strong chance of surviving to a good age, even approximating modern levels. The high number of older people also suggests a grim scenario – that they were the ones left behind!

Conversely, early excavations at Herculaneum suggested that the town was abandoned long before the final eruption since so few bodies had been found. That idea changed dramatically in 1982 when excavations on the waterfront of Herculaneum uncovered hundreds of skeletons in the arches facing onto the beach. These may reveal more details of population structure.

- http://www.cs.berkeley.edu/~jhauser/pictures/history/Rome/Pompeii/

Figure 11.18 *Wall painting from House of the Vettii, Pompeii*

Despite the destruction of the population these views of how the richer citizens wished to be portrayed have survived. In these strikingly modern looking examples we can learn much about appearance, class and gender.

worldwide progress flowing from more 'civilised' to 'backward' peoples, but it has been shown to be deeply flawed by the application of scientific techniques. Stonehenge is the most famous case. A generation of classically trained archaeologists had shown how the people of Bronze Age Wessex built monuments in imitation and with help from advanced Mediterranean civilisations. Yet radiocarbon dating has shown that Stonehenge predated the Mediterranean monuments it was supposed to have been influenced by. This cultural model of social change tends to undervalue the

KEY SITE

West Heslerton and Lechlade

Historical and linguistic sources suggest that Anglo-Saxon invaders slaughtered or displaced native Romano – British people from much of England in the fifth and sixth centuries AD. On the assumption that 'Germanic type' artefacts equalled Saxon invaders, archaeological material was used to trace the arrival and spread of migrants across the country. Similarly, areas where Saxon pottery or metalwork was absent were identified as places still held by Britons. Excavations of these two settlements present a rather different picture.

At West Heslerton in the early 5th Century some distinctive Anglo-Saxon grubenhauser (◀ p. 148) were built in what had been a typical Romano-British settlement. Around AD 450 this site was abandoned and a large, new settlement replaced it a short distance away. This too combined Romano-British and Anglo-Saxon elements but was a very different settlement. It included post- and plank-built buildings and a long hall. The whole site was laid out in an ordered way with distinct zones for agricultural processing, housing and industrial activity. This included bone and metal working and the manufacture of pottery and textiles. Imported pottery metal work and lava quernstones suggest some of this may have been for trade. The evidence of buildings and pottery suggested much continuity of population but the degree of planning and Scandinavian origin of the larger buildings suggested that the site had new, foreign leaders.

Burial evidence also appears to favour a mixed population. Amongst over 300 burials were many with weapons. Some of these seem to be female graves while others are individuals who do not have 'warrior' builds. This may support Härke's (1990) 'warband model'. His study of Anglo-Saxon cemeteries suggested that many included Romano-Britons, thus indicating co-existence. Male burials with swords were on average 1–2 inches taller than those without. This was not due to different diets and suggested two distinct ethnic groups. By the seventh century this distinction had disappeared, probably through intermarriage. DNA analysis of several cemeteries revealed two models of Anglo-Saxon immigration. In some, complete kin groups were represented, which suggests entire communities settled here, while in others, males with weapons existed alongside female skeletons which showed continuity with the Romano-British period. Harke terms this the 'warband' model. Over time, DNA evidence supports a mingling of the two populations into 'the English' while the dominant culture remained 'Anglo-Saxon'. This might suggest that weapons had a symbolic value rather than identifying male warriors. Oxygen and strontium isotope analysis of teeth enamel have also identified two distinct population groups, one with similar profiles to prehistoric burials from the area, the other with more distant origins. This suggests that many of the Anglo Saxons buried there were first generation immigrants.

The longevity of the site and the excavation of over 200 buildings means that changes in construction techniques can be traced over time. A massive assemblage of 750,000 animal bones offers the possibility of understanding the economy and diet.

The evidence from Lechlade covers another change in British history. This cemetery was both early and long lasting. Between 450 and 800AD over 200 people were buried and at least 29 cremated. Analysis of the feet from these burials by Jackson (1995) pointed to great local population continuity.

  **KEY SITE** *cont.*

West Heslerton and Lechlade

The early burials were classic pagan burials with grave goods including many with weapons. However, several of these were militarily useless and in one case an 11 year old was buried with an adult spear. Weapons may have been more symbolic than a sign of warfare. Although the Battle of Dyrham (577) is supposed to have occurred a few miles away, only one burial had died of trauma related to fighting. The richest burial was nicknamed Mrs Getty (◀ p. 272) but finds of valuables did come from several other graves which attested to exchange networks reaching far beyond England. The artefact traditions indicate that these people were ethnic Saxons rather than Jutes or Angles. In the 7th century the alignment of the graves shifted from NE/SW to NW/SE. This suggests they had converted to Christianity yet they continued to have grave goods. This is clear evidence of continuity and possibly people hedging their bets.

A few years after this excavation, the homes of these people were found in a nearby field. This settlement too was longlived. Its economy was based on mixed farming of cereals, beans and flax along with cattle and sheep. There was evidence too of metal working, weaving and leather working. This pattern is common on contemporary sites such as West Stow (◀ p. 148) but also is very similar to the picture we get from Iron Age settlements in the vicinity from 1000 years earlier.

Part of the problem with attempts to study ethnicity through material culture is the material itself. In some areas such as East Anglia or Oxfordshire it can be difficult to differentiate Saxon from Romano-British Greyware or Iron Age pottery, unless it is decorated. Where it can be identified, it sometimes turns up well before historical sources say the Saxons arrived, for example at Eynsham Abbey. This may illustrate the point that ethnically distinctive material may be used by other groups. Exchange, trade, small-scale migration or adoption and copying by indigenous people would also spread material.

For more on Anglo-Saxon cemeteries see

- www.gla.ac.uk/archaeology/staff/

Figure 11.19 *Grubenhaus from West Heslerton*

KEY SITE *cont.*

West Heslerton and Lechlade

Houses may be a better ethnic marker than pottery. Particularly since there is some evidence that Saxon settlers used containers made from wood and animals along with coarse grass-tempered wares which have not survived. These are very common finds on sites in the east of England from the mid 5th century onwards. It seems unlikely that native Romano-Britains would have adopted these small structures out of fashion. The same might not be true of Saxon metal jewellery. Experimental archaeology has established that these buildings had suspended floors (rather than being 'pit dwellings') and produced several models of the house superstructure.

Figure 11.20 *Reconstructed Grubenhaus at West Stow*

achievements of indigenous people as in the case of Iron Age brochs (◀ p. 215). In Neolithic studies the current orthodoxy has shifted away from seeing all change as due to migration. For example, while the spread of farming in central Europe is largely interpreted as colonisation, its eventual adoption after the Neolithic standstill (◀ p. 234) in north-western Europe is increasingly seen as the result of choices made by local foraging groups.

Even where we know invasions took place, the archaeological record is not always helpful. For example, there is little evidence for the Norman Conquest in sequences of medieval ceramics. Some evidence is ambivalent. Belgic coins found in South-east England from the late Iron Age have been used to support Caesar's description of immigration into the area from Gaul. However, there are other mechanisms by which the coins could have got there. As with other forms of identity, where ethnic allegiances were expressed in organic material such as textiles, evidence may not always survive.

SOCIAL CHANGE

Most periods will have examples of social changes to which you will be directed. The kind of evidence discussed in this chapter and those on economics and settlement will provide the focus for work on this area. Studying social change is likely to require you to discuss a range of different models to account for change. Essentially these will fall into two groups. External factors include immigration, diffusion, conquest and environmental change. Internal factors include evolution, competition and innovation. You need to ensure you examine and appraise an appropriate range of these. The adoption of agriculture exercise provides a good model (◀ p. 232) for this as does the Pizza exercise (▶ p. 290). In examining change don't forget the opposite: stasis. For much of the time things remain as they are, and that needs explaining too. A useful tool for examining forces for change or stasis is the force field diagram (◀ p. 234).

SOCIAL CONFLICT

Not all social conflict is violent. Probably its most common form is competition in either display or consumption. Our society is no different in this respect. Various attempts have been made to trace this sort of competition from the Neolithic onwards. Tilley (1996) suggested that developments in the design of Swedish passage graves might have been the product of local competitive emulation. Other writers have come to similar conclusions about the henges of Wessex, an idea that was taken up by Cornwell in his 1999 blockbuster novel, *Stonehenge*.

Warfare

In literate societies, warfare is one of the first things to be documented. It seems likely that in societies with oral traditions it forms a major part of their history too. From Homer we know something of the wars of Bronze Age Greece while medieval recording of Irish and Icelandic sagas

Figure 11.21 *Ruthven Barracks*

These barracks formed part of a chain of roads and forts built by the British Government to pacify the Scottish highlands after the 1715 Jacobite Rebellion. The site on a glacial feature was a natural defensive point dominating a junction of the new military road north to Inverness. The barracks initially held up to 120 infantry and a cavalry unit. Their function would be to patrol the area and suppress local problems whilst helping to give warning and delay more serious threats. However, cost cutting led to troop numbers being run down. By the time of the 1745 rebellion there were only 13 'redcoats' based there. They successfully drove off an attack by over 200 Jacobites who lacked the artillery needed to break through the defences. They surrendered in 1746 when retreating Jacobites with cannons arrived. The fort was reoccupied by Hanoverian forces soon afterwards but became the focus for thousands of regrouping Jacobites after their defeat at Culloden. When they heard that their leader, 'Bonnie Prince Charlie' had fled they burnt the barracks down before dispersing.

KEY SITES

Nimrud and Nineveh

The Assyrian Empire dominated present-day Iraq in the ninth to seventh centuries BC. The huge reliefs from the palaces of its great cities of Nimrud and Nineveh are interesting both as early propaganda and as evidence of early Iron Age warfare.

The use of sculpture to glorify kings in war had been common practice in the region for over 2000 years. As a result the imagery is highly stylised and intended to impress and intimidate. Rulers are shown larger than other people and they depicted the king as high priest linked to the gods. Other high ranking people have squared off beards and net skirts. The strength of rulers was emphasised through scenes of them hunting lions. Ashurnasirpal (reigned 883–859 BC) boasted in inscriptions to having killed 450.

The fate of those who displeased them was depicted in scenes of flaying, impaling and beheading. The cartoon strip style reliefs of their campaigns were also subject to conventions. No Assyrians were shown dead. The sculptures all show well equipped Assyrians trampling their foes under their chariots, beheading their leaders and bringing booty back to Assyria.

Despite all this there is unwitting evidence – that is evidence that was not deliberately distorted – about clothing, technology and warfare amongst other things. We see evidence of chariots, siege towers and inflatable skins being used to cross a river. We can see the lightly armed Aramaic forces who fought alongside the Assyrians and some of the different types of military units. The range of weapons including bows, spears and slings is evident as are some of their tactics. One panel shows a soldier holding a tall shield of wood or reeds as cover while others fire slingshots and arrows from behind it. The origin of the phrase 'taking a head count' is suggested in depictions of the aftermath of victory.

Figure 11.22 *Assyrian cavalry trampling their vanquished foes at the Battle of Til Tuba*

may provide insights into Iron Age warfare in north-western Europe. Tomb paintings and inscriptions in most of the classical civilisations of Eurasia and Mesoamerica provide graphic depiction of the nature of battles.

However, these very stylized accounts tend to concentrate on key heroic individuals and just tell the victor's version of events. Consequently, we approach them with some care as exact records of evidence. However, their unwitting evidence of equipment and organisation can be valuable. Trajan's Column in Rome provides a superb example. It commemorates the victorious campaigns of the Emperor Trajan against the Dacians. Scenes show in tremendous detail the equipment and organisation involved in the campaign. The battle scenes depict the tactics used by the legions and their effectiveness. The key events of the campaign are included and its effects, allowing for some bias, are also illustrated.

Apart from historic and artistic accounts, the physical evidence of weapons and fortification usually provide the main sources for identifying warfare. In some cases actual battles become visible. For instance, the 'war grave' at Maiden Castle with its famous iron arrowhead embedded in a defender's spine, or the mass grave at Towton. This was subjected to the same tests as a murder enquiry by forensic archaeologists. They were able to identify what happened to the individual soldiers and how each injury was caused. The exact location and sequence of the battle is also being revealed by archaeology. Towton shows how archaeology can add to and test historic

Figure 11.23 *Memorial to the dead at Flodden*

Rather unusually for a British battlefield we know exactly where the site of Flodden (1513) is from historic sources. This collective funerary monument overlooks it. In other cases these sources are less useful. Towton (1461) for example is being plotted through metal detection and fieldwalking. In the case of Tewksbury (1471), disputes about the location between archaeologists went to the High Court when development was being planned. The sites of many key battles such as Brunaburgh (937) are completely unknown.

sources, many of which are vague or unreliable in the accounts.

- http://mysite.wanadoo-members.co.uk/TowtonBattlefield

Of course, not everything that looks military may have been. Both weapons and fortifications can be symbolic. Early metal daggers and 'rapiers' were relatively fragile. While they could have been used to kill, they would have been less effective than flint-tipped spears or stone axes. The swords that emerge in the Bronze Age are quite a different matter. Their shape and balance suggest that they were ideal for slashing at opponents in fighting at close quarters. Analysis of their edges has shown that many have damage associated with metal-on-metal contact. Fortifications can also mislead us about the nature of warfare. 'Hill forts' with their massive circuits of ramparts suggest sieges. There is evidence of attack at a few, such as flint arrowheads around the entrance at Crickley Hill, but these are exceptions. Warfare in the Iron Age is more likely to have looked like a cattle raid than pitched battles between rival armies, at least until the Romans arrived. A similar bias would occur if we looked at the major physical evidence of warfare between France and Germany in 1940. The Maginot Line, bypassed by the Germans, is still visible while traces of mobile tank and infantry formations are harder to discern.

Figure 11.24 *Monea Castle*

It looks military but was it? Monea is a plantation era (1618) castle in Northern Ireland. It consisted of a large walled courtyard or bawn and a tall house with two round towers. These are topped with crow stepped 'Scottish corbels' supporting a rectangular top section. A virtually identical tower house exists at Claypotts near Dundee. There are gun-loops and it was built as part of a network of strong houses built across the region in case of rebellion. When rebellion came in 1641 it was captured. Perhaps what was more important was is symbolism. The verticality of the monument makes it seem more imposing than it is. Like the brochs (◀ p. 215) its main job was to reinforce status and social control.

Figure 11.25 *Iron Age coin*

Not all coins may have been used as money, some may have been used as tokens or symbols of power.

KEY SKILL

Evaluation exercises

Scales of justice

The ability to reach supported conclusions is expected at A Level and above. Learning how to reach judgements takes time and requires confidence building. One way of doing this is through short exercises where you get used to quickly summing up strengths and weaknesses. A simple task is to take three or four methods and list their advantages and disadvantages for particular tasks or in general. If you present the information in graphical form you are more likely to remember it. Adapting the scales of justice is a popular version. Try this as preparation for the next piece of work you have on methods.

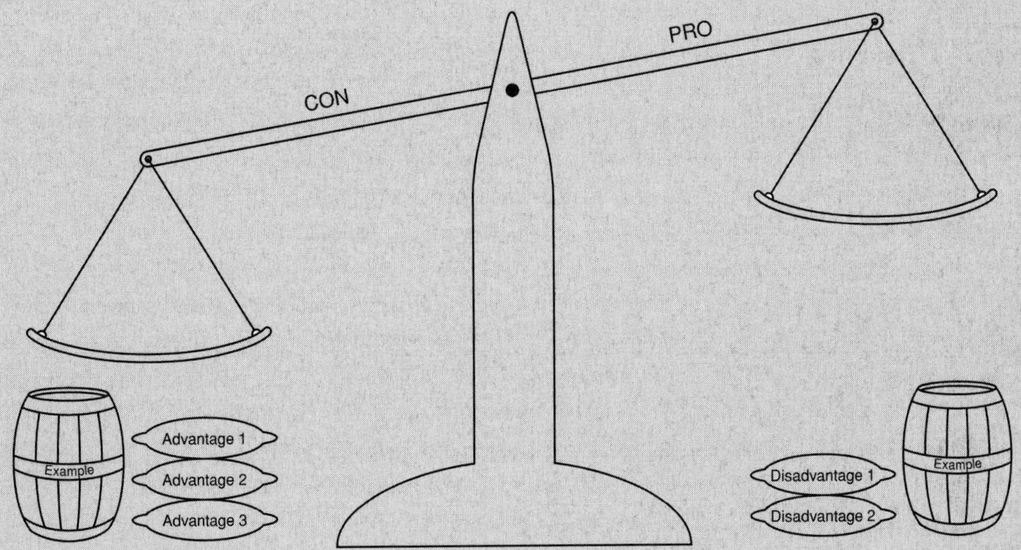

Figure 11.26 *A scales of justice diagram*

KEY SKILL *cont.*

Evaluation exercises

Archaeological pizza

This is a more sophisticated exercise. You can do this by yourself or it can be a team or whole class exercise. It will help you get used to using supporting evidence and prioritising points to reach a judgement.

1 Draw a large pizza shape with a circle of 'topping' in the middle.
2 Take an issue you have been studying where there is considerable debate and at least five different theories. For example, 'What happened to towns in Britain in the fifth century?' or 'What sort of social change were the Anglo-Saxon invasions?'
3 Put each theory into one of the inner sections of the pizza.
4 Research supporting evidence and enter it in the tomato or mushroom in the outer sections of the relevant slice.
5 Adjust the size of the slices so that the most convincing argument is the largest slice and so on.
6 If you have done this as a team exercise, each team has to argue for their version.

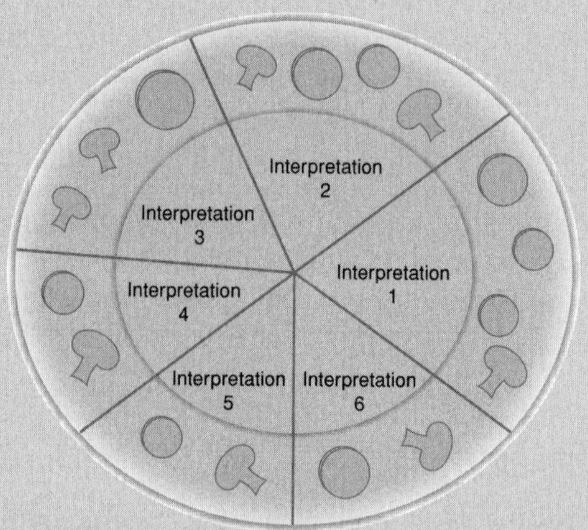

Figure 11.27 *An archaeological pizza diagram*

Part Three

Examination Success and Beyond

Chapter 12

Doing an Archaeological Project

YOUR GOALS

You need to understand

- how to choose an appropriate topic
- where to obtain help and evidence
- how to plan and manage your time
- how to record sites and materials
- what to include and how to present your study.

Most courses, including A Level, require students to undertake a piece of personal research and submit their findings for assessment. This may be called coursework, a personal study or simply an archaeological investigation. Whatever its title it will have a set of written instructions as to the precise nature of your task. This will include guidance on what you must eventually produce and in which format. This chapter covers issues which are common to most students' experiences and needs. You should keep your specific research brief to hand as you read through this section. The examples provided here are from good A Level projects. They could equally be good investigations undertaken out of general interest.

HOW TO CHOOSE A TOPIC

Study the assignment brief issued to you. It may include constraints such as the word 'local' or you may need to undertake some 'first-hand' observation. It is essential that you choose a subject that fits the requirements of your course, is based on evidence which is accessible to you and, most importantly, is something on which you will enjoy working.

It must be archaeological

Archaeology embraces many other academic disciplines and sources in attempting to understand past cultures. These range from biology through geology to architecture. It is common to find overlap emerging in a project. Graveyard surveys, for example, link strongly to social and economic history while studies of hedgerows will require some botanical knowledge. While links to other disciplines are clearly valid you must consider balance. Archaeological content should dominate the final work. For example, analysis of the structural evidence for different phases of building within a medieval castle is archaeological whereas exploring events and personalities linked to its use are usually of a historical nature. A general rule of thumb is that archaeology deals directly with the physical remains of the past whilst history is more concerned with analysing events using documentary sources.

You must be able to access your sources

Being able to visit your chosen sites, monuments, museum or archaeological unit should be high on your agenda. Research benefits from a first-hand approach and it is more than likely that you will need to make more than a single visit to your source(s) of evidence. A first visit – following initial research in the library – will familiarise you with the object of your study. You need to get a feel for the extent of the site(s) or the range of artefacts available. Follow-up visits will be required for more detailed research. This might include surveying earthworks or sorting and drawing artefacts. Often students find that there are points they missed on previous visits which can be checked on later ones. If you have chosen sites at too great a distance such opportunities to revisit may be impractical. This is particularly true when students are tempted to select sites overseas. Your holiday visit to Pompeii may have fired your archaeological imagination but is unlikely to have resulted in meaningful research. The cost of a later visit to check measurements makes this a rather expensive option. Sites within range of home, school or college are your best bet.

Access does not just mean closeness. There are other people such as landowners involved. Public rights of way can be found in OS maps while better known sites are listed in gazetteers, often with directions for access. But in many cases there is no easy or direct footpath. Despite 'right to roam' legislation, if the site is on somebody's land you will need their permission to survey it. In 1999 a gamekeeper chased a student away from a stone circle in Derbyshire. His project was delayed for months while he then tried to get written permission from the landowner. It would have been better to have done this first. It is sometimes difficult to discover who owns particular fields, so build in time to find out and consider fallback projects in case permission is refused or you don't receive a reply. If you hope to use an artefact collection, you need to check with the keeper that this is possible and determine when you can have access to it. To give yourself the best opportunity in all cases, write early in your research programme, explain briefly your reasons for wanting access to the land or collection and offer a range of suitable times when you could visit. A stamped self-addressed envelope may add a degree of success to the response rate. Permission should be obtained from the site manager if you are studying an excavation and want to record more than a few cursory notes or photographs.

It is easy to get caught out with access issues. A common excuse for poor studies is that sites or museums were closed at the time the student visited. Check it out in advance. A more difficult situation is where the site is accessible but it is overgrown with vegetation. Summer grass or bracken growth can easily mask relatively minor features such as hut circles or medieval village remains. Winter is often the best time to visit earthworks. Even then you can still be frustrated. One keen fieldworker had to wait several weeks for snow to melt on Bodmin Moor before his barrow survey could be undertaken.

Supporting literature will vary in quantity according to the topic selected. Key texts to establish a context for your research are usually essential. Most studies benefit from an understanding of the relevant background. If you find too many books on your subject it will run the risk of lacking originality and it might be better to reconsider your focus. On the other hand, it is possible, as the case studies show, to identify an aspect of our material past where there is little direct written material on which to draw. There are many untapped areas of archaeological potential.

Figure 12.1 *A lovely day, but not the best one to survey Kylesku Broch*

Summer vegetation totally obscures the interior and the entrances. The midges were bad too!

It is easier to say something new about the pattern of round barrows or pillboxes near your home than it would be to say something original about Hadrian's Wall. You should seek advice from your tutor on background reading and sources whatever your topic. Access to this material is also easier if it is a local site or collection. If your school or college does not have much, local museums and libraries probably will.

You also need to find the correct balance of available evidence to study. Too much and you run the risk of superficiality, too little and the problem will be achieving a meaningful outcome. The curator of your local museum might welcome an apparently sensible and enthusiastic student who offers to catalogue their Romano-British pottery collection; a concentration on just the Samian ware might in reality be more feasible and appropriate for your study. If you do work with a third party such as a local archaeologist be sure to seek their professional advice but always refer back to your tutor who will best understand the requirements of your study.

So the first stage in your research is to ensure adequate and appropriate sources and access to them. Often at this stage some change may be needed to the original title in the light of your findings.

BASIC RESEARCH OPPORTUNITIES

There is a vast range of subjects to choose from. Before you select one, look again at exactly what your course requires.

A Level students

- At A2 level each student selects an individual choice of topic and question. Access to HE assignments are likely to be similar.
- Students must develop an investigation of a question, issue or problem in an archaeological context. It has to be based on named sites, monuments or museums and must consider how archaeologists might approach such an investigation.
- Pass level responses must go beyond a straightforward factual account of evidence they have identified. Evaluation and analysis feature strongly in high level responses. Full details from AQA.

• http://www.aqa.org.uk/qual/gceasa/arc.html

Undergraduate or HND students

- No standard practice. Some courses require research diaries on summer excavation work, others set investigations similar to those at A level in year 1 or 2.
- Students may undertake research for their extended essay or dissertation. Requirements vary from one university to another but the focus of such work tends to be sharper the higher one proceeds up the academic ladder.

Sites and monuments

All sites can be studied in terms of spatial distribution and layout and their chronological development. Most can also be examined for typological development. Investigations can centre on any one, two or all of these factors to facilitate the depth of research needed. Whatever your choice of sites or monuments you should never go alone when doing fieldwork. Apart from the personal safety aspect, which cannot be over-stressed, a companion can hold tapes or discuss your observations with you.

The extent of the task should have a strong bearing on the selection of sites. Single sites may not always be sufficient. An Iron Age hill fort allows for both desktop research and field survey, a single pillbox would be too restrictive. A collection of coastal defences would be a sounder proposition. Studying a local group allows comparison and contrast to be developed which enables you to reveal your true archaeological investigative skills. Neolithic tombs provide such an opportunity. These monuments are widely distributed. For many students in the British Isles they are accessible and can be adapted to suit almost any purpose in terms of projects. A popular approach is to look at their distribution in terms of the Neolithic landscape, to establish original groupings or clusters, or to compare orientation. Other approaches include comparing inter-visibility or to report on the condition and current threats to the monuments.

Of course visible monuments, which include those you can find on OS maps, are rather like the tip of an iceberg. By far the greater proportion of evidence of past activity is hidden below ground. Those studies that only reflect on visible evidence may well fail to deal with the larger picture. Reference to aerial photographs and SMR documentation is useful in establishing evidence that cannot be recorded or accessed in other ways.

You may be also be able to consult the results – usually published – of previous excavations on the sites. You need to decide how much of your evidence will be derived from such sources and how much from your study of unexcavated sites. Few personal studies achieve high grades by simply paraphrasing the work of others. Excavation reports are also a particularly difficult medium to summarise effectively. However, if sites have been excavated then you have no option but to investigate via the site report or archive.

Including a well-known site in a group study of several sites such as Chedworth and other Cotswold villas can lead to a loss of balance. The

EXAMPLE 1

What evidence is there to suggest an Irish influence on the portal tombs of Wales?

'Kate' began with a comparative study of some portal tombs of south and north Wales and Ireland – leaving Cornish and Scottish examples outside the scope of the study. She combined a desktop survey of excavation reports with fieldwork. She hoped to discuss distribution, construction, orientation, typography, material culture, mortuary practices and chronology. However, few sites had 'comprehensive' excavation reports and therefore she reduced her commentary on finds and mortuary practice and placed greater emphasis on evidence from recording surviving remains in the field.

Figure 12.2 *Dolmen from Carrowmore Cemetery*

Sources

- SMRs
- Archaeological trusts
- Key sites: Pembrokeshire (4), Merioneth (3), Ireland (13)
- Museums: National Museum of Wales, National Museum and Library, Dublin
- Wide bibliography including prehistory texts and excavation reports
- Contacts: three practising archaeologists were contacted and all responded

Methodology

Kate established a background context from literature and produced distribution maps and commentary for the sites in Wales and Ireland. She reviewed academic arguments and established a hypothesis that there was an Irish origin/influence for Welsh sites. Her recording of sites included details of location, height above sea level, siting, orientation, style and material of construction. Where possible details of internal structure and reports on burial rites were also included.

Content/discussion

Kate began by considering definitions of portal tombs as types of megalithic structure and acknowledging the limitations of the evidence for burial rites. She then made a range of detailed comparisons and contrasts including statistical tables. She examined different theories in depth and commented on each against the evidence she had gathered. She went on to reflect on other Irish/Welsh influences of the time in terms of 'passage' graves and axe trade. Her conclusion noted that evidence is open to interpretation but having weighed the evidence she outlined a sustainable argument.

Additional illustrations included photographs of twenty-three sites, two site plans and drawings of typical Neolithic artefacts. She acknowledged help and included an extensive bibliography. Her field notes were placed in an appendix.

EXAMPLE 2

A survey of ground and polished stone and flint axes from East Kent

'Hamid' set out to examine finds from a small area in some detail and to catalogue quantity, type and distribution. He hoped this might shed some light on Neolithic settlement in the region.

Sources

- Kent SMR
- Canterbury Archaeological Trust
- Kent Archaeological Review
- Archaeologia Cantiana
- Museums: British Museum, Canterbury, Dartford, Dover, Folkestone, Herne Bay, Maidstone, Powell-Cotton
- Wide bibliography including general prehistory texts and articles in archaeological journals

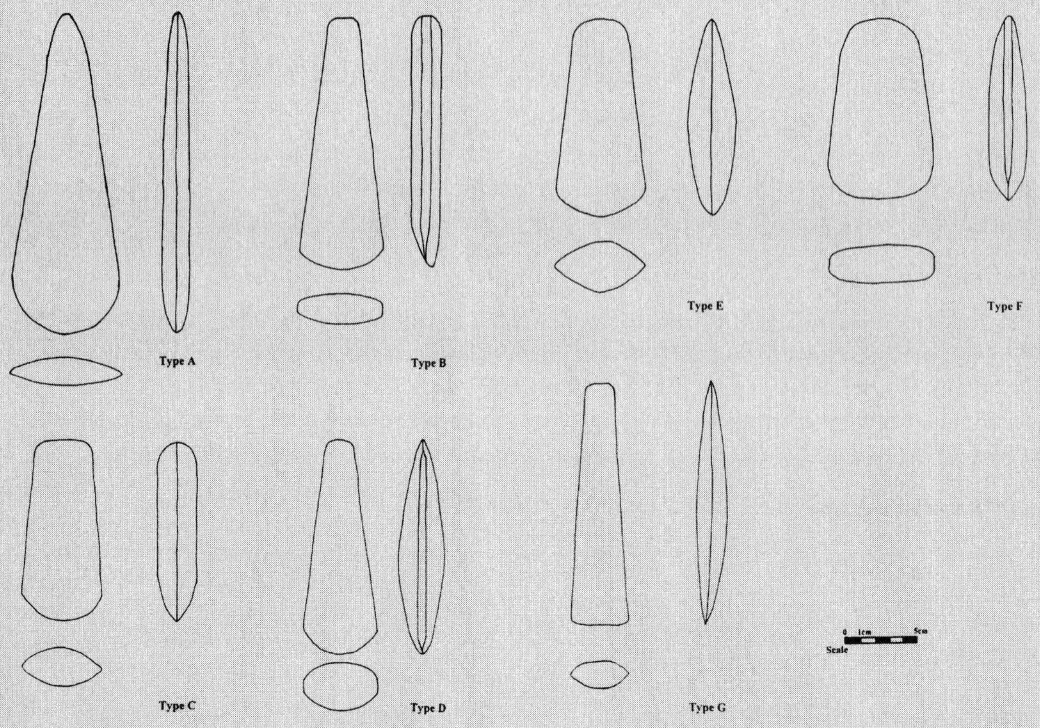

Figure 12.3 *A type series of stone axes: the seven profiles against which the axes were matched for typological analysis*

EXAMPLE 2 *cont.*

Methodology

Much previous research has been related to the petrological analysis (via thin sectioning) of axes to establish their source and the distribution patterns of products. Records on 125 axes were compiled from published data and museum records. Hamid used a self-devised sheet to list museum accession number; find spot; stone type; dimensions; completeness; condition; presence of cortex; other comments. The most complete were sketched in outline for shape comparison. Using typology and analysis of size and weight Hamid established a seven-type classification with description and illustration of one axe in each type. Charts were produced to show number of axes per group.

Having produced his catalogue, Hamid evaluated it and discussed its implications for understanding the archaeology of Neolithic Kent.

Content/discussion

Hamid acknowledged the difficulty in establishing an accurate number of axes. He observed that some are held outside Kent while others in Kentish museums were unprovenanced. More were likely to be in private collections and unpublished. Most were chance finds but others could be linked to archaeological sites or other Neolithic material. The section on raw materials acknowledged the work of others. Most axes were made from local flint but petrological analysis linked others to axe factories. He was able to construct distribution maps with links to known Neolithic sites and natural features. Further discussion centred on possible implications of the findings for exchange and identifying settlement and the function of the axes themselves.

Accompanying illustrations included location maps, six tables of data and typological drawings. No photographs were used; the project was acceptable without them. The project listed acknowledgements and had a comprehensive bibliography. The axe record sheets were placed in an appendix.

data on one site far outweighs that easily obtainable on the others. This imbalance can be countered by a title which lays the stress on the better known site or which focuses on conservation and preservation issues. Sites with guidebooks should carry a health warning for students. They can seem a bonus when you are hard-pressed for time but the availability of such material can tempt you into producing a study which owes too much to others' work. At worst this can turn into an archaeological version of I-spy.

Artefacts

The potential for studying artefacts is vast. These range from Palaeolithic stone tools to relatively recent objects like clay pipes or horseshoes. However, artefacts are less frequently used as source material for projects than sites and monuments. This may reflect the pull of the outdoors and landscape archaeology but probably also stems from the greater barriers that exist between the researcher and the guardians of material culture. Artefacts are most likely to be in museums or with archaeological units. Individual excavators or collectors are less easy to identify as resources for students.

Most museum material is in storage. Some of it will be fully catalogued. Curators tend to display their better items so these objects are often unusual rather than representative. To fully explore a museum's holding of any particular aspect of material culture will require museum staff to locate and get out appropriate evidence. Many will do this but will want sufficient notice and a clear idea of what it is you wish to study. Arrangements will have to be made for frequent visits to work on the material as cataloguing and drawing are time-consuming activities. These can only be done during opening times which may mean Saturday or holiday appointments.

Archaeological units hold most recently excavated material and their time is even more limited than that of museum staff. Their role is not curatorial and it will need a personal introduction to access their store of artefacts. Some students obtain work experience placements with units and may be able to develop links through such activity. Other sources include local societies who may do some excavation or, more rarely, local excavators. Some metal detectorists might allow a study of their findings – such a recording and analysis of them could well prove fruitful.

Fieldwalking

Some students use their links with museums, units, universities or landowners to identify sites under the plough and arrange their own fieldwalking exercise. If it is well researched and planned this can lead to excellent, original studies. Farmers need to be approached sensitively for permission and in good time. Their schedule of activity needs to be known so that you can organise the fieldwalk at a convenient time both to them and yourself. You also need an initial visit to check that archaeological material is visible in the topsoil. Try not to be overambitious and do get some help. It takes longer to set up and walk an area of a field systematically and gather the evidence than you might think. Two students fieldwalking a 200 metre square could walk up to 10 kilometres each. On ploughed land that represents a considerable expenditure of energy! Washing, identifying and analysing the finds will also take much time.

Archaeology from the modern period

Most archaeological texts focus on later prehistory to the medieval period. However, this should not limit you and particularly if you live in a built-up area, you may find it easier to focus on standing buildings or more recent structures. Students have studied buildings ranging from docks to petrol stations. The remains of the industrial age and also of the Second World War are particularly rich sources for studies.

Industrial archaeology including agricultural evidence

Early transport systems such as canals and railways often leave linear traces, now often fading, of their routes. A keen eye for landscape and interpretation backed by older Ordnance Survey maps can be just what a student researcher needs. Both wind and water mills survive in a range of conditions and often have constructional sequences that can be ascribed to different phases of development. Where they have been converted into homes you may find the owners rather proud to show off original elements of the building. Mines are often landscaped after their closure and the danger of hidden shafts should discourage their use as a source for study. However, harbours, their associated buildings and tramways may survive in sufficient state to warrant investigation. Despite urban regeneration it is quite possible to identify buildings whose original purpose has now given way to new uses. Breweries, maltings, cinemas and mills all fall in this category. They lend themselves to questions asking, 'To what extent can the development and function of the remains at X be identified by archaeological survey?'

Figure 12.4 *Fieldwalk finds presented with a scale*

There is a vast range of vernacular farm buildings in the countryside. Even on modern farms you may not have to look far to find some older features. Records of this diminishing archaeological resource are needed and your study could add to them. One rural structure which makes an ideal vehicle for manageable research to identify, record, illustrate, compare and produce distribution maps of is the dovecote. While there are some classic examples of free-standing structures (how many visitors to Avebury have noticed the circular dovecote opposite the entrance to the museum?), many are located in the end of barns or stables. Another disappearing feature are churn stands. Milk used to be collected from farms in churns placed at the roadside by farmers. They were put on stands so they could be easily lifted across to the lorries. Many stands still exist, though now redundant, and can be found, often rather overgrown, in hedgerows near to a farm's access onto a road. Styles vary (typology) and different materials were used. Very few are recorded.

The Defence of Britain

Research into modern military archaeology was boosted recently by the Defence of Britain project. It recorded some of the monuments slowly eroding away in the coastal and inland landscape. About 450 airfields were built during the Second World War particularly in the east. Coastal defences survive in many places simply because no one has bothered to remove them, for example the concrete blocks designed to slow a seaborne invasion at Fairbourne, Gwynedd. Running in lines across the countryside are numerous pillboxes

EXAMPLE 3

Industrial archaeology: the Dudley (No. 2) Canal from Selly Oak to Halesowen, Birmingham

'Tom' attempted to evaluate the archaeological significance of the surviving surface evidence for 8 km of a canal abandoned nearly fifty years ago. The line of the canal passed through a park and housing and industrial estates. A significant feature was the Lappal tunnel which collapsed in 1917. At nearly 4 km it was one of the longest canal tunnels ever built.

Sources

- Background texts and pamphlets on canals and industrial archaeology
- Maps: Birmingham Canal Navigations; 1:25,000 OS for modern information; 10 OS (1967) for canal route shortly after closure; 1:2500 OS (25″ to mile 1881–2) showing sites of spoil heaps from the tunnel
- Contacts: college library, Birmingham Central library archives, Country Park Ranger, local inhabitants with local knowledge/memories

Figure 12.5 *Students using tapes, ranging rods and clinometers to measure Painswick Beacon Hill Fort in order to construct profiles of the earthworks*

Methodology

Tom began with maps to establish the line of canal and accessibility. He planned to walk the length of the earthwork, observing and recording key features by note-taking, drawings (including profiles) and photography. He paid particular attention to bridges, wharves, overflows and tunnel spoil heaps, which had the appearance and the same fieldwork requirements as barrows.

Content/discussion

The first part of the line from the Worcester and Birmingham canal was easily identified in Selly Oak Park but the junction was obliterated in 1953 so Tom used local oral evidence and a dismantled towpath bridge to establish its position. Landscape interpretation revealed where the line of the old canal survived infilled between house gardens, which had been laid out when it was still a landscape feature.

Photographic evidence showed tunnel portals at the end of cuttings but like much of the canal these cuttings had been infilled. Locating boggy ground in the current landscape helped to reveal their original locations.

 **EXAMPLE 3** *cont.*

Industrial archaeology: the Dudley (No. 2) Canal from Selly Oak to Halesowen, Birmingham

The tunnel had been constructed by digging several shafts down to the proposed level of the canal and then cutting a bore on either side. The resulting spoil – red clay in this case – was brought to the surface. Once the tunnel had been cut and lined with brick the shafts were back-filled, but the bulk of the excavated material remained in heaps on the surface. Tom attempted to identify these 200-year-old spoil heaps from remains in a housing estate and adjacent Country Park by using an 1881 map. Erosion enabled him to determine the constituent material of the mounds and even retrieve reject bricks from the tunnel lining.

Towards Halesowen the canal ran on a huge earthwork embankment which was larger than the bank and ditch system at Maiden Castle. Tom was able to record profiles and compare them with eighteenth-century illustrations.

Tom's project included acknowledgements and a bibliography reflecting the Birmingham Canal Navigations and industrial archaeology. He produced plans, photographs and profiles of features, and map extracts were placed in an appendix.

designed to hold up an invading army. These could be studied for typology or distribution. In towns, metal was collected during the war to 'help the war effort'. Careful examination of the tops of garden walls reveals the extent of such activity and provides fresh and original archaeological evidence literally on the doorstep.

- http://www.britarch.ac.uk/projects/dob/index.html

Experimental archaeology

Planning, conducting and evaluating an archaeological experiment or reconstruction can seem an attractive option. It can make a worthwhile study but there are pitfalls to avoid. In many cases it is an advantage if you have some familiarity with the craft involved in the experiment. Prehistoric flint knappers or Romano-British potters had practice and experience on their side when they were making the artefacts we recover from excavations. Therefore if you don't have skills in knapping or wheel-made ceramics, you might be advised to avoid this type of project. Home-made hand-built pots, which do not resemble any archaeological material, 'fired' in a bonfire in the back garden do little to explain or extend understanding of ceramics, their manufacture or firing techniques.

However, a student adept at woodworking might reconstruct and fire a bow, testing draw strength and range with different arrows and arrowheads. The groove and splinter technique of bone working for slender items such as pins can be reproduced with animal bone from the butcher and some sharp flint flakes. If you are able to visit experimental centres such as the Peat Moors Centre near Glastonbury you may be able to get advice on opportunities for developing these skills.

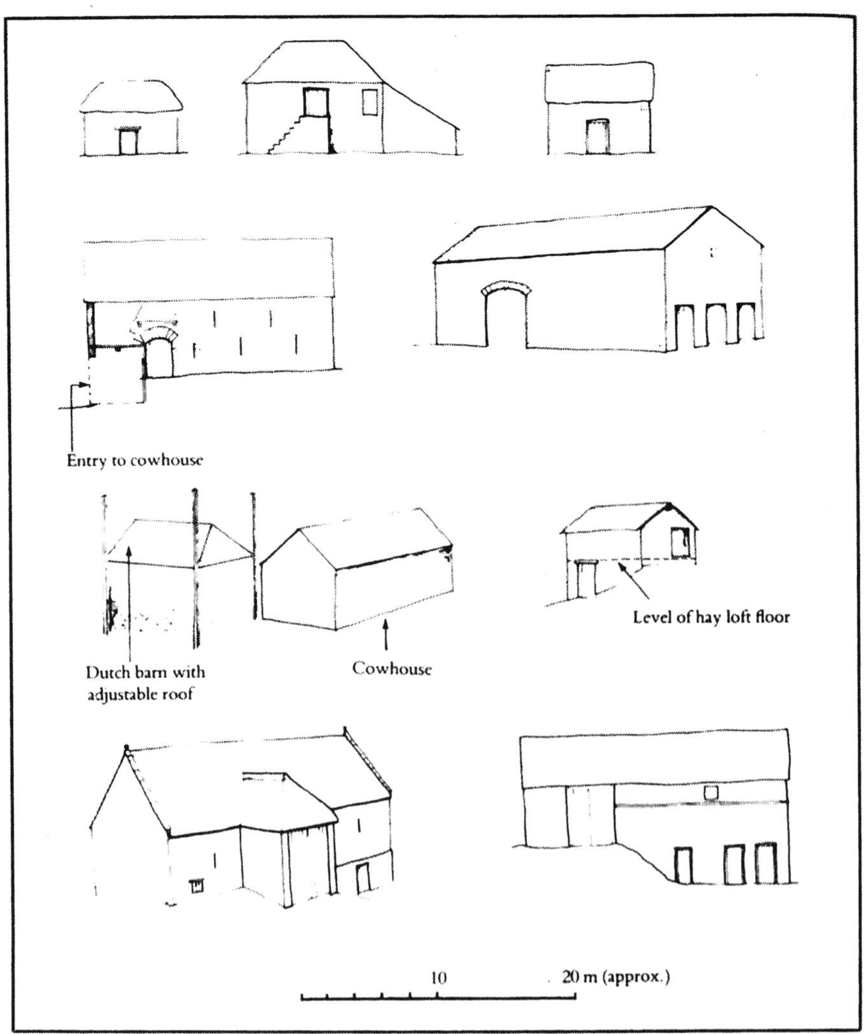

Figure 12.6 *Diagram of types of barn*

The range and typology of such structures offer opportunities for fieldwork in most parts of the UK. Identification of examples, establishment of distribution patterns and recording techniques are all valid exercises, which might form the basis of local studies (after Lake 1989)

WHERE TO GET HELP AND ADVICE

During the topic selection process you will have identified an accessible range of resources. Where this involves the services of others, for example museum staff or SMR personnel, any request needs to be as clear and succinct as possible. The best practice is to make it clear that you have already done some background research and focused on several questions to which you feel your contact might be able to offer answers. Don't pick a topic and send it to various possible sources of help expecting a completed project by return!

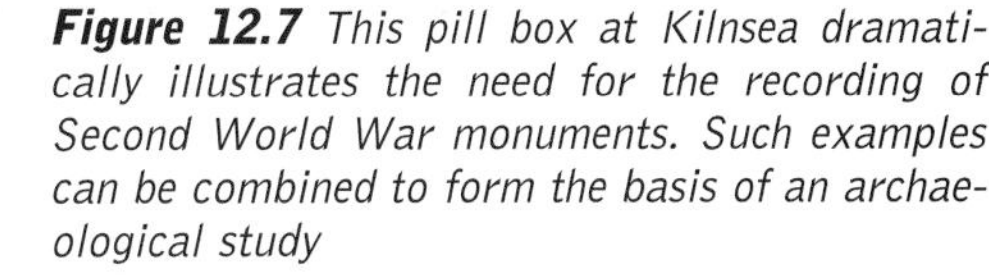

Figure 12.7 *This pill box at Kilnsea dramatically illustrates the need for the recording of Second World War monuments. Such examples can be combined to form the basis of an archaeological study*

Timing is also crucial. While you need to do exploratory work before making contact with requests for assistance or publications, you cannot afford to delay your approach for too long as agencies have their priorities and ordering material from them will involve a built-in time delay.

National resources

Whatever project you select there will inevitably be something of use on the Web. If nothing

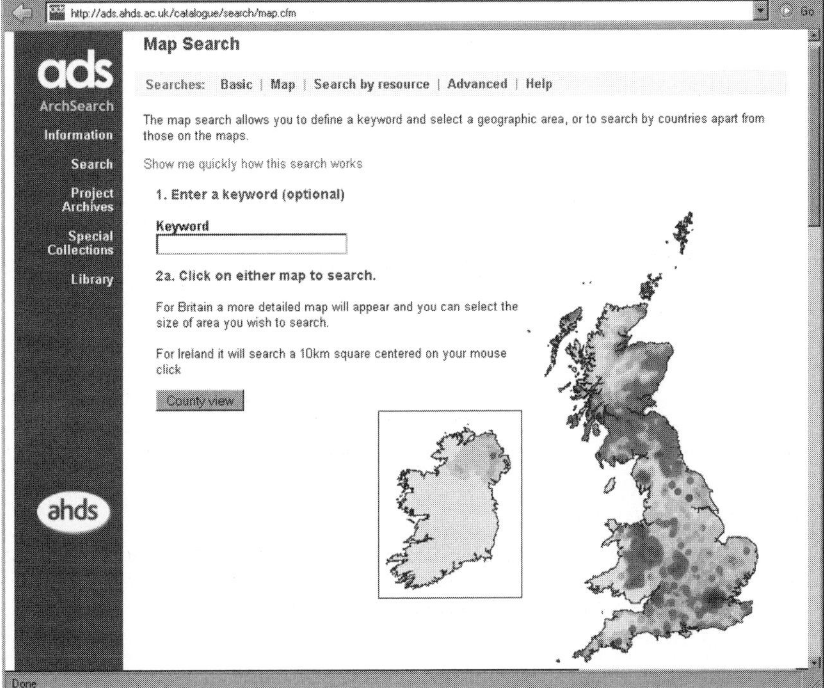

Figure 12.8 *Archaeological Data Service*

ADS is an unrivalled resource for archaeological researchers in the UK. The Archaeology Data Service provides free information on over 1 million sites. The online search engine provides short descriptive records. These can be used to access rich and detailed digital archives. Text resources include theses, monograph, journals and unpublished articles. There are also databases, images, CAD plans, survey plots, animations and virtual realities (◀ p. 143).

EXAMPLE 4

Sites and settlement patterns before 1900 in an Oxfordshire parish

'Marc' aimed to establish what continuity of occupation/settlement could be discovered by a survey of extant features and recorded sites. His fieldwork centred on an earthwork adjacent to Grims' Ditch, which had apparently not been studied or recorded previously.

Sources

- Oxfordshire SMR
- Centre for Oxfordshire Studies
- Texts on landscape archaeology and fieldwork
- 1841 Tithe map
- Ordnance Survey maps 1877–1914
- NMR in Swindon

Methodology

Marc used the SMR to create a comprehensive list of sites. He gained permission and visited them all before deciding to focus on two particular features for fieldwork survey. These were an earthwork and a surviving ridge and furrow near the village. After researching fieldwork techniques he recorded these features. He was able to use combinations of maps, documents, aerial photographs and hedgerow dating to establish the oldest boundaries in the area.

Content/discussion

Marc's summary of evidence was set against the geology and topography of the parish. He described a section of Grims' Ditch and other earthworks and discussed their possible age. He found documentary evidence for a Norman church but could find no physical evidence to support this. Similarly, there was an excavation report on an Anglo-Saxon cemetery but no evidence for contemporary settlement. He was able to use maps to suggest the possible development of the parish and suggest further possible study opportunities including excavation sites.

In addition to acknowledgements and a bibliography of landscape archaeology and fieldwork techniques, Marc included profiles and field plans, annotated maps and photographs and a distribution map of sites. Larger map extracts were placed in an appendix.

else, it can make access to sources of information faster. Start with one of the archaeological gateway sites (▶ p. 328). Of particular use for projects in England is the National Monuments Record (NMR) site. It is comprehensive and self-explanatory. It offers a search service, which is free 'subject to limitations', and free information packs. Topics available include 'Archaeology of England' and 'Aerial photographs of England'. A valuable link from NMR is to an alphabetical list of SMR addresses. These are your local sources of detail on known sites.

Museums

Museums often list 'supporting research', as part of their mission and many will have education officers who may be able to help. However, they are usually busy and their main focus is primary education so you need to book visits and be clear in advance about the help you want.

- http://www.mda.org.uk/vlmp/

Units

Archaeological units are less easy to discover as they are professional organisations in the business of offering archaeological services to those who need, and will pay for, them. Although their focus is not curation or education their staff may assist if approached sensibly. Units can be found on the CBA website or via your SMR.

Libraries

Libraries vary hugely in the archaeology stock they hold. Local libraries may hold local collections including an archaeological journal but are most used for background texts or the (rather slow) inter-library loan service. University libraries (where archaeology is studied) or national organisations such as the NMR are the best option and will hold excavation reports and journals. However, you will need special permission to enter some university libraries and they do not usually let you borrow. It is worth persevering particularly with excavation reports, which are as near as you may get to the evidence for some sites. Some older reports may be difficult to find. One last resort is to look for them at second-hand archaeological booksellers (▶ p. 328).

PLANNING AND MANAGING TIME AND WORD LIMITS

Every May, A Level projects are handed in with letters enclosed as appendices revealing that key information was still being sought only a few weeks earlier. There are many sources of information on time management and their advice is equally applicable to archaeological coursework. Once you have a plan, get started.

Archaeology differs from many other subjects in the mix of indoor and outdoor activity. You need to get the sequence right so that you don't have to make repeated visits because you didn't ask the right questions on earlier visits. After an initial visit to produce a description, most students carry out desktop research before returning to do detailed recording. That way they have more idea what they are looking for. You need to plan for delays. Letters from the SMR or landowner will not come back by return post. It may rain on the day you planned to do a fieldwalk. You need to start early, be patient and have other things to follow up while you wait.

PCs have made preparing studies much easier. You can collate information and notes as you go along, integrate visual images and perfect drafts more effectively. Try to ensure that you also record all sources used so that your references and bibliography are complete. Incidentally, nobody will believe that your hard disk crashed (and you forgot to make a back-up) the night you were printing the final copy. That excuse sounds like 'my dog ate it' to this generation of lecturers and examiners.

RECORDING EVIDENCE

How much of any site or range of artefacts you record will depend on the nature of the investigation and to what extent the site in question is central or more peripheral to the discussion. Wass (1999) is an excellent basic guide while Drewett (1999) provides a greater range of techniques.

Your record is likely to comprise four major types: drawn, written, photographic and diagrammatic. Drawings include location maps, plans of features or buildings, profiles of earthworks and elevations of structures. You may be able to illustrate relationships or phases through the medium of such illustrations. You will certainly need to make notes so that you can describe key features in your report. Photographs are useful in illustrating things you have identified and showing developments in the case of excavations. Tables and diagrams should be created where you have large amounts of data such as with fieldwork projects. They are also valuable for making comparisons and showing processes. A quick library search of archaeological texts will provide a wealth of examples.

Recording sites or features

Planning sites

You will probably wish to produce field drawings of earthwork sites. While drawing skills and surveying equipment obviously help, much can be achieved with simple gear: 20 or 30 metre tapes, ranging poles, a compass and marker arrows (try tent pegs with coloured ribbon) form a handy 'starter kit'. The simplest plans are likely to be made up from measuring or pacing the main features and roughly drawing hachures to indicate slopes.

For more accurate diagrams you will need to lay down a grid over the features to be recorded. A base line should be established and then a second main grid line should be fixed at right angles to the first. Parallel lines joined to each of these then form a grid. It is advisable to fix reference points so that you can return to the same grid, but you will need to do this sensitively and with permission from a landowner. You cannot leave obtrusive markers on public land or where grazing animals might damage themselves. Ideally this grid should be linked to reference points on OS maps. Once a grid is established you can plot

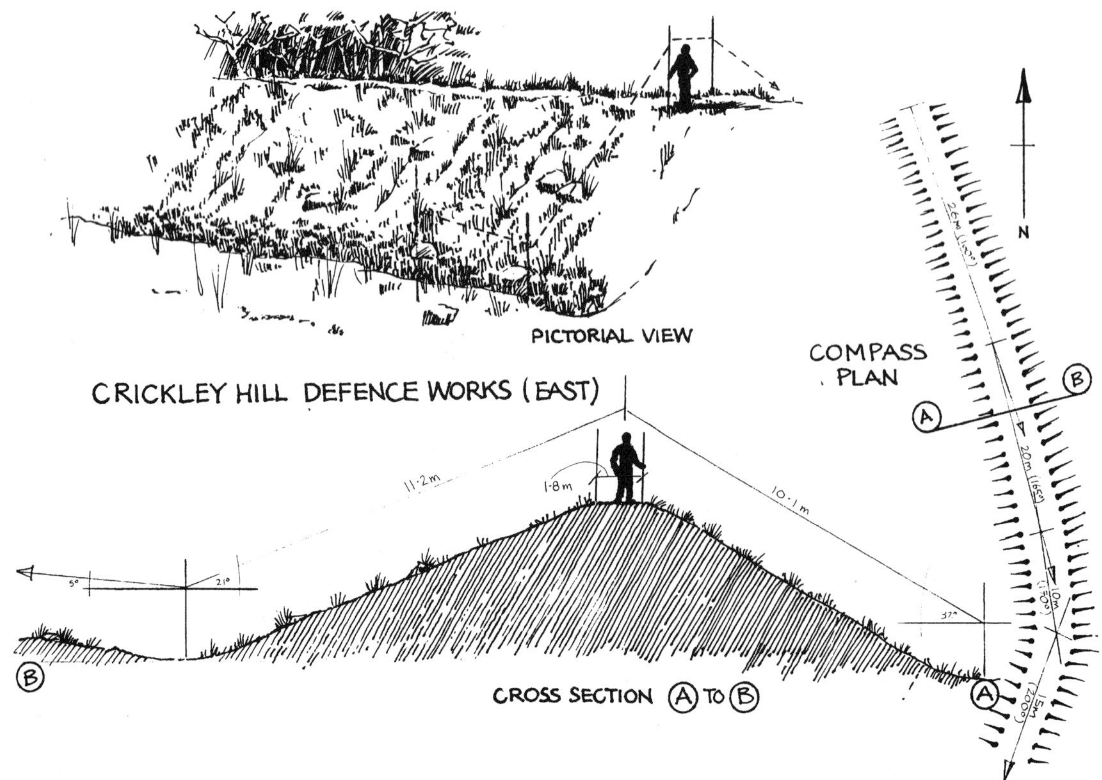

Figure 12.9 *A student drawing of the profile of earthworks at Crickley Hill including an example of the use of hachures*

it onto graph paper and by taking measurements from two fixed points to the feature, plot it by the process of triangulation.

When recording slopes, place marker arrows (one colour) along the upper edge and others (a different colour) at the lower extent of the slope. This enables the lines of the feature to be plotted and the arrows can be reused. Conventional hachures, where the head of the hachure represents the top of the slope and it gets thinner as the slope goes down, should be used. They indicate the direction and length of the slope. Steepness is indicated by heavier infill of the hachure, head shape or the closeness of the hachures.

Profiling features

If you want to draw a scale profile of an earthwork you may need more equipment. However, there are some simple methods which are effective. A horizontal line fixed across the earthwork at 90 degrees to its main alignment and kept level provides a baseline. Measurements are taken from it to the ground at fixed intervals that will establish the profile of your site. A series of shorter lengths may make maintenance of a level easier and can offer a solution for longer slopes as long as adjustments are calculated accurately. Ensure you record this. It is essential that you employ the same scale for both horizontal and vertical scales or your drawings will suffer from distortion. If you have access to more equipment, such as a level and measuring staff, your task will be quicker. Alternatively, your geography department may have clinometers or gradiometers which you could borrow and use to construct profiles in a series of angles and lengths.

If you follow the basic rules of setting out, measuring, plotting to scale and drawing up your field results it is possible for enthusiastic archaeology students to produce a decent original plan.

Recording excavations

Recording part of a current excavation site is similar to what the real excavation team will be doing. You need to consider how much detail you require in terms of plans, sections and photographs. You may need to ask about evidence relating to the various phases of occupation and to see particular finds, but it is unlikely that the specialist reports will be ready in time for you to see. A tape recorder might be a useful aid for when you have the chance to make enquiries.

Recording buildings

Photography and sketches of the lower levels and key external features are needed to illustrate building materials and phases. If you have internal access then room plans and details of construction and decoration can be added. You are unlikely to be able to get precise measurements for elevation drawings but using tapes, clinometers and some basic trigonometry can help produce a reasonable approximation.

Recording artefacts

There are archaeological conventions for the illustration of many finds and these can be studied in archaeological reports. Producing quality drawings is neither quick nor easy. You should consider the extent of your artistic skills and try them out against the recognised formulae for archaeological illustration so that you can judge your aptitude for this exercise. A reasonable alternative for those objects you may have collected yourself in fieldwalking is to scan them and trace the printout.

Often when there is a quantity of pottery to review attention is paid to what are called 'diagnostic' sherds. For example rims and decorated pieces. The less significant sherds can then be grouped and described as collections. Such sherds may be counted and weighed and the information about them given in tabular form rather than by illustration.

Smaller objects like bronze brooches or flint tools require careful treatment by the illustrator and will always need to be drawn from at least

Figure 12.10 *A scan of an artefact recovered by fieldwork*

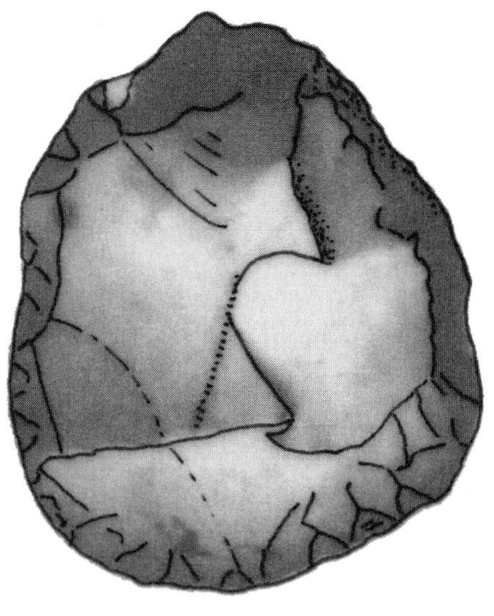

Figure 12.11 *A tracing made from the scan in Figure 12.10 with key features highlighted. This technique provides a good example of how those of us without good drawing skills can present illustrations*

	Quantity	Weight	Average Weight
Black Burnished Ware	77	676 gms	8.8 gms
Grey ware	70	457 gms	6.5 gms
White Ware	2	50 gms	25.0 gms
Severn Valley Ware	18	117 gms	6.5 gms
Samian Ware	5	19 gms	3.8 gms
Other	13	126 gms	9.7 gms
Totals	185	1445 gms	7.8 gms

Figure 12.12 *Presentation of fieldwork results*

two perspectives – front-on and side-on – to give a clear indication of their design. Sometimes in the case of objects, for example flint axes, it is the profile shape that is relevant in the report rather than a detailed drawing showing the flaking process. Each artefact should be drawn to a scale, shown in the drawing. Some description needs to be written to make clear to the reader matters relating to the object that the drawing does not necessarily convey, for example colour or texture.

A range of details should be used when cataloguing objects. These will include provenance, dimensions and description of key features.

WRITING UP

There are two considerations here: what does the reader of your study really need to know about your site? How can you best present the evidence? Assume that your reader has a sound archaeological understanding, but not necessarily knowledge of your site, and address your work to them on that basis.

Refer again to the assignment brief. There may be specific advice on structure and presentation. This may include instructions, title pages, abstracts and appendices. It will probably mention plagiarism and referencing.

It is essential that you plan to produce a project which meets the criteria set out by your tutor or the syllabus. In the case of A level this means about 4000 words. This is not long so it is important that you aim for depth of argument rather than the superficial treatment of a large number of sites or artefacts.

Plagiarism

This means using other people's work unchanged or without acknowledgement. Avoid it at all costs. It is particularly easy to slip into accidently where you are heavily reliant on one guidebook or report, or where you download material as notes from the internet. Be on your guard and if necessary adjust your question to avoid repeating somebody else's enquiry.

Presentation

Your original plan, probably somewhat adapted in the light of research, will form the basis for the work you submit. You will have sifted and sorted a range of materials and evidence and need a clear idea of the layout and balance of your work before you start writing. A flow diagram is useful.

Your illustrations should add to and explain points raised in your commentary. Avoid the temptation to put your photographs in just because you paid for them! Illustrations are probably best within or close to the text that refers to them. The ability to use a scanner is useful here. Always ensure that there is some annotation of any illustration. Transparent overlays are useful for illustrating distribution and your interpretation of phases. Maps can be traced as the base for these. Finally, if you are confident with IT think about a virtual walkabout (◀ p. 143).

KEY SKILL

Referencing

Referencing is an important part of a quality study and is insisted on at degree level. Get into the habit not only of listing your sources, both books and journals, but also of putting the page references into your draft notes as you select interesting comments or information. There are several referencing systems but the Harvard (author–date) version is becoming standard. Wherever you write something which is based on another's work you should reference that original work in a bracket immediately after your statement, giving the author's surname and the date of publication. In the bibliography you should list all your sources alphabetically by author. You also include date of publication, title, publisher and place of publication as shown below.

An example from case study X:

> 'The discovery of eight flint axes from Creteway Down at Folkestone can be associated with finds of Neolithic date from the same area. (Clarke 1982)'.

The study's bibliography contained the following entry:

> Clarke, A. F. (1982) *The Neolithic of Kent – A Review. Archaeology in Kent to* AD *1500*, CBA Research Report No 48, pp. 25–30.

There are some variations on the Harvard system in use in different universities, so check with your supervisors exactly which format they want. At A level, the version above is acceptable.

Websites must also be referenced. No standard has yet emerged. You should list full web addresses and what they are in the bibliography. You could number them and use (web1) etc. in the body of the text although some universities may want the full address in the text.

Chapter 13

Preparing for your Archaeology Examination

YOUR GOALS

You need to

- find out what you will be required to know and do
- organise your notes in order to revise
- ensure that you understand and have examples for all key areas
- train yourself to respond in a way that will be successful.

The key to successful revision is to be proactive. Start early and take charge, don't wait until the last moment. However, it is also possible to waste time revising ineffectively. Focus from the start on what you actually need to do and to revise actively. The key is to ensure that you understand your subject and can communicate that understanding in the format required by the examiners.

CATALOGUING YOUR PORTFOLIO

Ideally you will have been cataloguing and cross-referencing your notes as you went along. If you are like 90 per cent of students you won't have even thought about this. This should therefore be your first task.

- Start by putting your notes into an order. You may have a course content list supplied. If not, then you could organise your notes chronologically or by theme. The key is to get them organised.
- Now see what you have got. One way of doing this is to write out lists or grids. The latter are preferable because they will enable you to make connections and use the same material in several ways.
- Compare your lists with course or syllabus details. Are there gaps? If so then your next task will be to copy up notes from a friend or make some from a key text.
- Cross-reference your notes. You may be examined on methods, sources or topics so you need to have flexibility about how you use material. There are several ways of doing this such as colour coding, using Post-its or producing grids. A particularly useful way is to use index cards.

What do examiners

want to see?

not want to see?

Paragraphs
Clear structure
Argument
Detailed supporting evidence
A range of relevant case studies
Conclusions

Poor spelling
Long descriptions
Irrelevance
Few examples
Woolly sentences, e.g. 'the first chapter of the human story'

Figure 13.1 *What examiners want to see*

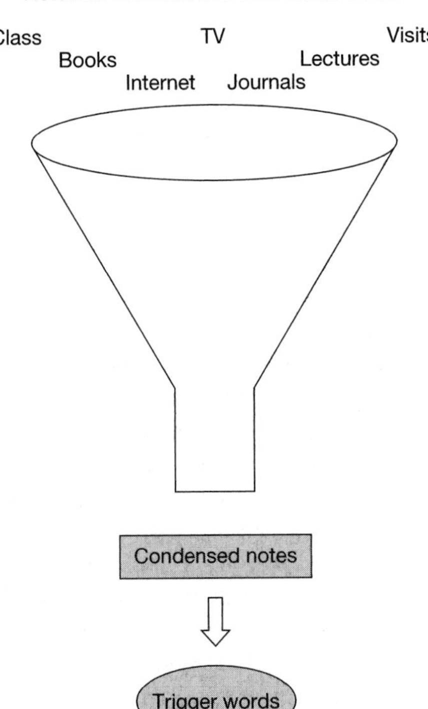

Reducing information onto cards

Many student find index cards useful for learning and condensing essential knowledge and to help them apply their understanding. To produce good cards you have to decide what is the essence of each topic, case or method you need to learn. This is a useful discipline in itself as it forces you to consider relevance to exam questions and to be selective. How much you write on each card will depend on your confidence in your ability to remember. Some students go through a process of reducing notes in this way several times until they are left with keywords or phrases. This process in itself helps with revision of knowledge. Because *you* have had to process the information it lodges in your memory much better than if you had just read or underlined notes. The words or phrases themselves will work as prompts and suggest additional material to you.

Figure 13.2 *Condense your notes*

Geophysics *Survey*	**Star Carr** *Settlement*
Resistivity: Deviation of electrical conduction due to resistivity of ground. Generally due to dampness. **Magnetometers:** Deviations in the magnetic field, caused by heating of hearths, kilns, filling in of pits, and solid features. **Metal Dectectors** **Radar and Sonar** **Remote Sensing:** Radar, infrared **Dowsing**	**Mesolithic** JGD Clark (1949–51) • Platform on swampy lake side. Birch and moss • 3–4 families, 20 people • Flint and antler tool making • Faunal remains indicate summer occupation • People probably based on the coast • Dogs kept for herding?
Head-Smashed-in *Kill Site* >5,500 BP	**Trade and Exchange** *Economics*
• Southern Alberta, Canada • Blackfoot Indians • 50 hectare animal processing area • Plains bison • Cairns to channel animals • Skin-lined boiling pits, drying, fires, • Seasonal kill site, feasting and storage	**Gift Exchange and Reciprocity** • *Kula network of Melanasia (Solomon Sea)* **Redistribution** • Tribute or appropriation • Central organisation • *Knossos, Danebury* **Market Exchange** • Internal or port-of-trade • *Ancient Greek Agora*

Figure 13.3 *Examples of revision cards. The process of selection involved in making these will help you remember the detail*

REVISION ACTIVITIES

Mix and match

This is one of several ways in which you can use the cards you have just made. It can be done individually or turned into a game with other students. Divide case study cards and themes or aspects of themes into two separate piles. Turn over one card from each pile and then try to make a connection, for example Boxgrove and Technology. This can be done with both sites and methods.

Make up mnemonics

Mnemonics are usually made by taking a number of linked words and then trying to make a new word from the first letter of each, for example Trench, Area and Box makes 'Tab'. Or develop formulae such as RIQI: recover, identify, quantify interpret. This can work as a prompt when you need to remember a list of detailed points. It is probably best for methods or 'what can be learned from . . .?' type questions. Use it sparingly. There is a limit to the number you will recall and exams are increasingly about applying understanding rather than remembering lists.

Mindmaps

A creative way to remember connections is to create a visual map of a subject in our minds. This works on the principle that we remember key images better than keywords. Start by placing a major concept, theme, site or method on a page. Identify four or five main aspects you wish to learn and mark them in bold on lines radiating out from the original word. Next draw something which each word suggests to you at the other end of the line. The more personal your choice of image, the more likely you are to remember. (It doesn't have to be sensible.) From here other connections can radiate out much like a spider diagram. ◄ examples on pp. 212 and 265.

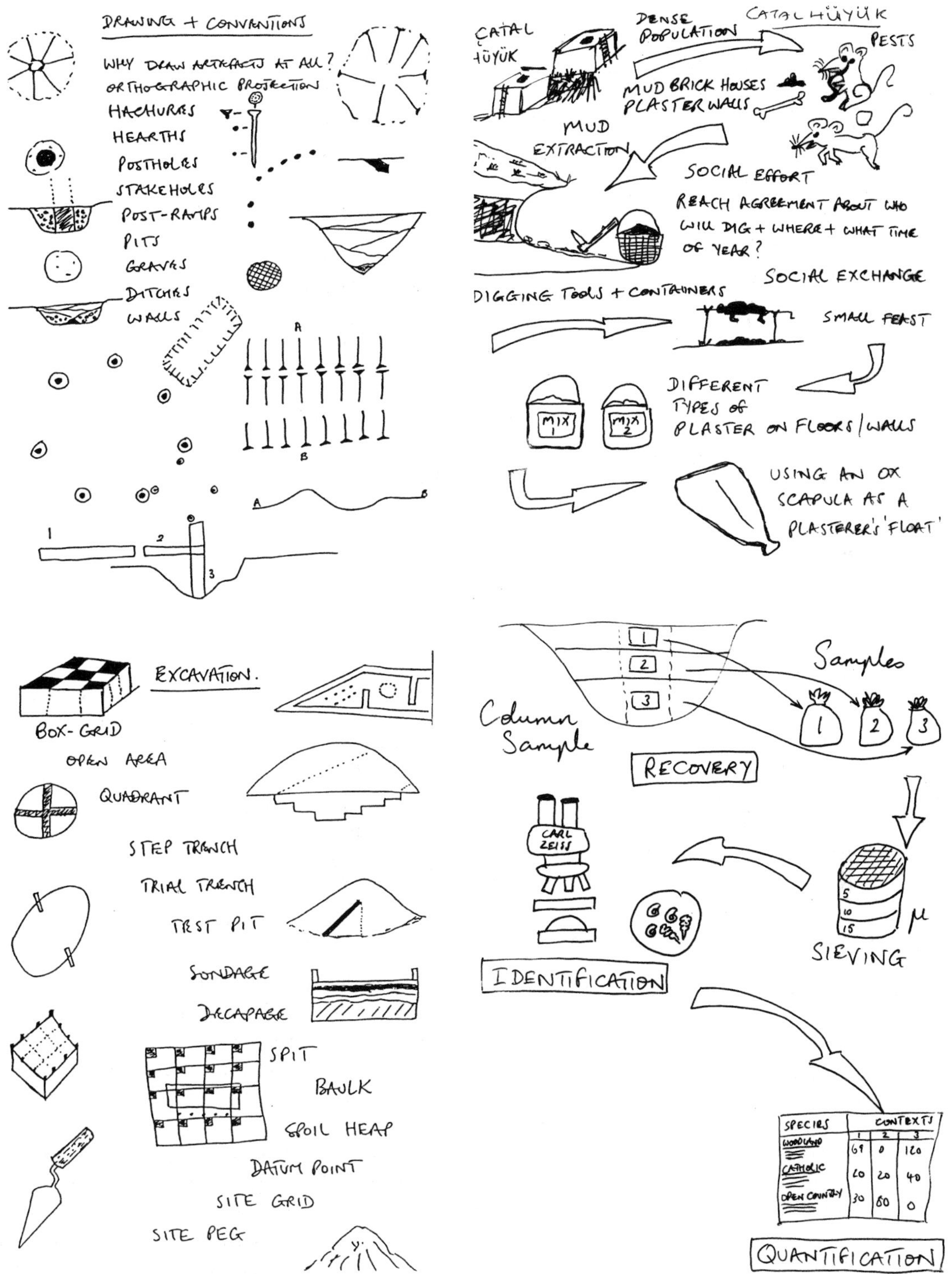

Figure 13.4 *Example of visual cue notes. If you are a visual learner, this may work for you*

Visual reminders

For archaeological methods, visual cues can be useful in revising and checking your understanding. One method is to produce your own sketches such as the examples in Figure 13.4.

Playing games

Many students find that games help them to remember and also encourage them to make links between areas of knowledge. They also break up the revision process. Many popular games can be adapted. These are just two you could try.

Archaeological dominos

Two archaeological words are put on each domino (card). Deal them out and play in the normal way with the following addition. Each time a player lays down a domino they have to make a connection between the two words.

Blockbusters

If you draw a hexagonal grid on a piece of acetate (OHT) the task of setting up this game becomes straightforward. The question setter inserts a letter into each hexagon and teams compete to make lines across the 'board', as in the popular television programme. All the clues should come from the syllabus.

TACKLING EXAM PAPERS

Ideally you should have become thoroughly familiar with the format and type of questions used in the exam during your course. Examiners do not try to catch students out and are highly unlikely to change their types of question without warning. The specific questions and any sources used are likely to be new to you but their format and what you are asked to do will be largely familiar. You need to work out what each paper or section wants you to do. To do this you need to look at the command words and the type of mark scheme used (▶ p. 319).

Command words

The way your essays are organised will reflect the command words in the question. For example, for the question, 'Compare the evidence for complex settlement from two areas that you have studied' the command words provide you with a ready-made structure.

Advice on essay writing (◀ p. 219) and improving style (◀ p. 257) during the course holds good for exams. It's never too late to improve.

Mark schemes

Mark schemes are increasingly published, so there is little excuse for not looking at them. Short questions which ask you to explain or describe usually reward you with one mark for each point drawn from a source that is linked to the question or for each occasion where you deploy your own knowledge in a relevant way. Most questions worth more than a couple of marks and essays are usually marked to 'levels of response' mark schemes where the levels are defined by set criteria. If there are five levels in a 25-mark essay you will not score high marks unless you write to suit the criteria for levels 4 and 5. Shorter structured questions are typical of schemes of assessment for AS level and larger structured questions and essays for A2. Both use levels.

Looking at mark schemes and doing practice assignments are obviously essential and you will do this as part of your course. One way of helping yourself is to play the role of examiner. Try setting questions in the style of the exam. Produce a mark-scheme, write responses and then mark your work. An alternative is to swap questions with a friend. Either way, by putting yourself into this role you will gain insights into what you need to do.

In the exam

Most of you will have taken many exams already. As always the same golden rules apply. In addition, don't forget your ruler and magnifying glass!

Take a watch in and use it. Divide the number of marks into the time available. Allocate time per question and try to stick to it.

Essay mark schemes

This shows in table form the hierarchy of levels for A Level and the undergraduate essays of two major university departments. Keywords and phrases have been extracted from the whole documents. Where statements sound similar they are shown at the same level.

Grade 25	A Level	Degree Level	Grade /16
		Critical thought and flair. Sound and relevant factual knowledge. Evidence of extensive reading, properly referenced. Logical, balanced and well supported arguments. Written without significant grammatical errors	15 or 73–9% Sound 1st
Level 5 21–25	Consistently analytical. Consistent corroboration with relevant detail from a range of contexts. Clear and consistent attempts to reach judgements. Strong communication skills. Strong conceptual understanding. Some evidence of independent thinking	Sound, competent, methodical and comprehensive. Lacking critical flair. Evidence of some reading beyond obvious texts which are referenced. Examples cited where relevant. Well written, without major grammatical errors	12 or 63–65% Solid 2:1
Level 4 16–20	Sustained analysis. Range of accurage and relevant supporting material. Covers main issues but may be unbalanced.Attempts to reach a judgement. Little narrative. Effective communication skills		
		Unoriginal and occasionally flawed. Where they are original they lack supporting evidence. Reading has been shallow. May be brief. Argument may be biased and not all may be relevant. May have significant grammatical or structural flaws. If several flaws are present it should be in a lower band	9 or 53–55% sound 2:2
Level 3 11–15	Understanding of relevant issues. Generally analytical with some narrative. Focused on the question but unbalanced treatment of it. Argued, but not consistently. Some relevant supporting material. Effective use of language	Not really satisfactory but shows just enough grasp of the subject. May be muddled and poorly argued. Weak and limited evidence with no sign of reading. Sections may be irrelevant. Arguments may be biased or simplistic. May be poorly written and structured	7 or 48–49% Solid 3rd
		Barely acceptable. Weak and shallow arguments. Lack of critical thought. Limited evidence. No reading. Poor English. Often confused or irrelevant although basic facts should be correct	5 or 45–47% Basic 3rd
Level 2 6–10	Some understanding of relevant issues. Lacking weight or balance. Relevant descriptions. Some irrelevance or inaccuracy. Some effective use of language		
Level 1 1–5	Largely narrative. Outline description. Very generalised. Lacking direction or links to the question. Limited communication skills	Unacceptably brief or muddled and flawed. Often irrelevant, difficult to understand and lacking basic understanding	3 or 30–39% Clear fail

Figure 13.5 *A level and undergraduate mark schemes*

Model A: *Compare* the evidence for *complex* settlement from *two* areas that you have studied

Introduction: define *key terms* in the title	
Aim for *breadth* in considering similarities and differences	
Region 1 Case study of Oaxaca Valley	Region 2 Case study of Palace of Knossos
Make explicit links to command words	
Discussion tries to identify common ground and major differences by reference to clear criteria such as size, specialisation, planning, etc.	
Degree of similarity and difference Conclusion: some/a lot/a little etc.	

Figure 13.6 *Planning a comparative essay*

Use your time effectively. Read the question paper before you start. Where you have a choice, make sure that you have understood all the questions before you make your choice. Often the longest questions, particularly those with quotations, look harder than they actually are. Try to avoid doing a question just because it contains a keyword you know about, you need to address the whole question.

On essay papers rough out a number of plans at once and add points later in case you forget them. They can save you time but don't spend too long doing this at the expense of the actual essay. If you finish early there is bound to be something you can improve on. Examiners are looking for:

- *Breadth*: have you considered all the ideas which might be appropriate to the question?
- *Relevance*: have you linked all your points to the command words in the question?
- *Support*: have you produced enough detailed specific evidence to illustrate the points you have made?

And finally . . .

Your battery of fluffy toys might bring you luck in the exam but sound preparation is a surer way to success. If you have absorbed the lessons in this book you should be able to cope with whatever you are asked. Don't forget that all examination essays will have flaws. No examiner expects perfection and if you have worked throughout your course you should succeed. The following examples give you an idea of the standard at A Level.

EXAMPLES OF MARKED RESPONSES TO EXAM QUESTIONS

These two essays were produced by students who attempted A2 questions under exam conditions. They illustrate common strengths and weaknesses and the difference between a poor and a reasonably strong answer. In reading them, bear in mind that the students were under pressure and had to write them in 45 minutes. The examiner's comments are italicised.

KEY SKILL

Understanding command words

All questions contain words or phrases which let you know what the examiner expects of you. It is important that you become familiar with the words and phrases used by archaeology examiners. The list below is roughly ranked in order of difficulty. Words in the top half of the list are usually used only for short or structured questions. Those in the lower half are also used for essays. The marks allocated will provide you with further clues. For example, for two marks the examiners will want a couple of words or sentences, for ten marks at least a paragraph.

Command words	What they mean	Examples
List	Simply write down names or examples.	List three methods of dating.
Describe	Say what something looks like using scales	Describe the feature shown at A.
Define	Give a precise meaning. (An example helps too.)	Define taphonomy.
Illustrate	Provide examples to support a definition or point.	Illustrate your argument.
Explain	Show how something works or give reasons.	Explain how the source of artefact A could be identified.
Outline	Describe with reasons.	Outline how an archaeologist might survey the field at X.
Account for	Explain clearly with supporting reasons.	Account for the lack of surviving evidence of X.
Compare (or Compare and contrast)	Identify similarities and differences.	Compare the sections of pits 23 and 46.
Synthesise (or summarise)	Reorganise materials to create a new version.	Synthesise the data in tables A to D
Analyse	Break down into parts, find patterns and links. Order the factors identified.	Analyse the data provided in tables B and C.
Justify	Give reasons for and provide supporting examples.	Justify your selection of method in question 2a.
What can archaeologists learn from . . .	This is a list type essay but it is not just a list. You have to provide examples and assess	What can be learned about societies in the past from the way they disposed of their dead?
Assess (or discuss)	Identify strengths and weaknesses to reach a judgement.	■ Assess the reconstruction drawing in source A. ■ 'Nucleated villages were a medieval development from the eleventh century onwards.' Discuss.
Evaluate	Assess and reach judgements about the relative value of some items.	Evaluate the evidence for industrial use of the site in source C.
How far (or to what extent)	Present both views, assess and reach a judgement.	■ How far can archaeologists be sure about when hominids began hunting animals? ■ To what extent does archaeology support historial views of the Vikings?

What is the evidence for the organisation of production for *one* type of artefact?

This is a 'list type' essay. The question offers the opportunity to bring in all the methods and sources used by archaeologists in investigating one type of artefact you are familiar with from your course of study. Note the word 'one'. Detailed knowledge will be required to do well and a high level answer would compare evidence for different aspects of production.

Pottery has been used to date and research past societies. It provides evidence of social development with specialisation by art and decoration. It is often found in burials which provides clues to its function.

This is not a good start. 'Axel' has not really addressed the question and has interpreted artefact as a type of material, which is not specific enough. It would have been better if he had selected Neolithic bowls or Samian tableware.

Through analysis of the inclusions in the clay, petrology can show the origin of the natural resources and suggest the location of pottery production.

This would be relevant to any ceramic material. A specific example should have been included.

Pottery was first produced in the Neolithic around 4000 BC. Early pottery was very heavy and coarse with round bottoms for example Grimston ware. Its basic shape was probably because there would have been no flat surfaces or tables so the rounded bottom would have prevented tipping on an uneven earth. [Diagram]

Excavations at Windmill Hill produced finds of Gabroic ware, which had lugs for holding or suspension. Inclusions included basalt which could be sourced to the lizard area of Cornwall. This suggests trade and distribution in the Neolithic. Windmill Hill pottery was another tradition of pottery making.

Axel has produced two relevant examples here and linked them to a method and hinted at how distribution might be studied. His diagram (not included here) also had some relevance.

Hearths and deposits of fired clay provides evidence of pottery production. Because it is so durable large quantities are often found on archaeological sites. Even though it is ususally damage, archaeologists can learn a lot from it.

Improvements in technology were accompanied by improved style and methods of decoration. The southern tradition of Peterborough wares included carination. It has been suggested that pots were not just functional items but also decorative. String was knotted and used to decorate pottery. This was called maggotting. Quills or reeds were also used to pierce and inscribe pottery. They may have been used as high prestige items to show a persons status or given as gifts in alliance making.

Much of this is relevant but it is not well focused. Axel should have discussed how archaeologists know how the pots were decorated. He is starting to narrate the development of pottery rather than address the question.

Black burnished ware is distinct and easily recognisable. It was produced in the Poole Harbour area of Dorset. Iron age settlements in Hamworthy have evidence of kiln sites and also at the Roman site at Lake Gales in Wimborne.

Again this is descriptive. It would have been better to discuss what can be learnt about production levels in those settlements.

Pottery continued to be produced and developed as a status item. Samian ware was decorated with a lion's head. It was very fine and produced for decorative use and for people to demonstrate their status. Beaker ware was also very fine. It is usually found often in burial sites which suggests it had a very specific purpose. Beaker ware may have been brought be immigrants or the idea imported from Europe. By the late Bronze Age British 'Beaker' pottery was produced. Both types being identified by thin section analysis of the original material and its inclusions.

This is largely descriptive and not made relevant. It could have been used earlier to illustrate petrology. It is not a conclusion. Overall, Axel has provided some material that is relevant to the question, and some limited examples. There is an attempt to organise the material into paragraphs, but it is not sustained. There is no direction to the essay aside from a loose chronological order. There are also some inaccuracies. While a specific artefact was not identified, much of the material could have been used. However, there was insufficient focus on methods. It is a high level 2 answer and scored a borderline 10/25.

'A sedentary way of life is necessary for storage practices.' Discuss.

This is a discursive type essay on a settlement and economic topic. It is more demanding conceptually than the previous question and so a lesser depth of knowledge might be required. It also requires you to reach a judgement in response to the statement in the question. It offers the opportunity to draw on examples across your course.

There is great variation in both storage methods and the substances which are stored. Food, wealth and other resources can all be stored to extend their availability and thus help in time of hardship or shortage. Storage is also an economic strategy. A sedentary way of life in fact makes storage practices necessary because people can no longer follow the seasons and forage for wild foods.

Even in the Palaeolithic and Mesolithic periods when a mobile, hunter-gatherer society is generally regarded as having existed there is evidence of storage. At the cave at Pontnewydd in Gwynedd animal bones have been discovered in recesses contemporary with occupation layers which suggests the cave had been used to deposit animal 'joints'.

'Zia' has not begun her response by defining the terms but it is clear that she has understood them. She has confidently provided an example that challenges the statement in the question.

Star Carr, which was excavated by Graham Clarke in 1949, was dated to the Mesolithic around 7000 BC. Like a number of other sites it seems to have been used as a seasonal base during the winter months. People seem to have used locations on estuaries, rivers and the coasts. At some there is evidence of tree clearing to provide grazing for red deer and to make hunting easier. This manipulation Of nature suggests a move towards storage. These mobile groups could not take much with them as they moved. Their choice of tools, personal jewellery, their dogs and possibly tent frames represents a storing of potentially useful material or curation. They may have used perishable forms of storage such as wicker or birch bark containers to carry or store thins such as honeycomb.

Not all relevant. More could have been made of the nature of evidence for this type of storage and whether absence of evidence means absence.

Palaeolithic people may have benefited from natural storage of mammoths in glaciers but the first type of storage the used was probably smoking. Stakeholes on some sites have been interpreted and drying or smoking racks. Salt may have also been used, but the early hard evidence usually comes from settled communities. Briquetage found in the Iron Age provides evidence of widespread use.

Zia is making up for a lack of specific knowledge with some generalised examples here. They are all relevant.

At Danbury and other hill forts from the Iron Age storage is seen in the large pits and the 'four poster' structures. Pits up to 20 feet deep and 7 feet across were dug down into the bedrock. Apparently they were used for grain although ritual purposes have also been suggested. Some pits provided enough grain to keep a large population fed for a year. In the pits the outer layers of grain decay giving off carbon dioxide which preserves the remaining grain by inhibiting bacteria. 'Four posters' are identified by four postholes in a square pattern. They are generally interpreted as granaries but may have had some other use such as chicken coops. This storage was only appropriate because of the agricultural surplus produced by large numbers of sedentary farmers. It provided them with insurance against the vagaries of the weather meant that time spent in travelling from one site to another could be used in production of foodstuffs.

A very relevant example with some depth of knowledge. There is a clear attempt to relate it to the question although not all the paragraph is relevant or accurate. She will not be penalised for this, but she has wasted a little time in writing it.

Earliest agricultural people in the early Neolithic also began to 'store' their dead. 'The mixed up remains in tombs and long barrows represent a form of macabre storage. Again this is linked to sedentism. A further type of storage is evident in individual burials during the Bronze Age. Personal ornamentation was a reflection of wealth and being kept on the person meant it could be safeguarded. People in earlier mobile societies did not seem to accumulate such wealth.

Zia raises two good points here. While she could be criticised for not knowing about alternative theories and evidence she will not be penalised. Many centres lack recent texts and this would not be fair. She is thinking laterally about storage and would gain credit even though points are underdeveloped.

Today coinage is the most recognisable form of storage of wealth. Coins appeared late in prehistory and like jewellery are easily transportable and concealed. They are not an encumbrance to mobility in the same way that herds of cattle might be.

This relevant, general point represents a lost opportunity. She could have discussed social storage and the contradictory idea of very mobile forms of storage developed in sedentary societies.

Mobile populations require small-scale storage of light and easily transportable products. Larger scale storage of bulky items are more appropriate to sedentary populations. 'Sedentary' and 'storage' are usually linked because if a group stores a high percentage of the wealth or resources in one place and then leaves them unattended for long periods the stored items are very likely to be exploited or damaged by other third parties be they animals or human. If you store a great deal you need to be sedentary.

The conclusion addressed the question and attempted to reach a judgement, which qualifies the initial statement.

Virtually all the essay was relevant, analytical and well focused. Zia demonstrated the ability to think widely about the concepts involved and structured her paragraphs in a logical way. She was low on examples and some sections were flawed, but there was still enough here to reach the bottom of band 4 and a mark of 16/25.

Chapter 14

Where to Next?

Studying Archaeology in the UK

BELOW UNIVERSITY LEVEL

There are plenty of opportunities to study archaeology although the range of qualifications is relatively small. To get further information on any of them either contact your local institution or the Council for British Archaeology (CBA) Education service.

- http://www.britarch.ac.uk/educate/ed1.html

Short courses are offered by Colleges of Further Education (FE) and the Workers Educational Association (WEA). Typically these will be 2 hours a week for ten weeks and are generally aimed at adults. Increasingly, colleges will offer an Open College Network (OCN) certificate for these courses.

Day schools or conferences are offered by university departments, FE colleges, local and national archaeological organisations and museums. Many of these involve lectures at university level although some are practically based. The two key sources on these are *Current Archaeology* (*CA*) and *British Archaeology* (*BA*) magazines.

Field schools, or training digs, are offered by universities and some local organisations in the summer. Details are advertised in *CA* and *BA* magazines.

AS and A Level Archaeology

These are offered by AQA. The AS can be taken separately or as the first stage of an A Level. Each award is broken down into three modules. Five of these modules are examinations which each last between one and one and a half hours.

AS Level (first half of A Level)

AS1
Finding and excavating archaeological sites

AS2
Post-excavation analysis, dating, interpretation and presentation

AS3
Religion and ritual
One from: Later British and Irish Prehistory, Roman Britain, Ancient Egypt, The Maya

AS level examinations consist of short questions focused on a series of sources. For AS1 and 2 you will have to interpret the sources, for AS3 you need to supply examples.

A2 (second half of A Level)

A4
Settlement and society
Thematic approach. No set content

A5
Material culture and economics
Thematic approach. No set content

A6
Coursework. A personal investigation. ◀ Chapter 12

A4 and A5 each have a stimulus-based question and a choice of essays. They can be approached through the study of any period.

AS and A Level are offered in some FE colleges and schools. To find your nearest centre, contact the AQA or CBA.

There are also some archaeology options in the Classical Civilisation A Level offered by OCR. There will also be archaeology options in the new hybrid history GCSE offered by OCR.

Access to higher education

These are general courses aimed at adults returning to education and offered in FE colleges. A few offer archaeology as an option.

AT UNIVERSITY

Most courses are offered at degree level although there has been an increase in the number of sub-degree programmes on offer such as HNDs and foundation degrees. Some of these are focused on practical archaeology. Degrees usually involve study at university, although some courses have also been franchised to FE colleges.

At degree level there is considerable variety. You can study archaeology as a BA or a BSc, or in Scotland for four years for an MA. Detailed information can be obtained from the CBA or from the institutions listed on p. 325. Archaeology can be studied on its own, in combination or as part of other subjects. The information here largely applies to where it can be studied as a single subject. All courses will include elements on the development of archaeology, its methods and techniques, as well as the theory used to make sense of archaeological evidence. Beyond that they will vary considerably in their choice of topics.

In considering university courses you may want to give thought to the following:

- Is the course thematic or period based?
- Which periods can I study?

Figure 14.1 *Although it is sometimes difficult to arrange, you should try to get some practical experience of archaeology prior to applying or going to university*

- Does the assessment pattern suit me? Is it continuous assessment or final exam based?
- What is the department strong in (E.g. science at Bradford, prehistory at Sheffield)?
- Does it have a practical or heritage element (for example Bournemouth)?
- What kinds of placements and excavation opportunities are on offer?
- How is it rated?
- Will I get the qualifications to get in?
- Do I need previous experience?

Market forces

Some courses have more applicants than others. They normally deal with this by asking higher grades from prospective students. If you are a standard A level student you simply have to get the grades. If you have a different educational background you should contact the department directly for advice before applying. Many are particularly keen on mature students, even if you haven't got A levels.

League tables

Universities are ranked on research and teaching. A good research record may tell you that the university has published good research or that it has a lot of researchers. You may not actually be taught by the key researchers. There also appears to be a bias towards larger departments in the way

University	Main degrees	Major specialist areas	Teaching grade	Research grade	Entry points
Queens, Belfast	Arch. Archaeology–Palaeoecology BA or BSc	Science, Prehistory	3	5	280
Birmingham	Ancient Hist and Arch.	Forensic	3	4	280–320
Bournemouth	Arch. BSc	Heritage Management	3	3a	240
Bradford	Arch. BSc	Science	3	5	280
Bristol	Arch	Classical	4	4	340
Cambridge	Arch and Anthropology	Theoretical, Early Medieval	4	5*	360
Kent, Canterbury	Classical and Arch Studies				
Wales, Cardiff	Arch	European Prehistory, Conserv	4	5	300
Trinity Coll, Carmarthen	Arch Heritage Conservation			3b	140
Durham	Arch BA and BSc	Prehistoric, Roman, Early Medieval	4	5	300
Edinburgh	Arch Environmental Arch MA	Prehistory and classical		3a	300
Exeter	Arch	Wetlands, Western Europe	4	5	300–320
Glasgow	Arch MA and BSc			4	280
Wales, Lampeter	Arch	Landscape		4	200–260
Leicester	Arch BA and BSc	Urban, Museum, Local	4	5	260–320
Liverpool	Arch BA and BSc E	Egyptology	3	5	260
London, SOAS	History of Art and Arch	World archaeology	4	5	280
London, University Coll.	Arch BA and BSc E	World archaeology	4	5	280–320
Manchester	Arch	Classical	4	5	280–320
Nottingham	Arch	Prehistory, Roman or Medieval	3	4	280
Newcastle	Arch	Practical	3	3b	
Wales, Newport	Arch Prehistory and Arch	Prehistory		3a	140
Oxford	Arch and Anthropology		3	5*	360
Reading	Arch	Prehistory and Roman	4	5*	260–280
Sheffield	Arch and Prehistory, Arch Science	Prehistory, World	4	5	300
Southampton	Arch	Prehistory, Maritime	4	5	330
King Alfred's Coll., Winchester	Arch BA and BSc	Heritage Management	4	2	220
York	Arch BA and BSc	Medieval	4	3a	320

On research, Archaeology departments as a whole were ranked very highly (5th of all subjects).

The grades indicate the following standards:

5* = International excellence in most areas
4 = National excellence in virtually all areas
3a = National excellence in a majority of areas
5 = International excellence in some areas
3b = National excellence in the large majority of area
2 = National excellence in up to half areas

Quality of teaching is rated on a 4 point scale. 4 is excellent.

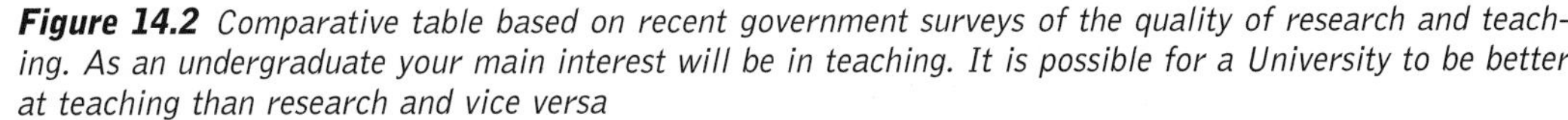

Figure 14.2 *Comparative table based on recent government surveys of the quality of research and teaching. As an undergraduate your main interest will be in teaching. It is possible for a University to be better at teaching than research and vice versa*

the tables are calculated. Bournemouth University in particular seems to have suffered in this respect despite producing important national research such as the MARS report. Teaching tables may reflect the quality of lecturing. One has to be a little careful interpreting these. Unlike A Level there is no systematic comparison of the quality of degrees from different universities. A 2:1 from one institution may or may not be as good as a 2:1 from another.

Figure 14.2 includes recent and information on A Level points asked for. It also lists some of the specialisms on offer but is not intended to be comprehensive. With over 100 different possibilities for joint or part honours courses in archaeology, there are many other opportunities to study archaeology in other university departments. Examples include Maritime Studies at St Andrews or Wetland Archaeology at Hull.

STEPPING UP TO DEGREE LEVEL

If you have studied A Level Archaeology, you may find that there is not much of an initial step up. You may even find that you have less to do at first. As with most subjects there is considerable overlap between A Levels and many first year undergraduate programmes. In considering your choice of programme it may be a good idea to select different topics or periods from those you did at A Level to broaden your knowledge and maintain your interest. If your chosen course has a practical scientific or statistical element you may find this new. You will generally get some support at the university, but it might be worth refreshing your memory before you go.

University lecturers and undergraduates have identified the following areas as different from A Level or where students sometimes struggle:

- Working more independently or in groups
- Making interesting oral presentations
- Coping with theoretical concepts
- Adjusting to the idea that knowledge is always the product of interpretation
- Coping with maths and science elements
- Coping with wide chronological and geographical ranges
- Adjusting to the precision required in excavation
- Using academic libraries, journals and texts
- Writing essays in an academic style
- Using academic referencing from books, journals and web pages (◀ p. 311)

Chapter 15

Finding the Best Information

There are so many excellent sites, museums and written and electronic resources available to archaeology students that we can only list a fraction of those available. Since selection is subjective we have included those resources that we have found most useful and which our students have made most use of. Although we have tried to provide a good range, our choice is clearly biased towards our own interests. Another person's list would undoubtedly look very different. Other sources, which provide additional depth on topics contained in the text, are listed in the bibliography.

TWENTY VERY USEFUL BOOKS

The focus is largely on Britain and Europe and full details of each text are in the bibliography. Make sure your school or college buys a copy of these books.

General texts

- Ashmore, W. and Sharer, R. (1999) *Discovering our Past*. A good text for the visual reader, with diagrams well used to illustrate methods and thinking.
- Fagan, B. (2000a) *In the Beginning*. A detailed introduction to archaeology from an American perspective.
- Greene, K. (2002) *Archaeology: An introduction*. This has good coverage of reconnaissance, excavation and post-excavation techniques.
- Orme, B. (1981) *Anthropology for Archaeologists*. A great little text for getting you to think beyond European norms.
- Renfrew, C. and Bahn, P. (2000) *Archaeology: Theories, methods and practice*. This has become *the* encyclopadia of cases studies for a generation of archaeology students.

Archaeological sources and methods

- Coles, J. and Lawson, A. (eds) (1987) *European Wetlands in Prehistory*. An excellent insight into differential preservation and the value of wet sites.
- Drewett, P. (1999) *Field Archaeology*. For detailed coverage and clear explanations of methods.
- Muir, R. (1981) *Reading the Landscape*. A book to open your eyes to evidence of past activity embedded in the countryside.
- Schick, K. and Toth, N. (1993) *Making Silent Stones Speak*. Good on the use of experimental archaeology in investigating early hominid activity in Africa.
- Wass, S. (1999) *The Amateur Archaeologist*. A good aid for project work.
- Wilkinson, K. and Stevens, C. (2001) *Environmental Archaeology*. At last, a clear introduction to the archaeology of economics and ecosystems.

Period studies

- Cunliffe, B. (ed.) (1994) *The Oxford Illustrated Prehistory of Europe*. Well illustrated and authoritative.
- Hunter, J. and Ralston, I. (eds) (1999) *The Archaeology of Britain*. An excellent introduction to each period of British archaeology since the Upper Palaeolithic.
- Parker-Pearson, M. (1993) *Bronze Age Britain*. A very accessible and well-illustrated introduction to the Neolithic and Bronze Age.
- Wenke, R. (1999) *Patterns in Prehistory*. An overview of the majority of human history from a world perspective.

Archaeological themes

- Binford, L. (1983) *In Pursuit of the Past*. The introduction to understanding the formation of the archaeological record.
- Bradley, R. (1984) *The Social Foundations of Prehistoric Britain*. A ground-breaking book which looks at how patterns in the archaeological record can be used to reveal the social and ritual nature of past societies.
- Fagan, B. (1995) *Time Detectives*. A very readable series of case studies including several mentioned in this text.
- Parker-Pearson, M. (1999) *The Archaeology of Death and Burial*. Wide-ranging and drawing on ethnography to examine past beliefs and practices.
- Sherratt, A. (1997) *Economy and Society in Prehistoric Europe*. A stimulating series of essays on topics from horses to alcohol.

ARCHAEOLOGY BOOKSELLERS

There are often only limited ranges of archaeological texts in general bookshops. If you know what you want but can't get it, try these two specialist companies:

- Castle Books: http://dspace.dial.pipex.com/town/square/fe63/index.htm
- Oxbow Books: http://www.oxbowbooks.com/

JOURNALS

In most subjects you would be unlikely to look at journals before university level. However, in archaeology it should be different. The first in this list are all very accessible and are often beautifully illustrated. The remainder are useful sources of case studies. Many good case studies only appear in journals.

British Archaeology (*BA*) http://www.britarch.ac.uk
Current Archaeology (*CA*) http://www.archaeology.co.uk/
Scientific American: http://www.amsci.org/amsci/amsci.html
Antiquity: http://intarch.ac.uk/antiquity/
Assemblage: http://www.shef.ac.uk/~assem/
Proceedings of the Prehistoric Society: http://www.britarch.ac.uk/prehist/

GATEWAY WEBSITES

We have listed websites throughout the book where they provide more information on methods and case studies. To find other information you should head for one of the many archaeology gateway sites. Each of these will provide you with a huge number of links. You should be able to find something on almost everything you are looking for. We usually do.

These are a selection of the very best:

World Archaeology:
http://archaeology.about.com/
http://archnet.asu.edu/
http://odur.let.rug.nl/arge/
http://www.discoveringarchaeology.com/
http://www.bbc.co.uk/history/ancient/archaeology/

Archaeology of the British Isles
http://www.britarch.ac.uk/info/uklinks.html
http://www.discoveryprogramme.ie/
http://www.cadw.wales.gov.uk/
http://www.english-heritage.org.uk/
http://www.historicscotland.gov.uk/
http://www.spoilheap.co.uk/

Our current favourite is the anthropology site of Mesa Community College, Arizona which has great world archaeology case studies including short ethnographic and archaeological film clips.

http://www.mc.maricopa.edu/dept/d10/asb/anthro2003/

If you want more, why not go online to the Archaeology Coursebook site www.routledge.com/textbooks/archaeologycoursebook. Unlike many of the sites listed, its focus will be on good case studies at the right level for seminars and essays.

PLACES TO VISIT

We have tried to ensure some regional coverage with our suggestions although there is inevitably a bias towards those which we have used and found useful.

Twenty museums to visit

There are two good websites which list many of Britain's museums:

- http://www.mda.org.uk/vlmp/
- http://www.museums.co.uk/

1 Ashmolean Museum, Oxford
2 British Museum, London:
3 Devizes Museum (Neolithic-Bronze Age)
4 Ipswich Museum (Anglo-Saxon)
5 Keiller Museum, Avebury (Neolithic-Bronze Age)
6 Museum of the Iron Age (Danebury), Andover
7 Museum of Archaeology and Anthropology, Cambridge
8 Museum of London
9 Museum of Wales, Cardiff:
10 National Museum of Scotland, Edinburgh
11 Newcastle University Museum (Roman)
12 Petrie Museum, London (Egypt)
13 Pitt Rivers Museum, Oxford (anthropology)
14 Salisbury Museum (Neolithic-Bronze Age)
15 Jewry Wall, Leicester
16 Lincoln Museum
17 Corinium, Cirencester (Romans and Saxon)
18 St Albans (Roman)
19 Manchester (Egyptian)
20 Tullie House, Carlisle (Roman)

Recreations and experimental sites

- Butser Ancient Farm, nr Petersfield
- Peat Moors Visitor Centre, nr Glastonbury
- West Stow Anglo-Saxon village, nr Bury St Edmunds
- Flag Fen, Peterborough
- Jorvik Centre, York
- St Fagins, Newport
- Bede's World, Jarrow
- Ironbridge Gorge, Telford

Visits to archaeological monuments

Where possible, several are grouped together to make a useful day out.

- Avebury–Keiller Museum–West Kennet–Windmill Hill
- Stonehenge–Durrington–Winterborne Stoke
- Arbor Low–Stanton Moor–Cresswell Crags
- Grimes Graves, West Stow–Thetford Castle
- Hadrian's Wall–Vindolanda–Housesteads
- Chedworth–Corinium Museum–Great Witcombe
- Fishbourne Palace–Butser–Mary Rose
- Maes Howe–Ring of Brodgar–Stones of Stenness
- Maiden Castle–Dorchester Museum–Cerne Abbas Giant
- Wharram Percy–Fountains Abbey–Rievaulx

Answers and Mark Schemes

Key task: test your understanding of geophysics (p. 20)

Resistivity area survey best for 2, 3, 4, 6, 8; also useful for 5, 9, 10.

Magnetometry area survey best for 1, 9, 5, 6, 10; also useful for 3, 4, 8.

Neither useful for 7.

Key skill: short questions test (p. 26)

1a Cropmarks (1 mk) circular enclosures or barrows (1 mk).

1b L1 Differential colour or tone due to buried features (1–2 mks).
L2 L1 plus explanation of reasons for effects (3–4 mks).
L3 L2 plus comment on possible type of crops and season (4–5 mk).

1c L1 Answers in list form or descriptive account of limited relevance (1–2 mks).
L2 At least one relevant method described. Top end for relation to this site (3–5 mks).
L3 Several relevant methods considered with consideration of appropriateness at top end (6–7 mks).

Key task: test your understanding of methods (p. 59)

1a Cropmarks (1mk), reason for them (1 mk).

1b L1 Answers that describe the differences or provide a brief list (1–2 mks).
L2 One or two points of contrast explained (3–4 mks).
L3 Several points of contrast explained. E.g., greater definition from the excavation, only partially excavated, some marks are not archaeological (5–6 mks).

1c L1 Generalised comments about excavation or evidence. Descriptions (1–2 mks).
L2 Focus on phasing. Some mention of dating or stratigraphy (3–4 mks).
L3 Stratigraphy and dating discussed (5–6 mks).
L4 L3 in detail, e.g. how might a layer be identified and relatively dated (7–8 mks).

Key task: test your grasp of dating methods (p. 102)

Spear (C14), shells (ESR, AAR, C14), seeds (C14), burnt flint (TL), mudbricks (archaeomagnetism, TL), Saxon bones (C14), kiln (archaeomagnetism), cave bones (uranium series or ESR for the calcite deposits), figurine (typology, TL, archaeomagnetism), boat timber (dendro, C14).

Glossary of Terms and Abbreviations

This list does not pretend to be precise in an academic sense. It is intended to give you a simple definition of words that may be new to you so that you can comprehend the sources you come into contact with. For greater sophistication you should use an archaeological dictionary. Every subject has a lexicon of acronyms and abbreviations. Archaeology (arx) is no different. The glossary contains those, which you are most likely to come across, and with which you should familiarise yourself.

Absolute dating: Giving the age of something according to a calendar or historic scale, e.g. BC, AD, BP. Also called as chronometric dating

Accelerator mass spectrometry (AMS): An advanced radiocarbon dating method which can work for tiny samples

Achieved status: Position or prestige in society earned through one's own efforts or qualities

Aerial survey: Locating and defining archaeological sites from the air. Photographing cropmarks and parchmarks during drought conditions usually produces the best results

Anaerobic conditions: Where there is insufficient oxygen for the bacteria, which normally break down organic matierals to thrive, for example waterlogged sites

Analogy: Interpreting something with reference to something else. For example, 'it is similar to X'

Animism: Belief in spirits

Anthropology: The study of humans. It has many subdivisions including Archaeology and Ethnography

Arable: Growing crops

Archaeological record: What survives in the ground before excavation or the records produced by archaeologists after the whole excavation and analysis process

Archaeology: The study of physical remains to help understand the behaviour of people in the past

Archaeometry: The application of scientific analysis to archaeological materials.

Artefacts: Can refer to anything made or modified by humans. Tends to be used most frequently for tools.

Ascribed status: Position or prestige in society due to inheritance

Assemblage: Artefacts from a particular period which typically appear together. Also used to describe a collection of materials, for example animal bones from a particular site

Atomic absorption spectrometry (AMS): Measuring light energy emitted by different elements. Different combinations provide different spectra

Attribute: A quality of an artefact which allows it to be grouped with others, for example colour, texture

Attritional bone profile: A table plotting the age and sex of animal bones which suggests that younger and old members of herds were killed. It suggests scavenging or selective hunting by humans or other predators

Augering: Using a drill to take a core through deposits in the ground

Band: A hunting and gathering based society with groups of under 100 people

Bigman: A non-hereditary position of status in some small-scale parties gained through the ability to amass and distribute resources – often through feasts.

BP: Before present (actually 1950). Absolute dating used for periods in the past where historical dates (BC and AD) are irrelevant, for example the Palaeolithic.

Cache: A store of food or artefacts

Calibration: Using one method to correct inaccuracies in another, for example using calendar dates from tree ring sequeces to calibrate raw radiocarbon dates

Catastrophic profile: A table plotting the age and sex of animal bones which shows the natural distribution of animals in a herd. It suggests a natural disaster or unselective slaughter

Central place theory: A geographic model developed by Christaller, which predicts that central places would develop at regular spaced in an ideal landscape

Characterisation: Identifying the origins of materials from their physical characteristics

Chiefdom: A ranked society with the inherited or elected role of chief at the top. Likely to have some specialisation in crafts and types of building

Clan: A system of social organisation based on blood and marriage ties

Context: The position of an artefact, the layer of soil it was found in and other artefacts found with it

Coppicing: Repeatedly cutting trees back to a stump in order to encourage them to grow long straight poles which can then be harvested

Coprolites: Preserved faeces

Core: A prepared lump of stone from which tools can be made

Coring: Driving a hollow tube into the ground to get a stratigraphic sample of the subsoil

Cropmarks: Variations in the tone or colour of crops due to underlying archaeological features

Curation: Deliberately preserving artefacts, for example jewellery or weapons. This can result in artefacts from an early period being discovered ‘out of sequence’ on a later site

Cursus: Linear monuments, sometimes several kilometres long, constructed in the Neolithic period

Debitage: Waste from the manufacture of stone tools

Dendrochronology: Tree ring dating

Depositional processes: The various means by which archaeological material becomes buried

Desktop study: An office based search of historical and existing archaeological records about a site

DHA: Direct historical approach. Using oral evidence and studies of a modern population to form hypotheses about an earlier culture in the same region

Diachronic change: Gradual change over a period of time

Disarticulated: Bones that are mixed up, no longer in the right places

Distribution patterns: Plots of archaeological finds either on a site or across a region which are analysed to determine the behaviour that caused them

DNA: Deoxyribonucleic acid. The material that makes up genes and determines the nature of living things

Earthworks: Literally a series of 'humps and bumps' on the surface that indicate the buried remains of buildings, boundaries and field systems

Ecofacts: Natural material that is of archaeological interest. It could include human remains, food waste or environmental material such as pollen or snails. Not artefacts

Entoptic: Internally produced. For example, entoptic images are generated by the brain itself rather than reflecting what has been seen

Ethnicity: Identity of different groups based on their distinctive cultures

Ethnoarchaeology: Studying modern groups of people to understand the behaviour that leads to particular patterns of deposition

Ethnography: Observation based study of modern social groups

Excarnation: Defleshing a corpse in some way as part of mortuary ritual

Exchange: Not just trade, but any interaction where something passes between people. It could include information, gifts or money

Fall-off analysis: measuring the rate at which the number of particular artefacts decline as the distance from their source increases. It is used to diagnose particular modes of exchange

Faunal dating: Relative dating based on the evolutionary sequence in which mammals have developed

Feature: Non-portable archaeological remain such as aspects of a site for example posthole, hearth

Fieldwalking: Systematically searching ploughed fields for the remains of artefacts and buildings to detect likely settlement areas

Foragers: Groups subsisting on wild foods. Plant foods are usually the most important

Formation processes: How archaeological material came to be created, buried and transformed to create the archaeological record

Funerary rites: Events to mark the final rite of passage of a person. Overlaps with, but is not the same as, *mortuary practice*

Glyphs: Reliefs of figures or signs carved on stone. Usually Mesoamerican

Geochemical survey: Using techniques derived from chemistry to detect traces of past activity from soil samples. See phosphate analysis

Geophysical survey: Using techniques derived from physics to detect remains under the ground. See resistivity and magnetometry.

GIS: Geographical Information Systems: linked maps and databases

GPS: Global Positioning System. A handheld device for locating your position using satellites

Hoards: Deliberately buried artefacts. May have been placed in earth or water for security, as offerings etc.

Horticulture: Encouraging particular plants to grow, for example by weeding round them. Used to identify a stage in food production before agriculture

Horticulturalist: Groups subsisting largely on plant foods, some of which they may plant. May be mobile and not using permanent fields

Hunter-gatherers: Groups subsisting on a mixture of wild animal and plant foods. May be mobile

Iconography: Art that may have a religious meaning

Inclusions: Material added to clay to provide strength and improve the firing process. Also known as temper

Inhumation: Burial

Intensification: Increasing production. Usually applied to food production but can apply to extraction or manufacture

Isotopic analysis: Identifying different ratios of isotopes in materials in order to pinpoint their source

Kin: Relatives through blood and marriage

Liminal: Something on the edge of normal society. May be a boundary or a group of people. May be seen as dangerous and likely to require ritual to deal with it

Lineage: A group sharing the same ancestor

Lithics: Stone tools

Magnetometry: Detecting buried remains through magnetic variations between them and the surrounding soil

Market exchange: A system of exchange where producers compete in terms of prices. It is often associated with money or bartering and particular exchange sites, for example shops or markets

Material culture: The total physical remains of a former society including artefacts, buildings, etc.

Matrix: The type of soil or other material in which an artefact is found

Mesolithic: A label given to the period from the end of the last Ice Age until the development of farming. Sometimes used to refer to groups living by hunting and gathering. In Britain dates range from around 8000 BC

Metallography: Studying the composition and structure of metals

Micro-contour survey: A detailed survey using accurate sensitive equipment to reveal subtle variations in the ground surface to reveal the plan of buried sites

Microliths: Tiny stone or flint blades. Associated with the Mesolithic period

Middens: A rubbish tip. In some periods may have had other functions including a source of fertiliser and a ritual site

MNI: Minimum number of individuals. The smallest number of animals that could have produced the bones in an assemblage

Moiety: Organisation of society based on the idea of two different subgroups

Monotheistic: Belief in one god

Mortuary practice: Ritual activity and preparation involving the disposal of a corpse

Neolithic: This label used to describe the period of the first farmers, before the use of metal tools. Increasingly it is used to describe the process of domestication including changing ideas about the world. British dates range from around 4500 BC

Neutron activation analysis (NAA): Highly sensitive analysis of trace elements undertaken within a reactor

NISP: Number of identified specimens. A count of all the bones of each species in an assemblage.

NMR: National Monuments Record

Obsidian: Volcanic glass that can be worked to produce hard, sharp edges

Organic residue analysis: Using chemicals to extract and identify traces of plant and animal materials from pottery

Ossuary: A place in which the bones of the dead are stored, for example a charnel house

Palaeolithic: The first archaeological period. Before 8000 BC but subdivided into Lower, Middle and Upper on the basis of stone technology

Palimpsest: A collection of archaeological artefacts, ecofacts and material that may not be related. For example, they are together through accident or natural forces rather than human activity. Also used for a site with a mass of intercut features of different periods

Palynology: Studying pollen for dating and environmental reconstruction

Pastoralists: People who subsist largely from the animals they herd. May be mobile

Petrology: Studying the minerals in archaeological material to identify their source of origin

Phosphate analysis: Analysing soil samples to detect high phosphate which can indicate human or animal habitation

Pollen dating: Using local pollen sequences to provide a relative date for a site

Polytheistic: Belief in many gods

Prestige goods chain: Where valuable items are exchanged between high status individuals, often over a considerable area

Primary products: The material gained by killing an animal, for example meat, skin

Probing: Using metal rods to detect walls and other buried features close to the surface

Propitiation: Offerings to gods, for example offerings in pits or deposited in water

Radiocarbon dating (RC): Absolute dating technique based on the known rate of decay of Carbon 14

Reciprocity: Exchange between social equals. Balanced reciprocity implies things of equal value are exchanged

Redistribution: A form of exchange where goods are collected by a central authority and then given to other people or places

Regression: Using clues from the earliest known maps and documents from an area and projecting them back in time to produce a picture of an earlier period

Relative dating: Determining where a site or artefact sits in a sequence in relation to other sites or artefacts

Remote sensing: Detecting archaeological remains from above the surface of the earth, usually from a satellite

Resistivity: Detecting buried remains through differences between them and the surrounding soil in their ability to carry an electrical current

Rites of intensification: Ritual to mark times of change or danger

Rites of passage: Ritual to mark events in the lives of individuals

Sampling: The careful selection of areas to investigate or materials to analyse. Usually based on mathematical probability to ensure that what is selected is representative of wider evidence

Secondary products: Materials gained from animals without killing them, for example milk, wool

Sedentary: Where a group is settled, that is staying in one place. Semi-sedentary groups stay for considerable periods, perhaps moving between sites on a seasonal basis

Segmentary society: Small, relatively self-contained social groups who may sometimes combine with similar groups to form wider alliances

SEM: Scanning electron microscope

Shadow sites: Sites that survive as low earthworks and are seen from the air in conditions of low sunlight

Shaman: Individual who can communicate with, and often interact with, spirits

Shovel pit testing: An alternative to fieldwalking for woods, pasture and gardens. Samples of soil from carefully selected test pits are sieved for artefacts

Signature: Traces in the archaeological record that can be linked to particular patterns of activity

Site: A place where human activity has taken place

Site catchment analysis: Reconstructing the available natural resources within easy reach of an archaeological site to help construct a model of its economy and the diet of its people

SMR: Sites and Monuments Record

Social storage: When an individual gives something of value to another individual, creating an obligation on the part of the second person to return something at a later date. What is exchanged can vary enormously from an exotic gift to a meal, from military service to a bride.

Soil marks: Variations in the tone or colour of ploughed soil due to the destruction of buried features

Sonar: Form of underwater detection based on sound waves

Specialisation: This term can be used in several ways. Economic specialisation can be used to describe a group who rely on one primary means of supporting themselves, for example pastoralists. It can also mean a division of labour where different individuals perform particular tasks rather than working in similar ways, for example miners, iron smelters and smiths in the production of iron tools

State: Society with a territory, central authority and permanent institutions

Stelae: Carved stone pillars or statues

Stratification: A series of layers, strata or deposits laid down over time. Stratigraphy is the analysis of stratification or its use in relative dating

Structured deposition: Material entering the archaeological record through specific (possibly ritual) activities or behaviour patterns (not random). For example, particular animal bones being placed in ditches

Superposition: The principle that in undisturbed stratification, the oldest layer in the sequence is at the bottom

Surface collection: American version of field-walking. It can usefully be applied to the systematic recovery of artefacts from places other than fields

Surface survey: Examining the landscape for evidence of underlying archaeological remains

Surveying: Precisely measuring the dimensions, position and orientation of archaeological sites and features

Taphonomy: 'The law of burial'. The processes which transform organic archaeological material in the ground

TAQ: Terminus ante quem. The latest possible date for a site or layer

Tell: A large mound created by successive settlement layers on a site over thousands of years

Temper: Material added to clay to give it strength and prevent it cracking during firing

Thiessen polygons: Shapes created by joining the mid-point between economic centres to provide models for exploring territories

Thin sections: Samples of rock taken for petrological analysis

TL: Thermoluminescence dating

Totemism: A natural object is adopted by a group as their emblem and as an object of worship

TPQ: Terminus post quem. The earliest possible date for a site or layer

Trace elements: Tiny amounts of rare elements within stone and metal. The balance of trace elements varies according to the geological source of the material

Transect: Walking or taking a sample across a landscape

Trend surface analysis: A way of illustrating the distribution of artefacts by using mathematical formulae to create a contour map

Tribe: A society that is larger than a band but still linked together by kinship ties. May number between several hundred and a few thousand people. Likely to be farmers or pastoralists. Unlikely to have wide variations in wealth and status

Typology: Organising artefacts into types based on similar attributes

Unit: An archaeological trust or commercial company that bids to do survey and excavation work

Use wear analysis: Using high-powered microscopes to study marks on tools and bones in order to identify the activity that caused them

Votives: Artefacts deposited as offerings to gods or spirits

X-ray fluorescence (XRF): A non-destructive method of analysing the mineral composition of the surface of artefacts

Bibliography

Anderson, S. (1985) 'Tybrind Vig' *Journal of Danish Archaeology* 4 Odense: Odense University Press

Ashmore, W. and Sharer, R. (1999) *Discovering our Past,* Mountain View, Calif.: Mayfield

Aston, M. (1985) *Interpreting the Landscape,* London: Routledge

Bahn, P. and Vertut, J. (1988) *Images of the Ice Age,* Leicester: Windward

Barclay, Gordon J. & Russell-White, Christopher J. (1993) Excavations in the ceremonial complex of the fourth to second millennium BC at Balfarg/Balbirnie, Glenrothes, Fife in *Proceedings of the Society of Antiquaries of Scotland* 123, 43–211

Barnett, J. (1998) 'Monuments in the landscape: thoughts from the Peak', Lecture at conference on Prehistoric Ritual, Oxford

Barrett, J. (1994) *Fragments from Antiquity,* Oxford: Blackwell

Barrett, J. and Bradley, R. (eds) (1980) *Settlement and Society in the British Later Bronze Age,* Oxford: BAR 83

Bayliss-Smith, T. (1996) 'People–plant interaction in the New Guinea highlands' in D. Harris, (ed.) *The Origins and Spread of Agriculture and Pastoralism in Eurasia,* London: UCL

Binford, L. (1978) *Nunamiut Ethnoarchaeology,* Orlando: Academic Press

Binford, L. (1983) *In Pursuit of the Past,* New York: Thames and Hudson

Binford, L. (1989) *Debating Archaeology,* San Diego: Academic Press

Bradley, R. (1984) *The Social Foundations of Prehistoric Britain,* London: Longman

Bradley, R. (1997) *Rock Art and the Prehistory of Atlantic Europe: Signing the Land* London: Routledge

Bradley, R. (1998) *The Significance of Monuments,* London: Routledge

Bradley, R. (2000a) *The Good Stones,* Edinburgh: The Society of Antiquaries of Scotland

Bradley, R. (2000b) *An Archaeology of Natural Places.* London: Routledge

Brück, J. (1995) 'A place for the dead: the role of human remains in late Bronze Age Britain, *Oxford Journal of Archaeology* 61: 245–77

Buckland, P. (1976) 'The use of insect remains in the interpretation of archaeological environments', in D. Davidson and M. Shackley (eds) *Geoarchaeology,* London: Duckworth

Champion, T. and Collis, J. (eds) (1996) *The Iron Age in Britain and Ireland: Recent trends,* Sheffield: Sheffield Academic Press

Chapman, R., Kinnes, I. and Randsborg, K. (eds) (1981) *The Archaeology of Death,* Cambridge: Cambridge University Press

Clarke, D. (ed.) (1972) *Models in Archaeology,* London: Methuen

Clark, R. (2000) *Mesolithic Hunters of the Trentino.* Oxford: BAR 832

Coles, B. and Coles, J. (1976) *Sweet Track to Glastonbury,* London: Thames and Hudson

Coles, J. (1979) *Experimental Archaeology,* London: Academic Press

Coles, J. and Lawson, A. (eds) (1987) *European Wetlands in Prehistory,* Oxford: Clarendon Press

Collis, J. (1984) *The European Iron Age,* London: Batsford

Collis, J. (1996) 'Hillforts, enclosures and boundaries' in T. Champion and J. Collis (eds) *The Iron Age in Britain and Ireland: Recent trends,* Sheffield: Sheffield Academic Press

Cooper, N. (2000) *The Archaeology of Rutland Water: Excavations at Empingham 1967–73 and 1990*, Leicester: Leicester University Press

Cornwell, B. (1999) *Stonehenge*, London: HarperCollins

Crossley, D. (1994) *Post Medieval Archaeology in Britain*, Leicester: Leicester University Press

Cunliffe, B. (1992) 'Pits, preconceptions and propitiation in the British Iron Age', *Oxford Journal of Archaeology* 11: 69–83

Cunliffe, B. (1993) *Danebury*, London: English Heritage

Cunliffe, B. (ed.) (1994) *The Oxford Illustrated Prehistory of Europe*, Oxford: Oxford University Press

Cunliffe, B. (1995) *Iron Age Britain*, London: Batsford

Darvill, T. and Fulton, A. (1998) *MARS: The monuments at risk survey of England*, Bournemouth and London: Bournemouth University and English Heritage

Darvill, T. and Thomas, J. (eds) (1996) *Neolithic Houses in North-west Europe and Beyond*, Oxford: Oxbow

Davidson, D. and Shackley, M. (eds) (1976) *Geoarchaeology*, London: Duckworth

Drewett, P. (1982) 'Later Bronze Age downland economy at Black Patch, East Sussex', *Proceedings of the Prehistoric Society* 48: 321–409

Drewett, P. (1999) *Field Archaeology*, London: UCL Press

Ellison, A. (1980) 'Settlements and regional exchange: a case study' in J. Barrett and R. Bradley (eds) *Settlement and Society in the British Later Bronze Age*, Oxford: BAR 83

Fagan, B. (2000) *In the Beginning*, New York: Prentice-Hall

Fagan, B. (1995) *Time Detectives*, New York: Simon and Schuster

Fash, W. L. (1991) *Scribes, Warriors and Kings*, New York: Thames and Hudson

Fleming, A. (1988) *The Dartmoor Reaves*, London: Batsford

Fleming, A. (1998) *Swaledale, Valley of the Wild River*, Edinburgh: Edinburgh University Press

Fried, M. (1978) 'The State, the chicken and the egg' in Cohen, N. and Service, E. *Origins of the State*, ISHI, Philadelphia

Gamble, C. (1986) *The Palaeolithic Settlement of Europe*, Cambridge: Cambridge University Press

Gamble, C. (2000) *Archaeology: The basics*. London: Routledge

Giddens, A. (1989) *Sociology*. London: Polity

Gilchrist, R. (1995) *Contemplation and Action: The other monasticism*, London: Leicester University Press

Gimbutas, M. (1991) *The Civilization of the Goddess*, New York: Harper Collins

Graslund, B. (1994) 'Prehistoric soul beliefs in Northern Europe', *Proceedings of the Prehistoric Society* 60: 15–26

Green, M. (2000) *A Landscape Revealed*, Stroud: Tempus

Greene, K. (2002) *Archaeology: An introduction*, London: Routledge

Grogan, E. (1999) 'Hilltop Settlement in South West Ireland', Lecture at conference on Late Bronze Age Landscapes, Oxford

Härke, H. (1990) 'Warrior graves? The background of the Anglo-Saxon burial rite', *Past and Present* 126: 22–43

Harris, D. (ed.) (1996) *The Origins and Spread of Agriculture and Pastoralism in Eurasia*. London: UCL

Haviland, W. (2000) *Anthropology*, New York: Harcourt Brace

Hawkes, C. (1954) 'Archaeological theory and method: some suggestions for the Old World', *American Anthropologist* 56: 155–68

Hill, J. D. (1996) 'Hillforts and the Iron Age of Wessex' in T. Champion and J. Collis (eds) *The Iron Age in Britain and Ireland: Recent trends*, Sheffield, Sheffield Academic Press

Hunter, J. and Ralston, I. (eds) (1999) *The Archaeology of Britain*, London: Routledge

Jackson, P. (1995) 'Footloose in archaeology', *Current Archaeology* 144: 466–70

Kemp, B. J (1993) *Ancient Egypt*, New York: Routledge

Kent, S. (1989) *Farmers as Hunters*, Cambridge: Cambridge University Press

Knecht, L. (1994) 'Late Ice Age hunting technology', *Scientific American* July: 82–7

Lake, M. (1989) *Historic Farm Buildings*, London: Blandford Press

Leroi-Gourhan, A. and Brézillion, M. (1966) 'L'habitation Magdalénienne No. 1 de Pincevent pres Monereau', *Gallia Préhistoire* 9(2): 263–385

Lewis-Williams, J. D. and Dowson, T. A. (1988) 'The signs of all times: entoptic phenomena in Upper Palaeolithic Cave Art', *Current Anthropology* 29 201–45

Loveday, R. (1998) 'Mother Dunche's Buttocks: a focus for Neolithic interest', Lecture to Neolithics Studies Group, London

Marcus, J. and Flannery, K. (1994) *Zapotec Civilization*, London: Thames and Hudson

Mays, S. (1998) *The Archaeology of Human Bones*. London: Routledge

Mithen, S. (1990) *Thoughtful Foragers: A study of prehistoric decision making*, Cambridge: Cambridge University Press

Moore, A., Hillman, G. and Legge, A. (2000) *Village on the Euphrates*, Oxford: Oxford University Press

Muir, R. (1981) *Reading the Landscape*, London: Michael Joseph

Orme, B. (1981) *Anthropology for Archaeologists*, London: Duckworth

Orton, C. *et al.* (1993) *Pottery in Archaeology*, Cambridge: Cambridge University Press

O'Shea, J. (1981) 'Social configurations and the archaeological study of mortuary practices: a case study' in R. Chapman, I. Kinnes and K. Randsborg (eds) *The Archaeology of Death*, Cambridge: Cambridge University Press

Parker-Pearson, M. (1993) *Bronze Age Britain*, London: Batsford

Parker-Pearson, M. (1999) *The Archaeology of Death and Burial*, Stroud: Sutton

Pitts, M. and Roberts, M. (1997) *Fairweather Eden*, London: Century

Price, N. (2001) *The Archaeology of Shamanism*, London: Routledge

Prior, F. (1991) *Flag Fen*, London: Batsford

Rackham, O. (1986) *The History of the Countryside*, London: Phoenix

Rackham, O. (1990) *Trees and Woodland in the British Landscape*. London: Phoenix

Reece, R. (1998) research in progress on the potential of hedges for locating early medieval settlement

Renfrew, C. (1973) *Before Civilization*, London: Jonathan Cape

Renfrew, C. (1984) *Approaches to Social Archaeology*, Edinburgh: Edinburgh University Press

Renfrew, C. and Bahn, P. (2000) *Archaeology: Theories, methods and practice*, London: Thames and Hudson

Reynolds, P. J. (1979) *Iron Age Farm: The Butser Experiment*. London: British Museum Publications

Rue, D. (1989) 'Archaic Middle American agriculture and settlement: recent pollen dating from Honduras', *Journal of Field Archaeology* 10: 177–84

Schele, L. and Matthews, P. (1983) *The Code of Kings*, New York: Thames and Hudson

Schele, L. and Miller, M. (1986), *The Blood of Kings*, Austin: University of Texas Press

Schick, K. and Toth, N. (1993) *Making Silent Stones Speak*, London: Weidenfeld and Nicolson

Service, E. (1971) *Primitive Social Organisation: An evolutionary perspective*, New York: Random House

Sharples, N. (1991) Maiden Castle, London: Batsford

Shennan, S. (1975) 'The social organisation at Branc', *Antiquity* 49: 279–88

Sherratt, A. (1997) *Economy and Society in Prehistoric Europe*, Edinburgh: Edinburgh University Press

Strudwick, N. and Strudwick, H. (1989) *Thebes in Egypt*, London: BM Press

Taylor, T. (1997) *The Prehistory of Sex*, London: Fourth Estate

Thomas, J. (1991) *Understanding the Neolithic*, London: Routledge

Tilley, C. (1994) *A Phenomenology of Landscape*, Oxford: Berg

Figure Bib.1 *King Redwald from Sutton Hoo?*

From the evidence we have, this is what King Redwald from Sutton Hoo might have looked like if he had done Archaeology A Level.

Tilley, C. (1996) *An Ethnography of the Neolithic,* Cambridge: Cambridge University Press

Trigger, B. (1989) *A History of Archaeological Thought,* Cambridge: Cambridge University Press

Van Gennep, A. (1909) *Les rites de passage,* Paris: E. Nourry

Waddington, C. (1998) 'Cup and Rings in Context', *Cambridge Archaeological Journal* 8(1): 29–54

Wass, S. (1999) *The Amateur Archaeologist,* second edn, London: Batsford

Watson, A. (1997) 'Hearing again the sound of the Neolithic' *British Archaeology* 23 (April)

Welch, M. (1992), *Anglo-Saxon England,* London: Batsford

Wenke, R. (1999) *Patterns in Prehistory,* Oxford: Oxford University Press

Whittle, A. (1996) *Europe in the Neolithic,* Cambridge: Cambridge University Press

Whittle, A. (1998) *Sacred Mound, Holy Rings.* Oxford: Oxbow

Wilkinson, K. and Stevens, C. (2001) *Environmental Archaeology* Stroud: Tempus

Wilkinson, R. (2000) *The Temples of Ancient Egypt,* London: Thames and Hudson

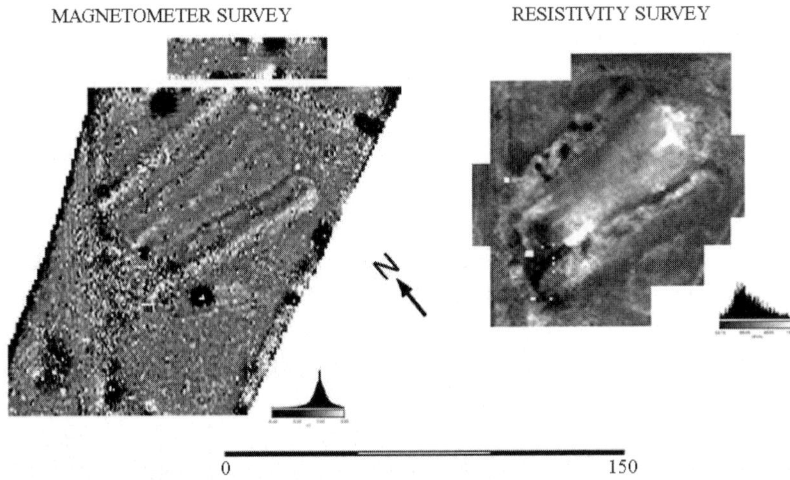

Figure 1.17
Resistance and Magnetometer plots compared

The essential complementary nature of these techniques can be seen in these plots from English Heritage's survey of White Barrow.

Figure 6.17
Archaeology on a massive scale

Excavations on the site of the Heathrow extension. Only the largest units are capable of bidding for projects such as this and often only in collaboration with others. Amongst the discoveries on this site was this linear feature, not an earlier runway but the Heathrow Cursus, a Neolithic ritual monument.

Index